Multilingualism and Assessment

Achieving transparency, assuring quality, sustaining diversity

Proceedings of the ALTE Berlin Conference, May 2005

Multilingualism and Assessment

Achieving transparency, assuring quality, sustaining diversity

Proceedings of the ALTE Berlin Conference, May 2005

CAMBRIDGE
UNIVERSITY PRESS

CAMBRIDGE UNIVERSITY PRESS
Cambridge, New York, Melbourne, Madrid, Cape Town, Singapore, São Paulo

Cambridge University Press
The Edinburgh Building, Cambridge CB2 8RU, UK

www.cambridge.org
Information on this title: www.cambridge.org/9780521711920

First published 2008

Printed in the United Kingdom at the University Press, Cambridge

A catalogue record for this publication is available from the British Library

ISBN 978-0-521-711920

Contents

Section Three
Sustaining Diversity

Acknowledgements

We would like to express our thanks to all the volume contributors for developing and writing up their original presentations given at the ALTE Berlin Conference in May 2005, and for their willingness to make subsequent revisions in line with our editorial suggestions. This volume has taken longer to reach publication than we had hoped so we are especially grateful to the authors for their patience.

The volume could not have reached publication without the professional, technological and administrative assistance of various staff based at Cambridge ESOL including: Barbara Stevens and Jacqui Wright in the ALTE Secretariat; Rowena Akinyemi and, more recently, Kirsty Sylvester in the Research and Validation Group; and Sally Downes in the Stakeholder Relations and Legal Affairs Group. We are grateful to all of them for their support throughout the production process.

Finally, the publishers are grateful to the copyright holders for permission to use the copyright material reproduced in this book. Cambridge University Press for Figure 1 from *Training Foreign Language Teachers. A Reflective Approach* by Michael J. Wallace, 1991.

Series Editors' note

The 1st International Conference of the Association of Language Testers in Europe (ALTE) was held in Barcelona in July 2001, hosted by the Generalitat de Catalunya. The event celebrated the European Year of Languages that year and took as its theme 'European Language Testing in a Global Context'. Following the success of this inaugural conference, plans were quickly put in place for a second conference to be held in 2005. The Goethe-Institut hosted ALTE's 2nd International Conference in Berlin from 19 to 21 May 2005 in support of the 50th Anniversary of the European Cultural Convention and focusing on the theme of 'Language Assessment in a Multilingual Context'. *Multilingualism and Assessment* – the 27th volume in the now well-established and highly regarded *Studies in Language Testing* series – is a direct outcome of the Berlin conference.

Members of ALTE were delighted to obtain the patronage of the Secretary General of the Council of Europe, Terry Davis, for the major 3-day language testing conference in Berlin; the event provided members of the international language testing and teaching community with a key forum for exploring the impact of multilingualism on language assessment, focusing on the needs to set common standards while at the same time sustaining linguistic diversity. The conference considered ways of describing and comparing language qualifications to establish common levels of proficiency, and offered a forum for the discussion of issues associated with quality, ethics and transparency in assessment. The fundamental aims of the ALTE members have always been to work on common levels of proficiency and common standards for the language testing process designed to support the mutual recognition of language certificates in Europe and the increase of quality and standards in their production and delivery.

The Council of Europe declared 2005 the European Year of Citizenship through Education and one of the aims of the year was to support democratic citizenship and participation in order to promote social cohesion, intercultural understanding and respect for diversity and human rights. In that context, the Council of Europe (Language Policy Division, Strasbourg) and ALTE set up a joint forum at the 2005 Berlin conference, focusing on political and ethical issues involved in defining and assessing the language proficiency required for citizenship and active participation of newcomers in social, occupational and democratic processes. Some of the papers in this volume explore in detail the key themes addressed during that forum.

ALTE, an International Non-Governmental Organisation (INGO) of the Council of Europe since 2003, has been in existence for almost 20 years, having been founded in 1990 following a proposal by the Universities of Cambridge and Salamanca. There were eight founder members, including the Goethe-Institut, and membership has grown over the intervening years to the present total of 31 members, who between them represent the testing of 26 European languages. Additionally, ALTE currently has more than 30 institutional affiliate organisations participating in its activities.

A key achievement of ALTE's work since the early 1990s has been the development of the ALTE Framework of Language Examinations, linked to the Council of Europe's Common European Framework of Reference for Languages (CEFR), using work carried out in the ALTE 'Can Do' Project. Close co-operation with the Council of Europe has continued in recent years with work on the Pilot Manual for Relating Language Examinations to the CEFR. Also important has been the development of a multilingual glossary of testing terms. The glossary, originally produced in 10 languages, is published as Volume 6 in the *Studies in Language Testing* series, and has since been developed in a further 10 European languages. More recently, ALTE working groups have been set up to look in more detail at projects such as testing younger learners, development of a Breakthrough level, as well as issues related to quality assurance in the test development and delivery process. Many of the projects undertaken by these groups and many of the documents developed by ALTE have been supported by the European Union Lingua Fund. ALTE has also worked closely with the European Association for Quality Language Services (EAQUALS) in recent years to produce a European Language Portfolio (ELP) for adult language learners, validated by the Council of Europe, and has with EAQUALS developed an electronic version of the ELP in English and French, available at www.eElp.org

A full listing of all the presentations given at the ALTE 2005 Conference can be found at the end of this volume. As will be apparent, the 20 conference papers presented here represent a selection of the many excellent presentations made in Berlin reflecting a wide range of topics and concerns; they provide a flavour of the key themes addressed at the conference. The Introduction to this volume by Lynda Taylor and Cyril Weir helps to highlight and summarise for readers the various strands which resonated throughout the conference, and points to implications for the language testing community.

At the time of writing, we look forward to ALTE's 3rd International Conference hosted by University of Cambridge ESOL Examinations in April 2008, on the theme of the social and educational impact of language assessment. We anticipate this will provide an invaluable opportunity for the European and wider international language testing community to revisit some enduring concerns of shared interest as well as to explore some new ones.

Michael Milanovic
Cyril J Weir
March 2008

Introduction

Lynda Taylor and Cyril J Weir

This volume brings together a selection of 20 edited papers based on presentations given at the 2nd ALTE Conference, Berlin, in May 2005, to explore the impact of multilingualism on language testing and assessment. The papers consider ways of describing and comparing language qualifications in order to establish common levels of proficiency, balancing the need to set shared standards and ensure quality, and at the same time sustain linguistic diversity. Grouped according to three broad themes, these edited papers address some of the substantive and complex issues in the current assessment of language ability around the world.

Against the backdrop of a globalised environment where populations are increasingly mobile and qualifications need to be transferable, **Section One** of the volume examines issues of *transparency and diversity*, and especially the role of the Common European Framework of Reference for Languages (CEFR) in this regard. Introductory contributions by Waldemar Martyniuk and Brian North helpfully set the scene for five papers that describe projects seeking to align tests and set standards in relation to the CEFR in differing European contexts (Norway, France, Germany, Spain) and across different European languages (English, French, German, Catalan, Italian, Spanish and Portuguese).

In his opening paper **Waldemar Martyniuk** provides us with a clear overview of the aims and work of the Council of Europe (CoE) and its development of the Common European Framework of Reference for Languages: Learning, Teaching, Assessment (CEFR). He describes the original intentions behind the CEFR and how it has been implemented through the European Language Portfolio (ELP) as well as other initiatives of the European Union. Growing acceptance throughout Europe of the levels and standards presented in the CEFR led to recognition of the need for practical guidance on how to relate language examinations to the Framework. The outcome was a set of specified recommended procedures in the form of a Draft Manual produced in 2003, together with an emerging 'toolkit' including a reference supplement, a DVD with sample speaking/writing performances, a CD-ROM with reading/listening test items, and various content analysis grids. Since 2003 the Draft Manual has been widely piloted throughout Europe by ALTE partners and other language testing specialists; it is expected to be released in a revised, updated version in 2008. **Brian North** builds upon Martyniuk's paper by tracing in much greater depth the origin and purpose of the CEFR; he discusses in some detail the CEFR descriptive scheme, the Common Reference Levels and the CEFR descriptors in whose development he was very closely involved. North also suggests ways in which the current descriptors might be further validated and developed through qualitative research. **Eli Moe** then reports on an attempt in Norway to set CEFR standards for a test of reading in English within the national schools context. Her detailed description of the procedures adopted in the project demonstrate how complex can be the process of standard setting of tests in terms of the CEFR; to be effective, it requires a combined approach that balances statistical analysis, rigorous training and informed judgement. **Patrick Riba and Marianne Mavel** report their experience of undertaking a similar, nationally initiated alignment project in France for the DELF and DALF exams of French as a Foreign Language. They describe some of the theoretical and practical challenges faced and the decisions made as they sought to link their suite of exams to the CEFR. **Guenter Nold, Henning Rossa and Johannes Hartig** describe the development and validation of tests of listening and reading comprehension in DESI, a large-scale assessment project in Germany. They offer an informative account of a data-driven approach to setting standards, involving ratings of task characteristics and application of the Dutch CEFR Grids to specify test content, to predict item difficulty, and to relate both test tasks and proficiency scales to CEFR levels and descriptors. The focus on listening comprehension in their paper sheds welcome light on an often neglected area of language testing. The following paper by **Montserrat Montagut and Pilar Murtra** reports how they used the CEFR for writing level descriptors when revising the higher level certificate in the Catalan language. This is one of relatively few accounts of test developers trying to use the CEFR to develop test specifications; they reflect upon the need for flexibility in its use, even to the point of local customisation, and comment critically on problems encountered and how these were overcome at C1 and C2 level. Finally in this section, **Peter Hardcastle, Sibylle Bolton and Francesca Pelliccia** explore some of the challenges that arise when attempts are made to link tests in different languages – Italian, Spanish, German and Portuguese – onto a single frame of reference. They argue that lexico-grammatical realisations of functions may well vary in difficulty across languages making the quantification and comparison of difficulty across languages and language tests a major problem. Their paper reminds us that the linguistic description component of the CEFR is generic rather than language-specific, and that the CEFR will need to be 'interpreted' when used for specifying reference levels for any particular language. This has already been accomplished for German, for example, through *Profile Deutsch*. The specification of reference levels for English, partially achieved through earlier initiatives such as *Waystage 1979/1990* and *Threshold*

1979/1990, is currently being extended through the *English Profile* project (www.englishprofile.org). The papers grouped in Section One thus explore the role and value of the CEFR in achieving transparency and coherence across multiple languages, multiple skills, multiple testing purposes and diverse socio-educational contexts, from both a theoretical and a practical perspective. The application of the CEFR in this regard is consistent with one of the fundamental aims of the ALTE members, i.e. to work together on common levels of proficiency and common standards for the language testing process designed to support the mutual recognition of language certificates across Europe. From the mid-1990s ALTE worked on placing the examinations of ALTE members within a common framework; more recently, effort has focused on relating the emerging ALTE Framework to the Common European Framework of Reference through empirical investigation as well as extensive work on the content analysis of examinations, guidelines for assuring the quality examinations and empirically validated performance indicators in different European languages.

Section Two of the volume considers the theme of *quality and diversity.* Papers in this section reflect contemporary concerns among language testers over quality management processes in test development and administration, including the application of testing standards and codes of practice; the notion of quality assurance and fairness review extends to embrace research into examination impact in various contexts. In the first paper in this section **Cyril Weir and Stuart Shaw** propose a comprehensive framework for establishing the various types of evidence needed to build a sound and convincing validity argument to underpin examinations. They demonstrate how a socio-cognitive framework can be applied to tests of second language writing and how such an approach may also assist in the process of linking exams to the CEFR in a transparent and coherent way. **Thomas Eckes** describes the complex process of assuring the quality of a high-stakes writing examination of German as a Foreign Language; he focuses on the application of *a posteriori* advanced statistical procedures such as multi-faceted Rasch measurement (MFRM) to provide a detailed view of how the rater-mediated performance assessment system functions. In his discussion of rater variability and the potential threat this poses for quality assurance, he speculates on possible factors underpinning rater variability and identifies avenues for further research. **David Coniam's** paper also addresses the critical quality assurance issue of rater severity/leniency but this time in the context of oral examinations in Hong Kong. Like Eckes, he uses MFRM to explore the impact of rater variability on scoring validity and argues for more careful consideration to be given to the process of using assessors' raw scores to report final grade outcomes. **Hanan Khalifa** continues the focus on quality assurance in this section by describing the cycle of activities undertaken by Cambridge ESOL in establishing their new Teaching Knowledge Test

(TKT). She explains how the generic Test Development Model developed by ESOL since the mid-1990s provides a rational and transparent basis for planning, managing and auditing exams, in order to maximise their validity and to ensure they are consistent with accepted professional standards in the field. **Maurizio Gotti and Carol Taylor Torsello** report on the development of a certification system (CERCLU) for tests of English and Italian within the context of university reform in Italy. They describe the procedures involved in creating and validating the test instruments, and discuss some of the diverse problems encountered with regard to technical (i.e. weighting) and technological (i.e. computer implementation) features. **Roger Hawkey** examines issues of test quality and test taker diversity in relation to an impact study of the International English Language Testing System (IELTS). Findings from the three-phase study conducted worldwide provide us with some useful insights into perceptions of test fairness, test anxiety and motivation, and test difficulty. The final paper in Section Two is by **Antony Kunnan** and deals with the concept of test fairness and the wider contexts in which tests operate. Building on his earlier Test Fairness Framework presented at the Barcelona 2001 conference, he proposes a complementary macro framework – the Test Context Framework – capable of analysing the wider context in which tests function, which can include political and economic, educational, social and cultural, legal and ethical, and even technological and infrastructure factors. Kunnan suggests that together the two Frameworks offer test agencies and institutions a comprehensive model for evaluating tests and testing. All the papers in this second section resonate with ALTE's long-established commitment to the concept of quality assurance in language testing and to continual improvement. In the early 1990s, for example, ALTE developed a Code of Practice which became the basis for elaborating professional standards for ALTE members and their stakeholders as well as for developing quality assurance systems and quality management tools that could be applied to the development, administration and validation of tests produced by ALTE members. Developing the concept of quality assurance and its management has to be a collaborative venture between partners and is not prone to imposition in the ALTE context. ALTE recognises that the field of language testing in different languages will be at different stages of development and that developing a language testing capacity in the European context, albeit in a relatively narrow domain, is an ongoing venture. Similarly, in a context where participants are free to walk away at any time, progress cannot be achieved through force or coercion but rather through involvement, greater understanding and personal commitment. Nevertheless, ALTE members are keenly aware that as test providers they carry significant responsibility and have sought to play a leading role in defining the dimensions of quality and how an effective approach to quality management can be implemented. Work on quality assurance has been in progress for several years now, more recently in the hands of an ALTE sub-group. Much of this has been presented at conferences and is publicly available in documented form, including on the ALTE website (www.alte.org).

As assessment interfaces increasingly with language proficiency requirements for participating in social, occupational and democratic processes, **Section Three** of the volume focuses on *ethics and diversity*, especially the complex relationships between linguistic identity and diversity on one hand, and immigration and citizenship policy on the other. In the opening paper of this section, **Joseph Sheils** outlines the Council of Europe's policy on social integration and citizenship. With regard specifically to its language policy he identifies a number of European Conventions and factors relating to language provision for integration and citizenship purposes, highlighting some common issues in member states concerning language provision and testing for residence or citizenship. Finally he explores the contribution the CEFR has to make in this area. **Nick Saville and Piet van Avermaet** continue this important theme, reporting on the political and ethical issues involved in defining and assessing the language proficiency required for citizenship and for active participation in society. They helpfully re-examine some commonly held assumptions in this area and consider the current role being played by language tests as well as the contribution members of the language testing community can make to political debate and public discourse. **Lynda Taylor** examines the issues that linguistic diversity raise for language testing in light of a preliminary survey of perceptions, policy and practice among European language test providers. She goes on to suggest how testing agencies might adopt a principled and pragmatic approach that affirms linguistic diversity while at the same time maintaining essential standards of quality and fairness. **Anne Lazaraton** explores another important strand relating to ethics and diversity, that of the non-native speaker in the role of language assessor. She reflects critically on what the available literature tells us about the traditional native speaker construct and about the issues which are perceived to surround the use of non-native speakers in language testing; and she highlights a number of useful implications and recommendations for language testers to consider. **Helen Sunderland and Chris Taylor** take us back to the relationship between language learning and citizenship. They provide a fascinating account of how test developers in the UK set about developing citizenship materials for ESOL learners as public policy and government legislation moved towards far greater regulation in relation to immigration and social cohesion in the early 2000s. Sunderland and Taylor offer a commentary on the problems they encountered and explain how they attempted to overcome these. Although the context has continued to evolve since this paper was first presented in 2005, it gives us a valuable insight into how key stakeholders in the process – both teachers and learners – can participate collaboratively and creatively in what may be a controversial initiative. In the final paper in this volume **Liz Hamp-Lyons** reflects on possible assessment trends for the future, specifically in the context of writing assessment. She considers notions of standards, diversity, individualism, local norms, equity and equality, suggesting that if we are to be 'ethical educators' we need to hold these notions in balance with one another as we strive for best practice in our approach to and use of assessment.

The field of language assessment is extremely broad today; assessment issues are dealt with in different ways by national and regional authorities throughout Europe and the world. ALTE was originally formed when a few organisations sought to establish a forum for the discussion of common issues and challenges in assessment. ALTE's direct interests and aims were at that time on a much smaller scale. It is important to underline that it brought together those interested in the assessment of their own language as a European foreign language. This might be in an international context, particularly with the more widely spoken languages but also in a national context, as is the case with lesser spoken languages in particular. While some ALTE members are located within ministries or government departments, others are within universities and cultural agencies. As a group, ALTE has always aimed to provide a benchmark of assessment quality in the particular domain in which it operates and to operate as a capacity builder in the multilingual European context, but ALTE does not set out to establish or police the standard for European language assessment in general. Increasingly, however, ALTE's work is perceived as having relevance outside its own immediate context. The two international conferences held in Barcelona in 2001 and in Berlin in 2005 (and the third to be held imminently in Cambridge in April 2008) attracted considerable interest and support not only from across Europe but also from much further afield, suggesting that these events provide a welcome forum for the international language testing community to come together and discuss shared interests and concerns. With its broad coverage of key issues, combining theoretical insights and practical advice, we believe that this proceedings volume on *Multilingualism and Assessment* will be a valuable reference for academics and policy-makers, e.g. immigration bodies, not only throughout Europe but in the wider international community. It will also be a useful resource for postgraduate students in language testing and for all practitioners who are seeking to define language proficiency levels in relation to the CEFR and similar frameworks.

Lynda Taylor and Cyril J Weir
March 2008

Section One
Achieving Transparency

1 Relating language examinations to the Council of Europe's Common European Framework of Reference for Languages (CEFR)

Waldemar Martyniuk
Council of Europe
Language Policy Division, Strasbourg

About the Council of Europe

The Council of Europe is the continent's oldest intergovernmental organisation, founded in 1949, with its permanent headquarters in Strasbourg, France. At the time of writing, it serves 800 million people in 46 member states, with five observers (Canada, Japan, the Holy See, Mexico and the United States).

The main aim of the Council of Europe is to achieve a greater unity between its members. It was created to: protect human rights and the rule of law in all member states; consolidate democratic stability in Europe by backing political, legal and constitutional reforms undertaken nationally, regionally and locally; seek solutions to social problems such as intolerance, discrimination against minorities, human cloning, drugs, terrorism, corruption and organised crime; promote and develop a European cultural identity, with special emphasis on education; and promote social cohesion and social rights.

The Council of Europe has been active in the area of languages for over 40 years now. Its programmes are co-coordinated by two complementary bodies: the Language Policy Division in Strasbourg and the European Centre for Modern Languages in Graz (Austria). The Division in Strasbourg focuses on instruments and initiatives for the development and analysis of language education policy for the countries which have ratified the European Cultural Convention and provides a forum for debate on policy development. The Centre in Graz (ECML), established in 1995, has as its mission the implementation of language policies, including support for the policy instruments developed in Strasbourg, and the promotion of innovative approaches. Its strategic objectives include the practice of modern language learning and teaching and the training of language educators.

Language education policy aims and principles

The Council of Europe language education policies aim to promote:

- PLURILINGUALISM: all are entitled to develop a degree of communicative ability in a number of languages over their lifetime in accordance with their needs.
- LINGUISTIC DIVERSITY: Europe is multilingual and all its languages are equally valuable modes of communication and expressions of identity; the right to use and to learn one's language(s) is protected in Council of Europe Conventions.
- MUTUAL UNDERSTANDING: the opportunity to learn other languages is an essential condition for intercultural communication and acceptance of cultural differences.
- DEMOCRATIC CITIZENSHIP: participation in democratic and social processes in multilingual societies is facilitated by the plurilingual competence of individuals.
- SOCIAL COHESION: equality of opportunity for personal development, education, employment, mobility, access to information and cultural enrichment depends on access to language learning throughout life.[1]

The following guiding principles define the CoE language education policy:

- Language learning is for *all*: opportunities for developing their plurilingual repertoire is a necessity for all citizens in contemporary Europe.
- Language learning is for the *learner*: it should be based on worthwhile, realistic objectives reflecting needs, interests, motivation, abilities.
- Language learning is for *intercultural communication*: it is crucial for ensuring successful interaction across linguistic and cultural boundaries and developing openness to the plurilingual repertoire of others.
- Language learning is for *life*: it should develop learner responsibility and the independence necessary to respond to the challenges of lifelong language learning.
- Language teaching is *co-ordinated*: it should be planned as a whole, covering the specification of objectives, the use of teaching/learning

materials and methods, the assessment of learner achievement, and the development of appropriate convergences between all languages that learners have in their repertoire or wish to add to it.

- Language teaching is *coherent and transparent*: policy makers, curriculum designers, textbook authors, examination bodies, teacher trainers, teachers and learners need to share the same aims, objectives and assessment criteria.
- Language learning and teaching are *dynamic* lifelong processes, responding to experience as well as changing conditions and use.[2]

The Common European Framework of Reference for Languages: Learning, Teaching, Assessment (CEFR)

The CEFR was developed by a Council of Europe international working party between 1993 and 1996 with a view to promoting transparency and coherence in language learning and teaching in Europe. After a pilot scheme, it was officially published in 2001, the European Year of Languages.[3] In addition to the two official Council of Europe versions in English and French, the document is now (September 2005) available in Basque, Catalan, Croatian, Czech, Finnish, Friulian, Galician, Georgian, German, Hungarian, Italian, Japanese, Moldovan, Polish, Portuguese, Romanian, Russian, Serbian, Spanish and Ukrainian. Further versions are in preparation. The document quickly became one of the most influential publications of the last decade in the field of language learning, teaching and specifically language testing in Europe and elsewhere.

The CEFR is a comprehensive descriptive scheme offering a tool for reflecting on what is involved not only in language use, but also in language learning and teaching. The Framework provides a common basis and a common language for the elaboration of syllabuses, curriculum guidelines, textbooks, teacher training programmes, and for relating language examinations to one another. It allows the different partners involved in planning and delivering language provision and in assessing language progress and proficiency, to co-ordinate and situate their efforts.

The CEFR is based on an action-oriented approach to language learning and use. One of its aims is to help partners to describe the levels of proficiency required by existing standards, tests and examinations in order to facilitate comparisons between different systems of qualifications. For this purpose a Common Reference Level system was developed, a system of six ascending levels of proficiency with specific outcomes – a compendium of descriptors of language proficiency (proficiency implying not only the knowledge of a language, but also the degree of skill in using it). The scheme proposed in the

CEFR adopts a 'Hypertext' branching principle, starting from an initial division into three broad levels:

- Basic User: A1 and A2
- Independent User: B1 and B2
- Proficient User: C1 and C2.

The CEFR is in effect a common reference tool across languages – the Framework is non-language specific, i.e. it is not referring to any single, concrete language but to the concept of language as such – and meant to be used in developing coherence in provision across different languages. It is also used in policy making as a means of ensuring coherence and transparency through the different sectors or stages in language education. Many countries have used the opportunity of the appearance of the Framework to stimulate curriculum and examination reforms in different educational sectors. The application of the principles laid out in the Framework may significantly contribute to the improvement of quality in language education.

The use of the CEFR

A survey on the use of the CEFR conducted in May 2005 by the Council of Europe Language Policy Division produced the following results[4]:

- the CEFR is fairly widely known in the responding institutions (3.16 on a 0–4 scale) and it is quite widely used (2.24 on a 0–4 scale)
- it is used mostly by teachers, teacher trainers, test writers, and materials writers
- it is used mostly in the domains of teacher training (pre-service and in-service), language testing/assessment, language curriculum development, textbook/materials production, and communication with stakeholders (learners, parents, teachers, staff, clients, etc.)
- clearly the best known/most frequently used parts of the CEFR are the Common Reference Levels of language proficiency (the global scale, the self-assessment grid, and the scales of illustrative descriptors)
- the usefulness of the CEFR has been rated at 2.44 on a 0–3 scale
- the CEFR proved to be most useful in the domains of testing/assessment/certification (2.70 on a 0–3 scale) and curriculum/syllabus development (2.66 on a 0–3 scale)
- institutionally, the CEFR proved to be most useful for the examination providers (2.88 on a 0–3 scale).

In general, the results of the survey indicate that the document's major impact is in the areas of teacher training and testing/assessment, with its Common Reference Scales of language proficiency being the part mostly looked at.

European Language Portfolio (ELP)

The most successful implementation of the approach proposed in the CEFR is the European Language Portfolio (ELP), launched during the European Year of Languages 2001. The ELP is a document in which those who are learning or have learned a language – whether at school or outside school – can record and reflect on their language learning and cultural experiences.[5]

The Portfolio contains a language passport which its owner regularly updates. A grid – adapted from the Common Reference Level scales of the CEFR – is provided where a learner's language competences can be described to serve as a complement to customary certificates. The document also contains a detailed language biography describing the owner's experiences in each language and which is designed to guide the learner in planning and assessing progress. Finally, there is a dossier where examples of personal work can be kept to illustrate one's language competences.

The Ministers of Education of the Member States of the Council of Europe have recommended that governments, in keeping with their education policy, support the introduction of a European Language Portfolio.[6] Several different models of the ELP have been or are being developed in Council of Europe Member States for specific groups of learners and for national contexts. However, all models must conform to the agreed principles and be approved by the European Validation Committee in order to use the Council of Europe logo.[7] The Validation Committee is an organ appointed by the Education Committee of the Council of Europe to assure the conformity of European Language Portfolio models to the common European Principles and Guidelines set down in document CC-ED (2000) 20.

European Union initiatives

In a communication from the Commission of the European Communities regarding the Action Plan 2004–2006 for Promoting Language Learning and Linguistic Diversity, the CEFR is mentioned as an important reference document:

> The Common Reference Scales of the Council of Europe's Common European Framework of Reference for Languages provide a good basis for schemes to describe individuals' language skills in an objective, practical, transparent and portable manner. Effective mechanisms are needed to regulate the use of these scales by examining bodies. Teachers and others involved in testing language skills need adequate training in the practical application of the Framework. European networks of relevant professionals could do much to help share good practice in this field.[8]

The CEFR Common Reference Level scales have been included in the Europass CV and in the Europass Language Passport (adapted part of the European Language Portfolio). Europass is a scheme which aims to facilitate mobility for those who wish to work or study abroad.[9]

At the European Council meeting in Barcelona, Heads of State and Government called for the establishment of a European Indicator of Language Competence. The purpose of the indicator is to measure overall foreign language competencies in each Member State. It is intended to have high levels of accuracy and reliability, with political acceptance to follow. The objective is to provide Member States with hard data on which any necessary adjustment in their approach to foreign language teaching and learning can be based. The CEFR Common Reference Scales are used as reference:

> The indicator should record the proficiency at each of the six levels of the scales of the Common European Framework of Reference for Languages (Council of Europe). This is already widely accepted and used by several Member States for determining their own benchmarks in this area.[10]

National and institutional level

The CEFR Common Reference Levels are widely used by ministries, examination bodies and providers, curriculum developers, textbook writers and publishers. One example of this is the objectives set in France by the French Ministry of Education for the academic year 2007/8 onwards:

- at the end of primary education, learners should reach Level A1 of the CEFR in the language studied
- at the end of compulsory schooling, learners should reach Level B1 of the CEFR in the first language studied and A2 in the second language studied
- at the Baccalaureate level, learners should reach Level B2 of the CEFR in the first language studied and B1 in the second language studied.[11]

More and more examination providers, language schools, textbook authors and publishers are using the CEFR Common Reference Levels.

International level

In addition to a growing number of non-European countries using the CEFR (Australia, China, Japan, Korea, New Zealand, USA, etc.) the United Nations has also adopted the Common Reference Level system, using it for teacher training and staff in-service training in all United Nations institutions across the world.

Relating language examinations to the CEFR

The growing acceptance of the standards presented in the Common European Framework of Reference for Languages has created a situation in which public bodies, examination institutes, language schools and university departments concerned with the teaching and testing of languages are increasingly interested in relating their curricula and examinations to the Common Reference Levels. A problem that arises in this regard is the question of assuring a consistent interpretation of the levels in different contexts.

The Language Policy Division is already responding in a comprehensive manner to the increasing number of requests from Member States for further guidance concerning the use of the Common Reference Level system. A pilot version of a Manual for relating language examinations to the Common European Framework of Reference for Languages[12] was developed in order to assist Member States, national and international providers of examinations in relating their certificates and diplomas to the CEFR in a reliable and proven manner.

In 2002, an authoring group of experts in the field of language assessment was nominated to draft, revise and deliver a pilot version of the Manual. An initial set of reference material already calibrated to the CEFR has been made available (CD-ROM + DVD) for the piloting. Several international benchmarking events are being planned to produce further CEFR calibrated reference material for a variety of languages. A range of language examining bodies and institutions from different CoE member countries and diversified educational contexts have been approached to participate in the pilot phase. They are asked to provide feedback from the piloting and to prepare full scale case study reports for selection of examples of good practice.

By September 2005 38 institutions from 19 countries were registered for the pilot phase of the Manual. Their work is supported by a Reference Supplement containing quantitative and qualitative considerations in relating certificates and diplomas to the CEFR and presenting different approaches to standard setting (its first draft is already available on the web pages of the Language Policy Division) – as well as by a growing set of multilingual reference materials accompanying the preliminary draft of the Manual: CD-ROMs with calibrated illustrative test items for listening and reading and calibrated samples of written performances, and DVDs/videos with calibrated illustrative samples of spoken performances. The final version of the Manual is planned to be published as a CoE document in 2008.

The preliminary draft of the Manual envisages the process of linking an examination to the CEFR in three stages:

• Specification: define the coverage of the examination in categories of the CEFR.

- Standardisation: ensure a consistent interpretation of the Common Reference Levels, using illustrative test items and samples of performances already calibrated to the CEFR elsewhere.
- Empirical Validation: check that the results produced by the examination relate to the levels of the CEFR in the way foreseen.

The general aims of the Manual project are to improve the quality of language education and to achieve transparency and comparability in language assessment. The project is intended to assist ministries of education and examination bodies to plan and measure student progress and to facilitate transparency and comparability in language assessment.

The specific objective is to provide reference material, tools and procedures for relating local language examinations to the CEFR. The expected results (outputs) are:

- sets of reference material for different languages (CEFR benchmarked test items and performance samples)
- case study reports from the piloting phase, with examples of good practice
- a Manual for relating language examinations to the CEFR – piloted, revised, published, promoted and disseminated by 2008
- a Reference Supplement to the Manual.

In a parallel project, the Common Reference Levels are being described in linguistic details for specific languages, referred to as '*Reference level descriptions for national or regional languages*' (such as *Profile Deutsch* or *B2 pour le français*, etc.). All these documents and tools are part of the *CEFR-toolkit* currently being developed by the Language Policy Division. The European Commission is contributing to the project as well, and it is currently producing a reading and listening item bank at Level B1 in English, French and German.

The following materials developed to support the piloting have been made available so far by the Language Policy Division of the Council of Europe (as of September 2005):

a) Reference Supplement to the Preliminary Pilot version of the Manual

The Reference Supplement, published by the Council of Europe Language Policy Division in December 2004 accompanies the Pilot Manual.[13] Its aim is to provide the users of the Pilot Manual with additional information which will help them in their efforts to relate their certificates and diplomas to the CEFR.

The Reference Supplement contains three main components: a) quantitative and b) qualitative considerations in relating certificates and diplomas to the CEFR and c) different approaches in standard setting.

The authors note that the link between language examinations and the Common European Framework of Reference for Languages (CEFR) can be established in at least three different ways:

- direct linkage to the CEFR scales of language proficiency
- indirect linkage via linkage to some local scales of language proficiency which have already been linked to CEFR scales
- indirect linkage via equation to an existing test already linked to the CEFR scales.

Whatever approach is adopted in the particular concrete situation, the authors stress that the linkage always requires standard setting and thus standard setting is a key element in the linkage process.

The editor of the Reference Supplement is confident that it will prove very useful for the language testing and assessment community in general. It contains information which is not readily available in the mainstream language testing literature. More specifically, it provides good support for those who wish to contribute to the development of the Manual by providing feedback, by piloting the Manual and by writing case studies of some aspects or the whole process of linking examinations to the CEFR and hopefully will contribute to the improvement of language testing quality.

b) DVD with French spoken performance samples illustrating the CEFR levels (including a report on the rating seminar in Sèvres and a guide for organising benchmarking events)

Users piloting the Manual have been encouraged to contribute towards collecting a set of videos and scripts of learner performances, whether or not they are writing up a case study. Such performances should be graded and documented in relation to CEFR levels following the procedures outlined in the Manual. A representative selection from samples collected will be very useful in illustrating future editions of the Manual for different languages, in different educational sectors and including speakers of different mother-tongues. A *Guide for the organisation of a seminar to calibrate examples of spoken performances in line with the scales of the CEFR* is available.[14] It is based on the experiences gathered during a seminar organised in Sèvres by the Centre International d'Etudes Pédagogiques (CIEP) and Eurocentres aimed at calibrating samples of oral performances in French to the CEFR levels.[15] A DVD resulting from this seminar is already available.[16]

c) CD-ROM with listening and reading items (and a grid to classify them)

The materials made available on this CD-ROM[17] are intended to facilitate the standardisation process for reading and listening described in the preliminary pilot version of the Manual.

The activities described in the standardisation phase of the Manual are expected to foster discussion amongst professionals piloting the Preliminary Version during the training sessions and as a result to contribute to building a common understanding in order to relate locally relevant test items to the CEFR levels and gain insights into developing test items that can eventually claim to be related to the CEFR levels.

The CD-ROM will also be useful for institutions and examination boards preparing Case Studies which will follow and document the process of validating the linking of a particular language examination to the CEFR levels. The feedback and materials resulting from the Piloting and the Case Studies will inform the main text of a revised version of the Manual, and provide standardised exemplar items to be included in a revised version of the CD-ROM.

The items and tasks contained in this CD-ROM are for English, French, German, Italian, and Spanish. They have been kindly supplied by examination providers operating in different contexts and for different languages: Cambridge ESOL, Goethe-Institut, WBT, TestDaF, CIEP, a recent EU-funded project with a pan-European perspective (DIALANG), and a national examination system from a Ministry of Education (YKI, Finnish Matriculation Examination Board).

To facilitate the use of the CD-ROM, the institutions characterised their items and tasks according to an agreed framework – the summary page of the Grid developed by the Dutch CEFR Construct Project – in order to analyse texts, items and tasks in terms of the CEFR descriptive scheme and levels. The Project aimed to help test developers and other language professionals to construct or relate test items to the CEFR. Since the CEFR is not directly relevant for the construction of test specifications, or the evaluation of test items, it was necessary to supplement guidance provided in the CEFR itself with information from other sources on what reading and listening tests might contain. One major outcome of the Project was an Internet-based Grid which can be used to help characterise reading and listening texts, items and tasks, and this Grid has been used in this way with the samples on the CD-ROM. The Grid can be accessed at: www.ling.lancs.ac.uk/cefgrid

It should be noted that the items in the CD-ROM should be considered to be a pilot in the same way as the Manual, and as part of a process which will feed into a new version of the Manual. Hence, the CD-ROM provides examples of good and appropriate practice in linking examinations to the CEFR.

d) Grid for the analysis of writing tasks and performances

In addition to the grid to analyse the content of reading and listening items and tasks, a CEFR Writing Content Analysis Grid was developed by the following process:

- A draft Grid was produced from a) the ALTE Checklist (produced in the early 1990s) adapted to the CEFR and b) the Dutch CEFR Construct Project Grid for Reading at a small ALTE workshop.
- The Ad Hoc group was consulted by email on the Grid. ALTE members tested the Grid.
- The final version of the Grid is now available on the Language Policy Division web page: www.coe.int/lang An online version is also available on the ALTE web page: www.alte.org

A Content Analysis Grid for Speaking is currently being developed by a similar process.

More information on the work of the Council of Europe Language Policy Division and its Manual project can be found on the following web pages:

www.coe.int/lang

www.coe.int/portfolio

Notes

1 Plurilingual Education in Europe. 50 years of international co-operation. A draft paper on the occasion of the 50th anniversary of the European Cultural Convention, CoE Language Policy Division, Strasbourg 2004, p. 6.
2 Op. cit. p. 8.
3 *Cadre européen commun de référence pour les langues: apprendre, enseigner, évaluer*, Editions Didier 2001; *Common European Framework of Reference for Languages: Learning, Teaching, Assessment*, Cambridge University Press 2001.
4 The results are based on questionnaires sent in by 111 respondents from 37 European states, Egypt and Mexico. They represent the views of the following types of institutions: Higher education (39); Central authority (29); Teacher training centre (18); Teacher education/Teacher college (18); Examination provider (16); Language school/centre (14); Adult education (12); Other: Further education, publisher, primary or secondary school, cultural agency/centre (28).
5 Recommendation N° R (98) 6 of the Committee of Ministers to Member States concerning Modern Languages from 1998 suggested, among other measures, the development and use by learners of a personal document (European Language Portfolio) to record their qualifications and other significant linguistic and cultural experiences in an internationally transparent manner as part of an effort to extend and diversify language learning at all levels from a lifelong perspective.
6 Resolution on the European Language Portfolio (adopted at the 20th Session of the Standing Conference of the Ministers of Education of the Council of Europe, Kraków, Poland, 15–17 October 2000).

7 74 versions of the ELP have been validated so far (September 2005), among them the first online version produced jointly by ALTE and EAQUALS.

8 Commission of the European Communities, COM (2003) 449, Brussels, 24/07/2003, p. 11.

9 For more information on the Europass project see: www.europass.cedefop.eu.int.

10 Commission of the European Communities, COM (2005) 356, p. 7, Brussels 1/8/2005.

11 Décret gouvernemental, J.O. n° 197 du 25 août 2005, texte n° 15.

12 DGIV/EDU/LANG (2003) 5, available as a downloadable PDF file in English or French from: www.coe.int/lang.

13 DGIV/EDU/LANG (2004) 13, downloadable as a PDF file from: www.coe.int/lang.

14 *Guide for the organisation of a seminar to calibrate examples of spoken performances in line with the scales of the CEFR*, by Sylvie Lepage and Brian North, Council of Europe, Language Policy Division, Strasbourg, May 2005 DGIV/EDU/LANG (2005) 4.

15 *Seminar to calibrate examples of spoken performances in line with the scales of the CEFR, CIEP, Sèvres, 2–4 December 2004*, report by Brian North and Sylvie Lepage, Council of Europe, Language Policy Division, Strasbourg, February 2005 DGIV/EDU/LANG (2005) 1.

16 Exemples de productions orales illustrant, pour le français, les niveaux du Cadre européen commun de référence pour les langues, DVD, Council of Europe/CIEP/Eurocentres, 2005.

17 *Relating Language Examinations to the Common European Framework of Reference for Languages: Learning, Teaching, Assessment.* Reading and Listening Items and Tasks: Pilot Samples illustrating the Common Reference Levels in English, French, German, Italian, and Spanish, a CD-ROM, Council of Europe, Language Policy Division 2005.

2 The CEFR levels and descriptor scales

Brian North
Eurocentres and EAQUALS, Switzerland

This paper describes the origin and purpose of the CEFR, discusses the CEFR descriptive scheme, the Common Reference Levels and the CEFR descriptors and concludes by suggesting ways in which the descriptors might be further validated and developed through qualitative research, taking a recent Cambridge ESOL writing project as an example.

Origin and purpose of the CEFR

The '*Common European Framework of Reference for Languages: Learning, Teaching, Assessment*' (CEFR) was developed between 1993 and 1996 by a Council of Europe international working party following the recommendation of an intergovernmental Symposium '*Transparency and Coherence in Language Learning in Europe*' hosted by Switzerland and coordinated by Eurocentres at Rüschlikon, near Zurich in November 1991. The main aim of the Symposium had been to investigate the feasibility of relating language courses and assessments in Europe to each other through some kind of common framework. Many school certificates awarded for language learning contained statements like 'followed a course of English at intermediate level' or 'successfully completed a course in Foundation French,' whilst others reported 'Grade C' or '4.5' or 'sehr gut'. Examination certificates tended to follow a similar pattern. It was very difficult to relate such results to each other because what they said was not very *transparent*: you have to be familiar with the particular course or exam to make sense of the result. Since no person or institution can be familiar with more than a few of the courses and exams around, this caused a lack of *coherence* in the organisation of language learning and in the reporting of results achieved at it.

The main outcome of the Symposium was the recommendation that a transparent and coherent Common European Framework should be produced to assist in the definition of language learning objectives. The text was produced by an authoring group consisting of John Trim (project director), Daniel Coste (CREDIF), Brian North (Eurocentres) and Joe Sheils (Council of Europe Secretariat). After piloting with two internal editions distributed by the Council of Europe in 1996 and 1997, the CEFR was published with Cambridge University Press for English and with Didier for French (Council of Europe 2001) and by May 2005 was available in 23 languages. In the past few years it has been increasingly widely adopted by schools in mainstream and adult education, by publishers and by examination providers.

The CEFR was written with three main aims:

- To establish a metalanguage common across educational sectors, national and linguistic boundaries that could be used to talk about objectives and language levels. It was hoped that this would make it easier for practitioners to tell each other and their clientele what they wish to help learners to achieve and how they attempt to do so.
- To encourage practitioners in the language field to reflect on their current practice, particularly in relation to learners' practical language learning needs, the setting of suitable objectives and the tracking of learner progress.
- To agree common reference points based on the work on objectives that had taken place in the Council of Europe's Modern Languages projects since the 1970s.

In time, the existence of such a common reference framework would, it was hoped, help to relate courses and examinations to each other and thus achieve the 'transparency and coherence' that had been the subject of the Rüschlikon Symposium. This was not seen as a harmonisation project. The aim of the CEFR was to provide a mental framework that can value and encourage diversity. It was intended to provide a tool that would enable people to say where they were, not a specification telling them where they ought to be. It was intended as a compendium or thesaurus, not as a cook-book. Right at the very beginning, the authors emphasise:

> We have NOT set out to tell practitioners what to do or how to do it. We are raising questions not answering them. It is not the function of the CEF to lay down the objectives that users should pursue or the methods they should employ. (Council of Europe 2001: xi Note to the User).

The Rüschlikon Symposium also recommended that a reporting instrument called the European Language Portfolio (ELP) should be developed for learners to self-assess and document their plurilingual proficiency in relation to the CEFR. Since 1997, dozens of versions of Portfolios have been produced for different countries and educational sectors. The EAQUALS/ALTE[1] electronic version for the adult sector has recently been made freely available (www.eelp.org).

It is worth returning to the full title of the CEFR 'Common European Framework of Reference for Languages: *Learning, Teaching, Assessment*' and noticing the deliberate order of the three words in the sub-title. It would probably be true to say that in the 10 years since the simultaneous internal publication of the CEFR and the 1997 Swiss prototype for the ELP, the CEFR became most widely known through the attention paid to the ELP in teacher training institutes and national educational ministries. The ELP prototype presented the CEFR descriptors in a way that made them accessible to teachers. One could argue that the ELP has in fact been highly successful as a tool for (a) operationalising in teacher training what a communicative approach means, (b) encouraging discussion of self-directed learning and above all (c) introducing the CEFR Common Reference Levels to language teachers in the state and private sectors throughout Europe. The link between the CEFR and ELP may also have been helped by the fact that the descriptors in the 1996 and 1997 internal editions of the CEFR were grouped in an appendix, making perusal a simple matter.

In the mid to late 1990s, the issue of linking assessments, tests and examinations to the CEFR was still hardly discussed at an academic level. Several projects funded by the EU took what might be described as a pragmatic approach and claimed relationships of examinations to the CEFR based on little more than self declaration, the personal opinions of small groups of experts or committee discussions in relation to descriptive frameworks that were not necessarily related to the CEFR. There were exceptions, of course, notably the efforts in Finland in Sauli Takala (a member of the original CEFR Working Party) and his colleagues. Therefore it is not surprising that it was the Finnish authorities that took the initiative and organised an intergovernmental seminar in Helsinki in July 2002 on the subject of relating examinations to the CEFR. This seminar led to the development by a project group co-ordinated by the current writer of the Manual '*Relating Language Examinations to the Common European Framework of Reference for Languages: Learning, Teaching, Assessment (CEFR)*' (Council of Europe 2003; Figueras North, Takala, Verhelst & Van Avermaet 2005). This manual, henceforth referred to as the Manual, is currently being piloted, not least by several ALTE members. The Manual proposes a linking process undertaken through three sets of procedures: *specification* of the context and purpose of the examination plus of the coverage of its tests and sub-tests in relation to the CEFR, *standardisation* of the interpretation of the CEFR levels by those involved with the examination, plus *empirical validation* including external validation that the results reported by the test-in-operation relate to the CEFR in the manner intended.

One must emphasise that the CEFR is not and was not intended to be a test specification or a blueprint to harmonise the content of language examinations in Europe. One could perhaps compare the CEFR to the European Monetary Union (EMU: currency snake) but not to the Euro. The CEFR is a translation device – not a super-specification. There is no 'Official European

Test' around the corner. This would be completely against the tradition of the Council of Europe, which after all is a political body dedicated to giving value and respect to cultural diversity. Even EU plans do not extend beyond (a) a modest project to create a small item bank of test items calibrated to the CEFR levels that could be used to help 'anchor' national tests to one another and thus support the *external validation* of claims to linkage based on *specification* and *standardisation*, and (b) a PISA-style snapshot of the foreign language proficiency of school leavers – the so-called 'Barcelona indicator'.

There is in fact an inherent contradiction in the idea of a pan-European test specification since any test should surely be designed for a particular context: a specific type of learner in a certain educational sector in a particular pedagogic culture. The CEFR tries to be 'comprehensive' (in the sense of including what is of relevance to everyone rather than in the sense of exhaustive) and in so doing deliberately adopts a stance that is as context-free as possible. It discusses parameters that are involved in language use and language learning (Chapter 4 'Language use and the Language User/learner') and the competences that the user/learner needs to have (Chapter 5 'The Competences of the User/learner'). It does not attempt to define all the aspects necessary in a test specification. The descriptor scales in Chapters 4 and 5, as is generally the case with scales of language proficiency, describe the proficiency shown by the learner. They are of only limited use as a specification of what the learner should actually be required to do in an examination: the test tasks. Test method and item type, for example, are not even mentioned in the CEFR. It is not a handbook for language testers. It is a compendium intended to be shared by the wider professional community concerned with teaching, learning and assessment.

The core of the CEFR is a *descriptive scheme* defining relevant activities and relevant qualities of language and a set of **Common Reference Levels** defining proficiency at six levels (A1, A2, B1, B2, C1, C2) in as many of these categories as has so far proved possible. The descriptive scheme is introduced in Chapter 2 and then fleshed out in Chapters 4 and 5. The Common Reference Levels are introduced in Chapter 3, and used to present descriptor scales for aspects of the descriptive scheme in Chapters 4 and 5.

Descriptive scheme

The descriptive scheme can be considered to be, in Mislevy's terms, a learner model '. . . a simplified description of selected aspects of the infinite varieties of skills and knowledge that characterise real students' (Mislevy 1995:343)

> A learner's state of competence at a given point in time is a complex constellation of facts and concepts, and the networks that interconnect them; of automatized procedures and conscious heuristics, . . .; of

perspectives and strategies, and the management capabilities by which the learner focuses his efforts. There is no hope of providing a description of such a state. Neither is there any need to. (Mislevy 1993:28).

The CEFR authors were actually careful to avoid the theoretical connotations of the word 'model' preferring to talk of a taxonomic 'scheme' covering domains, activities, strategies and competences. North (1997, 2000) describes the relation of the scheme to descriptive theory in applied linguistics. The scheme provides a principled set of categories, with open-ended lists of subcategories and possible elements. The 'action-oriented approach' taken is summarised by this paragraph from Chapter 2 written by Daniel Coste:

> Language use, embracing language learning, comprises the actions performed by persons who as individuals and as social agents develop a range of **competences,** both **general** and in particular **communicative language competences**. They draw on the competences at their disposal in various **contexts** under various **conditions** and under various **constraints** to engage in **language activities** involving **language processes** to produce and/or receive **texts** in relation to **themes** in specific **domains**, activating those **strategies** which seem most appropriate for carrying out the **tasks** to be accomplished. The monitoring of these actions by the participants leads to the reinforcement or modification of their competences. (Council of Europe 2001: 9)

Strategies are thus seen as a kind of hinge between competences on the one hand and the exigencies of the relevant task in the language activity one is undertaking, not unlike the Bachman model (Bachman 1990). Illustrative scales are in fact provided for Reception Strategies, Interaction Strategies and Production Strategies. The former area (Reception Strategies) is, however, under-defined as the vast majority of descriptors in this area were unfortunately found to be interpreted very inconsistently.

The core of the scheme is the set of *communicative language activities* plus the set of *communicative language competences*.

Communicative language activities are organised in three main categories: *reception, interaction, production*, each subdivided for spoken and written mode. Each of these macro categories has lists of activities that come under that heading. This tri-partite division reflects the thoughts of several applied linguists. Breen and Candlin (1980:92) posited three underlying abilities: 'Interpretation', 'Negotiation' and 'Expression', which they considered to be not primarily linguistic, but which Brumfit (1984:69–70; 1987:26) developed into 'Comprehension', 'Conversation or Discussion' and 'Extended Speaking' (with Extended Writing as a supplementary category appropriate on some occasions) which he described as 'independent modes of behaviour' (1984:70). Swales (1990) considered these issues from a genre angle, arguing that certain types of language use can be regarded as pre-generic and common to all societies: casual conversation or 'chat', and 'ordinary' narrative story-telling (Swales 1990:58–61). The former 'chat', is interactive with short turns, its coherence provided through the way participants weave their contributions together. It can be related to Cummins' (1979; 1980) concept BICS (Basic Interpersonal Communications skills), tending to low cognitive complexity and high contextual support (implicature). It can be considered to underlie all the genres of more specialised communicative interaction developed in different cultures (Swales *ibid*). The latter, storytelling, is productive, often prepared, rehearsed (or redrafted), its coherence provided in the text by the speaker/writer. It can be considered to underlie literacy and can be related to Canale's (1984) concept 'autonomous competence' (as opposed to communicative competence), tending to high cognitive complexity and low contextual support. This distinction between interactive and productive language is also related to the distinction made by Brown, Anderson, Shilock & Yule (1984) between short and long turns. 'Long turns which are used to transfer information – to recount an anecdote, justify a position, give instructions about how to take some medicine, describe a route – demand skill in construction and practice in execution.' Very young children do not attempt long turns, and young people in general (and some adults) have great difficulty organising them when under communicative stress (Brown et al 1984:15). Storytelling, production, long turns, then create an inverse receptive role as an auditor/recipient. North (1992) as a result proposed summary scales for the 'macro-skills' Reception, Interaction and Production at the Rüschlikon Symposium.

The development can be summarised by Table 1. A fourth category Processing (integrated skills) was later developed by the Framework Working Party into the concept of Mediation.

Table 1: Alternative categories to the four skills

Underlying abilities	Major activities	Pre-genres	Macro-skill
Interpretation	Comprehension	[Listening to storytelling]	Reception
Negotiation	Conversation	Conversation	Interaction
Expression	Extended speaking/writing	Storytelling	Production
			Processing
Breen & Candlin 1980	**Brumfit 1984**	**Swales 1990**	**North 1992**

The categories for the CEFR sub-scales provided for Reception, Interaction and Production are influenced by the concept of *macro-functions*. In discussing language use, Brown and Yule (1983:13) make a distinction between the establishment and maintenance of human relations (interactional use) and the working out of and transference of information (primarily transactional use). The speaking and writing sub-scales in the 1983 version of the Eurocentres

Scale of Language Proficiency (Johnson and Scott 1984) were organised according to three macro-functions: 'Asking for and exchanging information' (*Information*); 'Expressing opinions and making judgements' (*Opinion*); 'Establishing and maintaining social relationships' (*Social*). Scales were also produced for 'Listening to authentic texts' and for 'Reading authentic texts'.

Other curriculum projects in the 1980s developed similar approaches, for example the following list of curriculum strands related to the Australian Language Levels (ALL) (Tuffin 1990):

1. Establishing and maintaining relationships and discussing topics of interest.
2. Participating in social interaction related to solving a problem, making arrangements, taking decisions with others, and participating in transactions to obtain goods, services and public information.
3. Obtaining information (a) by searching for specific details in a spoken or written text (b) listening to or reading a spoken or written text as a whole and then processing and using the information obtained.
4. Giving information in spoken (monologue) or written form on the basis of personal experience (talk, essay, instructions).
5. Listening, reading, viewing and then responding personally to a stimulus.
6. Creating (a story, dramatic episode, poem, play).

Macro-functions (e.g. Transactional) can be cross-referenced to macro-skills (e.g. Interaction) to produce the cells of Table 2. Each cell in Table 2 can be elaborated for spoken and for written mode with one exception, *Discussion*, since written discussion (though it might be argued that there are interactive aspects to it) would be absorbed into the Production category *Presenting a case*.

Table 2: Cross-referencing macro-function and macro-skill

	Reception	Interaction	Production
Transactional language use	Understanding information-carrying text	Obtaining information and services	Presenting information
Creative, interpersonal language use	Understanding fictional text	Maintaining social relationships	Describing, narrating and interpreting experience
Evaluative, problem-solving language use	*(Merged with info-carrying texts)*	Discussion	Presenting a case

Such an elaboration is shown in Table 3. The Production categories *Describing, narrating and interpreting experience* and *Presenting a case* appear for both spoken and written language. Such production often takes the form of spoken monologue embedded within the interaction.

Table 3: Categories for communicative activities

	Interaction		Production	
	Spoken	**Written**	**Spoken**	**Written**
Transactional	Service encounters Information exchanges Interviews Telephone transactions	Form-filling Notes & messages Formal letters	Formal presentations	Formal reports
Creative, Inter-personal	Conversation	Personal letters	Describing, narrating and interpreting experience	
Evaluative, Problem-solving	Discussion Negotiating Formal meetings	–	Presenting a case	

The categories in Table 3 were validated in a series of 32 workshops with Swiss teachers in 1994–95. In these workshops, teachers were given a pile of about 60 descriptors for three or four similar categories, (e.g. Conversation, Obtaining information and services, Discussion) with the descriptors presented individually on strips of paper like confetti. They were given empty labelled envelopes (e.g. labelled 'Conversation', 'Obtaining information and services' and 'Discussion' and asked to put each descriptor into an appropriate envelope. An extra envelope was supplied for descriptors the teachers found sub-standard or for which they could not decide which the appropriate category was. This tested not only the clarity of the descriptors, but also the feasibility of the categories. There is a strong similarity between the categories listed in the cells in Table 3 and sub-scales in the CEFR. This is because the categories for the CEFR descriptor scales emerged through an interplay between the work of the Council of Europe authoring group, and experimentation with categories in the workshops with Swiss teachers.

It has to be admitted that this process, in the workshops with teachers, worked better for Interaction and Production (in Year 1: 1994) than for Reception (in Year 2: 1995). Indeed, initial attempts to validate subcategories for Listening and Reading or to classify descriptor elements in terms of actions, text-types and conditions proved singularly unsuccessful. Teachers were unable to associate such analytic elements with proficiency level, a finding not dissimilar to that of Alderson, Figueras, Kuijper, Nold, Takala & Tardieu (2004).

The approach then taken for Listening was to fall back on a 'situational discourse' approach: in what sort of situations that are significantly different in discourse terms do people listen? This approach was to a considerable extent influenced by the work of Rost (1990) on learner roles as interactive participant, addressee or overhearer. It worked well: teachers could understand the descriptors and sort them into categories; the 'Listening in Interaction' descriptors, already well calibrated in relation to the construct Interaction/ Production (Tables 8 and 9), then provided a solid 'anchor' to calibrate the receptive listening items into the scale. The final categories were:

Overall listening comprehension

- Understanding conversation between native speakers
- Listening as a member of a live audience
- Listening to audio media and recordings
- Listening to announcements and instructions.

For Reading the distinction adopted between the CEFR descriptor scales is more by purpose (in order to maintain a relationship; in order to find something, in order to read and understand in detail, in order to do something), although the descriptors in the scales also deal with text types. As reported in North and Schneider (1998) the Reading descriptors then had to be calibrated in a separate 'Reception' analysis, using the now-calibrated Listening items as 'anchors'. Unfortunately, in this process all descriptors for Reading Literature, indeed all descriptors combining reading with either socio-cultural/socio-linguistic or strategic factors showed extremely high misfit (i.e. were interpreted inconsistently) and had to be dropped from the analysis. The categories that survived for Reading were then the following:

Overall reading comprehension

- Reading correspondence
- Reading for orientation
- Reading for information and argument
- Reading instructions.

Communicative language competences are again organised in three main categories: linguistic competences, pragmatic competences and socio-linguistic competences. Again, each of these macro-categories has lists of aspects that come under that heading, as shown in Table 4.

Space does not permit a detailed discussion as to why fluency is included as a scale category under pragmatic competence. This issue is covered at length in North (1997, 2000). The expression 'She's a really fluent speaker', especially if used of a native speaker, would suggest not just the linguistic automaticity of the actual 'fluency' scale, but also a high degree of flexibility and precision of formulation (speaker meaning), not to mention coherence, thematic development and, in conversation, turn taking skills (all aspects of discourse competence).

Socio-linguistic competence, and other aspects of socio-cultural competence, proved very difficult at the formulation stage, in the workshops with

Table 4: Scale categories for linguistic and pragmatic competence

Linguistic	Pragmatic
Language resources	*Language use*
Usage	*Usage*
What can be said (sentence/dictionary meaning)	*What people say (speaker meaning)*
Knowing a language	*Knowing how to use a language*

Scale Categories		
Range:	General	Fluency
(Knowledge)	Vocabulary	Flexibility
		Precision
Accuracy:	Grammatical	Turntaking
(Control)	Vocabulary	Coherence
	Pronunciation	Thematic Development

teachers, and in the (Rasch) statistical analysis of teachers using descriptors to assess their students. It was not clear how much the problems were caused (a) by the concept being a quite separate construct from language proficiency and hence not 'fitting' in a Rasch analysis, as also found in a Rasch analysis by Pollitt and Hutchinson (1987); (b) by rather vague descriptors; or (c) by inconsistent responses by the teachers in the data collection. In the 2001 published edition, a scale for socio-linguistic competence was included, but most of the descriptors lack an empirical base. We will return to descriptors for socio-linguistic competence at the end of the paper when discussing the Cambridge common scale for writing.

Common Reference Levels

The Common Reference Levels in the CEFR describe learner achievement in the communicative language activities and communicative language competences in 54 illustrative scales distributed in the relevant sections of Chapters 4 and 5. The 54 descriptor scales can be used to describe the kinds of attributes examinations require their learners to demonstrate and can thus be used to profile such examinations as recommended in the Manual referred to above (Council of Europe 2003, Figueras et al 2005). This obviates the need to compare tests directly to each other.[2]

As mentioned above, the levels are themselves introduced in Chapter 3, summarised with a global scale (CEFR Table 1), a self-assessment grid of levels by communicative activities taken from the European Language Portfolio (CEFR Table 2), and an oral assessment grid edited from CEFR descriptors and defining Range, Accuracy, Fluency, Coherence and Interaction for each level (CEFR Table 3).

Origin

The CEFR levels did not suddenly appear from nowhere. They have emerged in a gradual, collective recognition of what the late Peter Hargreaves (Cambridge ESOL) described during the 1991 Rüschlikon Symposium as 'natural levels' in the sense of useful curriculum and examination levels.

The process of defining these levels started in 1913 with the Cambridge Proficiency in English exam (CPE) that defines a practical mastery of the language for a non-native speaker. This level has become C2. In 1939, Cambridge introduced the First Certificate in English (FCE) – still seen as the first level of proficiency of interest for office work, now associated with B2. In the 1970s the Council of Europe defined a lower level called 'The Threshold Level' (now B1) that specified what kind of language an immigrant needed to integrate into society, quickly followed by 'Waystage' (now A2), a staging point half way to Threshold. The first time these concepts were described as a possible set of 'Council of Europe levels' was in a presentation by David Wilkins at the 1977 Ludwigshafen Symposium (Trim 1978) that represented the first – unsuccessful – attempt to move towards a common European framework in the form of a unit-credit scheme linked to common levels.

During the 1980s Cambridge ESOL exploited this Wilkins framework and the specifications Threshold and Waystage in order to create new examinations below the First Certificate in English: the Preliminary English Test (PET) related to Threshold, and the Key English Test (KET) related to Waystage. The third Council of Europe specification in the Threshold series, called Vantage (now B2) was directly related to First Certificate when it was developed in 1992. The Cambridge Certificate in Advanced English (CAE) completed the Cambridge ESOL series by filling the gap between FCE and CPE. The set of exams KET, PET, FCE, CAE, and CPE then formed the basis of the original ALTE Framework.

As a result of this process of convergence, the CEFR levels (e.g. A2) , the names of Council of Europe-related specifications (e.g. 'Waystage') and the levels of Cambridge ESOL exams (e.g. Key English Test) all relate to each other as shown in Table 5. Cambridge ESOL has over the past 10 years helped other examination boards in Europe to begin to standardise on these levels through ALTE.

Development

The descriptor scales for the CEFR were developed in a 1993–96 Swiss project for English, French and German. The project was set up to provide descriptors for the CEFR and the prototype Portfolio, the descriptors for the latter being self-assessment versions of those for the former. The self-assessment versions

Table 5: Emergence of Common Reference Levels

Wilkins 1977/8, Ludwigshafen	Cambridge 1992	Council of Europe/ Swiss Project 1992–97	CEFR Levels
Ambilingual proficiency			
Comprehensive operational proficiency	CPE	Mastery	C2
Adequate operational proficiency	CAE	Effective operational proficiency	C1
Limited operational proficiency	FCE	Vantage	B2
Basic operational proficiency (Threshold Level)	PET	Threshold	B1
Survival proficiency	KET	Waystage	A2
Formulaic proficiency		Breakthrough	A1

were then also used by DIALANG (a European project to develop a multi-lingual computer-based diagnostic language assessment system for the internet). The project is described in detail in North (1995, 2000), North and Schneider (1998) and Schneider and North (2000). The project had a principled methodology:

1. **Qualitative research:** The first drafts of the descriptors were edited in 1993 from a wide documentation of over 30 existing sets of language proficiency statements. Exact formulations and the viability of categories used were checked through the series of some 32 workshops with teachers referred to above when discussing the Descriptive Scheme. The categories used for scales were thus validated by checking that teachers could correctly assign descriptors to the category concerned and that they found the descriptors clear and useful.

2. **Quantitative research:** The best descriptors – those that were sorted consistently to the correct pile and that were marked as clear and useful – were then used to create a series of overlapping 50-item checklists of descriptors for different levels. The descriptors on the different questionnaires were 'calibrated' onto the same mathematical scale through an analysis of the way in which teachers interpreted them in using the checklists to assess learners in their classes at the end of the school year. Data was collected for English in 1994, and then for English, French and German in 1995 – using the descriptors in all three languages. Lower and upper secondary, vocational and adult sectors were involved in a reasonably representative manner and altogether some 2,800 learners, 500 classes and 300 teachers were involved. Each learner was rated by their teacher for each descriptor using a 0–4 rating scale that was glossed on the first page of the questionnaire as follows:

0   This describes a level which is definitely *beyond* his/her capabilities.
    Could *not* be expected to perform like this.

1   Could be expected to perform like this provided that circumstances are
    favourable, for example if he/she has some time to think about what to
    say, or the interlocutor is tolerant and prepared to help out.

2   Could be expected to perform like this without support in normal
    circumstances.

3   Could be expected to perform like this even in difficult circumstances,
    for example when in a surprising situation or when talking to a less co-
    operative interlocutor.

4   This describes a performance which is *clearly below* his/her level. Could
    perform better than this.

After a Rasch model analysis, each individual descriptor had a difficulty
value (e.g. 1.76 or 0.53) that represented its position on the scale. Since,
unless otherwise specified, items in a Rasch model analysis are
calibrated at the point on the scale where learners have an equal chance
of getting them right or wrong, i.e. at 50%, this means that the difficulty
value of each descriptor was set at the point at which learners 'could be
expected to perform like this without support in normal circumstances'.
Descriptors calibrated higher up the scale were thus those descriptors
that were perceived by teachers to be more difficult than those lower on
the scale. The highest descriptor scale value was 4.68 (*Has a good
command of idiomatic expressions and colloquialisms with awareness of
connotative level of meaning*) and the lowest was way below A1 at −5.68
(*Can use some basic greetings; can say yes, no, excuse me, please, thank
you, sorry*). The overall length of the descriptor scale, from −5.68 to
4.68, is thus over 10 logits (10.36) with the learner ability scale being
considerably longer. The relatively long scale helped to ensure that the
descriptors were accurately separated out in rank order, with descriptors
describing similar things coming out close to each other. There was in
fact a marked tendency for descriptors that described something very
similar, and which had been deliberately put on different checklists, to
come out calibrated adjacent to each other. This confirmed that the
calibration had worked successfully.

3. **Exploitation:** The final step was to identify where on this mathematical
   scale one level stopped and the next level started. In other words the
   continuous scale of descriptors had to be 'cut' into levels. A conscious
   effort was made in this process to match up the descriptors to the set of
   levels that had gradually become established in Council of Europe
   circles in the 1970s and 1980s as discussed above and shown in Table 5.
   The 'cut-off points' were established by an interactive process of:

   (a) marking out units of approximately equal size on the scale

(b) identifying 'jumps' in the content described or gaps between clusters of descriptors

(c) comparing the content described to the levels adopted by ALTE examinations, the Council of Europe's Waystage and Threshold Level specifications

(d) comparing with the intentions of the original authors of the descriptors.

The resulting series of ascending levels, discussed in more detail in CEFR Section 3.6, can be briefly summarised as follows:

Level A1 is the point at which the learner can:

- *interact in a simple way; ask and answer simple questions about themselves, where they live, people they know, and things they have; initiate and respond to simple statements in areas of immediate need or on very familiar topics rather than relying purely on a rehearsed repertoire of (tourist) phrases.*

Level A2 reflects the Waystage specification with:

- the majority of descriptors stating social functions: *greet people, ask how they are and react to news; handle very short social exchanges; ask and answer questions about what they do at work and in free time; make and respond to invitations; discuss what to do, where to go and make arrangements to meet; make and accept offers*
- plus descriptors on getting out and about: *make simple transactions in shops, post offices or banks; get simple information about travel; ask for and provide everyday goods and services.*

Level B1 reflects the Threshold Level, with two particular features:

- maintaining interaction and getting across what you want to: *give or seek personal views and opinions in an informal discussion with friends; express the main point he/she wants to make comprehensibly; keep going comprehensibly, even though pausing for grammatical and lexical planning and repair is very evident, especially in longer stretches of free production*
- plus coping flexibly with problems in everyday life: *deal with most situations likely to arise when making travel arrangements through an agent or when actually travelling; enter unprepared into conversations on familiar topics; make a complaint.*

Level B2 reflects three new emphases:

- effective argument: *account for and sustain opinions in discussion by providing relevant explanations, arguments and comments; explain a viewpoint on a topical issue giving the advantages and disadvantages of various options*

- holding your own in social discourse: *interact with a degree of fluency and spontaneity that makes regular interaction with native speakers quite possible without imposing strain on either party; adjust to the changes of direction, style and emphasis normally found in conversation*
- plus a new degree of language awareness: *correct mistakes if they have led to misunderstandings; make a note of 'favourite mistakes' and consciously monitor speech for them.*

Level C1 is characterised by access to a broad range of language that results in fluent, spontaneous communication:

- *express him/herself fluently and spontaneously, almost effortlessly; has a good command of a broad lexical repertoire allowing gaps to be readily overcome with circumlocutions; there is little obvious searching for expressions or avoidance strategies – only a conceptually difficult subject can hinder a natural, smooth flow of language*
- *produce clear, smoothly flowing, well-structured speech, showing controlled use of organisational patterns, connectors and cohesive devices.*

Level C2 represents the degree of precision and ease with the language of highly successful learners:

- *convey finer shades of meaning precisely by using, with reasonable accuracy, a wide range of modification devices*
- *and a good command of idiomatic expressions and colloquialisms with awareness of connotative level of meaning.*

Unfortunately only six descriptors were calibrated at C2. These consisted of the two cited above, plus the following four:

> *Can backtrack and restructure around a difficulty so smoothly the inter-locutor is hardly aware of it.*
> *Can substitute an equivalent term for a word he/she can't recall so smoothly that it is scarcely noticeable.*
> *Shows great flexibility reformulating ideas in differing linguistic forms to give emphasis, to differentiate and to eliminate ambiguity.*
> *Can understand and summarise orally information from different spoken sources, reconstructing arguments and accounts in a coherent presentation of the overall result.*

All but the last (lowest) are concerned with the impression of precision and naturalness. Only the last concerns a communicative language activity. Most of the descriptors for C2 were therefore drafted intuitively. Unfortunately, neither DIALANG nor the ALTE 'Can Do' project produced descriptors for C2 that could noticeably enrich the current set. To do so, one may have to turn to a different methodology as discussed at the end of the paper.

'Plus' levels

The research project actually identified 10 rather than six bands of proficiency. The middle CEFR levels (A2–B2) proved to take twice as much space on the scale as the bands of proficiency at the top and the bottom (C1–C2; A1 and a beginner band below it, referred to in the CEFR as 'Tourist').

To put this another way, between what can be described as the criterion level for A2 and the criterion level for B1 there was found to be what came to be described as a 'plus level'. The same was the case for between B1 and B2 (B1+) and between B2 and C1 (B2+). Such 'plus levels' were characterised by a stronger performance in relation to the same features found at the criterion level, plus hints of features that became salient at the next level. This phenomenon can be seen clearly in reading CEFR Section 3.6.

The relationship between the six CEFR Common Reference Levels and the 10 empirical bands of proficiency produced in the Swiss research project is shown in Table 6. As can be seen from the right hand column, when the plus levels are included, the 'size' of each band is virtually identical at approximately 1 logit, with a slight, symmetrical distortion.[3]

Table 6: CEFR levels and 'plus' levels

Levels		Cut-off	Range on logit scale
C2		3.90	
C1		2.80	1.10
	B2+	1.74	1.06
B2		0.72	1.02
	B1+	−0.26	0.98
B1		−1.23	0.97
	A2+	−2.21	0.98
A2		−3.23	1.02
A1		−4.29	1.06
	Tourist	−5.39	1.10

Objective scale values

The CEFR levels are thus related to a measurement model, the Rasch model. As is the case with Mislevy's 1995 student model, mentioned in relation to the Descriptive Scheme, a 'model' here does not imply theoretical perfection but a working model with certain drawbacks. Nevertheless, the majority of the CEFR descriptors have published item characteristics including a scale value on the logit scale shown in Table 6 (North 2000): they are calibrated in the technical meaning of the term. Certain features are not described at particular levels just because of the opinions of authors, teachers, testers or members of an authoring or construct group. Their placement on the scale is objective.

The existence of objective scale values (based on a measurement model) rather than subjective scale values (based on personal opinion(s)) is an important prerequisite for a valid descriptor scale that was identified as long ago as 1928:

> . . . the scale values of the statements should not be affected by the opinions of the people who helped to construct it. This may turn out to be a severe test in practice, but the scaling method must stand such a test before it can be accepted as being more than a description of the people who construct the scale. At any rate, to the extent that the present method of scale construction is affected by the opinions of the readers who help sort out the original statements into a scale, to that extent the validity of the scale may be challenged (Thurstone 1928:547–8).

With the exception of the descriptors for C2, as discussed above, the vast majority of the CEFR descriptors can be claimed to fully meet Thurstone's test, as is discussed further below.

Descriptors

The CEFR descriptors are relatively concrete descriptions with a 'Can Do' formulation. Here are some typical examples that were calibrated to Level B2. The three appear together as the entry for Level B2 in the sub-scale for 'Informal Discussion (with friends)' (English: page 77):

> Can take an active part in informal discussion in familiar contexts.
>
> Can with some effort catch much of what is said around him/her in discussion, but may find it difficult to participate effectively in discussion with several native speakers who do not modify their language in any way.
>
> Can account for and sustain his/her opinions in discussion by providing relevant explanations, arguments and comments.

As mentioned above, B2 showed a concentration of descriptors concerned with effective argument, for example *explain a viewpoint on a topical issue giving the advantages and disadvantages of various options* (a classic FCE task). A B1 user cannot do this effectively, a B2 user can – but may still have some comprehension problems. The content of the three descriptors could be presented schematically, as in Table 7.

Comprehension in interaction, as illustrated by the calibrated descriptors, actually develops in a very systematic way. This can be seen by the schematic representation of this descriptor scale in Table 8, which breaks descriptors up into the elements 'Setting', 'Speech' and 'Help'.

Table 7: Informal discussion at B2

Global	Comprehension	Expression of opinions	Reaction to other views
take an active part in informal discussion in familiar contexts	• catch much of what is said around him/her in discussion (by several native speakers) – but with some effort • *may* (nonetheless) find it difficult to participate effectively in discussion with several native speakers who do not modify their language in any way	• put point of view/ opinion clearly • account for and sustain his/her opinions/point of view • make hypotheses • provide relevant explanations • provide relevant arguments	• evaluate alternative proposals • make relevant comments • respond to hypotheses

Table 8: Listening in interaction – elements calibrated to different levels

Level	Setting	Speech	Help
B2+	– animated conversation between native speakers		
B2	– even noisy environments	– standard spoken language	– some recognition in discussion between natives that not a native speaker
B1+	(topics which are familiar)	– clearly articulated standard speech	– some recognition in discussion between natives that not a native speaker
B1	– extended everyday conversation	– clearly articulated standard speech	– ask for repetition & reformulation
A2+	– simple, routine exchanges – familiar matters	– clearly articulated standard speech	– ask for repetition & reformulation
A2	– simple everyday conversation	– clear, slow, standard, directed at him	– if partner will take the trouble
A1	– everyday expressions aimed at the satisfaction of needs of a concrete type – short, simple questions & instructions	– very clear, slow, carefully articulated, repeated speech directed at him	– sympathetic partner – long pauses to assimilate meaning

A very clear progression is visible in all three columns. Speech must at first be *very clear, slow, carefully articulated, repeated speech* that is *directed at* the recipient. Then comes *clear, slow, standard speech directed at him/her* followed by *clearly articulated standard speech* (which no longer has to be especially slowly or carefully adjusted for him/her) and finally the *standard spoken language* – even when this is *animated conversation between native speakers*. Proficient users (C1 and C2) do not have comprehension problems in interaction.

This progression can also, if desired, be presented in an even more schematic form as in Table 9, which shows simplifying factors that are prerequisites for the user to understand.

Table 9: Prerequisites for comprehension in interaction

	some recognition by several NSs that not a NS	low background noise	familiar, everyday topics	clear articulation	chance to get repetition	non-standard = simplified	directly to user	overtly helpful interlocutor	slow	careful articulation with pauses	very concrete, immediate topic
A1	√	√	√	√	√	√	√	√	√	√	√
A2	√	√	√	√	√	√	√	√	√		
A2+	√	√	√	√	√	√					
B1	√	√	√	√	√						
B2	√										
B2+											

In the context of developing a set of test content specifications, there has been some recent criticism (e.g. Alderson et al 2004:7–11) that the descriptor scales do not explicitly describe in a systematic way the presence or absence of the same features for each level in this way. Indeed Alderson et al take the difficulty of speech in listening comprehension as an example of such a lack of systematicity. Yet as Tables 8 and 9 show, there is a systematic progression in listening in interaction. In fact a content analysis of the calibrated descriptors for Interaction (including comprehension in interaction) and Production made it clearer and clearer that what had been calibrated had been content elements in descriptors. An example for the treatment of 'topic' is given in CEFR Document B5 in CEFR Appendix B (Coherence in descriptor calibration). This contrasts the treatment of topic in content analysis charts for the descriptor scales Describing and Narrating (personal experience), for Information Exchange with the column for 'settings' from the analysis of Linguistic competence: Range. The content demonstrates a high degree of coherence, reflected throughout the set of calibrated descriptors. This consistent scaling of the *content elements* in descriptors was exploited to create scales for categories not included in the original survey (e.g. Public Announcements) by recombining descriptor elements. The coherence is further demonstrated in a series of charts published by North (2000:290–309).

Returning to the citation from Thurstone made at the end of the last section, it can therefore be claimed that the vast majority of the CEFR descriptor scales do meet the test he sets as either the descriptor itself or the elements from which it is made up have been objectively calibrated. This explains why the replication of the rank order of descriptor scale values found in follow-up projects has been so high: in the second year of the Swiss

CEFR research project with French and German (0.99: North 2000: 339), in conjunction with ALTE 'Can Do' statements in their self-assessment format (0.97: Jones 2002:176), in relation to listening, reading and writing descriptors used in their self-assessment form by DIALANG (0.96 for Listening and Reading, 0.92 for Writing: Kaftandjieva and Takala 2002:114–121) and in a self-assessment instrument at university entrance (0.90: North 2002:162).

A weaker claim, not backed by empirical data, must be made for the majority of C2 descriptors, as discussed above, plus Socio-linguistic Appropriateness, Phonological Control and Orthographic Control. Some of the descriptors for Socio-linguistic Appropriateness are already included in other descriptor scales; a few were calibrated in the project reported in North (2002) and several were written by the author and John Trim in 2000. Orthographic Control was added for the sake of completeness, using descriptors edited from existing scales.

The issue with regard to Phonological Control is more complex. The descriptors showed noticeable misfit for English from B1 downwards – when the descriptors are phrased in a more negative fashion. When used simultaneously in English, French and German for those three target languages, all the phonology descriptors showed very high Rasch misfit (inconsistent use). This was the only category for which descriptors behaved significantly differently in and for different languages. This is the reason why this descriptor scale was excluded from the assessment grid presented as CEFR Table 3.

Possible limitations of the descriptor scales

Alderson et al (2004:7–11) give a list of apparent shortcomings in the CEFR descriptor scales highlighted in their project to develop specifications for test item development and classification:

1. Terminological problems: synonymy or not – especially with verbs – especially with listening and reading, e.g. understand/recognise, find/locate.
2. Gaps: (a) areas of the descriptive scheme for which no descriptor scale exists, and (b) a lack of coverage of tasks, especially (i) comprehension tasks and (ii) test tasks in the sense of task and item types.
3. Inconsistencies: the inclusion of verbs, content elements or provisos at one level and not at another level. Here paradoxically complexity of speech for listening (shown schematically in Tables 8 and 9 above) is taken as the example.
4. Lack of definition: What do, for example, 'simple' or 'frequent' mean, and what they mean for, e.g., French vocabulary – and surely the meaning may be different depending on how similar or different the learner's first language is to the (French) language.

Taking the last point first, it would in fact seem unwise for a common framework scale, used for different languages, different linguistic regions and different educational sectors to attempt such definition. Such definitions, used for test specifications, must surely be context bound. Even then it would appear wise to base such definition on an analysis of performances by the learners concerned.

As pointed out at the beginning of this paper, the CEFR descriptor scales are not test specifications. Like any scale of language proficiency, they describe the learner rather than the task the learner is doing. This makes them useful for subjective assessment – whether self-assessment, teacher assessment or profiling of examinations as suggested in the Manual (Council of Europe 2003). Furthermore, even if valid content specifications can be developed for different languages (e.g. Profile Deutsch), tests and the specifications for them are more valid for a context if they are developed for the needs of that context. Finally the omission of any discussion of test task and item types in the CEFR is deliberate: the CEFR is a compendium on objectives, not a cookbook on test development.

The 'gaps' are admitted and indeed highlighted by the authors of the CEFR. One of the problems is perhaps that because the scales are distributed through the text precisely in order to be honest about this point and stimulate further research, people don't always find all of them. For example three of Alderson et al's list of 10 missing areas do have at least one modest descriptor scale (study skills, text-to-text activities, strategies).

The CEFR levels and descriptor scales have an empirical basis in a relatively large-scale, multi-lingual, multi-sector project combining intuitive, qualitative and quantitative analysis. This is probably why they have met largely positive feedback. However an empirical base brings distinct disadvantages: things always turn out differently to what you intended. Descriptors on a certain feature targeted at, for example, B2 sometimes landed at, for example, B1 – leaving two descriptors at B1 and a 'gap' at B2. Several of these gaps were successfully plugged in Year 2, but some remain. Why? Maybe there is nothing new to say at this level; maybe there is, but no one has yet successfully formulated it. Strategies (especially receptive strategies like 'getting gist', 'inferring' 'deducing unknown words'), plus sociolinguistic competence and socio-cultural knowledge were very problematic in all stages of the project. Reading and Listening were very complicated at the qualitative stage of defining categories. Attempts to edit descriptors systematically from content elements rather like Alderson et al's (2004) charts and get teachers to sort them into categories or levels ran into a complete cul-de-sac as stated when discussing the Descriptive Scheme.

The other two points raised by Alderson et al ('Inconsistencies', 'Terminology: when synonymous') are a result of the scale construction method used and a reluctance to tinker arbitrarily with empirical results without having collateral evidence. Alderson et al's criticism assumes that a descriptor scale should systematically cover the same features at all levels. However, there are in fact two contrasting schools of thought for the development of descriptor scales. The first is a more abstract, systematic approach under which something is found to be said about the same set of features at every level. The second approach focuses on more concrete, salient features, describing what is new that is significant at each level.

The main disadvantage of the abstract, more systematic approach is that it can produce descriptors that spread the feature across the pre-designated number of levels by systematically alternating qualifiers like 'very', 'somewhat', 'a little' or 'simple', 'standard', 'complex' or 'fully', 'mostly', 'partly'. Cohen and Olshtain offer a good example of this approach (Cohen and Olshtain 1993; Cohen 1994:283–7). Their scale for socio-linguistic ability reads as follows:

Socio-linguistic ability

5 *the speaker uses linguistic forms that are fully appropriate for expressing the intended speech act*

4 *the speaker uses linguistic forms that are mostly appropriate for expressing the intended speech act*

3 *there is some use of inappropriate linguistic forms for expressing the intended speech act*

2 *there is much use of inappropriate linguistic forms for expressing the intended speech act*

1 *there is continuous use of inappropriate linguistic forms for expressing the intended speech act*

This scale relies upon alternating qualifiers to such an extent that it can just as effectively be presented as the kind of labelled scale used on questionnaires.

	1	2	3	4	5
Socio-linguistic ability: Appropriateness of linguistic forms for expressing the intended speech act	*fully app.*	*mostly app.*	*some inappr.*	*much inappr.*	*continuous inappr.*

One could imagine the scale being used effectively in a speaking test aimed at a certain level, in which the examiners already have an internalised standard. But could one really try to match up Bands 1–5 on such a scale to curriculum and examination levels like A1, A2, B1, B2 etc?

Carroll and West (1989) do attempt to differentiate examination levels systematically by giving more detail in their English Speaking Union (ESU)

Framework scale. Their descriptors alternate key qualifiers in standard sentences in order to create systematic links in the formulation of descriptors for adjacent bands. The ESU scale has nine bands and each descriptor is made up of eight content elements as shown in the descriptor for Speaking for Band 5:

> Handles moderate speech situations with adequate confidence and competence. Message is broadly conveyed but with little subtlety and some loss of detail. Some difficulties in initiating and sustaining conversation. Interaction needs repetition and clarification. Spoken text organisation is adequate but with fairly frequent stylistic lapses. Fairly frequent hesitations and lapses in fluency, but these do not interfere with basic communication. Uses a moderate language repertoire, but has to search for words and use circumlocutions. Fairly frequent errors in accuracy. Obvious L1 accent and speech features. Limitations impair communication at times.

Each content element is distinguished from the elements at the band above and below by switching two or three qualifiers in otherwise very similar sentences. The first sentences from the descriptors for Bands 3–6 are as follows:

6 Handles *moderate* speech situations with *good* confidence and competence but some problems with *higher* level situations.

5 Handles *moderate* speech situations with *adequate* confidence and competence.

4 Handles *simple* speech situations with *good* confidence and competence, but *some* problems with *moderate* level situations.

3 Handles *simple* speech situations with *adequate* confidence and competence, but *many* problems with *moderate* level situations.

The same sort of approach is also used with the subsequent seven sentences in each band descriptor.

This may provide the kind of systematic mentioning of a given set of features that Alderson et al (2004) found missing in the CEFR descriptors – though they would of course like all the terms 'simple', 'moderate', 'good' etc. need to be defined. However, it is not exactly an easy read. This type of approach (with definitions) may well be appropriate to a set of test specifications, but whether it is appropriate as a style for formulating descriptors in a common framework is another matter. It is difficult to envisage this kind of approach being successfully exploited for self-assessment, teacher assessment or curriculum development.

In fact, this approach perpetuates three main problems found with many proficiency scales:

- Wording often creates a semantic appearance of a scale, without really describing anything.

- Wording tends to be relative. The descriptors are seldom stand-alone criteria to which one could rate 'Yes' or 'No' independently on a checklist (e.g. a portfolio checklist).
- Descriptors for lower levels tend to be worded negatively and are thus unhelpful as objectives.

The alternative approach based on salient features highlights what is significant at each level, deliberately not cluttering the description when there is nothing new to say. It tends to use 'Can Do' formulation. Basically this approach starts with individual descriptors that can be considered as target behaviours (= objectives) and then decides the relative difficulty of each such behaviour. Such an approach originated in occupational evaluation of health professionals in the 1960s and 1970s (Bernadin and Smith 1981, Borman 1986, Landy and Farr 1983, Smith and Kendall 1963). The approach came into language teaching from two directions: in America with the 1950s Foreign Service Institute scale (Wilds 1975) and its successors including the Australian Second Language Proficiency Ratings (ASLPR: Ingram 1981), both four skills based, and in Europe through 'English for Specific Purposes' in the 1970s, exemplified by the 1974 IBM France scale presented at the 1978 Ludwigshaven Symposium (Trim 1978) and the ELTDU scale (ELTDU = English Language Teaching Development Unit, originally part of Oxford University Press). Unlike the American 4-skills scales, the IBM and ELTDU scales each had a relatively large number of descriptor scales for different types of activities. The ELTDU scale had a direct impact on the development of the Eurocentres scale (Johnson and Scott 1984, North 1993). The IBM, ELTDU and Eurocentres scales were used for curriculum development, language audits (what categories are relevant? where do you need to be? where are you now?) and self-assessments.

Descriptor scales developed by both approaches were presented to the Rüschlikon Symposium. The Symposium made a very clear decision that, because the European Framework was to build on the 1970s work in the Modern Languages project and be primarily concerned with learning and teaching objectives, and because it was to produce a scale that should be usable for self-assessment in the European Language Portfolio, the 'salient features' approach should be adopted.

The main disadvantage of the salient features approach is that the placement of descriptors at a particular level could well be arbitrary, based on unvalidated conventions and clichés being copied from scale to scale through a process of systematic plagiarism. This was Thurstone's point: '. . .the scale values of the statements should not be affected by the opinions of the people who helped to construct it' (Thurstone 1928:547). This is why a Rasch model analysis of data from checklists made up of descriptors was used to break the circle of subjectivity.

As discussed above, this provides impressive coherence in the content calibrated to different levels, a very high agreement between different projects on where specific content should be placed and high correlations between the difficulty values for CEFR descriptors used in different projects. But it also provides some inconsistencies caused by decisions taken in formulating individual descriptors (here: 'find', there: 'locate') and between what is mentioned at different levels: ('find'/'locate' mentioned at level X but not at level Y) that irritated Alderson et al – and translators.

Enriching the description

However, it seems unwise to undertake any editing or further elaboration of the descriptor scales without some collateral evidence. Otherwise one risks falling back into the clichéd mistakes the CEFR has so far avoided. One could, of course, analyse the ALTE 'Can Do' statements and the DIALANG reporting statements, both currently in CEFR appendices and see if they have anything significant that could be added within the CEFR structure. But it is likely that any radical enrichment would need to come from a new methodology, not from more of the same.

North and Schneider (1998:243) emphasised that the production of a scale was only the first step in the implementation of a common framework, and that ensuring a common interpretation through standardised performance samples and monitoring data from tests was necessary. The Manual (Council of Europe 2003) now has calibrated video samples for the two official languages of the Council of Europe, English and French, with further samples for German, Spanish and Italian planned. In addition, there are projects collecting writing performance samples and sample reading and listening items that are considered by the institutes they originate from to represent the CEFR levels.

Therefore a very useful next step could be to:

a) Define key assessment criteria and salient features in those categories at each level as seen in samples; this is a common technique to develop a writing scale, but it presumably could also be done with video recordings or calibrated test items with scripts and possibly think-aloud protocols.

b) Compare the scale that is the result of the above analysis to the content of the CEFR descriptor scales; this process might lead to:
   - confirmation of existing illustrative descriptors
   - enrichment of existing illustrative descriptors
   - identification of weak points in the CEFR descriptors, and contradictions with what is defined qualitatively from the samples.

c) Strengthen the connection between the formulation of descriptors and the features observed in calibrated exemplars by:

- identifying key features that appear to distinguish between levels and checking that these are salient in the descriptors
- offering documented examples of what is meant by expressions in descriptors like 'simple language', 'a wide range of vocabulary' etc.
- developing definitions of such terms (as wished by Alderson et al) on the basis of such examples.

Hawkey and Barker (2004) have recently reported a qualitative study developing a writing assessment scale from writing samples from the Cambridge ESOL examinations PET, FCE, CAE and CPE, which are related to the CEFR levels B1–C2 as shown in Table 5. The aims of the project encompass points (a) and (c) listed above.

To conclude, I would like to simulate step (b) above in relation to the Cambridge writing scale so reported. I would suggest that such a methodology could be valuable to the future enrichment of the CEFR descriptors, particularly at levels (e.g. C2) and for categories (e.g. socio-linguistic competence, receptive strategies) that have so far proved elusive. Readers will need to refer to the appendix to follow the argument.

Table 10, the CEFR writing assessment scale (Table 5.8 in the Manual – Council of Europe 2003), is also provided to show the current CEFR descriptor tool for this area. Elements on Table 10 shown in italics have been added by Sauli Takala. In creating what became CEFR Manual Table 5.8, Takala himself drew on a qualitative analysis of writing samples from Finnish national examinations, in order to supplement the main descriptors drawn from CEFR scales.

A descriptor on the draft Cambridge scale (Appendix 1) looks like the following:

ALTE 5 (C2)
Can write extensively and enhance impact on the reader through the effective use of sophisticated language resources such as:

- the ability to vary style of expression and sentence length for effect
- the use of advanced vocabulary and word order
- the use of idiom and humour

Can write with only very rare errors of grammar or vocabulary
Can organise extended writing effectively, linking ideas appropriately with or without explicit words

The first step taken was to classify each descriptor by CEFR categories and reformulate it in CEFR style (Appendix 2), giving the reformulation of the above descriptor shown in Table 11.

The next step was to sort these descriptors by category so as to give CEFR-style descriptor scales like the one shown in Table 12.

Table 10: CEFR written assessment criteria grid: CEFR Manual Table 5.8

	Overall	Range	Coherence	Accuracy	Description	Argument
C2	Can write clear, *highly accurate and smoothly* flowing complex texts in an appropriate and effective *personal* style *conveying finer shades of meaning.* *Can use a* logical structure which helps the reader to find significant points.	Shows great flexibility in *formulating* ideas in differing linguistic forms to convey finer shades of meaning precisely, to give emphasis and to eliminate ambiguity. Also has a good command of idiomatic expressions and colloquialisms.	Can create coherent and cohesive texts making full and appropriate use of a variety of organizational patterns and a wide range of connectors and other cohesive devices.	Maintains consistent *and highly accurate* grammatical control of even *the most complex language forms.* *Errors are rare and concern rarely used forms.*	Can write clear, smoothly flowing and fully engrossing stories and descriptions of experience in a style appropriate to the genre adopted.	Can produce clear, smoothly flowing, complex reports, articles and essays which present a case or give critical appreciation of proposals or literary works. Can provide an appropriate and effective logical structure which helps the reader to find significant points.
C1	Can write clear, well-structured *and mostly accurate* texts of complex subjects. *Can underline* the relevant salient issues, *expand and support* points of view at some length with subsidiary points, reasons and relevant examples, and *round* off with an appropriate conclusion.	Has a good command of a broad range of language allowing him/her to select a formulation to express him/herself clearly in an appropriate style on a wide range of general, academic, professional or leisure topics without having to restrict what he/she wants to say. *The flexibility in style and tone is somewhat limited*	Can produce clear, smoothly flowing, well-structured text, showing controlled use of organizational patterns, connectors and cohesive devices.	Consistently maintains a high degree of grammatical accuracy; *occasional errors in grammar, collocations and idioms.*	Can write clear, detailed, well-structured and developed descriptions and imaginative texts in an assured, personal, natural style appropriate to the reader in mind.	Can write clear, well-structured expositions of complex subjects, underlining the relevant salient issues. Can expand and support point of view with subsidiary points, reasons and relevant examples.
B2	Can write clear detailed *official and*	Has a sufficient range of language to be able	Can use a limited number of cohesive	Shows a relatively high degree of	Can write clear, detailed	Can write an essay or report that develops an

Table 10: (continued)

	Overall	Range	Coherence	Accuracy	Description	Argument
	semi-official texts on a variety of subjects related to his field of interest, synthesising and evaluating information and arguments from a number of sources. *Can make a distinction between formal and informal language with occasional less appropriate expressions*	to give clear descriptions, express viewpoints on most general topics, using some complex sentence forms to do so. *Language lacks, however, expressiveness and idiomaticity and use of more complex forms is still stereotypic.*	devices to link his/her sentences into clear, coherent text, though there may be some 'jumpiness' in a longer text.	grammatical control. Does not make errors which cause misunderstandings.	descriptions of real or imaginary events and experiences marking the relationship between ideas in clear connected text, and following established conventions of the genre concerned. Can write clear, detailed descriptions on a variety of subjects related to his/her field of interest. Can write a review of a film, book or play.	argument systematically with appropriate highlighting of significant points and relevant supporting detail. Can evaluate different ideas or solutions to a problem. Can write an essay or report which develops an argument, giving reasons in support of or against a particular point of view and explaining the advantages and disadvantages of various options. Can synthesise information and arguments from a number of sources.
B1	Can write straightforward connected texts on a range of familiar subjects within his/her field of interest, by linking a series of shorter discrete elements into a linear sequence. *The texts are understandable but*	Has enough language to get by, with sufficient vocabulary to express him/herself with some circumlocutions on topics such as family, hobbies and interests, work, travel, and current events.	Can link a series of shorter discrete elements into a connected, linear text.	Uses reasonably accurately a repertoire of frequently used 'routines' and patterns associated with more *common* situations. *Occasionally makes errors that the reader usually can*	Can write accounts of experiences, describing feelings and reactions in simple connected text. Can write a description of an event, a recent	Can write short, simple essays on topics of interest. Can summarise, report and give his/her opinion about accumulated factual information on familiar routine and non-routine matters, within his field with some confidence.

	occasional unclear expressions and/or inconsistencies may cause a break-up in reading.		interpret correctly on the basis of the context.*		Can write very brief reports to a standard conventionalised format, which pass on routine factual information and state reasons for actions.
A2	Can write a series of simple phrases and sentences linked with simple connectors like 'and', 'but' and 'because'. *Longer texts may contain expressions and show coherence problems which makes the text hard to understand.*	Uses basic sentence patterns with memorized phrases, groups of a few words and formulae in order to communicate limited information in simple everyday situations.	Can link groups of words with simple connectors like 'and', 'but' and 'because'.	Uses simple structures correctly, but still systematically makes basic mistakes. *Errors may sometimes cause misunderstandings.*	trip – real or imagined. Can narrate a story. Can write straightforward, detailed descriptions on a range of familiar subjects within his/her field of interest. Can write short simple imaginary biographies and simple poems about people. Can write very short, basic descriptions of events, past activities and personal experiences.
A1	Can write simple isolated phrases and sentences. *Longer texts contain expressions and show coherence problems which makes the text very hard or impossible to understand.*	Has a very basic repertoire of words and simple phrases related to personal details and particular concrete situations.	Can link words or groups of words with very basic linear connectors like 'and' and 'then'.	Shows only limited control of a few simple grammatical structures and sentence patterns in a memorized repertoire. *Errors may cause misunderstandings.*	Can write simple phrases and sentences about themselves and imaginary people, where they live and what they do.

Table 11: Cambridge writing scale with CEFR classification and formulation (see Appendix 2 for full scale)

	ALTE 5 (C2) Can write extensively
Socio-linguistic: Style	Can enhance impact by effectively varying style of expression and sentence length for effect
Linguistic: Range	Can enhance impact through the use of advanced vocabulary and word order
Socio-linguistic: Idiomatic	Can enhance impact through the use of idiom and humour
Linguistic: Grammatical Accuracy; Vocabulary Control	Shows only very rare errors of grammar or vocabulary
Pragmatic: Coherence and Cohesion	Can organise extended text effectively, linking ideas appropriately with or without explicit words

Table 12: Cambridge writing scale as CEFR-style descriptor scales, example (see Appendix 3 for full scale)

	Linguistic: Range
C2	Can enhance impact through the use of advanced vocabulary and word order
C1	Can make a positive impact through the use of advanced vocabulary and word order
B2	Can only occasionally show limited use of advanced vocabulary
B1	Communicates meaning on chosen topics without using advanced vocabulary

The final step was to compare the new information from the Cambridge scale to the existing CEFR descriptors for the categories concerned. Was there any significant enrichment of the description? Was there a complementary approach? Were there contradictions? The result is shown in Appendix 4 with a comment in the right hand column. They can be briefly glossed as follows:

1. **Writing (Globally):** The global statements for C2 and B1 do not really add anything. B1 is also negatively formulated. However, the current CEFR descriptors for Written Production focus only on the communicative activity undertaken, whereas the Cambridge ones focus on the quality side as well. One could thus imagine mentioning qualitative factors too, though these are available in other CEFR descriptors (see Table 10 where they appear in separate columns).

2. **Linguistic–Range:** The CEFR description seems considerably richer. The Cambridge formulation is not adding anything significant.

3. **Linguistic–Grammatical Accuracy & Vocabulary Control:** Here the main point is a possible contradiction at C1 and C2. At C2, whereas the CEFR makes a fairly absolute (non-empirical) statement: *Maintains*

consistent grammatical control of complex language. Consistently correct and appropriate use of vocabulary, the Cambridge CPE-based descriptor says: *Shows only very rare errors of grammar or vocabulary*. That seems truer of CEFR C1: *Consistently maintains a high degree of grammatical accuracy; errors are rare and difficult to spot. Occasional minor slips, but no significant vocabulary errors.*

Is the CEFR maybe too strict here in an effort to differentiate from the calibrated descriptor for C1? Or are the Cambridge CAE and CPE standards slightly more lenient than the CEFR on accuracy?

4. **Pragmatic–Coherence/Cohesion & Thematic Development:** Here the Cambridge descriptors for B1 and B2 have a focus complementary to that in the CEFR descriptors. The CEFR descriptors on thematic development are very 'macro', and those on Cohesion/Coherence are very 'micro'. The Cambridge ones – talking about text organisation – slot quite nicely into the middle. The C2 descriptor is particularly clear and concise, making the valid point that more cohesive devices do not necessarily mean better text. (The C2 CEFR descriptor here is not empirically based.)

5. **Socio-linguistic Appropriateness:** This is where the comparison begins to get even more interesting. The CEFR scale for Socio-linguistic Appropriateness was added in the 2001 edition and has a very limited empirical base, as reported above. At all four levels, the current CEFR description could be improved by incorporating insights from qualitative analysis in the Cambridge scale.

However, at B2 there is a clear contradiction. Whilst the CEFR says: *Can express him or herself appropriately in situations and avoid crass errors of formulation* (not empirically calibrated) and whilst the CEFR does have a descriptor calibrated at a very low B2+ that says: *Can vary formulation of what he/she wants to say*, the Cambridge descriptor is far more modest, saying: *Can only occasionally and quite often inappropriately match style of expression to the topic or use idioms.*

The question with socio-linguistic appropriateness at B2, as with linguistic control at C2, is 'Who is right?'. And could there be a spoken/written distinction here: that it is easier to formulate something appropriately face-to-face in a foreign language and more difficult to adopt the more complicated conventions applied in writing? The CEFR illustrative descriptors were calibrated in relation to a construct dominated by spoken language (North 2000).

This little exercise is not intended to give a definitive answer to the questions posed. It is intended to demonstrate that, once sets of exemplars are available that have been directly benchmarked to the CEFR, with this benchmarking confirmed and so standardised by international benchmarking conferences, there will be lots of potential for qualitative research.

Another possible source of future enrichment for the CEFR descriptor scales is the work that has been done in the Portfolio network to collect and document well-formulated descriptors. The problem of using them, however, could be to add to the problems caused by the existing non-calibrated descriptors (socio-linguistic competence, orthographic control – and many at C2), plus the risk of reintroducing clichés. However, a way around the problem could be found by collecting assessment data with such new descriptors presented on checklists with about 50% already calibrated descriptors and then expanding the calibrated 'descriptor bank' with a Rasch analysis of the data. This can work well, even with descriptors for totally different categories, as reported by North (2002).

Conclusion

We are still several years away from a wider CEFR toolkit of standardised exemplars, empirically validated examination comparisons, supplementary descriptors, curriculum and test specifications etc. What is important is to realise that this phase of the Common European Framework project only started in earnest in 2002 as a reaction to the external publication in 2001. We have come a very long way in only a few years.

What is very encouraging is how well what we already have works in practice. For example the seminar organised by Eurocentres and the Centre international d'études pédagogiques at Sèvres in December 2004 to produce calibrated spoken samples for French was remarkably successful both in terms of process (principled reflection) and product (a DVD of standardised performance samples). A total of 38 teachers, testers and administrators, native speakers and non-native speakers, experts in French and non-experts in French were involved as raters. A decade ago such a representative, heterogeneous group might not have been capable of carrying out a benchmarking/standard-setting event. It worked because we are beginning to establish a transparent and coherent European common framework shared by language professionals across linguistic and cultural barriers. One reason for this success is that this framework is based on comprehensible, validated descriptor scales that reflect the way such professionals think about learner proficiency.

Notes

1 EAQUALS: European Association for Quality Language Services.
www.eaquals.org
ALTE: Association of Language Testers in Europe. www.alte.org
2 It would be exaggerated to claim on this basis that two tests for the same language related to the same CEFR level, even with the same skills profile, would be equivalent and thus interchangeable. This issue is discussed in

Figueras et al 2005. Nevertheless such profiling of exam results in terms of a common metric can be of great help to test users.

3 Logit scales produced with the Rasch model are always distorted towards infinity at the top and bottom. Opinions differ as to the point at which the distortion becomes significant and as to whether one should take corrective action.

References

Alderson, J C (Ed.) (2002) *Case Studies in the Use of the Common European Framework*, Strasbourg: Council of Europe, ISBN 92–871–4983–6.

Alderson, J C, Figueras, N, Kuijper, H, Nold, G, Takala, S and Tardieu, C (2004) *The Development of Specifications for Item Development and Classification within the Common European Framework of Reference for Languages: Learning, Teaching, Assessment; Reading and Listening (Final Report of the Dutch Construct Project)* unpublished paper.

Bachman, L F (1990) *Fundamental Considerations in Language Testing*, Oxford: Oxford University Press.

Bernardin, H J and Smith, P C (1981) A Clarification of Some Issues Regarding the Development and Use of Behaviourally Anchored Rating Scales (BARS), *Journal of Applied Psychology* 66, 458–463.

Borman W C (1986) Behaviour-based Rating Scales, in Berk, R A (Ed.) *Performance Assessment: Methods and Applications*, Baltimore: John Hopkins Press, 100–120.

Breen, M P and Candlin, C N (1980) The Essentials of a Communicative Curriculum in Language Teaching, *Applied Linguistics* 1, 89–112.

Brown, G and Yule, G (1983) *Discourse Analysis*, Cambridge: Cambridge University Press.

Brown, G, Anderson, A, Shilock, R and Yule G (1984) *Teaching Talk: Strategies for Production and Assessment*, Cambridge: Cambridge University Press.

Brumfit, C (1984) *Communicative Methodology in Language Teaching. The roles of fluency and accuracy*, Cambridge: Cambridge University Press.

Brumfit, C (1987) Concepts and Categories in Language Teaching Methodology, *AILA Review* 4, 25–31.

Canale, M (1984) On Some Theoretical Frameworks for Language Proficiency, in Rivera, C (Ed.) *Language Proficiency and Academic Achievement*, Clevedon: *Multilingual Matters*.

Carroll, B J and West, R (1989) *ESU Framework. Performance Scales for English Language Examinations*, Harlow: Longman.

Cohen, A (1994) *Assessing Language Ability in the Classroom (2nd edition)*, Rowley Mass: Newbury House/Heinle and Heinle.

Cohen, A and Olshtain, E (1993) The production of speech acts by EFL learners, *TESOL Quarterly* 27, 33–56.

Council of Europe (2001) *Common European Framework of Reference for Languages: Learning, Teaching, Assessment*, Cambridge: Cambridge University Press.

Council of Europe (2003) *Relating Language Examinations to the Common European Framework of Reference for Languages: Learning, Teaching, Assessment (CEFR), DGIV/EDU/LANG (2003) 5*, Strasbourg: Council of Europe.

Cummins, J (1979) Cognitive Academic Language Proficiency: Linguistic interdependence, the optimum ages question and some other matters, *Working Papers on Bilingualism* 19, 197–205.

Cummins, J (1980) The Cross-lingual Dimensions of Language Proficiency: Implications for bilingual education and the optimal age issue, *TESOL Quarterly* 14, 175–187.

Figueras, N, North, B, Takala, S, Verhelst, N and Van Avermaet, P (2005) Relating Examinations to the Common European Framework: a Manual, *Language Testing* 22, 1–19.

Hawkey, R and Barker, F (2004) Developing a Common Scale for the Assessment of Writing, *Assessing Writing* 9, 122–159.

IBM (1974) IBM France Performance Charts in Trim J L M (1978) *Some Possible Lines of Development of an Overall Structure for a European Unit/Credit Scheme for Foreign Language Learning by Adults*, Appendix B, Strasbourg: Council of Europe.

Ingram, D E (1981) The Australian Second Language Proficiency Ratings: Their Nature, Development and Trialling, in Read, John A S (Ed.) *Directions in Language Testing*, Singapore: University Press, 108–138.

Johnson, C and Scott, R (1984) Formulating Objectives for Heterogeneous Groups of Learners, *IATEFL (International Association of Teachers of English as a Foreign Language) Newsletter* January 1984, 42–44.

Jones, N (2002) Relating the ALTE Framework to the Common European Framework of Reference, in Alderson, J C (Ed.) *Case Studies in the Use of the Common European Framework*, Strasbourg: Council of Europe, 167–183.

Kaftandjieva, F and Takala, S (2002) Council of Europe Scales of Language Proficiency: a validation study in Alderson, J C (Ed.) *Case Studies in the Use of the Common European Framework*, Strasbourg: Council of Europe, 106–129.

Landy, F J and Farr, J L (1983) *The Measurement of Work Performance*, New York: Academic Press.

Mislevy, R J (1993) Foundations of a new test theory, in Frederiksen, N, Mislevy, R J and Bejar, I I (Eds) *Test Theory for a New Generation of Tests*, Hillsdale NJ: Lawrence Erlbaum Associates, 19–40.

Mislevy, R J (1995) Test theory and language learning assessment, *Language Testing* 12, 341–369.

North, B (1992) *European Language Portfolio: Some Options for a Working Approach to Design Scales for Proficiency, in Council of Europe (1992) Transparency and Coherence in Language Learning in Europe: Objectives, assessment and certification.* Symposium held in Rüschlikon, 10–16 November 1991. (Edited by North, Brian), Strasbourg: Council for Cultural Co-operation, 158–174.

North, B (1993) Transparency, coherence and washback in language assessment, in Sajavaara, K, Lambert, R, Takala, S and Morfit, C (Eds), *National Foreign Language Planning: Practices and prospects*, Jyväskylä: University of Jyväskylä, 157–193.

North, B (1995) The development of a common framework scale of descriptors of language proficiency based on a theory of measurement, *System 23*, 445–465.

North, B (1997) Perspectives on language proficiency and aspects of competence, *Language Teaching 30*, 92–100.

North, B (2000) *The Development of a Common Framework Scale of Language Proficiency*, New York: Peter Lang.

North, B (2002) A CEF-based self-assessment tool for university entrance, in Alderson, J C (Ed.) *Case Studies in the Use of the Common European Framework*, Strasbourg: Council of Europe, 146–166.

North, B and Schneider, G (1998) Scaling Descriptors for Language Proficiency Scales, *Language Testing* 15, 217–262.

Pollitt, A and Hutchinson, C (1987) Calibrating Graded Assessments; Rasch Partial Credit Analysis of Performance in Writing, *Language Testing* 4, 72–92.

Rost, M (1990) *Listening in Language Learning*, London: Longman.

Schneider, G and North, B (2000) *Fremdsprachen können – was heisst das?* Skalen zur Beschreibung, Beurteilung und Selbsteinschätzung der fremdsprachlichen Kommunikationsfähigkeit, Chur/Zürich.

Smith, P C and Kendall, J M (1963) Retranslation of Expectations: An Approach to the Construction of Unambiguous Anchors for Rating Scales, *Journal of Applied Psychology* 47.

Swales, J M (1990) *The Genre Analysis: English in Academic and Research Settings*, Cambridge: Cambridge University Press.

Thurstone, L L (1928) Attitudes can be measured, American Journal of Sociology 33, 529–554, cited in Wright, Benjamin D and Masters, Geoffrey N (1982) *Rating Scale Analysis: Rasch Measurement*, Chicago: Mesa Press, 5.

Trim, J L M (1978) *Some Possible Lines of Development of an Overall Structure for a European Unit/Credit Scheme for Foreign Language Learning by Adults*, Appendix B, Strasbourg: Council of Europe.

Tuffin, P (1990) Response to Alderson, in De Jong, John H A L and Stevenson, Douglas K (Eds) *Individualizing the Assessment of Language Abilities*, Clevedon: Multilingual Matters, 28–37.

Wilds, C P (1975) The Oral Interview Test, in Spolsky, B and Jones, R (Eds.) *Testing Language Proficiency*, Washington DC: Center for Applied Linguistics, 29–44.

Wilkins, D A (1978) *Proposal for Levels Definition, in Trim J L M Some Possible Lines of Development of an Overall Structure for a European Unit/Credit Scheme for Foreign Language Learning by Adults*, Appendix C, Strasbourg: Council of Europe, 71–78.

Appendix 1

**Draft 4-level scale for writing
(Hawkey, R and Barker, F (2004) Developing a common scale for the
assessment of writing,
Assessing Writing 9, 122–159.)**

ALTE 5 (C2)
Can write extensively and enhance impact on the reader through the effective use of sophisticated language resources such as:

- the ability to vary style of expression and sentence length for effect
- the use of advanced vocabulary and word order
- the use of idiom and humour.

Can write with only very rare errors of grammar or vocabulary.
Can organise extended writing effectively, linking ideas appropriately with or without explicit words.

ALTE 4 (C1)
Can write extensively and make a positive impact on the reader through sophisticated language resources such as:

- the ability to vary style of expression and sentence length for effect
- the use of advanced vocabulary and word order
- the use of idiom and/or humour though the use of these resources is not always completely appropriate.

Can write with impact on the reader only occasionally reduced by errors of grammar or vocabulary, which, however, do not impede communication.
Can organise extended writing in a generally sound way, linking most ideas appropriately, with or without explicit linking words.

ALTE 3 (B2)
Can write extensively, but with only occasional evidence of limited and quite often inappropriately used language resources such as:

- matching style of expression to the topic
- the use of advanced vocabulary
- the use of idiom.

Can communicate meaning on chosen topics although the impact of the writing may be reduced by quite basic errors of grammar or vocabulary although these do not significantly impede comprehension.

Can organise extended writing but weaknesses of organisation and some inappropriate linking of ideas, tend sometimes to reduce impact.

ALTE 2 (B1)

Can write on an extended topic although without the use of sophisticated language resources such as style of expression, advanced vocabulary or idiom. Impact of the writing may be reduced and the message may be sometimes impeded by frequent basic errors of grammar or vocabulary.

Can attempt to organise writing, but quite frequent weaknesses of organisation and inappropriate linking of ideas, weaken and occasionally impede the message.

Appendix 2

Appendix 1 classified by CEFR categories and formulated in CEFR style

---

ALTE 5 (C2)

Can write extensively

Socio-linguistic: Style — Can enhance impact by effectively varying style of expression and sentence length for effect

Linguistic: Range — Can enhance impact through the use of advanced vocabulary and word order

Socio-linguistic: Idiomatic — Can enhance impact through the use of idiom and humour

Linguistic: Grammatical Accuracy; Vocabulary Control — Shows only very rare errors of grammar or vocabulary

Pragmatic: Coherence and Cohesion — Can organise extended text effectively, linking ideas appropriately with or without explicit words

ALTE 4 (C1)

Can write extensively

Socio-linguistic: Style — Can make a positive impact by effectively varying style of expression and sentence length for effect

Linguistic: Range — Can make a positive impact through the use of advanced vocabulary and word order

Socio-linguistic: Idiomatic — Can make a positive impact through the use of idiom and/or humour though the use of these resources is not always completely appropriate

Linguistic: Grammatical Accuracy; Vocabulary Control — Impact only occasionally reduced by errors of grammar or vocabulary, which, however, do not impede communication

Pragmatic: Coherence and Cohesion — Can organise extended text in a generally sound way, linking most ideas appropriately, with or without explicit linking words

ALTE 3 (B2)

Can write extensively
Can communicate on chosen topics

Socio-linguistic: Style — Can only occasionally and quite often inappropriately match style of expression to the topic

Linguistic: Vocabulary Range — Can only occasionally show limited use of advanced vocabulary

Linguistic: Vocabulary Control — Occasional attempts to use advanced vocabulary are quite often inappropriate

Socio-linguistic: Idiomatic — Can only occasionally show limited and quite often inappropriate use of idiom

Linguistic: Grammatical Accuracy; Vocabulary Control — Can communicate meaning on chosen topics although the impact may be reduced by some quite basic errors of grammar or vocabulary although these do not significantly impede comprehension

Appendix 1 (*continued*)

Pragmatic: Coherence and Cohesion	Can organise extended text but weaknesses of organisation and some inappropriate linking of ideas, tend sometimes to reduce impact

ALTE 2 (B1)

	Can write on an extended topic
Socio-linguistic: Style	without variation in style of expression
Linguistic: Vocabulary Range	without using advanced vocabulary
Sociolinguistic: Idiomatic	without using idiom
Linguistic: Grammatical Accuracy; Vocabulary Control	Impact may be reduced and the message may be sometimes impeded by frequent basic errors of grammar or vocabulary
Pragmatic: Coherence and Cohesion	Can attempt to organise text, but quite frequent weaknesses of organisation and inappropriate linking of ideas, weaken and occasionally impede the message

Appendix 3

	Writing
C2	Can write extensively and enhance positive impact on the reader through variation in style, use of advanced vocabulary, idiom and humour
C1	Can write extensively and make a positive impact on the reader through variation in style, use of advanced vocabulary, idiom/humour, though use of the latter is not always appropriate
B2	Can write extensively on chosen topics with occasional evidence of limited and often quite inappropriate matching of style to topic, use of advanced vocabulary and of idiom
B1	Can communicate meaning on an extended topic although without variation in style, idiomatic use of language or use of advanced vocabulary

Linguistic: Range
C2	Can enhance impact through the use of advanced vocabulary and word order
C1	Can make a positive impact through the use of advanced vocabulary and word order
B2	Can only occasionally show limited use of advanced vocabulary
B1	Communicates meaning on chosen topics without using advanced vocabulary

Linguistic: Grammatical Accuracy; Vocabulary Control
C2	Shows only very rare errors of grammar or vocabulary
C1	Impact only occasionally reduced by errors of grammar or vocabulary, which, however, do not impede communication
B2	Can communicate meaning on chosen topics although the impact may be reduced by some quite basic errors of grammar or vocabulary although these do not significantly impede comprehension. Occasional attempts to use advanced vocabulary are quite often inappropriate
B1	Impact may be reduced and the message may be sometimes impeded by frequent basic errors of grammar or vocabulary

Socio-linguistic
C2	Can enhance impact by effectively varying style of expression and sentence length for effect and by using idiom and humour
C1	Can make a positive impact by effectively varying style of expression and sentence length for effect, and through the use of idiom and/or humour though the use of the latter is not always completely appropriate
B2	Can only occasionally and quite often inappropriately match style of expression to the topic or use idioms
B1	Communicates in a straightforward manner without variation in style of expression or use of idiom

Pragmatic: Coherence and Cohesion
C2	Can organise extended text effectively, linking ideas appropriately with or without explicit words

Appendix 2 (*continued*)

C1	Can organise extended text in a generally sound way, linking most ideas appropriately, with or without explicit linking words
B2	Can organise extended text but weaknesses of organisation and some inappropriate linking of ideas, tend sometimes to reduce impact
B1	Can attempt to organise text, but quite frequent weaknesses of organisation and inappropriate linking of ideas, weaken and occasionally impede the message

Appendix 4

Comparison between Appendix 3 and existing CEFR scale content

	ALTE draft writing scale (reformulated)	Common European Framework of Reference – 2001	Enrichment?
	Writing	Overall Written Production	
C2	Can write extensively and enhance positive impact on the reader through variation in style, use of advanced vocabulary, idiom and humour.	Can write clear, smoothly flowing, complex texts in an appropriate and effective style and a logical structure which helps the reader to find significant points.	No significant enrichment
C1	Can write extensively and make a positive impact on the reader through variation in style, use of advanced vocabulary, idiom/ humour, though use of the latter is not always appropriate.	Can write clear, well-structured texts of complex subjects, underlining the relevant salient issues, expanding and supporting points of view at some length with subsidiary points, reasons and relevant examples, and rounding off with an appropriate conclusion.	Different emphases: tasks/qualities. Qualitative aspects could be added
B2	Can write extensively on chosen topics with occasional evidence of limited and often quite inappropriate matching of style to topic, use of advanced vocabulary and of idiom.	Can write clear, detailed texts on a variety of subjects related to his field of interest, synthesising and evaluating information and arguments from a number of sources.	Different emphases: tasks/qualities. Qualitative aspects could be added
B1	Can communicate meaning on an extended topic although without variation in style, idiomatic use of language or use of advanced vocabulary.	Can write straightforward connected texts on a range of familiar subjects within his field of interest, by linking a series of shorter discrete elements into a linear sequence.	No significant enrichment

	Linguistic: Range	Linguistic: Overall Linguistic Range, Vocabulary Range	
C2	Can enhance impact through the use of advanced vocabulary, word order and idioms.	Can exploit a comprehensive and reliable mastery of a very wide range of language to formulate thoughts precisely, give emphasis, differentiate and eliminate ambiguity. No signs of having to restrict what he/she wants to say. Has a good command of a very broad lexical repertoire including idiomatic expressions and colloquialisms; shows awareness of connotative levels of meaning.	No significant enrichment
C1	Can make a positive impact through the use of advanced vocabulary and word order and idioms.	Can select an appropriate formulation from a broad range of language to express him/herself clearly, without having to restrict what he/she wants to say. Has a good command of a broad lexical repertoire allowing gaps to be readily overcome with circumlocutions. Good command of idiomatic expressions and colloquialisms.	No significant enrichment
B2	Can only occasionally show limited use of advanced vocabulary.	Has a sufficient range of language to be able to give clear descriptions, express viewpoints and develop arguments without much conspicuous searching for words, using some complex sentence forms to do so. Has a good range of vocabulary for matters connected to his field and most general topics. Can vary formulation to avoid frequent repetition, but lexical gaps can still cause hesitation and circumlocution.	No significant enrichment
B1	Communicates meaning on chosen topics without using advanced vocabulary.	Has enough language to get by, with sufficient vocabulary to express him/herself with some hesitation and circumlocutions on topics such as family, hobbies and interests, work, travel, and current events, but lexical limitations cause repetition and even difficulty with formulation at times.	No significant enrichment

Comparison between Appendix 3 and existing CEFR scale content (*continued*)

ALTE draft writing scale (cont.)	Common European Framework of Reference – 2001	Enrichment?
Linguistic: Grammatical Accuracy; Vocabulary Control	**Linguistic:** Grammatical Accuracy; Vocabulary Control	
C2 Shows only very rare errors of grammar or vocabulary.	Maintains consistent grammatical control of complex language. Consistently correct and appropriate use of vocabulary.	CEF formulation may be too absolute
C1 Impact only occasionally reduced by errors of grammar or vocabulary, which, however, do not impede communication.	Consistently maintains a high degree of grammatical accuracy; errors are rare and difficult to spot. Occasional minor slips, but no significant vocabulary errors.	CEF formulation may be too absolute
B2 Can communicate meaning on chosen topics although the impact may be reduced by some quite basic errors of grammar or vocabulary although these do not significantly impede comprehension. Occasional attempts to use advanced vocabulary are quite often inappropriate.	Shows a relatively high degree of grammatical control. Does not make mistakes which lead to misunderstanding. Lexical accuracy is generally high, though some confusion and incorrect word choice does occur without hindering communication.	No significant enrichment
B1 Impact may be reduced and the message may be sometimes impeded by frequent basic errors of grammar or vocabulary.	Uses reasonably accurately a repertoire of frequently used 'routines' and patterns associated with more predictable situations. Shows good control of elementary vocabulary but major errors still occur when expressing more complex thoughts or handling unfamiliar topics and situations.	Different emphases. Scope for improved description through qualitative method
Pragmatic: Coherence/Cohesion, Thematic Development	**Pragmatic:** Coherence/Cohesion & Thematic Development	
C2 Can organise extended text effectively, linking ideas appropriately with or without explicit words.	Can create coherent and cohesive text making full and appropriate use of a variety of organisational patterns and a wide range of cohesive devices.	ALTE 'descriptor' clearer. CEF not empirically calibrated
C1 Can organise extended text in a generally sound way, linking most ideas appropriately, with or without explicit linking words.	Can produce clear, smoothly flowing, well-structured text, showing controlled use of organisational patterns, connectors and cohesive devices. Can use a variety of linking words efficiently to mark clearly the relationships between ideas.	No significant enrichment

B2	Can organise extended text but weaknesses of organisation and some inappropriate linking of ideas, tend sometimes to reduce impact.	Can develop a clear description or narrative, expanding and supporting his/her main points with relevant supporting detail and examples. Can use a limited number of cohesive devices to link his/her utterances into clear, coherent discourse, though there may be some 'jumpiness' in a long contribution.	ALTE-type 'descriptor' based on qualitative method could also be added to Coherence/Cohesion
B1	Can attempt to organise text, but quite frequent weaknesses of organisation and inappropriate linking of ideas, weaken and occasionally impede the message.	Can link a series of shorter, discrete simple elements into a connected, linear sequence of points.	Different emphases. Scope for improved description through qualitative method

Comparison between Appendix 3 and existing CEFR scale content (*continued*)

	ALTE draft writing scale (cont.)	Common European Framework of Reference – 2001	Enrichment?
	Socio-linguistic Appropriateness	**Socio-linguistic Appropriateness/Flexibility**	
C2	Can enhance impact by effectively varying style of expression and sentence length for effect and by using idiom and humour.	Has a good command of idiomatic expressions and colloquialisms with awareness of connotative levels of meaning.	Style could be mentioned as in Production descriptor: 'in an appropriate and effective style'[?]
C1	Can make a positive impact by effectively varying style of expression and sentence length for effect, and through the use of idiom and/or humour though the use of the latter is not always completely appropriate.	Can use language flexibly and effectively for social purposes, including emotional, allusive and joking usage. Can express him or herself confidently, clearly and politely in a formal or informal register, appropriate to the situation and person(s) concerned. Can adjust what he/she says and the means of expressing it to the situation and the recipient and adopt a level of formality appropriate to the circumstances.	**Possible contradiction.** ALTE seems more limited. Only part of CEF descriptors empirically calibrated – and concerned face-to-face social situation
B2	Can only occasionally and quite often inappropriately match style of expression to the topic or use idioms.	Can express him or herself appropriately in situations and avoid crass errors of formulation. (*Can vary formulation of what he/she wants to say: was very low B2+.*)	**Relatively clear contradiction.** ALTE considerably more limited CEF not empirically calibrated
B1	Communicates in a straightforward manner without variation in style of expression or use of idiom.	Can perform and respond to a wide range of language functions, using their most common exponents in a neutral register.	Different emphases. Scope for improved description through qualitative method

3 Juggling numbers and opinions: An attempt to set CEFR standards in Norway for a test of reading in English

Eli Moe

University of Bergen, Norway

Background

The University of Bergen, Norway, is responsible for developing computerised national reading tests of English for school children in Norway in four different grades (4th, 7th, 10th and 11th grade). The tests are compulsory for all pupils in these grades. Test specifications are based on the National Curriculum in Norway as well as on the Common European Framework of Reference (CEFR). The pupils get their results reported as CEFR levels, or in-between levels – i.e. A2/B1 etc., and the standard setting procedures conducted aim to confirm the link between the actual tests and the CEFR.

The reading tests are regarded as something new and quite unconventional partly because pupils have to do the tests on computer, and also because many item formats are designed specially for this medium.

The tests for the 7th, 10th and 11th grade are adaptive at the level of the test taker age group. When pupils at a particular grade log in to take a test, they are given one of three pretests randomly chosen by the computer. These three pretests have the same level of difficulty. Depending on their result on the pretest, the pupils continue to one of three main tests with different levels of difficulty. Pupils with a good command of English (for their age group) are given the most difficult main test, while weak pupils are given the easiest main test. The test results are based on the students' achievement on the main test only, and standard setting concerns main test items.

Aim

The main aim of this study is to explore the quality of the standard setting procedures applied when linking test results to the CEFR scale. Insights gained from the study should inform judgement as to the effectiveness of the standard setting procedures applied, and what operational procedures need to be put in place to ensure a valid and reliable linking to the CEFR in the future.

Piloting of items

Data collection

A total of 288 main test items were piloted on computer in 10 reading tests or booklets using an incomplete linked design. Of these 288 items, 105 (36%) had already been piloted and used previously in the 10th grade tests run in 2004, while 183 items (64%) were new. In this way the current piloting results could be linked to the earlier analyses.

Each reading test booklet consisted of both old and new items, approximately 22 old and 35 new items in each booklet. Each item appeared in two booklets, something which enabled us to link all booklets to the same difficulty scale when analysing the results. The booklets were piloted on a total of 2,622 pupils in 2004. Each test item was answered by an average of 525 pupils (minimum: 496/maximum: 542).

Item characteristics

In order to express item difficulty parameters and student proficiency parameters on a common scale, IRT-modelling was applied to calibrate the items (OPLM, Verhelst, Glas and Verstralen 1995). Of the initial 288 items, 216 items 'survived' the calibration, fitting the chosen model. The misfit of 72 of the items was mainly due to one or more of the following reasons:

- unacceptable level of difficulty
- low discrimination
- high level of guessing factor.

The summary statistics for item parameters, based on classical item analysis Classic Test Theory (CTT), are presented in Table 1.

According to Table 1 the mean difficulty is a little above 60% both in the initial pool of items and in the calibrated item pool. Some of the most difficult items did not survive the calibration. These items were too difficult and did not discriminate well among the pupils. When these items were discarded, minimum discrimination estimates increased as well as the mean discrimination. Because of good discrimination indices, some very easy items survived calibration. These items were considered suitable for the easiest version of the main test.

Table 1: Item statistics (CTT)

Statistics		Initial Item Pool	Calibrated Items
Number of items		288	216
Item Difficulty	Min	7%	20%
	Mean	62%	64%
	Max	95%	95%
Item Discrimination	Min	−0.11	+0.22
	Mean	+0.45	+0.48
	Max	+0.79	+0.79

Standard setting

In order to establish valid cut-off scores and create bands representing different levels of reading competence in agreement with the CEFR levels, the application of human judgement through a process of standard setting is required. 'The term "standard setting" in the field of educational measurement refers to a decision making process aiming to classify the results of examinations in a limited number of successive levels of achievement, (Kaftandjieva 2004:2). A large number of different standard setting methods exist. Kaftandjieva (2004:12) mentions more than 50. Jaeger (1989: 493) classifies the different standard setting methods into two main groups: test centred methods and examinee centred methods. This classification is the most commonly accepted in standard setting today. However, not all methods fit this classification. Some methods focus on the distribution of scores or students on a particular scale and do not fit Jaeger's classification. The fact that different methods tend to yield different cut-off scores prompts Jaeger to suggest the application of different standard setting methods (1989:500). This means different cut-off scores should be considered. The procedure for arriving at final cut-off scores is a process of human decision-making, a matter of the strength of the arguments supporting the decision.

Where the aim is to link a test to the CEFR scale, a test centred method would imply letting judges assess individual test items against the CEFR scale. An examinee centred method, on the other hand, would mean letting teachers assess the English reading competence of individual students taking the test against the CEFR scale.

Researchers agree that a positive relationship between observed item difficulty and judges' estimates of the probabilities of success on the items is an adequate objective criterion; it constitutes 'a reality check', or evidence of support for the validity of judgements. At the same time, however, several studies show that judges' ability to estimate item difficulty is questionable. Most of the research reports modest correlations between item difficulty and its estimations, usually between +.40 and +.60 (DeMauro & Powers 1993, Impara & Plake 1998, Smith & Smith 1998).

Since the piloting data was collected some time before standard setting took place, it was not possible to go back and let teachers assess pupils who took part in the piloting. An examinee centred method could therefore not be applied. In order to compensate for the lack of data on the level of reading proficiency of individual pupils, we asked the judges who took part in the test centred standard setting procedures to make an estimation of the frequency distribution (in percentages) on the CEFR scale.

The main method for establishing cut-off scores is a test centred method, described below.

The Kaftandjieva and Takala Compound Cumulative Method

The Kaftandjieva and Takala Compound Cumulative Method (Kaftandjieva and Takala 2002) is a test centred method. It is a modification of the yes/no Angoff method (Angoff 1971). The method implies four stages of judgement:

1. A number of judges assess individual test items, in our case on the CEFR scale answering the question: *At what CEFR level can a test taker answer the following item correctly?*
2. Based on the aggregated judgements, the 'core' difficulty bands for each level are established. Items are assigned to corresponding CEFR levels depending on the band in which the item difficulty falls.
3. Some items are reassigned to CEFR levels because the original assignment given by the judges does not match the empirical difficulty.
4. Cut-off scores are established on the basis of the cumulative frequency distribution of items into CEFR levels.

Judges

Ten judges were selected to take part in the standard setting process. All judges were well acquainted with the CEFR. All of them had a background in language teaching even though not all of them were practising teachers at the time of standard setting. Some were language teachers, while others were language test developers (see Table 2).

Table 2: Judges' background

Current occupation Judge no	1	2	3	4	5	6	7	8	9	10
Language teacher	x	x	x	x	x	x				
Language test developer			x	x	x	x	x	x	x	x

All 10 judges assigned all 216 items to the CEFR scale. As mentioned above, all judges in addition estimated the percentage of students per level.

All judges had taken part in the initial standard setting procedures a year earlier. On that occasion they all spent one day familiarising themselves with the CEFR, particularly with the level descriptions for reading. They also had an introduction to standard setting in general, and to their own standard setting job in particular, as well as some initial training in assessing items on the CEFR. This time the judges had a short refresher training on what was expected of them; then they assessed some reading items with different degrees of difficulty and discussed what made these items easy/difficult.

Results

Judges' assessment of item difficulty

All judges assessed all 216 calibrated items (see Table 3). According to their assessment, all judges agreed completely on three items, which they assigned to B2. According to standard setting procedures these three items were later assigned to B2.

Table 3: Judges' assessment of items

Items assessed by judges			
Range*	Frequency	%	Cumulative %
0	3	1	1
1	146	68	69
2	65	30	99
3	2	1	100
Total	216	100	

* Range in terms of CEFR levels between maximum and minimum level assignment

For 146 items there was a maximum of one level difference between the judges, while for 65 of the items the range was two levels. For two of the items the judges' range of assignment was three CEFR levels, A2–C1. These two items were mistakenly included in the piloting; both items were 'true/false' items, a format we had dropped earlier due to the high guessing frequency. A possible explanation for the high range of level assignment for these two items may be that different judges put different weight on the guessing factor when assessing these two items.

Other indices of inter-rater reliability are as follows:

The internal consistency between the raters is high with a Cronbach's alpha of 0.93. Kendal W, Kendal's coefficient of concordance which is an index of concordance between all 10 judges, is 0.62. These two indices demonstrate that the aggregated rating of the judges' assessments is at a satisfactory level of reliability, while the agreement between any two judges is moderate (the average inter-rater correlation is 0.55). On the other hand, the average inter-rater correlation is close to the correlation between the judges' assessment and the observed empirical difficulty of the items which ranges from 0.41 to 0.76. This means that on an individual level judges vary considerably in their perception of item difficulty. This tells us that there is a need for more and better training of judges.

Judge 7 is the most successful judge in terms of the highest correlation between CEFR level assignments and observed empirical item difficulty.

Figure 1: Mean item difficulty per CEFR level – Judge 7 (the 'best' judge)

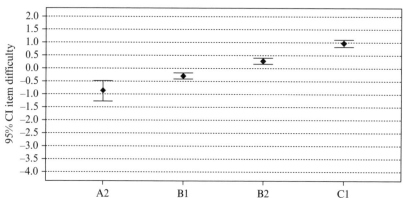

Figure 2: Item difficulty distribution per CEFR level – Judge 7 (the 'best' judge)

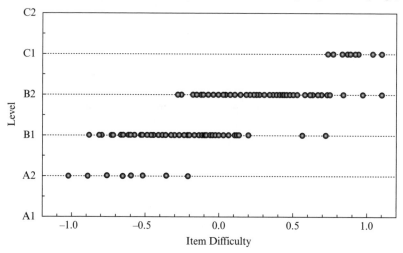

As can be seen from the mean level assignment estimates in Figure 1, it seems like judge 7 clearly manages to distinguish between different levels of item difficulty. However, on looking more closely at judge 7's level assignments of individual items (Figure 2), it is clear that mean indices disguise important information. Not all assignments match the empirical difficulty. Some items with the same empirical difficulty have for instance been assigned to A2, B1 and B2 by this judge.

Even though judge 7 in terms of standard setting is quite a successful judge, there is surely room for improvement both for this judge as well as for the other not so successful judges. To improve future standard setting training sessions, it is necessary to explore characteristics of items which were not successfully assigned to levels. A future recommendation would also be to include an examinee centred method in the standard setting procedures.

Judges' assessment of distribution of pupils on the CEFR scale

The judges also estimated how the 11th grade population of students would spread across the CEFR scale to answer the question: *How large a proportion of the population of 11th grade pupils (in per cent) do you think have a reading competence in English comparable to the descriptions for the different CEFR levels?*

The terms 'min' and 'max' estimation refer to minimum/maximum judge estimations (in %) of the proportion of students with a reading competence in English corresponding to the descriptions for the different CEFR levels.

Figure 3: Judges' assessment of population across CEFR levels

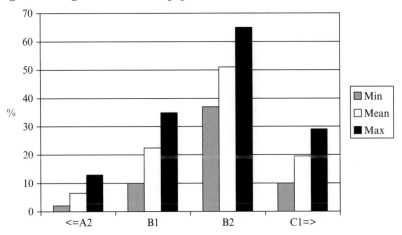

According to the aggregated judge estimation, the majority of pupils, 70%, would have a reading competence in English above B1, and around 50% of these are predicted to have a B2 competence.

Final level assignment of items

Comparing the judges' estimation of item difficulty, spread of population across CEFR levels and the observed item difficulty, some interesting issues appear. While the aggregated judgement of items shows that close to half the items are assessed to be B1 or lower (Table 4, reading from left to right), the estimation of the ability of the population across CEFR levels indicates that more than 70% of the students would have an English reading ability of B2 or above. This should indicate that the items piloted were too easy for the group of pupils. The analysis of the data piloted, however, does not give the same impression (Tables 2 and 3). On the contrary, the item analysis referred to earlier indicated that the items piloted seemed to suit the piloting population well. Therefore there is a need for some sort of adjustment.

We chose to make the final level assignment of items on the basis of all the different types of information we had: the observed empirical item difficulty, the judges' assignment of items to the CEFR scale and their estimation of population across CEFR levels. The result of this adjustment is found in Table 4. While for 95 of the items (44%) there is a match between the judges' assessment of items and the observed empirical difficulty, there is a discrepancy of one CEFR level for 111 items (51%).

Table 4: Aggregated judgement and final CEFR level assignment

			Final CEFR level assignment				Total
			A2	B1	B2	C1	
Aggregated judgement	A2	Count	2	1	0	0	3
		% of total	1%	0%	0%	0%	1%
	B1	Count	32	42	18	8	100
		% of total	15%	19%	8%	4%	46%
	B2	Count	1	27	34	28	90
		% of total	0%	13%	16%	13%	42%
	C1	Count	0	1	5	17	23
		% of total	0%	0%	2%	8%	11%
Total		Count	35	71	57	53	216
		% of total	16%	33%	26%	25%	100%

For 10 items (5%) the discrepancy is more than one CEFR level between the aggregated judgement and the final level assignment. Eight of these items were assessed as very difficult items by the judges (C1), while the observed empirical difficulty turned out to be much lower (B1). Two of the items the judges assessed to be quite easy (A2 and B1), while the empirical difficulty was much higher (B2 and C1).

While the aggregated judging shows that the judges assigned the majority of items to B1 and B2, in the final level assignment, which was also affected by the observed empirical difficulty from the piloting and the judges' assessment of population across levels, the majority of items are assigned to B1, B2 and C1. The cut-off scores were established on the basis of the final level assignment of items.

Reality check

The 'real' tests were administered in the spring of 2005. Data from these tests will show how well the standard setting procedures worked. Figure 4 shows the estimated spread of population across levels compared to the 'real' spread.

Figure 4: Population of pupils across CEFR levels – piloting and real examination

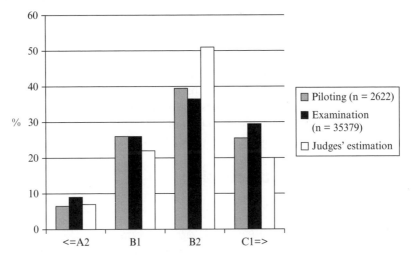

Figure 4 shows that there is a reasonable match between the distribution of pupils predicted from the standard setting procedures in connection with the piloting and the real test. According to the judges' prediction of distribution of pupils' results, more results were predicted at B2 and fewer at C1. Future standard setting procedures will have to investigate this issue further, for instance by also including examinee centred methods in the standard setting procedures.

Additional results

Table 4 showed that there is agreement between the aggregated judgement of item difficulty and the final level assignment for 95 items. For 111 items there is a difference between the two of one level. In Table 5 the mean difficulty and the standard error of measurement is calculated for 1) the 95 items for which there was a match between aggregated judgement and

Table 5: Absolute difference between aggregated rating and final CEFR level assignment

No of levels	No of items	Mean difficulty	SE mean	t test
0	95	+0.09	0.04	t=2.82
1	111	−0.11	0.06	p=0.005

observed empirical item difficulty, and 2) for the 111 items where the difference between the two was one level. The indices for the 10 items where the difference between judgement and empirical difficulty was two levels is not reported because the number of items in this group is too small for making valid statistical inferences. The mean difficulty is reported in terms of IRT modelling (in logits).

Table 5 shows how item difficulty affects the agreement between the judges. Agreement increases with item difficulty. The difference in item difficulty is statistically significant. This means that the judges who took part in the standard setting procedures are better at estimating the difficulty of difficult items, while estimating very easy items is more problematic for them. A possible reason for this might be that some judges are unaware of certain clues in item stems or distractors which make some items easy.

Conclusions and discussion

Findings

The aggregated mean estimation of item difficulty predicted by the judges is a reliable measure (0.93). This means that the test centred method applied (Kaftandjieva and Takala 2002) worked well.

Judges differ considerably in their ability to assign items to the CEFR and thus predict item difficulty (0.41–0.75). Thus there is a need for improvement regarding individual judges' ability to predict item difficulty. To be able to train judges more effectively, a specific training programme should be developed where judges learn to assess items and item difficulty. In addition to focusing on CEFR level descriptions and finding good examples of items which represent CEFR levels, it is also important to focus specifically on what characterises a) items on which judges disagree when assessing item difficulty, and b) items where there is a large discrepancy between judges' perception of difficulty and observed empirical difficulty.

Judges are better at estimating distribution of students across CEFR levels than item difficulty. This finding may lead to the conclusion that examinee centred methods could be more suitable than test centred methods. This possibility should be explored further.

Item difficulty affects intra-judge consistency. Our judges were more successful predicting the level of difficulty for difficult items than easy ones. This is an interesting finding which underlines the necessity of scrutinising easy items in particular to be able to guide the judges in a qualitatively better way.

Standard setting – concluding remarks

Cut-off scores were mainly established by a test centred method, the Kaftandjieva and Takala Compound Cumulative Method, and slightly adjusted by an additional procedure, the judges' prediction of the distribution of pupils across CEFR levels. Each procedure indicated different cut-off scores, but the combination of the two seems to have worked. When checking the predicted distribution of pupils across the CEFR from the piloting against the population taking the 'real' test, there is a reasonable match between the two. This means that there is empirical evidence to support the cut-off scores that were decided upon. However, it does not mean that our decisions are the 'right' ones or the only possible ones. Applying an examinee centred method could yield different cut-off scores, a possibility which will be explored further in the next round of standard setting.

When judges assign individual items to CEFR levels, they do this by comparing individual items to CEFR level descriptions. To some extent this secures the connection between items and tests on the one hand, and the content of the CEFR level descriptions on the other. But there is also a certain vagueness about such an action. Judgements are predictions – about something or someone. The CEFR is a mental concept of levels of language proficiency. Assigning items to CEFR levels therefore involves making predictions in relation to a mental concept – the nature of which is not very concrete. This could lead us to the conclusion that by applying an examinee centred method, judges would do something more concrete. They would then make predictions about the proficiency of human beings, i.e. teachers would assess pupils they know. This would add valuable information to the standard setting procedures.

Studies involving judges or raters show that they often disagree and vary in their judgements. This is the main argument against using examinee centred methods as the only approach in a process of standard setting. Relying only on information from one teacher about each pupil's proficiency could therefore be dangerous. Even though a test centred method involves assessing more abstract concepts than with an examinee centred method, it still allows us to let several judges assess each item.

The two approaches both have their strengths and drawbacks. Since researchers seem to agree that there is no best or worst method, we have to collect all the information we have access to, and improve our procedures all the time. Trying to set CEFR standards which are as correct as possible may well turn out to be 'a never ending story'.

References

Angoff, W H (1971) A Latent-Variable Modeling Approach to Assessing Interrater Reliability, Topic Generalizability and Validity of Content Assessment Scoring Rubrics, *Educational & Psychological Measurement* 55, 701–716.

DeMauro, G and Powers, D (1993) *Logical Consistency of the Angoff Method of Standard setting*, RR–93–26, Princeton: Educational Testing Service.

Impara, J C and Plake, B S (1998) Teachers' Ability to Estimate Item Difficulty: A Test of the Assumptions in the Angoff Standard Setting Method, *Journal of Educational Measurement* 35, 69–81.

Jaeger, R M (1989) Certification of student competence, in Linn R L (Ed.) *Educational Measurement* (Third Edition), Washington DC: American Council on Education, 485–511.

Kaftandjieva, F (2004) Standard Setting, in Reference Supplement B to the *Preliminary Pilot version of the Manual for Relating Language Examinations to the Common European Framework of Reference for Languages: Learning, Teaching, Assessment*. Strasbourg: Council of Europe.

Kaftandjieva, F and Takala, S (2002) *Relating the Finnish Matriculation Examination in English Test Results to the CEF Scales*, paper presented at Helsinki Seminar on Linking Language Examinations to Common European Framework of Reference for Languages: Learning, Teaching, Assessment.

Smith, R and Smith, J (1998) Differential Use of Item Information by Judges Using Angoff and Nedelsky Procedures, *Journal of Educational Measurement* 25, 259–274.

Verhelst, N, Glas, C and Verstralen, H (1995) *One Parameter Logistic Model OPLM*, The Netherlands: Cito.

4 L'harmonisation du DELF et du DALF sur les niveaux du Cadre européen commun de référence pour les langues

Patrick Riba et Marianne Mavel
Pôle évaluation et certifications, Centre international
d'études pédagogiques, France

Résumé

Lorsque le Ministère de l'Education nationale français a chargé le Centre international d'études pédagogiques – CIEP – d'harmoniser les certifications en français langue étrangère DELF et DALF sur les six niveaux du Cadre européen commun de référence pour les langues, cela impliquait l'application des spécifications proposées par la division des politiques linguistiques du Conseil de l'Europe et des standards d'ALTE.

L'un des enjeux de cette réforme est bien la possibilité d'aller vers un système commun d'évaluation basé sur les valeurs fondamentales du Conseil de l'Europe dans la conception qu'il a de la citoyenneté européenne, tout en préservant notre culture de l'évaluation. Mais l'approche retenue ne saurait cependant se limiter à l'application de simples procédures et le CIEP a été conduit à faire un certain nombre de choix théoriques et fonctionnels pour aboutir à la mise en place d'un système de six certifications cohérentes. Nous présentons ces choix, les résultats de certaines phases d'expérimentation et un bref descriptif de la structure des nouveaux examens du DELF et du DALF.

Introduction

La convention culturelle européenne que célèbre la 2ème conférence internationale d'ALTE – Association of Language Testers in Europe – l'affirmait déjà il y a 50 ans, l'un des enjeux majeurs de l'enseignement et de l'apprentissage des langues est de soutenir la citoyenneté et la participation démocratiques en vue de promouvoir la cohésion sociale, la compréhension interculturelle et le respect de la diversité et des droits de l'homme.

Le centre international d'études pédagogiques, CIEP, établissement public du ministère français de l'Education nationale, l'a compris depuis longtemps comme le démontrent les nombreuses actions de prospective didactique et de formation de formateurs en français langue étrangère qu'il conduit, souvent en collaboration avec ses partenaires européens et mondiaux, et depuis plusieurs années en adhérant à ALTE. Cet engagement est particulièrement important dans le domaine des certifications et diplômes en français langue étrangère.

Le DELF et le DALF de 1985 à nos jours

Le DELF, Diplôme d'études en langue française, et le DALF, Diplôme approfondi de langue française, ont été créés par arrêté ministériel en 1985 et sont les seuls diplômes officiels du ministère de l'éducation nationale français en français langue étrangère, FLE.

Depuis leur création, ces certifications ont connu un succès croissant. 400 000 unités sont présentées chaque année dans 900 centres d'examen répartis dans 154 pays, et le taux de progression en 2003–2004 était de près de 8%. Le réseau des centres d'examen, solide et géographiquement bien implanté sur les cinq continents, est constitué par les centres et instituts culturels français ainsi que les alliances françaises, et il est placé dans chaque pays sous la responsabilité des services culturels de l'Ambassade de France qui en garantissent le fonctionnement quantitatif et qualitatif. Sur le plan administratif, deux ministères en gèrent le devenir du DELF et du DALF (ministère de l'éducation nationale et ministère des affaires étrangères au sein d'une Commission nationale présidée par le directeur du CIEP), et un 3ème ministère est en passe de les rejoindre, celui des affaires sociales et de l'intégration, avec la création du DILF, diplôme d'initiation en langue française.

Le CIEP a été chargé d'harmoniser ces certifications sur le *Cadre européen commun de référence pour les langues – CECR –* en 2005. Ce document, élaboré collectivement par différents pays européens, rend en effet possible un rapprochement des enseignements de langues en autorisant « une détermination partagée, sur la base de définitions communes de la nature des compétences d'enseignement et d'apprentissage en langues et des niveaux de maîtrise dans ces compétences ».[1] Les travaux de Christine Tagliante, responsable du pôle évaluation et certifications, dans l'élaboration pour le français du portfolio des langues[2] et dans la mise en place du test de connaissance du français, TCF, déjà calibré sur le CECR, ont servi d'ancrage à ce projet.

Le processus d'harmonisation du DELF et du DALF sur le Cadre européen commun de référence pour les langues

Planification et définition des spécifications initiales

Harmoniser le DELF et le DALF sur le Cadre européen commun de référence pour les langues signifie les rendre lisibles et conformes aux critères du CECR. C'est la première spécification qui a été retenue ; elle implique une refonte en profondeur du dispositif actuel :

• création de six diplômes correspondant aux six niveaux du CECR
• élaboration basée sur la perspective actionnelle en adéquation avec les référentiels pour le français édités par le Conseil de l'Europe[3]
• respect des procédures d'élaboration du Conseil de l'Europe et d'audit de ALTE (manuel « relier les examens au Cadre européen »[4], « *Can Do statements* » de ALTE, etc.).

Cela signifie également de prendre en compte l'ancienne formule (2ème spécification) et de concevoir des épreuves en corrélation avec les attentes du public ciblé, qu'il soit issu des instituts français ou alliances françaises, d'établissements scolaires en partenariat avec le Ministère des affaires étrangères ou encore d'universités ou centres d'enseignement supérieur partenaires.

L'équipe DELF DALF devait également susciter une réflexion sur les pratiques de classe et l'offre de cours dans les centres de langue/centres d'examen (3ème spécification), tout en insistant sur la nécessaire continuité entre l'ancienne et la nouvelle version (4ème spécification).

Enfin, trois autres éléments ont été pris également en compte :

• allégement des procédures de gestion (5ème spécification)
• formation et habilitation des correcteurs et examinateurs afin de rendre plus fiables les certifications (6ème spécification)
• respect du chronogramme pour une mise en place au 1er septembre 2005 (7ème spécification).

Etude sur les anciens diplômes « relier des examens au Cadre européen »

Le calibrage sur le CECR d'épreuves déjà existantes, qui répond à la deuxième spécification énoncée, visait à faciliter la réutilisation de typologies d'exercices dont la pertinence était avérée, inscrivant ainsi les nouvelles certifications dans une dynamique sans rupture avec le dispositif antérieur (il a par ailleurs permis de structurer un tableau d'équivalences avec l'ancien dispositif). Les postes diplomatiques français ont pu s'appuyer sur cet argumentaire pour la reconnaissance locale de ces certifications.

Le DELF et le DALF ont été analysés et calibrés selon les spécifications du chapitre 4 du Manuel « *Relier les examens au Cadre européen de référence pour les langues* » publié par le Conseil de l'Europe. Pour chaque épreuve de chaque unité nous avons indiqué:

- les domaines et les situations dans lesquelles les candidats devaient prouver leurs compétences (voir CECR 4.1)
- les thèmes de communication que les candidats devaient être capables de traiter (CECR 4.2)
- les activités communicatives (CECR chapitre 4)
- les types de textes ou supports utilisés
- les tâches à effectuer.

A titre d'exemple nous proposons ici l'analyse de la production écrite de l'Unité A1 de l'ancienne formule qui stipulait *la rédaction d'une lettre d'environ 100 mots dans laquelle le candidat racontera des événements de la vie quotidienne et formulera une invitation ou une proposition.* Cette épreuve a été située au niveau A2.2 car elle correspond principalement à la partie supérieure du descripteur de A2 pour l'écriture créative :

	ECRITURE CREATIVE
A2	**Peut écrire sur les aspects quotidiens de son environnement, par exemple les gens, les lieux, le travail ou les études, avec des phrases reliées entre elles.** **Peut faire une description brève et élémentaire d'un événement, d'activités passées et d'expériences personnelles.**
	Peut écrire une suite de phrases et d'expressions simples sur sa famille, ses conditions de vie, sa formation, son travail actuel ou le dernier en date. **Peut écrire des biographies imaginaires et des poèmes courts et simples sur les gens.**
A1	**Peut écrire des phrases et des expressions simples sur lui/elle-même et des personnages imaginaires, où ils vivent et ce qu'ils font.**

Le même travail a été fait pour les épreuves de compréhension orale, de production et d'interaction orales, et les résultats ont été synthétisés dans une série de graphes tels que celui-ci :

Fiche A23: Schéma de la relation de l'Unité A1 aux niveaux du CECR

B1

	Compréhension de l'oral	Production orale	Entretien	Production écrite	Compétence linguistique	Compétence sociolinguistique
A2.2						
A2.1						
A1						
Niveaux du CECR	Compréhension de l'oral	Production orale	Entretien	Production écrite	Compétence linguistique	Compétence sociolinguistique

Ce schéma montre que la première unité de l'ancienne formule se situait au niveau A2 du CECR. Nous avons donc repris ces typologies d'exercices pour le DELF A2 avec quelques modifications pour que les tâches proposées permettent de tester des savoir-faire différents.

Ce schéma montre aussi que le niveau A1 du Cadre n'était pas testé, d'où la création d'un nouvel examen. Cette innovation, qui permet d'obtenir un diplôme dès le début de l'apprentissage, vise à stimuler et à fidéliser les apprenants.[5]

Elaboration de nouvelles épreuves, opérationnalisation et contrôle

Les premières spécifications nous ont amenés à concevoir six diplômes claire-ment référencés sur le CECR, reprenant les intitulés antérieurs:

Version tout public	**DELF junior/scolaire**
DELF A1 pour le niveau A1 du CECR	DELF A1
DELF A2 pour le niveau A2 du CECR	DELF A2
DELF B1 pour le niveau B1 du CECR	DELF B1
DELF B2 pour le niveau B2 du CECR	DELF B2

DALF C1 pour le niveau C1 du CECR
DALF C2 pour le niveau C2 du CECR

Structure des examens

La détermination du profil de compétences d'un individu au travers de tâches pose un certain nombre de problèmes dès lors que ces tâches ne s'étalent pas sur un continuum allant de la plus simple (niveau A1) à la plus complexe (niveau C2). Rappelons à la suite de Lussier et Turner[6] que « trois conditions sont essentielles pour parler d'évaluation sommative: un jugement sur le degré de maîtrise des objectifs d'apprentissage, un jugement sur l'ensemble ou une partie du programme et finalement la décision d'octroyer une note pour la reconnaissance des acquis ». En délivrant un diplôme de niveau X, avec toute la valeur sociale que cela représente, l'institution atteste donc que le candidat est au moins, ou plutôt moyennement, de niveau X, ce qui signifie:

- qu'il doit avoir été évalué dans toutes les activités langagières représentatives de ce niveau
- qu'il a globalement satisfait à l'ensemble des épreuves proposées, l'une pouvant compenser l'autre
- qu'il a satisfait à des tâches qui se situent à une hauteur suffisamment représentative du niveau X, sans toutefois en exiger la maîtrise complète.

Nature des épreuves	Note sur
Compréhension de l'oral	/25
Compréhension des écrits	/25
Production écrite	/25
Production orale	/25

Nous avons donc imaginé la structure suivante pour chaque examen :
Note totale sur 100
Seuil de réussite pour l'obtention du diplôme : 50/100
Note minimale requise par épreuve : 5/25

Tâches et exercices retenus

Nous sommes convenus que les tâches proposées seraient d'un niveau de difficulté correspondant aux descripteurs les plus élevés dans le continuum de chaque niveau (équivalent aux notes TCF incluses entre x80 et x99) et nous avons enfin reconduit le principe d'une interprétation critérielle du niveau de performance qui existait déjà dans l'enseigne formule.

Afin de garantir la validité des contenus, nous avons retenu pour chaque activité langagière des tâches explicitement mises en relation avec les descripteurs de compétence du CECR, tels qu'ils sont présentés dans le chapitre 5 ; chaque épreuve est composée d'un nombre de tâches suffisant pour mesurer plusieurs compétences. Un conseil d'orientation pédagogique[7] a veillé à ce que cette structure soit en adéquation avec les modèles théoriques retenus (**validité de construct**), mais aussi avec les référentiels existant pour le français.[8] Voici à titre d'exemple deux tâches retenues pour le niveau A1.

■ **Exercice de production écrite, DELF A1**

Exercice de compréhension de l'oral, DELF A1

Consigne:
Vous allez entendre 2 fois un document. Vous aurez 30 secondes de pause entre les 2 écoutes puis 30 secondes pour vérifier vos réponses. Lisez d'abord les questions.

Document sonore :
« Le train TGV n°6866 à destination de Paris partira à 15 h 18, quai numéro 5. »

Questionnaire :
Vous allez à Paris en train. Répondez aux questions.
1. Le train part du quai :
        numéro 6.
        numéro 16.
        numéro 5.
2. À quelle heure part le train ? _____

Complétez votre fiche d'inscription à l'hôtel :

Nom : . . . .
Prénom : . . . .
Nationalité : . . . .
Adresse personnelle : . . . .
Profession : . . . .
Date d'arrivée à l'hôtel : . . . .**Date de départ :** . . . .

Ces tâches correspondent aux descripteurs suivants du CECR (niveau A1) :

Compréhension générale de l'oral
COMPRENDRE UN LOCUTEUR NATIF
Peut comprendre des questions et des instructions qui lui sont adressées lentement et avec soin et suivre des consignes simples et brèves.

Interaction écrite générale
NOTES, MESSAGES ET FORMULAIRES
Peut écrire chiffres et dates, nom, nationalité, adresse, âge, date de naissance ou d'arrivée dans le pays, etc. sur une fiche d'hôtel par exemple.

Nous avons en outre décidé de différencier systématiquement dans nos épreuves de production orale une phase de monologue suivi avec une phase d'interaction, et d'ajouter des tâches relevant par exemple de la coopération à visée fonctionnelle alors que les épreuves antérieures du DELF et du DALF privilégiaient souvent l'échange de biens et de services ou encore l'interview.

De même nous avons décidé de ne pas évaluer, faute d'outils pour le faire, les compétences socio culturelles en dehors de leur manifestation dans le fait linguistique (socio linguistique). En effet, si des savoir, savoir-faire et savoir-être caractérisent sans doute le développement progressif d'une personnalité interculturelle, convertissant ainsi ces notions en objet éducatif explicite, il ne nous a pas semblé possible pour l'heure d'évaluer sommativement des compétences de médiation culturelle telles que le Conseil de l'Europe les met en évidence.[9] Il y a là sans aucun doute un travail de réflexion auquel le CECR nous invite.

Fiabilité des notations

L'organisation d'un examen à l'échelle mondiale pose des problèmes relatifs à la fidélité de la notation. Les équipes d'examinateurs et correcteurs proviennent en effet d'espaces culturels très différents et l'on sait combien il est difficile de garantir une fidélité de notation inter évaluateurs sur des épreuves de productions écrite et/ou orale.

Nous considérons cependant que l'évaluation des compétences en langue ne peut faire l'impasse sur ces activités langagières et nous avons donc mis en place un dispositif pour améliorer la fiabilité de la notation.

Des grilles critériées, directement reliées aux descripteurs du CECR et aux référentiels pour le français ont été créées, et un plan massif de formation des correcteurs et des examinateurs a été mis en place pour l'ensemble des centres d'examens. L'inspection générale du Ministère de l'Education nationale évaluera la qualité de ce dispositif dans le courant de l'année 2006.

Grille d'évaluation de la production orale au niveau DELF A1

1ère partie - Entretien dirigé

Peut se présenter et parler de soi en répondant à des questions personnelles simples, lentement et clairement formulées.	0	0,5	1	1,5	2	2,5	3	3,5	4

2ème partie – Echange d'informations

Peut poser des questions personnelles simples sur des sujets familiers et concrets et manifester le cas échéant qu'il/elle a compris la réponse.	0	0,5	1	1,5	2	2,5	3	3,5

3ème partie – Dialogue simulé

Peut demander ou donner quelque chose à quelqu'un, comprendre ou donner des instructions simples sur des sujets concrets de la vie quotidienne.	0	0,5	1	1,5	2	2,5	3	3,5	4
Peut établir un contact social de base en utilisant les formes de politesse les plus élémentaires.	0	0,5	1	1,5	2	2,5	3		

Pour l'ensemble des 3 parties de l'épreuve

Lexique (étendue)/correction lexicale Peut utiliser un répertoire élémentaire de mots et d'expressions isolés relatifs à des situations concrètes.	0	0,5	1	1,5	2	2,5	3
Morphosyntaxe/ correction grammaticale Peut utiliser de façon limitée des structures très simples.	0	0,5	1	1,5	2	2,5	3
Maîtrise du système phonologique Peut prononcer de manière compréhensible un répertoire limité d'expressions mémorisées.	0	0,5	1	1,5	2	2,5	3

L'épineuse question des seuils de réussite (*cut-off scores*) sera prochaine-ment abordée dans une communication où le CIEP présentera ses choix.

Opérationnalisation des nouvelles épreuves

Afin de garantir la validité de ces épreuves plusieurs phases expérimentales ont été menées dans le monde (Viêt-Nam, Norvège, Italie, Espagne, République Tchèque, Malaisie, Grèce) et en France avec des apprenants de plus de 40 nationalités différentes. Tous ces étudiants ont tout d'abord passé le TCF – test de connaissance du français – qui a servi d'ancrage aux mesures effectuées, puis ils ont été évalués par leurs enseignants et par des experts du CIEP, avant de passer le DELF ou le DALF. Le rapport psychométrique réalisé met en évidence l'adéquation qui existe désormais entre ces épreuves et le TCF et donc, selon nous, sur le TCF.

Comparaison des niveaux du TCF et ceux du DELF-DALF

La première étude comparative entre les niveaux attribués par le TCF et ceux du DELF-DALF a été réalisée sur un échantillon de 250 personnes. Nous

souhaitions savoir si les niveaux des candidats au DELF-DALF corre-
spondaient à ceux qu'ils avaient obtenus au TCF. Nous avons utilisé le test
du Kappa de Cohen qui permet de chiffrer l'accord entre deux ou plusieurs
observateurs ou techniques. Cette étude montre qu'il y a une très forte corre-
spondance entre les niveaux globaux des deux examens.

Tableau des correspondances entre le TCF et le DELF-DALF

Niveaux TCF	Niveaux DELF-DALF
1	A1
2	A2
3	B1
4	B2
5	C1
6	C2

Le Kappa général est significativement différent de 0, c'est-à-dire que les
jugements de niveaux du TCF et du DELF-DALF ne sont pas indépendants.
Il est élevé (0,803), ce qui signifie que le taux d'accord entre les deux examens
est important. Les accords catégoriels (par niveau) sont tous significatifs au
risque 5% (p<0,05).

**D'après notre analyse, on peut considérer que les niveaux globaux du DELF-
DALF et du TCF sont en accord.**

Méthodologie et procédure d'analyse des items

Le calibrage des items

Le calibrage des items des épreuves de compréhension orale et écrite des nouveaux examens du DELF-DALF est réalisé par l'équipe des psychométriciens
du CIEP, Marianne MAVEL et Sébastien GEORGES. L'objectif est de créer
à moyen terme une banque d'items.

Les analyses psychométriques seront réalisées régulièrement sur les items des
différentes versions du nouveau DELF-DALF afin d'alimenter au fur et à
mesure la banque d'items. Ces analyses permettront de déterminer la qualité, le
niveau de difficulté des items, et de vérifier qu'il n'existe pas de biais dus à certaines caractéristiques des candidats (langue maternelle, sexe, centre d'examen,
. . .). La banque d'items facilitera la fabrication de nouvelles versions du DELF-
DALF, et garantira l'équivalence des versions à l'intérieur d'un même niveau.

Théorie classique des tests

Avant de procéder au calibrage des items, on applique le modèle de mesure
classique sur les données. Ce modèle permet de repérer les items qui ne convi-
ennent pas au construit (ici la connaissance du français) et de mettre en évidence les erreurs de construction de l'item :

- la clé n'est pas reconnue par les candidats (seule la clé doit avoir un r_{ptbis} positif)

- un ou plusieurs distracteurs ne fonctionnent pas ou mal (ils ne sont presque pas ou jamais sélectionnés, leurs r_{ptbis} sont positifs)
- l'item est trop facile ou trop difficile (taux de réussite)
- l'item n'est pas assez discriminant (r_{ptbis} trop faible).

Exemple:

Item validé
Répartition des réponses des candidats par groupe de niveau

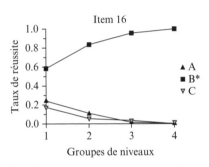

Item rejeté
Répartition des réponses des candidats par groupe de niveau

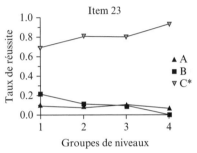

On observe une croissance continue du taux de réussite, plus le niveau du groupe de candidats est élevé en français, plus le taux de réussite est élevé.

Les candidats du groupe 4 ont un taux de réussite légèrement inférieur à celui du groupe 3, alors qu'il devrait être supérieur.

Distracteurs	A	B	C
r_{ptbis}	-28	**43**	-31

Distracteurs	A	B	C
r_{ptbis}	**2**	-29	**21**

Seule la clé B a un r_{ptbis} positif, elle est bien reconnue par les candidats.

Le distracteur A a un r_{ptbis} positif, donc un certain nombre de candidats de niveau élevé (dont les scores au test sont forts) ont pensé que la bonne réponse était A.

Vérification de quelques hypothèses préalables au modèle de Rasch

L'unidimensionnalité

On vérifie aussi la fidélité du test grâce à l'indice suivant : alpha de Cronbach. Cet indice varie entre 0 et 1, une valeur supérieure à 0,80 indique que le test a une bonne cohérence interne. Si cet indice est trop faible, on retirera les items qui le font diminuer.

On souhaite savoir s'il est pertinent, en terme de mesure, d'additionner les différentes parties du test, autrement dit de résumer tous les items via une appréciation globale. Pour cela, on applique sur nos données une analyse en composante principale.

Repérer les choix heureux par ignorance

On regarde si les candidats dont les scores sont faibles ont réussi aux items les plus difficiles. Le cas échéant, on les retire.

Calibrage des items avec le modèle de Rasch

Qualité de l'ajustement

L'indice OUTFIT est la variance, pour chaque item, des écarts standardisés au modèle. Cet indice sera d'autant plus élevé si les réponses sont inattendues compte tenue de l'habilité des candidats et de la difficulté de l'item : un individu fort qui échoue à un item facile ou un individu faible qui réussit un item difficile contribuent donc de manière plus importante à cet indice. Si l'indice est trop faible (inférieur à 0,7), cela peut indiquer que les réponses des candidats sont trop redondantes.

L'indice INFIT est calculé de manière à minimiser l'importance des réponses des individus pour lesquels l'item est inapproprié. Cet indice est une variance pondérée des écarts standardisés au modèle. Il est associé à la recherche des réponses trop redondantes. Les valeurs de ces deux indices « doivent » être comprises **entre 0,7 et 1,3**.

Comparaisons des probabilités prévues aux probabilités observées

Afin de décider de l'adéquation d'un item au modèle, les indices infit et outfit ne sont pas suffisants. Pour chaque item, on compare les probabilités prévues et celles observées en fonction du niveau des candidats en français. Les probabilités de succès prévues par le modèle doivent être les plus proches possibles des probabilités observées.

Exemple:

Item validé	**Item rejeté**
Probabilité de la réponse observée et prévue aux probabilités observées	*Probabilité de la réponse observée et prévue aux probabilités observées*

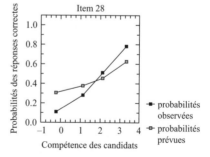

Les courbes représentant les probabilités prévues et observées sont très proches.

Les courbes représentant les probabilités prévues et observées ne se superposent pas sur l'ensemble des quatre niveaux. Il y a une trop grande différence entre ce qui a été prévu et ce qui a été observé.

Infit (msq)	Outfit (msq)
0,98	0,98

Infit (msq)	Outfit (msq)
1,37	1,7

Ces indices sont supérieurs à 1,3, il semble donc qu'il y ait trop de réponses inattendues.

Étude des biais

On recherche s'il n'existe pas de biais liés à certaines caractéristiques des individus : âge, sexe, langue maternelle, etc... Nous partageons notre échantillon en sous catégories, et pour chacune de celles-ci, nous estimons avec le modèle de Rasch la difficulté des items.

Exemple
Nous étudions ici l'existence de biais lié au sexe des candidats.
L'équation de la droite de régression entre les estimations des niveaux des items pour les femmes et celles des hommes est la suivante :
femme = 0,000410291174 + 0,984698817 x *homme*

Le coefficient directeur et l'ordonnée à l'origine de la droite de régression sont respectivement proches de 1 et de zéro, on considère alors que les estimations des niveaux de difficultés varient très peu entre les femmes et les hommes. Sur le graphique ci-dessous, la droite de régression n'a pas été tracée, il s'agit de la droite d'invariance ($y = x$).

Les points se regroupent tous autour de la droite d'invariance, donc il ne semble pas y avoir de biais sur l'estimation de la difficulté des items par rapport au sexe.

Etude des résidus

Les résidus représentent la part des données non expliquée par le modèle de Rasch. Ils doivent non seulement être peu élevés mais également ne pas révéler de dimension mathématique sous-jacente. Dans un tel cas, cela signifierait qu'une autre dimension, différente de la compétence en français est susceptible de rendre compte des données recueillies par le test auprès des candidats, et par conséquent que le test ne mesure pas ce qu'il est censé

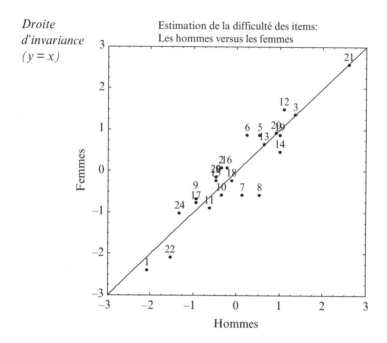

Droite d'invariance (y = x)

Estimation de la difficulté des items:
Les hommes versus les femmes

mesurer (problème de validité de contenu). Pour vérifier qu'il n'y a pas de dimension dominante sous-jacente, on réalise une ACP sur nos résidus.

Processus d'ancrage

Le recours à l'ancrage est indispensable pour la construction puis l'alimentation d'une banque d'items. Afin de construire une échelle commune à tous les items provenant de prétests différents, on utilise des items ancres. Chaque prétest est relié à un ou plusieurs autres par un certain nombre d'items en commun, il s'agit des ancres.

Un item ancre ne doit laisser aucun doute quant à la validité de son contenu, à sa forme et à toutes les qualités psychométriques qui le caractérisent. Il doit en quelque sorte symboliser l'invariance propre aux items de l'échelle. L'idée est de sélectionner des items qui répondent à ces exigences.

Les choix effectués ainsi que les procédures d'analyse sont désormais systématisés pour la mise en place de la banque de sujets que le CIEP utilise pour envoyer à ses 900 centres les épreuves des sessions. Le CIEP qui a déjà obtenu la norme ISO 9000 pour le TCF travaillera en 2006–2007 à l'obtention de cette norme pour le DELF et le DALF.

Conclusions

Il reste bien évidemment à analyser la validité apparente de ces épreuves, leur acceptabilité par celles et ceux qui passent le test comme par ceux qui le font passer. En éducation un instrument de mesure peut influencer les pratiques et la perception que les enseignants ont du processus d'enseignement / apprentissage, voire susciter des changements dans la progression des apprentissages et dans l'élaboration des instruments d'enseignement. Le DELF et le DALF ont contribué depuis 20 ans à créer non seulement une culture commune de l'évaluation au sein de la communauté FLE, mais aussi à intégrer l'approche communicative dans les pratiques de classe.

Entre un souci de validation de l'excellence et une logique de régulation des apprentissages, le diplôme connaît aujourd'hui un succès social indéniable et représente un marché non négligeable. N'oublions cependant pas que cette réforme est bien d'introduire la perspective actionnelle et derrière elle la dimension de politique éducative et linguistique du CECR dans les dispositifs d'enseignement apprentissage des langues.

Nous émettons le vœu que cette réforme contribuera à la promotion et à la diffusion de langue française et au respect de la diversité linguistique à laquelle nous sommes tous attachés.

Pour plus d'information : www.ciep.fr

Notes

1 Référentiels pour les langues nationales et régionales, niveau B2 pour le français, un référentiel, Beacco, Bouquet, Porquier, Didier éd, 2004.
2 Portfolio européen des langues, Conseil de l'Europe, Castellotti, Coste, Moore, Tagliante, CIEP, ENS, Didier, 2004.
3 Beacco, Bouquet, Porquier, op cite.
4 « Relier les examens all Cadre européen », Conseil de l'Europe.
5 « Une certification pour un niveau de découverte », B. Dupoux, Le français dans le monde, n° 336, novembre-décembre 2004, pages : 29–35.
6 «Le point sur l'évaluation en didactique des langues », Lussier, Turner, CEC éd, Anjou, Canada, 1995, p. 164.
7 La liste des membres du Conseil d'orientation pédagogique est consultable sur le site: www.ciep.fr
8 Un référentiel pour le français, niveau B2, Beacco, Bouquet, Porquier, Didier, 2004. A1 à paraître.
9 « Médiation culturelle et didactique des langues », Zarate, Gohard-Radenkovic, Lussier, Penz, CELV COE, Strasbourg, 2003.

5 Proficiency scaling in DESI listening and reading EFL tests: task characteristics, item difficulty and cut-off points

Guenter Nold

University of Dortmund, Germany

Henning Rossa

University of Dortmund, Germany

Johannes Hartig

German Institute for International Educational Research, Frankfurt, Germany

Abstract

This paper is concerned with the development and evaluation of tests of listening and reading comprehension in DESI, a large-scale assessment project. A procedure was developed that involved ratings of task characteristics and application of the Dutch CEFR GRID (Alderson, Figueras, Kuijper, R Nold, Takaala & Tardieu 2004). This process was directed towards three interconnected goals: the specification of the contents of the tests, the prediction of item difficulty and relating both the test tasks and the proficiency scales derived from them to the descriptors and the levels of the Common European Framework of Reference for Languages (Council of Europe 2001).

A system of task characteristics was developed to define what the language test items demanded from the test takers. These task characteristics were validated by comparing ratings done by internal experts with those performed by an external group of linguistically informed students. It was then possible to match the specific test items with facets of the listening and reading constructs and, more specifically, the respective cognitive operations involved in performance on the tasks. As a result, it was also possible to assign a presumed difficulty value to a given task. Furthermore, the assumed difficulty resulting from the ratings was then compared with the empirical difficulty parameters derived from administering the test (N=10,543). This investigation led to the development of scales of listening and reading proficiency as assessed by the test tasks. The three authors have worked as a research team within the DESI project.

Introduction

DESI (German-English-Student-Assessment-International) is a large-scale research project in the tradition of PISA (Baumert, Klieme, Neubrand, Prenzel, Schietele, Schneider, Stanat, Tillmann & Weiß 2001). It was funded by the Committee of Education Ministers of Germany to investigate the language competences of students at 9th form in all types of schools in all the states of Germany, and it was planned to also include additional countries such as Austria and parts of Italy. The students' abilities to be assessed range from mother tongue reading and writing and language awareness to listening and reading, speaking and writing and language awareness in English as the first foreign language. As it is a major objective of the project to investigate the possible causes that underlie the different levels of student achievement, various background data was collected and the respective competences were assessed in 2003 and 2004 (N=10,543), namely at the beginning and at the end of year 9, in order to be able to observe in which way and to what extent students developed their proficiency.

In this paper it is the aim to focus on the steps that were taken to develop the listening and reading comprehension test constructs in English as the first foreign language (EFL), a system of task characteristics, and to arrive at cut-off points and descriptors for proficiency scales of EFL reading and listening in a way that is less arbitrary than traditional approaches would have allowed (Beaton and Allen 1992). Due to the limits of this paper, and contrary to popular practice in the research community, we will mainly focus on listening as an example of how we linked construct, tasks, task characteristics and proficiency scaling rather than emphasising reading. We will add, in a piecemeal fashion, aspects of reading comprehension that differed from the listening module.

Test development and specifications

In this part of the paper we respond to two items on Alderson's 'wishlist for the future of language testing' (2004:14), presented at the ALTE conference in Barcelona, by describing how test specifications were developed and how constructs were identified in two modules of the DESI tests. The constructs and test tasks for the DESI tests of listening and reading have drawn on three main sources both in the initial phases of test development and during the process of revising the piloted tests and constructs:

- Applied Linguistics research on communicative competence and the specific skills of listening and reading in a foreign language

- German curricula specifying content areas and achievement goals for foreign language skills in year 9
- CEFR specifications and scales for receptive communicative activities.

As the DESI English tests were developed for the assessment of EFL proficiency in the German context it was imperative to not only consider the research done in the field of listening and reading comprehension and in testing in general, but also to look at the specific demands that are stated for all the school types in the curricula of the 16 states of Germany. Education is the special responsibility of the states rather than the central government. A synopsis of the various curricula revealed the amount of overlap between the school types and among the states. For the English part of DESI it became more and more obvious what the possible range of achievement in listening and reading might be and how this would relate to linguistic and content requirements described in the curricula. What all the curricula more or less share is the focus on listening and reading as a communicative skill in its own right. They also lay great store by the inclusion of authentic texts. Where they tend to differ are the linguistic complexity of the texts, the variety of topics and text types (e.g. the use of literary texts mentioned especially in the grammar school curricula) and the amount of creativity and guidance in dealing with the texts. So it was the special task for the research team to develop tests that would, on the one hand, cover a wide range of listening and reading subskills and that would, on the other hand, be based on a variety of topics and text types which would be an expression of what the different curricula share.

In addition to analysing the curricula it was decided also to take into account the descriptions of the Common European Framework of Reference for Languages (Council of Europe 2001). This decision proved to be very useful and appropriate because a curriculum of national standards for language education in Germany was created while the research in DESI was under way (Klieme 2003). In this document the national standards in EFL were clearly based on the CEFR and so the latest changes in the state curricula in Germany all reflect the influence of the CEFR at all levels. The descriptors of the CEFR scales were found to be relevant guidelines during the process of test development. However, as the CEFR is not primarily a tool for test development (Alderson et al 2004) it was soon found that the level descriptions of the CEFR had to be interpreted and selected in the light of the research on listening and reading comprehension. Otherwise it would not be possible to show how the test constructs would focus on the processes and competences involved. This explains why the DESI listening and reading tests and the proficiency levels they address have their roots in the theory of comprehension, in the curricular requirements for 9th form students and in the level descriptions of the CEFR. An analysis of the level descriptions in DESI and the CEFR reveals to what extent the scales overlap. And, it is the

Dutch CEFR GRID (Alderson et al 2004) that helps to link the tests to the CEFR more specifically by applying standard setting procedures (Council of Europe 2004: Section B).

The listening construct in DESI

Even though research findings strongly suggest that listening plays a central role in language acquisition the wide majority of empirical studies in cognitive psychology, applied linguistics and language education which investigate receptive skills and their assessment focus on reading rather than listening. In attempts at describing the state of the art of assessing listening this phenomenon has led to the contradictory notion that 'the assessment of listening abilities is one of the least understood, least developed and yet one of the most important areas of language testing and assessment' (Alderson and Bachman in their preface to Buck 2001: x).

Several studies indicate the apparent similarity of listening and reading processes (Bae and Bachman 1998, Buck 2001, Freedle and Kostin 1999, Grotjahn 2000, Hagtvet 2003, Rost 2002, Tsui and Fullilove 1998). Freedle and Kostin, for example, compare TOEFL listening and reading modules and conclude that 'both these receptive skills are measures of a general underlying language comprehension ability' (1999:23). However, all sources mentioned above also demonstrate that both forms of comprehension can be assessed as distinct factors, which suggests that we need to account for a number of significant differences between processing a printed page and an aural input. Grotjahn argues that listeners rely much more on 'real-time processing' than readers do (2000:7). This is clearly due to the transitory non-permanent nature of the language input. A participant in an introspective study on listening describes comprehension processes in listening as 'the continuous modification of a developing interpretation in response to incoming information' (Buck 1991:80). It seems that the key difference between listening and reading is the lack of control of incoming information: while a reader can re-read parts of the text to infer the meanings of unknown words (cf. Grotjahn 2000:7), listeners encounter comprehension problems when 'the on-line processing is somehow taxed or interrupted' (Hagtvet 2003:528). A synopsis of relevant research (Buck 2001, Rubin 1994) creates an image of listening that is in line with Celce-Murcia's conclusion: listening is a 'complex, dynamic and rather fragile' process (1995: 366).

Listening in a foreign language is especially fragile because bottom-up processes are usually restricted to the availability of proceduralised language knowledge, which – as far as many L2 learners are concerned – is deficient (cf. Tsui and Fullilove 1998). Buck neatly summarises the challenges that are unique to L2 listening: 'When second-language listeners are listening, there will often be gaps in their understanding. [. . .] Of course, gaps occur in first-language listening too, but the gaps in second-language listening usually have a far more significant impact on comprehension' (Buck 2001:50).

Following the suggestions in Buck (2001) and Rost (2002) the listening construct in DESI reflects theoretical models of communicative competence as well as the specific characteristics of situations of target language use. Buck argues for the integration of both sources in construct development on the grounds of present conceptions of language use that emphasise the interconnections between knowledge and contexts in which knowledge is applied:

> This approach is most appropriate when we think that the consistencies in listening performance are partly due to some underlying knowledge and ability, partly due to situational factors, and partly due to the interaction between them. In other words, we see performance in terms of underlying language competence, but this is influenced by contextual factors. [. . .] this is probably a theoretically more defensible position than either the competence-based or task-based approach (Buck 2001:109)

In language assessment the contextual factors Buck points out above can be identified in the situations of language use the test impresses on the test taker by means of different test tasks. Whether the test actually succeeds in conveying what the test taker is expected to do with his language skills in the test situation is an additional question that cannot be addressed here. Since DESI is both an assessment study and an evaluation study of EFL education in the German school system, the test specifications reflect to some extent the situations of language use German students encounter in EFL classrooms. An analysis of EFL curricula for all German *Bundesländer* has shown that the listening subskills German students are expected to develop in language use situations in class basically aim at understanding auditory texts for learning and following classroom discourse. The samples of spoken language students are exposed to in these situations may at times resemble authentic oral interaction among native speakers of English; generally, however, they are dominated by recordings of people reading aloud simplified and scripted texts. Accordingly, the listening construct in DESI encompasses both the comprehension of aural texts that belong to the oral and the literate end of the continuum which Shohamy and Inbar (1991:29) have used for the analysis of listening texts.

Along the lines of the Council of Europe's CEFR the test construct views listening as a receptive communicative activity which includes comprehension purposes such as 'listening for gist, for specific information, for detailed understanding, for implications, etc.' (Council of Europe 2001:65). These purposes are mirrored in the test construct and in the test tasks operationalising the construct. The DESI listening construct in its most explicit form draws on Buck's 'default listening construct' (2001: 114) and specifies the following facets of listening ability:

- processing short and extended samples of spoken language (English [Near-RP and General Canadian], authentic speech rates, generally clear articulation, scripted texts) in real time
- understanding the linguistic information that is presented on the local level of the input text (understanding details)
- connecting pieces of information in order to develop a mental model which allows comprehension on the global levels of the input text (understanding gist)
- matching explicitly and implicitly presented information (actions, emotions, intentions) with language knowledge and background knowledge to recognise and retrieve, to infer, and to interpret this information
- constructing a representation of information presented in the aural mode that allows the listener to understand paraphrases of that information in other (written) contexts.

The assessment of listening ability assumes that the listener's competences are measured against test tasks of variable difficulty. This entails that we need to specify which competencies listeners have to activate in listening situations and which tasks will most probably elicit specific processes of knowledge activation and utilisation that resemble these situations.

Buck's (2001) framework of listening ability adapts the much quoted Bachman model of communicative language ability (Bachman 1990, Bachman and Palmer 1996) and provides a framework of competences involved in listening comprehension. According to Buck's model, successful listening mainly depends on language knowledge and strategic competence (Vandergrift 2003). World knowledge is an additional variable that affects whether listening ability can actually be applied in a given context as listeners have to test the developing representation of the input for plausibility (Buck 1991, Rubin 1994). The theoretical background for the measurement model in DESI integrates all three types of knowledge and recognises their relevance for successful performance on test tasks as shown in Figure 1. Generally, all types of knowledge will interact during comprehension. For the sake of specification, however, the measurement model breaks challenges posed by test tasks down to distinguishable elements of task characteristics. These characteristics are likely to challenge specific types of knowledge more than others.

Since input texts and test tasks differ with regard to variable task demands, the deduction of task characteristics from the measurement model allows test developers to assign a profile of task demands for each item. These profiles would make explicit which competences are mainly assessed by specific items. Depending on the quantitative and qualitative levels of competences on the side of the test taker performance on such tasks will be more or less successful (cf. the quantitative and qualitative dimensions in the

Figure 1: The DESI listening measurement model

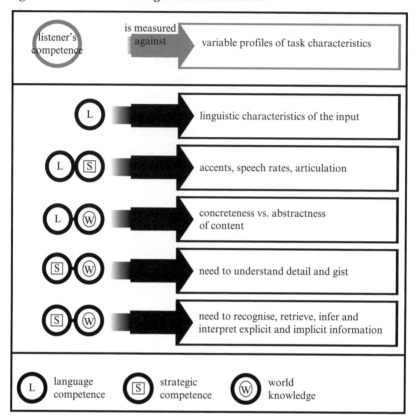

CEFR level descriptors, Council of Europe 2001). Task profiles for DESI listening and reading items were identified using the system of task characteristics described later in this paper.

The reading construct in DESI

The reading comprehension test construct takes into account the theoretical findings of research on reading and the curricular requirements that were explained above. The competences that are needed to perform successfully on the tests correspond to the following requirements.

In response to narrative and expository texts and extracts from drama and in response to texts that differ with regard to their linguistic and text-pragmatic levels of complexity it is necessary to:

- understand linguistic information (e.g. reference to incidents) at the local level (understanding detail)

- infer unknown linguistic elements from context
- connect pieces of information in order to develop a mental model so as to understand the text on the global levels (understand main idea, gist)
- match explicitly and implicitly presented information (actions, emotions, intentions) with language knowledge and background knowledge, in order to recognise and retrieve, to infer, and to interpret this information at the level of text parts and the whole text.

The test construct underlines that reading requires active student behaviour. The students need to process texts and while doing so to access and activate various types of knowledge in order to make sense of text details and to develop mental models that relate to certain parts or the whole of a text. And it is the test items that determine and restrict the number of interpretations in view of the fact that other types of interpretations may theoretically be possible. This is in line with Buck (2001:114), who points out that comprehension tests need to go beyond the level of literal meanings, although they do not include the '. . . full range of implied meanings'.

Moreover, a further aspect of the test construct is determined by the number of texts that the students were asked to read. Overall, four texts with a total of 46 multiple-choice-test items were used. Each student had to cope with two texts and their items. Students at the various types of schools had to perform on different texts and test items. However, an anchor design was employed to make sure that all the texts and their items were linked to one another so as to make comparisons and statistical analyses possible. In this way texts with different topics and belonging to different textual varieties (narrative, expository, drama) could be given to every student.

What could not be taken care of in the test construct are different types of reading. The time restrictions (approx. 20 minutes) did not allow the inclusion of a greater variety of reading types systematically. However, as the tests required a greater amount of inferencing and interpreting it can safely be assumed that from a reading strategies perspective it was necessary to make use of intensive reading in addition to skimming and scanning in order to successfully complete the tasks.

Developing a system of task characteristics for the DESI listening and reading tests

In order to establish a link between test constructs, tasks, and scale descriptors, we developed a system of task characteristics. This development process had three subgoals. Firstly, and most importantly, the specification of tasks based on the system of characteristics systematically documented the extent to which facets of the construct were actually represented in the tasks. Second, and crucially for this paper, is our intention to use task specifications in combination with item difficulty to arrive at cut-off points on proficiency scales in a more informed and less arbitrary manner than other approaches would permit. The third goal is to provide a scheme of task analysis for the receptive skills to be applied in future test development and evaluation.

Listening task characteristics

Research into task characteristics affecting difficulty in listening tests from various methodological backgrounds has tried to group characteristics according to item and text characteristics and those reflecting the interaction between item and text (Brindley and Slatyer 2002, Brown 1995, Buck and Tatsuoka 1998, Grotjahn 2000, Solmecke 2000). Characteristics of the *interaction* type defined in the DESI system assess the comprehension processes the test taker has to engage in to successfully solve the item and as a result reflect aspects of content, lexical and grammatical complexity, comprehension purposes and depth of information processing. A prerequisite for rating these aspects is the identification of what Buck and Tatsuoka termed 'necessary information' (*NI*) in their rule-space-analysis of a listening test (1998:134). *NI* is defined as parts of the input text that must be comprehended to solve the item. This analytical procedure is based on the following hypothesis: 'The basic idea is that the characteristics of this particular part of the text, especially its comprehensibility, will have a considerable impact on the difficulty of the item and the abilities necessary to respond correctly' (Buck and Tatsuoka 1998:134). A finding from our study supports this claim to some extent. We found that item ratings using characteristics that assess the entire input text disregarding which aspects items actually focus on resulted in very weak correlations with item difficulty, which suggests that these characteristics could not suitably predict difficulty in DESI listening items. Buck and Tatsuoka report similar conclusions: 'Generally, it seemed that the characteristics of the whole text had little effect on individual items, but the characteristics of the text immediately surrounding the necessary information had more, although not as much as the necessary information itself'. (Buck and Tatsuoka 1998:134) The analysis of a pilot version of the DESI system of task characteristics has led to six characteristics which showed the strongest correlations (Spearman) with item difficulty. Five of these characteristics take into account the *NI*. It is fitting that the weakest correlation can be found in the single characteristic (TC2) which focuses on the item disregarding the input text.

The six elements of the system, which are specified on a 3-value scale, are presented below, following a format that provides information on four aspects that should guide raters in rating items[1]:

Table 1: Correlation coefficients (Spearman) for predictors of listening item difficulty TC1–TC6

Label	Task Characteristic	r
TC1	Task: Focus on concrete vs. abstract content	.558
TC2	Task: Lexical and grammatical complexity of item stem/options	.377
TC3	Comprehension: Purposes	.706
TC4	Comprehension: Depth of processing	.625
TC5	Passage (*NI*): Speech rate and articulation	.479
TC6	Passage (*NI*): Lexical and grammatical complexity of the input	.453

1. Title of the characteristic.
2. A paraphrase of the title in the form of a question.
3. Further explanation of the question if deemed necessary.
4. Descriptors for the three parameter values.

TC1 Task: focus on concrete vs. abstract content

Do the item stem and response options direct test takers' attention to abstract or concrete information conveyed by the input text? (Freedle and Kostin 1999:21)

This central question is based on research arguing that concrete words are easier to understand than abstract words (Dell and Gordon 2003, Freedle and Kostin 1999, Weir 2005).

In the process of deciding the parameter value for this characteristic with regard to a given task it is important to assess the interaction between the item and the *NI*. Consider an item stem such as 'What happened when the man left the store?' One may feel tempted to rate this as an item that focuses on a concrete event. However, if the respective *NI* in the aural input is 'I had just left the store when I suddenly realised how much I really hated shopping' it appears that the item actually focuses on an emotional reaction, which, in turn, should result in selecting parameter value 1 rather than 0 from the table below.

Parameter value	Descriptors
0	concrete aspects in everyday contexts (e.g. actions, persons, objects)
1	more abstract aspects (e.g. utterances about emotions, judgements) or unfamiliar content (e.g. how a student was able to use special language skills to translate English into Elvish)
2	abstract aspects (e.g. beliefs, intentions, contradictions, textual structures)

TC2 Task: lexical and grammatical complexity of item stem/options

What is the linguistic complexity of the item stem and the response options?

Parameter value	Descriptors
0	Vocabulary: only frequent words Grammar: only simple syntactic structures
1	Vocabulary: mostly frequent words Grammar: mostly simple syntactic structures
2	Vocabulary: rather extended Grammar: limited range of complex structures

TC3 Comprehension: purposes

Is it necessary to understand detail (listening for specific information) to solve the item or does the test taker have to integrate several pieces of information (listening for gist) to arrive at the correct answer?

The mere distinction between local and global comprehension does not account for a sufficient amount of variance in item difficulty. TC3 therefore distinguishes the linguistic and propositional complexity of the information that has to be comprehended and recalled.

Parameter value	Descriptors
0	Understanding a linguistically and propositionally simple detail
	Understanding a linguistically complex detail (local comprehension)
	or
1	Integrating details presented in a short passage of the text to construct global comprehension
	Understanding a propositionally and linguistically complex detail (local comprehension)
	or
2	Integrating several details scattered all over the text (global comprehension)

TC4 Comprehension: depth of processing

How deeply must the relevant text information be processed? Is it sufficient to recognise and retrieve – in the aural input – a word or a phrase and match it with the correct written option, or does the test taker have to make inferences beyond the literal wording?

Parameter value	Descriptors
0	Recognise and retrieve explicit information
1	Bridging inferences to match information recalled and clear paraphrases and synonyms in the item
	Elaborative inferences on explicit information in contexts of competing information surrounding the *NI*
	or
2	Bridging inferences to compensate for gaps in the text

TC5 Passage (*NI*): speech rate and articulation

How do you rate the phenomena of spoken language in the *NI*?

Parameter value	Descriptors
0	Low speech rate, usually coincides with very clear articulation
1	Normal speech rate, usually coincides with normal articulation
2	Fast speech rate, sometimes unclearly articulated

Buck (2001:40) expands the notion that speech rate is an important variable in listening comprehension by referring to research that suggests a limited impairment of comprehension 'until a threshold level is reached, at which time an increased speech rate leads to a more rapid decline in comprehension'. This parallels results of a regression analysis we did of ratings of task characteristics (independent variables) and item difficulty parameters (dependent variable). Only value parameter 2 of TC5 was integrated into the regression model, while value 1 was assigned a regression weight that was not significantly higher than value 0.

TC6 Passage (*NI*): lexical and grammatical complexity of the input

What is the linguistic complexity of the necessary information that item focuses on?

Parameter value	Descriptors
0	Vocabulary: only frequent words Grammar: only simple syntactic structures
1	Vocabulary: mostly frequent words Grammar: mostly simple syntactic structures
2	Vocabulary: rather extended Grammar: limited range of complex structures

An ongoing validation study, which has recently completed the phase of data collection, poses the critical question whether the system of task characteristics laid out above can reliably be applied to test tasks by raters who have not been involved in the development of the tasks and the system.

Reading task characteristics

The task characteristics of the reading tests share a great deal with the respective characteristics of listening comprehension. However, as in reading there is a focus on the written rather than the oral medium, text processing and the strategic reading behaviour of the students are bound to be different. Thus it was possible for the students to go back and forth in their reading, as the reading time was only determined by the overall testing time. However this was not possible in listening. This explains why the linguistic and textpragmatic complexity of the whole text is an essential task characteristic in reading, but not in listening. This finding is also in line with research results on reading that state that the language level of a test text is a powerful predictor of successful comprehension (Alderson 2000:104).

TC5 Text Level: linguistic and textpragmatic complexity

The reading texts can be rated in line with certain language-related scales of the CEFR. This means that their complexity corresponds to level descriptors that focus on linguistic and textpragmatic aspects in the respective scales (cf. Council of Europe 2001:69–71). What is meant by defining the text level of a reading text in terms of A2 or B1 is that such a text can typically be understood by a reader whose reading proficiency is at that particular level. At the same time the test items that are related to the text can be one level below or above the respective text level.

Parameter value	Descriptors
0	(A2/B1) Vocabulary: more or less frequent words Grammar: mostly simple syntactic structures (paratactic structures, few subordinating structures) Textpragmatics: coherent text with marked cohesive elements
1	(B1) Vocabulary: a certain amount of less frequent words Grammar: mostly simple syntactic structures, Textpragmatics: coherent text with marked cohesive elements

2	(B2) Vocabulary: rather extended, also special vocabulary Grammar: limited number of complex structures Textpragmatics: less coherent presentation, fewer cohesive ties

As can be detected here, the lexical complexity and the syntactic properties of the texts play an important role in distinguishing different levels. In addition, the question whether a text presents information in a coherent way with clear cohesive elements has also to be considered in the differentiation of language-related text characteristics.

IRT scaling and estimation of difficulty parameters

In DESI, item response theory (IRT) models were used to obtain estimates for student proficiency under the assumption that latent unidimensional proficiency dimensions determine the probabilities of observable responses within each test. Specifically, the DESI test data was analysed within the framework of a generalised Rasch model implemented in the IRT software ConQuest (Wu, Adams and Wilson 1998). ConQuest uses a marginal maximum likelihood algorithm to estimate item and person parameters despite the incomplete data due to the matrix sampling design used in DESI. The generalised Rasch model allows the analysis of both dichotomous and ordinal responses within the same test. However, since the listening and reading comprehension tests contain only dichotomously scored multiple-choice items, the model used here corresponds to the standard dichotomous Rasch model (e.g. Fischer 1995). Based on data from the DESI field test (N=462), items for listening and reading comprehension had been selected to fit the Rasch model. The weighted fit statistic index provided by ConQuest was used as a criterion for item selection. This fit index compares the observed response frequencies with those predicted by the model (Wu et al 1998). Values near one indicate close fit between data and model for a particular item parameter, values greater than one indicate poor item discrimination. Items with values greater than 1.20 were dropped from the tests (Adams and Wu 2002).

One main conceptual strength of IRT methodology is that item difficulties and proficiency scores are linked on a common scale, allowing the description of a test taker's proficiencies in terms of their mastery of specific tasks. The response probabilities are modelled as a logistic function of the latent proficiency variable, higher proficiency being associated with increasing probabilities of correct responses. The dichotomous Rasch model used in DESI contains one difficulty parameter for each item and assumes parallel functions for each item, which means that the item characteristic function is completely determined by the item's difficulty alone (for advantages of this model compared with more complex models see Wilson 2003). Within the Rasch model, item difficulty is defined as the point on the latent variable scale at which the probability to solve a particular item is 50%; this point locates items on the proficiency scale. However, 50% correct answers seems a rather low criterion to accredit the mastery of a certain task to test takers with the corresponding proficiency score. Instead, a probability of 65% was used as the criterion to locate items on the DESI proficiency scales (65%–threshold). The item difficulties for DESI listening and reading comprehension were estimated based on the total data available, that is data from both points of measurement in the case of listening comprehension and data from the second point of measurement for reading comprehension. For identification purposes, the mean student proficiency was restricted to zero. Since the matrix sampling design employed in DESI does not allow for classical reliability estimates, an IRT based reliability index for the test was obtained using the relation of expected *a posteriori* variance between persons and the measurement variance within persons. This estimate yields results in a similar range as the classical Cronbach's alpha coefficient (Rost 2004).

IRT scaling: Listening comprehension

To estimate item parameters for listening comprehension, all responses from the first and second point of measurement were used in one common analysis. All 51 items proved to fit the Rasch model satisfactorily, the maximum weighted fit statistic was 1.15. Classical item discrimination indices (item–total correlations) ranged from .21 to .53 with a mean of .48. Overall reliability of the listening comprehension test was moderate but still acceptable (Rel=.68), given the relatively small number of items answered by each student due to the matrix sampling design. Item difficulties ranged from −2.46 to 1.44 on the logit scale with a mean of −0.33, indicating that the tasks were relatively easy for the average student.

IRT scaling: Reading comprehension

For reading comprehension, data from the second point of measurement was analysed. Again, all items fit the Rasch model satisfactorily, the maximum weighted fit statistic was 1.19; classical item discrimination indices ranged from .11 to .56 with a mean of .41. Overall reliability was acceptable with Rel = .74. Item difficulties range from −3.05 to 1.15 with a mean of 0.24, indicating that tasks were relatively easy for the average student in the DESI sample.

Multiple linear regression analysis to determine cut-off points

A linear additive model was assumed adequate to represent the relations between task characteristics and item difficulties: the greater the number of demanding characteristics combined in one task, the more difficult this task is predicted to be. For each test linear regression was used to model this relation; differences in item difficulties were explained using the task characteristics as predictors (cf. Hartig 2007). The 65%-threshold of the items was used as the dependent variable. To integrate the task characteristics into the regression models, dummy variables for each characteristic were created. These variables code the presence or absence of any value greater than zero. For example, one dummy variable codes whether a listening comprehension task is rated as '1' in 'TC4 Comprehension: depth of processing', and another codes whether the task is rated as '2' in the same characteristic. The dummy coding takes into account that the levels of the task characteristics are of ordinal character.

Due to collinearities between the task characteristics, not all of them were included in the final regression model for each test. This led to a restricted selection of those task characteristics that have the strongest explanatory power for differences in item difficulties. For some characteristics, it seemed adequate to differentiate between fewer levels than originally defined. For example, the easy and medium level (0 and 1) were collapsed and only the presence of the highest value (2) was included in the model. It is important to note that significance of the regression weights was not used as a criterion for the selection of characteristics. The primary aim of the analysis was to attain an adequate *description* of the proficiency scale in terms of task characteristics, not necessarily to generalise the results beyond the actual tasks used in the DESI tests. As a criterion, predictors with a regression weight greater than 0.10 logits, corresponding to approximately 10% of a standard deviation in the students' proficiencies, were kept in the model.

The regression analysis serves two main purposes: firstly, the overall explanatory power of the task characteristics is estimated. The amount of explained variance in differences between item difficulties indicates the quality of the assumptions expressed by the definition of the task characteristics. The second and more important aim of the regression analysis was to estimate expected difficulties for combinations of task characteristics' value parameters. For each task characteristic's value parameter, a specific regression weight is estimated. The expected difficulty for a specific combination of task characteristics can be obtained as the sum of the corresponding regression weights. The regression constant corresponds to the expected difficulty of a task that was rated on the lowest difficulty level (0) regarding all characteristics that were included in the model. Table 2 shows regression weights for listening task characteristics' parameter values.

Table 2: Regression weights for predictors of listening item difficulty TC1, TC3, TC4 and TC5 ($R^2 = .57$).

Task Characteristics	Regression Weight
Regression constant; **TC1, 3, 4, 5** parameter value 0	−0.59
TC1 Task: focus on concrete vs. abstract content; parameter value 1	0.16
TC1 Task: focus on concrete vs. abstract content; parameter value 2	0.18
TC3 Comprehension: Purposes; parameter value 2	0.72
TC4 Comprehension: Depth of processing; parameter value 1	0.63
TC4 Comprehension: Depth of processing; parameter value 2	0.98
TC5 Passage: Speech rate and articulation, parameter value 2	0.25

The expected difficulties for certain combinations of task characteristics' parameter values are used to define cut-off points between proficiency levels. The main idea is that student proficiency can be interpreted in terms of general task characteristics instead of individual item difficulties. A student with an estimated proficiency that corresponds to a specific expected item difficulty should master the demands of the respective combination of task characteristics' levels. For example, a student with an estimated proficiency matching the regression constant should master tasks at the lowest difficulty levels in respect to all relevant task characteristics.

To define cut-off points, combinations of task characteristics that were particularly suitable to distinguish between students at different proficiency levels were selected. Additionally, the following empirical criteria were applied:

• the test has to contain several tasks that actually implement the specific combination of task characteristics

• the differences between the expected and observed difficulties (regression residuals) should be negligible for at least some of these tasks

• the cut-off points should be selected with a sufficient distance on the scale between each point to allow for a reliable differentiation between the resulting proficiency levels.

Cut-off points on the DESI scale 'proficiency in listening comprehension'

The DESI scale for proficiency in listening comprehension has three larger levels and three levels that represent a qualitative development of proficiency within each level (see Table 3). As laid out above, these qualitatively different descriptions of proficiency are deduced from qualitatively different task characteristics' parameter values of items that are consequently at a higher predicted difficulty level than those items with value combinations of the cut-off point on the scale. The thresholds of 'developmental' sub-levels do not function as genuine cut-off points, because there was only an insufficient number of tasks in the test that actually fulfilled the empirical criteria laid out above.

Table 3: Cut-off points and combinations of task characteristics' value parameters for listening comprehension proficiency levels in DESI. Shaded cells refer to levels which feature a specific value parameter that cannot be found on lower levels. Values in parentheses were not integrated into the regression model.

Level	Logit	TC1	TC3	TC4	TC5
LC1	−0.59	0	0	0	0
LC1+	0.04	0	(1)	1	(1)
LC2	0.20	1	(1)	1	(1)
LC2+	0.39	0	(1)	2	(1)
LC3	1.16	1	2	1	2
LC3+	1.54	2	2	2	2

Logit: predicted IRT item difficulty parameter
TC1 Task: focus on concrete vs. abstract content
TC3 Comprehension: purposes
TC4 Comprehension: information processing
TC5 Passage: speech rate and articulation

While level one is characterised by the ability to understand simple details when speech rate is low and articulation is clear, higher levels are first distinguished by higher level cognitive processes in TC3 and TC4 (global comprehension and making inferences) then by phenomena of spoken language (TC5) and finally by the abstractness of the content in focus (TC1) and the need to interpret and elaborate on information (TC4).

Cut-off points on the DESI scale 'proficiency in reading comprehension'

The DESI scale for proficiency in reading comprehension is significantly different from the listening scale both in its structure and the distinguishing combinations of task characteristic parameter values that make up the levels. It was possible to identify four combination clusters and one 'developmental' cluster in level four (see Table 4).

Table 4: Cut-off points and combinations of task characteristics' value parameters for reading comprehension proficiency levels in DESI. Shaded cells refer to levels which feature a specific value parameter that cannot be found on lower levels. Values in parentheses were not integrated into the regression model.

Level	Logit	TC1	TC3	TC5	TC6
RC1	−0.59	0	0	0	0
RC2	−0.36	(1)	0	0	1
RC3	0.49	(1)	1	(1)	1
RC4	0.87	(1)	1	2	(2)
RC4+	1.23	2	(2)	2	(2)

Logit: predicted IRT item difficulty parameter
TC1 Task: focus on concrete vs. abstract content
TC3 Comprehension: purposes
TC5 Text level: linguistic/textpragmatic complexity
TC6 Passage (*NI*): lexical/grammatical complexity

Reading levels above level one are first determined by lexical and textpragmatic complexity of the necessary information, then characterised by higher level cognitive processes in TC3 and higher text levels (TC5) and finally defined by the abstractness of the content in focus (TC1).

The road ahead: a link with the CEFR?

As a result of the procedure described above, listening and reading comprehension scales are now available in DESI. These scales can function as yardsticks for future tests and consequently can be regarded as standards to relate to. However, in the meantime the curricula in Germany have been linked to the CEFR as indicated above. So it is desirable to show how the DESI standards compare with the levels of the CEFR. This involves a linking procedure as delineated in the CEFR Manual of the Council of Europe (2003). The test specifications in DESI that have been described in detail above can be analysed in terms of the suggested linking procedure. As a first step the descriptors of the DESI scales can be compared with those of the CEFR. For example, the scale descriptions of LC1+, LC2 and LC2+ of DESI can be related to similar scales of the CEFR. If the two scales are compared it becomes obvious that the overlap between the DESI and the CEFR scales ranges from only a partial fit to a more or less perfect match. Whereas the scale descriptions of LC1+ are defined by descriptors that can be found in CEFR level descriptions ranging from A2+ to B1+ with a clear midpoint in B1, the descriptions of LC2 and LC2+ in DESI more or less match those of Level B2 in the CEFR.

DESI

LC1+: Can understand <u>concrete details</u> in contexts of <u>everyday communication</u> (narrative, radio report, conversation) and infer apparent paraphrases of this information, even if these details are presented at a normal speech rate with a wider range of lexical items and syntactic structures.

Can connect a limited number of concrete details in order to <u>understand main ideas</u> in parts of the text.

CEFR

A2+: Can understand enough to be able to meet needs of a concrete type, provided <u>speech is clearly and slowly articulated</u>.

B1: Can <u>understand the main points</u> of clear standard speech on familiar matters <u>regularly encountered in work, school, leisure</u> etc., including short narratives.

B1+: Can understand straightforward factual information about common everyday topics, identifying both general messages and <u>specific details,</u> provided speech is clearly articulated in a generally familiar accent.

DESI

LC2: Can develop an understanding of concrete details by <u>inferring implicitly stated information or interpreting</u> explicitly stated <u>information</u>.

LC2+: Can understand <u>more abstract information</u> in contexts of everyday communication (e.g. utterances about emotions), even if these <u>details are linguistically complex</u> and are presented at a normal speech rate.

CEFR

B2: Can understand the <u>main ideas</u> of propositionally and linguistically complex speech on both <u>concrete and abstract topics</u> delivered in a standard dialect, including technical discussions in his/her field of specialisation.

Can follow <u>extended speech</u> and <u>complex lines of argument</u> provided the topic is reasonably familiar, and the direction of the talk is sign-posted by explicit markers.

These findings may prove relevant to educators who want to judge the level of achievement of their students in relation to the CEFR scales. If the linking procedure is to be made more transparent and valid, however, a procedure of standard setting is needed as described in the Reference Supplement to the Manual for Relating Examinations to the CEFR (Council of Europe 2004). This will involve the rating of each DESI test item based on the scale descriptions of the CEFR and statistical analyses that reveal the extent to which the item level corresponds to a level on the respective CEFR scale. The levels of the items in both the DESI scales and the CEFR scales can then be systematically compared. In order to rate the items, the Dutch CEF GRID can be used to ensure that the rating procedure is consistent. Whereas the standard setting procedure in DESI can be called data-driven, as it is based on task characteristics and their match with difficulty parameters, the standard setting procedure suggested by the Reference Supplement to the Manual for Relating Examinations to the CEFR makes use of a descriptor-based approach by applying a rater-driven process in assigning level descriptions to test items. For the test takers, the teachers and the educational administrators this latter approach provides valuable information as it allows the assessment of test takers on a continuum of proficiency levels that has been agreed on in the European context.

Note

1 Jan Hulstijn (Universiteit van Amsterdam) has helpfully provided suggestions for alternative terminology to specify titles and focuses of task characteristics. Descriptors for TC2 and TC6 were developed along the lines of the Dutch CEF GRID (Alderson et al 2004).

References

Adams, R and Wu, M (Eds) (2002) *PISA 2000 technical report*, Paris: OECD.

Alderson, J C (2004) The shape of things to come: will it be the normal distribution?, in Milanovic, M and Weir, C (Eds) *European Language Testing in a Global Context,* Cambridge: UCLES/Cambridge University Press, 1–26.

Alderson, J C, Figueras, N, Kuijper, H, Nold, G, Takala, S and Tardieu, C (2004) *The Development of Specifications for Item Development and Classification within The Common European Framework of Reference for Languages: Learning, Teaching, Assessment: Reading and Listening, Final Report of The Dutch CEF Construct Project*, Amsterdam, unpublished document.

Alderson, J C (2000) *Assessing Reading*, Cambridge: Cambridge University Press.

Bachman, L F (1990) *Fundamental Considerations in Language Testing*, Oxford: Oxford University Press.

Bachman, L F and Palmer, A (1996) *Language Testing in Practice*, Oxford: Oxford University Press.

Bae, J and Bachman, L F (1998) A latent variable approach to listening and reading: Testing factorial invariance across two groups of children in the Korean/English Two-Way Immersion Program, *Language Testing* 15, 380–414.

Baumert, J, Klieme, E, Neubrand, M, Prenzel, M, Schiefele, U, Schneider, W, Stanat, P Tillmann, K-J and Weiß, M (Eds) (2001) *PISA 2000: Basiskompetenzen von Schuelerinnen und Schuelern im internationalen Vergleich,* Opladen: Leske und Budrich.

Beaton, E and Allen, N (1992) Interpreting scales through scale anchoring, *Journal of Educational Statistics* 17, 191–204.

Beck, B and Klieme, E (Eds) (2007) Sprachliche Kompetenzen, Konzepte und Messung, DESI-Studie, Weinheim und Basel: Beltz.

Brindley, G and Slatyer, H (2002) Exploring task difficulty in ESL listening assessment, *Language Testing* 19, 369–394.

Brown, G (1995) Dimensions of difficulty in listening comprehension, in Mendelsohn, D J and Rubin, J (Eds) *A guide for the teaching of second language listening,* Carlsbad, CA: Dominie Press, 59–73.

Buck, G (1991) The testing of listening comprehension: An introspective study, *Language Testing* 8, 67–91.

Buck, G (2001) *Assessing Listening,* Cambridge: Cambridge University Press.

Buck, G and Tatsuoka, K (1998) Application of the rule-space procedure to language testing: Examining attributes of a free response listening test, *Language Testing* 15, 119–157.

Celce-Murcia, M (1995) Discourse analysis and the teaching of listening, in Cook, G and Seidlhofer, B (Eds) *Principle and Practice in Applied Linguistics,* Oxford: Oxford University Press, 363–377.

Council of Europe (2001) *Common European Framework of Reference for Languages: Learning, Teaching, Assessment,* <http://culture2.coe.int/ portfolio//documents/0521803136txt.pdf [accessed 11 July 2004]>

Council of Europe (2003) *Relating Language Examinations to the Common European Framework of Reference for Languages: Learning, Teaching, Assessment (CEF).* <www.coe.int/T/E/Cultural_Cooperation/education/ Languages/Language_Policy/Manual/Manual.pdf?L=E [accessed 11 July 2004]>

Council of Europe (2004) *Reference Supplement to the Preliminary Pilot version of the Manual for Relating Language Examinations to the Common European Framework of Reference for Languages: Learning, Teaching, Assessment.* <www.coe.int/T/E/Cultural%5FCo%2Cooperation/education/Languages/ Language_Policy/Manual/CEF%20reference%20supplement%20version%203. pdf?L=E [accessed 11 April 2005]>

Dell, G S and Gordon J K (2003) Neighbors in the lexicon: Friends or foes?, in Schiller, N O and Meyer, A S (Eds) Phonetics and Phonology in Language Comprehension and Production, Berlin: Mouton de Gruyter, 9–37.

DESI-Konsortium (Eds) (2008) *Unterricht und Kompetenzerwerb in Deutsch und Englisch, Ergebnisse der DESI-Studie,* Weinheim und Basel: Beltz.

Fischer, G H (1995) Derivations of the Rasch Model, in Fischer, G H and Molenaar, I W (Eds) *Rasch models,* New York: Springer, 15–38.

Freedle, R and Kostin, I (1999) Does the text matter in a multiple-choice test of comprehension? The case for the construct validity of TOEFL's minitalks, *Language Testing* 16, 2–32.

Grotjahn, R (2000) Determinanten der Schwierigkeit von Leseverstehensaufgaben: Theoretische Grundlagen und Konsequenzen für die Entwicklung des TESTDAF, in Bolton, S (Ed.) *TESTDAF: Grundlagen für die Entwicklung eines neuen Sprachtests. Beiträge aus einem Expertenseminar,* München: Goethe-Institut, 7–56.

Hagtvet, B (2003) Listening comprehension and reading comprehension in poor decoders: Evidence for the importance of syntactic and semantic skills as well as phonological skills, *Reading and Writing* 16, 505–539.

Hartig, J (2007) Skalierung und Kompetenzniveaus, in Beck, B and Klieme, E (Eds) *Sprachliche Kompetenzen, Konzepte und Messung,* DESI-Studie,Weinheim und Basel: Beltz, 83–89.

Klieme, E (2003) Bildungsstandards. Ihr Beitrag zur Qualitätsentwicklung im Schulsystem, *Die Deutsche Schule* 95, 10–16.

Rost, J (2004) *Lehrbuch Testtheorie – Testkonstruktion,* Bern, Göttingen: Huber.

Rost, M (2002) *Teaching and Researching Listening,* London: Pearson Education.

Rubin, J (1994) A Review of Second Language Listening Comprehension Research, *The Modern Language Journal* 78, 199–221.

Shohamy, E and Inbar, O (1991) Validation of listening comprehension tests: The effect of text and question type, *Language Testing* 8, 23–40.

Solmecke, G (2000) Faktoren der Schwierigkeit von Hörtests, in Bolton, S (Ed.) *TESTDAF: Grundlagen für die Entwicklung eines neuen Sprachtests. Beiträge aus einem Expertenseminar,* München: Goethe-Institut, 56–74.

Tsui, A B M and Fullilove, J (1998) Bottom-up or Top-down Processing as a Discriminator of L2 Listening Performance, *Applied Linguistics* 19, 432–451.

Vandergrift, L (2003) Orchestrating Strategy Use: Toward a Model of the Skilled Second Language Listener, *Language Learning* 53, 463–496.

Weir, C J (2005) *Language Testing and Validation. An Evidence-Based Approach,* New York: Palgrave Macmillan.

Wilson, M (2003) On choosing a model for measuring, *Methods of Psychological Research Online* 8, 1–22.

Wu, M, Adams, R and Wilson, M (1998) *ConQuest: Generalized item response modelling software,* Melbourne: Australia Council for Educational Research.

6 The Common European Framework of Reference for Languages and the revision of the Higher Level Catalan Language Test

Montserrat Montagut and Pilar Murtra
Secretariat of Language Policy, Evaluation Section,
Generalitat of Catalonia, Spain

Background

When the Catalan language certificates were created over 20 years ago, their aim was to help standardise the language. At the time, the higher level certificate, like the intermediate and advanced certificates, was essentially aimed at the Catalan-speaking population residing in Catalonia who had not learned Catalan at school because of the lack of a standardised linguistic environment, and who wished to accredit their knowledge of Catalan.

The needs of Catalan society have changed a great deal since then and the certificates of Catalan have been gradually adapted to these changes. In recent years, the types of candidate applying for the intermediate, advanced and higher level certificates have increased to include Catalan speakers wishing to accredit specific linguistic knowledge and also individuals whose mother tongue is not Catalan but who would like to obtain accreditation of this language for different reasons.

Updating the higher level certificate

The difficulty of updating the higher level certificate was that it had been designed so long ago (20 years ago) that now it was not enough simply to update the format of the test; the certificate needed to be thoroughly reworked. It was necessary to revise the communicative competence required by the certificate, to describe the level of this competence in detail, and to update the test.

We have now reached the end of the first stage, i.e. we have made a preliminary proposal for the competence level description, which has been approved by the technicians at the Evaluation Section where we work.

To carry out our task, the first source we consulted was the document entitled Specifications of the advanced level Catalan certificate. We consulted this document because it describes the competence level of the certificate immediately preceding the higher level one. However, we found the document to be lacking in many areas; for example, the four language skills were not described separately and the language content being tested was not explicitly indicated.

In fact, we had set ourselves two aims in our reworking of the higher level certificate: to explain clearly and precisely what the user had to be able to do in each language skill, and to specify what we could actually assess. Achieving these aims meant answering questions such as:

- What oral and written texts must the user understand and produce?
- What is the nature of these texts and what is their degree of difficulty or complexity (meaning, structural, lexical)?
- In which domains must the user be able to act?
- Which communicative tasks must the user be prepared to take on and carry out effectively?
- What should the degree of difficulty of these tasks be?
- What strategies or microfunctions must the user be able to use efficiently?

The document we found most helpful for answering these questions – also for posing new ones – was the Common European Framework of Reference for Languages (Council of Europe 2001). To date, the Framework has helped us in two ways:

- firstly, it helped us to define in significant detail the level of communicative competence required to obtain the higher level Catalan certificate
- and, secondly, it helped us to define and structure the language content (discursive, lexical, syntactic, morphological, etc.) assessed in the new test.

In this article we will discuss the first point, the description of the competence level, which we have structured in the following way:

1. **General description of the competence level.** In this section we identify the user of the certificate. Based on the communicative tasks that he/she can carry out, we provide a very general description of the types of text that the user can understand or produce, we list the expressive resources that he/she should use correctly, and we establish the degree of grammatical correction of his/her production.
2. **Description of the linguistic competence level skill by skill.** The aim of this section is to describe the four skills in detail – listening comprehension,

reading comprehension, oral production and written production. In this case, our description is based on three points:

a. *General description of the texts that the user must be able to deal with at this level.*

b. *Specifying the texts and classifying them into domains.*

c. *Strategies and microfunctions the user must be able to manage.*

We will focus our attention on skills because this is the area where the Common European Framework was more useful to us and because the general description of the level works as a synthesis of the four skills.

Description of the competence level

From the outset we were certain the description of the competence level had to take into account the context of the certificate and the users at whom it was aimed. This is why we've been quite flexible in our use of the Framework. In fact, we have used it as a working tool, adapting it to suit our needs. Therefore, for the skills description, we used a number of scales from the Framework and focused particularly on the top two levels of these scales: Levels C1 and C2. The descriptions were made by combining descriptors from different scales in the Framework, by modifying some of these descriptors and by creating new ones. We had to modify and adapt some Framework descriptors because we came across certain difficulties when we consulted them, such as:

a) Descriptors that, due to the way in which they are written, seem to indicate a higher or lower competence level than that suggested by the scale. For instance:

- 'Can write clear, well-structured texts of complex subjects, underlining the relevant salient issues, expanding and supporting points of view at some length with subsidiary points, reasons and relevant examples, and rounding off with an appropriate conclusion' C1

- 'Can write clear, smoothly flowing, complex texts in an appropriate and effective style and a logical structure which helps the reader to find significant points' C2.

Both are descriptors on the Overall Written Production scale. To us – and here we seem to agree with other studies conducted in Catalonia – these descriptors are the wrong way round, i.e. C1 would appear to be C2 and vice versa.

b) Descriptors that seem to require a very high command of the language. For instance:

- 'Can follow specialised lectures and presentations employing **a high degree of** colloquialism, regional usage or **unfamiliar terminology**' (Descriptor of C2, Listening as a Member of a Live Audience)
- 'Can understand any native speaker interlocutor, even on **abstract and complex topics of a specialist nature beyond his/her own field**, given an opportunity to adjust to a non-standard accent or dialect' (Descriptor of C2, Understanding a Native Speaker Interlocutor).

These two descriptors are for C2 and found on two activity scales. As we can see, no limits are set as regards the specialisation of the discourse in either case. In our opinion, these descriptors require a command of the language that goes beyond what we would expect of a certificate of general knowledge of language, which is the case with the higher level Catalan certificate.

c) Descriptors with vague or poorly defined concepts. For example:

- 'I can read with ease virtually all forms of the written language, including abstract, **structurally or linguistically complex texts** such as manuals, specialised articles and literary works' (Descriptor of C2 of the Self-Assessment Grid, Spoken Interaction)
- 'Can express him/herself spontaneously, very fluently and precisely, differentiating finer shades of meaning even in more **complex situations**' (Descriptor of C2, Global Scale: Common Reference Levels).

There's a vague concept in both cases: complexity. When we reached this point we thought we had to answer two questions before going on: What do we mean when we say that a text is 'structurally or linguistically complex'? And what types of situation could be qualified as 'complex situations'?

It is not our intention to suggest that the Framework has not been useful – on the contrary. It has enabled us to produce a very thorough description of each skill thanks to the diversity of scales and broad range of concepts and variables it contains. And what is most important: the lack of definition in some cases required us to stop and think, to explain certain concepts in detail and to set down the limits of language fluency in relation to our context. Therefore, what could have been a drawback actually turned out to be an advantage.

General description of the types of text

The first aspect we concentrated on in order to make a deep description of each skill was the types of text the users should be able to understand or produce at this level. As we said before, the descriptors of the Framework helped us to achieve this goal, though we had to make some changes considering the context where the certificate falls.

Below you can see an example of the attempt we made to adapt the Framework to our context. It is the description of the types of text that users need to be able to comprehend orally. So, we are referring here to the Listening Comprehension skill.

In the new specifications this description is a continuum. However, in order to make it easier to understand the aspects we took into account, we have divided the description as follows:

- language variety and speed of production
- type of text, topic and degree of formality, and finally
- complexity of the discourse.

- **Language variety; speed:**

The descriptor of C2 on the Overall Listening Comprehension scale of the Framework does not distinguish between the types of oral discourse that can be understood at this level: '[The user] Has no difficulty in understanding any kind of spoken language whether live or broadcast, delivered at fast native speed.' Our certificate, however, distinguishes between standard variety and other varieties as you can see below.
[Higher level user . . .]

- Can understand almost any oral text in the standard variety despite it being delivered at fast native speed.
- Can also understand texts in other varieties so long as he/she is given time to become familiar with the accent.

Therefore, the user of our certificate should have no difficulty in understanding discourse in the standard variety, but may need a little time to familiarise him/herself with the accent in the case of other varieties. In fact, this condition is included in other descriptors of the Framework, such as those of C2 on the Self-Assessment Grid and the Understanding a Native Speaker Interlocutor Grid.

- **Type of text, topics, formality:**

Many descriptors of C2 in the Framework do not restrict the area of knowledge of the text. In our case, despite considering that users must be able to understand texts from areas of knowledge or work that are not their own, we believe that our higher level certificate should not be excessively out of the latter's reach. This is because, as we said earlier, our certificate is of general language knowledge and our certification system contains other certificates aimed at evaluating specialist linguistic knowledge. Therefore:

- Oral texts at this level can be individually managed (conferences, speeches, reports, announcements, etc.) or plurally managed (colloquial conversations, film dialogues, and theatrical performances, debates, seminars, etc.) in all domains and for a wide range of formality levels.

They can be on a variety of topics, though not too far away from the user's area of knowledge or work.

- **Complexity of the discourse:**

From our point of view, it is important to explain what defines the complexity of a text at any level. The Framework was very useful in specifying the factors involved in the complexity of a text, which are: the specificity of the topic (the more specific and removed from the area of knowledge or work of the user, the more complex the topic), the degree of abstraction with which the topic is dealt, the organisation of the discourse, the relationship between ideas (the more implicit the relationship, the more complicated the text) and the language used (the more colloquialisms, slang and terminology it contains the more complex it will be). All these factors were included in the wording of our descriptor:

- The complexity of the texts is greater than in the previous level. Complexity is determined by factors such as the specificity of the topic or the degree of abstraction with which it is dealt, the organisation of the discourse, the fact that the relationship between ideas is not always explicit, or the type of language used. As regards lexicon, for instance, oral texts can contain colloquialisms, slang, dialectisms and unfamiliar terminology.

In the specific case of terminology, we believe it is necessary to limit the amount of this lexicon in the texts used for evaluation purposes. That means we will not find oral texts containing 'a high degree of unfamiliar terminology' in the higher level Catalan certificate, as indicated in the C2 Framework descriptor of the Listening as a Member of a Live Audience Grid.

Lastly, we thought it was important to include a paragraph on the complexity of plurally managed oral activities because we believe that, in addition to factors influencing the complexity of any text or discourse, plurally managed communication is affected by two additional factors: the linearity of the conversation and interlocutors' attitude. The less linear the progression of topics in the conversation and the less co-operative the attitude of the interlocutors, the more difficult it is to understand the discourse:

- Plurally managed texts can have further complications because they can be the result of exchanges in which the progression of topics in the conversation is not always linear and the interlocutors may adopt unco-operative attitudes.

Specifying texts and language activities

Once we had written up the general description of the type of text or discourse the user had to be able to deal with in each skill, we collected the most representative language activities and texts for the level. It is important to clarify at this point that we make no distinction between text and language activity because we understand the text to be the result of language activities, as does the Framework. To be exact and in line with this document, we consider that the user carries out 'communicative tasks involving language activities that require the processing of oral or written texts'.

To select the activities and texts, we also used the Framework and its idea of communicative domains to classify them. Thus, for example, in writing, we find:

Selection of texts and language activities:

Personal domain	No linguistic limitation in any situation or text (letters and notes to congratulate, express sympathy, request or supply information, invite, thank, tell stories, explain events, etc.).
Occupational domain	Letters, circulars, certificates, calls to meetings and minutes, technical or specific reports, memorandums, summaries, complex instructions and indications (for appliances, machines, processes and procedures), email messages, etc.
Educational domain	Academic or research work, abstracts, criticisms, exams, etc.
Public domain	• Texts aimed at public and private organisations (governments, private companies, associations, etc.): applications and letters to request or offer a service, to request or supply information, to complain, thank, etc. • Different types of text typical of periodical publications with a small distribution (magazines or newsletters from institutions, associations, schools, etc.): news, reports, articles, reviews, etc. • Letters to the editors of newspapers with a wide distribution. • Written texts to be read aloud: brief addresses, speeches at celebrations, meetings, events, etc.

Since we have used all of the domains included in the *Framework*, the relationship with specifications of the certificate immediately preceding the higher level one has been changed, since that certificate only deals with professional and social domains.

It is true that some of these texts and language activities may already have been dealt with at advanced level. Higher level users, however, are required to demonstrate they can manage a wider range of communicative resources when writing this kind of texts and that they have a greater command of the language in order to deal effectively with any communicative situation. And how can we check this command of language? From our point of view, we can find the answer to this question by observing the strategies and microfunctions the user mobilises in order to understand or produce any text.

Description of the strategies and microfunctions that users must demonstrate

After determining the texts for each skill, we wondered about the possibility of creating descriptors for each of these texts, as the Framework does in its scales for language activities. However, we realised that this would not be very functional. Instead, we thought it would be much more useful to describe the communication strategies and microfunctions that the user would need to use correctly in order to understand or produce any of the texts. By describing these strategies and microfunctions, we were able to define in greater detail the competence level required and specify what higher level users know how to do and how they do so.

In line with the Framework, we classified the strategies into the metacognitive principles of planning, execution and evaluation. Thus, we categorised the applicable strategies into the four skills and into the metacognitive processes. This means each skill has a section where we describe the strategies the user must be able to manage in each one of these processes. In the case of the writing skill, for instance, we find strategies for planning, executing and evaluating the written production. We discussed the convenience of introducing planning and revision strategies, because we are aware of the fact that when we face the assessment of a written production we can only assess the final result. However, we thought it would be interesting to include all three processes because it was a way of adding importance to the whole process of producing a text and because the inclusion of this approach in the specifications of the test could have a positive effect on the teaching and learning environment.

Unlike the Framework, we only distinguish production and reception strategies. We do not deal with mediation strategies because they are used in a type of activity that will not be assessed. And in the case of the interaction strategies, they are dealt with mainly from the point of view of production, as they are strategies used in plurally managed activities.

As the Framework only includes illustrative scales for strategies, we consulted other reference works (such as Daniel Cassany's *Ensenyar llengua* 1996 and others), and adapted descriptors of other Framework scales, particularly those for competences. The oral production skill is a good example of how we used the Framework and other reference sources. In this particular skill we include strategies and microfunctions the user employs to plan, execute and evaluate or repair his/her oral production. In the case of planning, we collect in the same section the strategies used in individually managed activities and in plurally managed activities. And so we do in evaluation. However, we differentiate between the two in execution, as does the Framework.

In the section about strategies used during execution of individually managed activities (conferences, communications, presentations, etc.), we have pointed out actions the user performs to transmit information coherently and produce a cohesive, linguistically rich and varied discourse tailored to the communicative situation. This section contains strategies related to the selection of information, exposition of ideas, organisation of the discourse, use of cohesive mechanisms, control of the degree of formality and specialisation of the discourse, modalisation, compensation of lexical gaps, embellishment of discourse and improved communication, etc. There now follows a series of examples taken from the Execution section:

Individually managed production:

[Higher level users . . .]

- Show great flexibility in reformulating ideas with different linguistic forms to emphasise their words, eliminate ambiguity, etc.

This descriptor is based on the Flexibility scale of the Framework, under Discourse competence:

C2 'Shows great flexibility reformulating ideas in differing linguistic forms to give emphasis, to differentiate according to the situation, interlocutor, etc. and to eliminate ambiguity'.

[Higher level users . . .]

- Use a broad, varied and accurate lexical repertoire including genuine words, specific words to the topic of discussion, idiomatic expressions, synonyms, etc. and show awareness of the levels of semantic connotation.

The previous descriptor is based on the Lexical Competence scales of the Framework:

C2 'Has a good command of a very broad lexical repertoire including idiomatic expressions and colloquialisms; shows awareness of connotative levels of meaning' (Vocabulary Range).

C2 'Consistently correct and appropriate use of vocabulary' (Vocabulary Control).

We have seen above two descriptors adapted from the Framework Level C2. However, the next descriptors are based on level C1:

- Use circumlocation to substitute words or expressions that they cannot remember to avoid interrupting the Xow of the speech, and
- Produce a grammatically and phonetically correct speech: they speak clearly with a high degree of correction; errors are rare and difficult to spot.

The first one is based on the Compensating Scale of Production strategies: C1 (as B2+) 'Can use circumlocution and paraphrase to cover gaps in vocabulary and structure'.

And the second one is based on the Grammatical Accuracy scale of Grammatical Competence:

C1 'Consistently maintains a high degree of grammatical accuracy; errors are rare and difficult to spot' (Grammatical Competence: Grammatical Accuracy).

So, as you can see, we believe the user of this level can still make some mistakes.

Lastly, we have created some new descriptors such as the next one, which refers to the use of resources to embellish the text and improve communication:

[Higher level users . . .]

- Use resources to embellish the text and enhance communication (emphatic questions, figures of speech . . .

Clearly, many of the strategies typical of individually managed production are also used in plurally managed production. However, some of these are exclusive to interaction and are related to the process of the collective creation of meaning. The Framework offers three illustrative scales for interaction strategies (scales related to the execution process: 'Taking the floor or turntaking', 'Co-operating' and 'Asking for clarification'.) Our description of this type of production goes further than this document. On the one hand, we divide execution into three sections: 'Negotiating the topic', 'Directing the interaction' and 'Encouraging communication', which include adaptation of the Framework's descriptors for the scales mentioned above and new descriptors. On the other hand, we include a series of strategies for planning interactions and for evaluating and monitoring the effect and success of communication. Some examples are given below:

Plurally managed production:

Planning:
[Higher level users . . .]

- Foresee the schemata of interchange (communicative routine) likely to come into play during the activity, i.e. they foresee the organisation of turntaking.

Execution:
[Higher level users . . .]
  Negotiate the topic:

- They work together to select and develop topics: they start on a topic, build on it, divert it towards a new topic or avoid it and close it, they choose the detail in which to explain the topic, taking into account the interests or knowledge of the interlocutor.

This descriptor paraphrases the descriptor of C2 on the Framework's Co-operating scale we find in the Interaction strategies section:
C2 (as C1): 'Can relate own contribution skilfully to those of other speakers'.

[Higher level users . . .]
Direct the interaction:

- They control turntaking: they choose the right moment to take part in conversation, use their turn to say everything they need to, observe the conventions of the type of discourse, mark the beginning and end of their speaking, acknowledge when interlocutors wish to take the floor and allow them to speak at the right time.

In this case, we have created a descriptor that we could include on a Taking the floor/Turntaking scale like that of the Framework. There is no exclusive descriptor for C2 in the Framework, so we refer here to C1:
C2 (as C1): 'Can select a suitable phrase from a readily available range of discourse functions to preface his/her remarks appropriately in order to get the floor, or to gain time and keep the floor whilst thinking'.

[Higher level users . . .]
Encourage communication:

- They confirm the comprehension of the interlocutor and compensate for difficulties in oral communication: they reinforce their expression and help the receiver to understand the message, they encourage mutual comprehension by asking questions and getting clarification of ambiguous points or misunderstandings, they often correct themselves as they speak (they polish meanings, correct *lapsus linguae*), they use circumlocution to cover lexical gaps, repeat the most important points, synthesise their words or reformulate their discourse with other words in order to clarify the message.

Here, we have clearly developed a descriptor that appears in the Framework on a Reparatory scale: 'Asking for clarification' [C2 (as B2): 'Can ask follow-up questions to check that he/she has understood what a speaker intended to say, and get clarification of ambiguous points']. However, although our descriptor is similar to the C2 descriptor of the above scale, it goes further in that it does not only include strategies for clarifying the message and ensuring comprehension, but also strategies for controlling the user's own production and improving on this.

Finally, as we said earlier, we have not distinguished between individually managed oral productions and plurally managed oral productions in evaluation strategies or microfunctions. However, the write-up of the descriptors does differentiate to some extent between the former and the latter, as follows.

Evaluation:
[Higher level users . . .]

- During the conversation, they use information from discourse and facial expression, gestures, and movements to control the effect and success of communication.
- They consciously monitor production (particularly in non-interactive activities) both linguistically and communicatively, and correct the discourse where necessary.

Although the Framework does not develop scales to evaluate interaction, it does point out that the speaker monitors the progress of interaction on a communicative level, in the sense that he/she checks that the interaction is progressing according to the expected schema (monitoring schemata) and that the communicative targets are being met (monitoring effect and success). As we have seen, our first descriptor relates to the monitoring of interaction and focuses on monitoring the effect and success of communication, which is the most relevant aspect for us. The second descriptor, on the other hand, focuses on the conscious monitoring of production which, as pointed out in the Framework, is typical of individually managed communication, where the degree of planning and control of expression is greater. We will finish off this section by explaining why we have duplicated the reference to the speaker's ability to repair the discourse and hence correct him or herself. We have done so because we need to bear in mind that production is evaluated during communication, i.e. during the process of execution. Therefore, although the speaker mobilises repair strategies when he/she detects the need as a result of mental production monitoring, the effective use of these strategies really takes place in the communicative plan and hence, during the process of executing expression.

Conclusion

We would like to conclude this article by describing where we are now with the reworking of the certificate. In addition to the description of the competence level, we now have an almost complete list of the language content for testing. The classification of language content we propose is also based on the competences of the Framework. Therefore, they have been provisionally classified into: discursive competence, which includes aspects of coherence and text cohesion; socio-linguistic competence, which includes aspects of adaptation to the communicative situation, and linguistic competence, the contents of which are split into lexicon, semantics and grammar (which includes phonology, spelling and morphosyntax).

As you can see, the Common European Framework of Reference for Languages has been useful in many ways and for many purposes. For us personally, the revision of the certificate has enabled us to become familiar with the Framework in a practical way. We have used it flexibly and, probably, some might even say in a not very orthodox way. However, as we know the Framework aims to be open, dynamic, flexible and non-dogmatic, we are quite satisfied with our approach and we have no doubt we will carry on using it for our project. We encourage all of you to do the same.

Bibliography

Alderson, J C, Clapham, C, Wall, D (1995) *Language Test Construction and Evaluation,* Cambridge: Cambridge University Press.

Association of Language Testers in Europe (ALTE) *The Can-do statements.* <http://www.alte.org/can_do/>

Bassols, M, Torrent, A M (1996) *Models textuals. Teoria i pràctica,* Vic: Eumo Ed.

Cassany, D, Luna, M, Sanz, G (1996) Ensenyar llengua, Col. «*El Llapis*», Barcelona: Ed. Graó.

Coromina i Pou, E (1984) *Pràctiques d'expressió i comunicació,* Vic: Eumo Ed.

Council of Europe (2001) *Common European Framework of Reference for Languages: Learning, teaching, assessment,* Cambridge: Cambridge University Press.

Direcció General de Política Lingüística; Artigas, R, Bellès, J, Grau, M, (2003) *Tipotext. Una tipologia de textos de no-ficció,* Vic: Eumo Ed (Llengua i Text: 8).

Generalitat de Catalunya, Direcció General de Política Lingüística (1987) 2nd ed. *COM/Ensenyar Català als Adults. Extres. Núm. 2 Programes i orientacions per als cursos de llengua catalana (nivells de suficiència i proficiència).*

Generalitat de Catalunya, Secretaria de Política Lingüística (2005) *Programa de llengua catalana. Nivell de suficiència.* <www6.gencat.net/llengcat/aprencat/suficiencia.htm>

7 Test comparability and construct compatibility across languages

Peter Hardcastle – Cambridge ESOL
Sibylle Bolton – Goethe-Institut
Francesca Pelliccia – Università per Stranieri di Perugia

The University of Salamanca, the Università per Stranieri di Perugia, the University of Lisbon and the Goethe-Institut, in co-operation with University of Cambridge ESOL Examinations, have initiated a project to carry out validation studies relating to their four suites of European language tests. One of the objectives of this project, in accordance with the Council of Europe's recent initiatives, is to take measures to align their language tests to the *Common European Framework of Reference for Languages: Learning, Teaching, Assessment* (CEFR) (Council of Europe 2001). All four partners in this project either already produce, or intend to produce, a series of tests aligned to at least five levels of the CEFR, from A2 Waystage to C2 Mastery (see CEFR p. 23). The test suites currently involved in this project are:

- the Certificati di Conoscenza della Lingua Italiana (CELI), levels 1–5, owned by the Università per Stranieri di Perugia
- the Diplomas de Español como Lengua Extranjera (DELE), levels *inicial, intermedio, superior*, owned by the Instituto Cervantes and produced in co-operation with the Universidad de Salamanca
- the Goethe-Institut suite of German tests, including Start Deutsch 1, Start Deutsch 2, Zertifikat Deutsch (and Zertifikat Deutsch für Jugendliche), Zentrale Mittelstufenprüfung (ZMP)
- the five tests of Portuguese of the Centro de Avaliação de Português Língua Estrangeira (CAPLE), Universidade de Lisboa.

The project sets out to study the equivalence of individual tests over a given time frame examining issues of quality, stability, consistency, validity and reliability, as well as examining test comparability across languages. Validation of each examination individually is not too difficult to accomplish. Established procedures which have been followed for several years by Cambridge ESOL and by other institutions which have adopted similar methods are available as proven models. Of course, not all providers apply these procedures, but increasingly validation work is seen as an essential element of assessment. Without some form of validation it is difficult, or impossible, to make a convincing argument that a test is measuring the trait it purports to measure or at the level at which it purports to measure it. This is at the centre of the construct validity argument which ALTE has been addressing through its statement of minimum standards (ALTE 2004, and see Appendix 1), its Code of Practice (ALTE 2001) and its Quality Management System (2005). Recent initiatives at the Council of Europe have similarly been encouraging all European Language test providers to follow established procedures when validating tests and developing arguments to support claims of CEFR alignment; see the Manual for Relating Examinations to the CEFR (CoE 2003), its Reference Supplement (CoE 2004) and the illustrative samples of the European Language Test Benchmarking Project (CoE 2006).

When we extend the concept of validation to include cross-language elements, as is fundamental to CEFR alignment, then we are introducing another dimension to validation which adds an enormous amount of complexity to the arguments we are trying to develop. How can it be ascertained that the level of difficulty of a test in one language is in any way associable with a level of difficulty of a test in another language, in terms of observable and definable linguistic characteristics? In other words, the following fundamental question has to be addressed:

Where does difficulty reside and how can relative difficulty across languages be established?

This project is investigating three test dimensions in order to obtain a clearer understanding of what linguistic aspects of a test dictate the level at which it operates. These dimensions are:

1) The lexico-grammatical, or morpho-syntactic, dimension.
2) The performative dimension (pragmatic or functional dimension).
3) The cognitive dimension.

These three broad areas have been identified which contribute to overall difficulty, and the tests are being considered in the light of these. This is not to say that these dimensions are definitive, all-encompassing terms, incorporating all aspects of language competence. It would undoubtedly be possible to attribute elements of difficulty to other features of language as well, but we feel that these three are fundamental.

They are not mutually exclusive categories and interrelate with each other within the framework of context- and theory-based validity (Weir 2005), as suggested by Figure 1.

Figure 1: Dimensions of Cross-Language Comparability

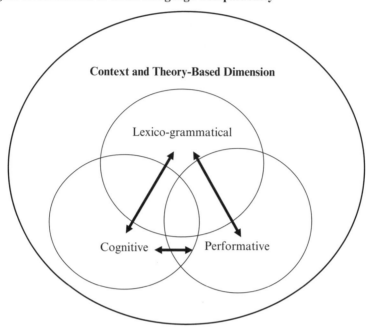

The lexico-grammatical or morpho-syntactic dimension

It may be unfashionable to talk about the importance of the study of grammar in language teaching and learning, but this is not to say that a thorough understanding of morpho-syntax and lexico-grammar is not a fundamental component of proficiency in any language. Obviously, without lexis and grammar there is no language at all. Grammatical and syntactic structures of a target language are executive resources to be internalised by learners before any form of structured verbal communication can take place. Although experience will tell any teacher of language that certain aspects of grammar are more 'difficult' than others, it is not clear how these aspects of grammar and syntax relate to difficulty level across languages. Is the difficulty involved in the assimilation and application of comparable grammatical categories similar in different languages? Is the future tense more difficult than the present tense, or is it simply that teaching present time before future time or past time has become a pedagogical convention in the language teaching profession due to the dominant role played by present time in human existence? More importantly with cross-language validity issues, can it be said that the future tense in French is more or less difficult to learn than the future tense in Spanish or Italian, or in English and German where the future tense does not, morphologically at least, exist? These are the kinds of grammatical issues which have to be addressed.

The following examples serve to illustrate the point. In an English pedagogical grammar, the example English sentence (in Example 1) would be referred to as an impossible or hypothetical (type 3) condition. The other sentences in French, Spanish, Italian, Russian, German and Arabic express the same meaning and adopt similar, but different, grammatical forms. Is it possible to assert that a 'type 3 unfulfilled condition' can be associated with a particular level of the CEFR regardless of the language in which it is expressed? Or is it easier to express this kind of conditionality in Russian (without the complication of subjunctive moods and auxiliary verbs) than it is in, say, Spanish?

Example 1

- If I had finished the book, I would have given it to you.
- Wenn ich das Buch gelesen hätte, hätte ich es dir gegeben.
- Si j'avais fini le livre, je te l'aurais donné.
- Si hubiera leido el libro, te lo hubiera dado.
- Se avessi finito il libro, te lo avrei dato.
- Если бы я прочитал книгу, я вам дал бы её.
- لو كنت أكملت قراءة الكتاب لأعطيته لك

Another similar discrepancy can be observed in the forms and functions of the verb(s) 'to be' in different languages (Example 2). Notice how in English one lexical form (the copula) suffices to express a temporary or permanent state of being, while in Portuguese (as in Spanish) there are two. In Russian (as in Arabic) the present tense of the verb *to be* is defective and, to all extents and purposes, is rarely used. It would, thus, not be an untenable claim to suggest that learning the correct use of 'be' in the present tense is easier to learn in English than in Portuguese. In Russian and in Arabic, where the form is largely elided, the task must be considerably easier.

Example 2

- I am a teacher. I am English. I am married. I am sick today.
- Sou professor. Sou inglês. Sou casado. Hoje estou doente.
- Я учитель. Я английский. Я женат. Я болен.

These are just two examples of how apparently equivalent grammatical cognates may place very different demands on the learner. It is not difficult to find many more examples, particularly as the languages concerned digress qualitatively from the Romance norm of many (southern-) European languages. From a grammatical perspective it is not easy to establish parallel or equivalent difficulty relating to the learning of formal or structural aspects of language. This kind of difficulty tends to be both language and learner specific.

The communicative (performance–based) dimension

'Can Do' statements and performance descriptors are useful tools for identifying and defining proficiency levels, but are they universal? And can they be used as instruments to quantify difficulty across languages? The CEFR implies that they might be. Our view is they are not. Although the CEFR has been and continues to be translated into several languages (a Galician version is the latest to appear in 2005), performance descriptors produced for one language may operate at different levels in another and, in truth, are probably not always very translatable. This view is endorsed by Jean-Claude Béacco:

> Chaque ensemble de descriptions peut tirer profit des descriptions déjà réalisées pour d'autres langues, mais celles-ci ne sont pas établies sur la seule base de la traduction d'inventaires concernant une autre langue (Béacco 2005).

In other words, the translation of performance descriptors may be a useful starting point, but further work needs to be done before levels can be definitively exemplified in terms of morpho-syntactic, lexical and pragmatic categories. Such work has been carried out before in English (Van Ek and Trim 1990a, 1990b, 1990c) and in French (Coste, Müller, Schmitz and Rusch 1987) and the more recent Profile Deutsch (Glaboniat, Müller, Schmitz and Rusch 2002) addresses this issue in German, but other languages need to follow suit.

One problem which has to be surmounted lies in the semantics of the concept 'ability', which itself varies from language to language. In English the modal auxiliary 'can' is fairly general in meaning, indicating the capacity to fulfil a particular action or function over a broad range of competence. In other languages 'ability' is broken down into two or even three categories. Note the distinction in French between 'savoir' and 'pouvoir' and the elision of modality in such utterances as '*Parlez-vous anglais?*' *(Can you speak English?)*. '*Pouvez-vous parler en anglais?*' means something entirely different. German is similar (*Sprechen Sie Deutsch?* rather than *Können Sie auf Deutsch sprechen?*). In Russian we have three verbs expressing distinctly different aspects of ability, introducing an additional dimension of difficulty to addressing the cross-linguistic applicability of the 'Can Do' statement. It is important to call into question whether it is possible to impute validity into a set of descriptors for one language when they have been developed to describe performance in another.

The concept of 'Can Do' has been translated into many European languages. Here are some examples of how it has been done. Few attempts retain the simplicity and succinctness of the English equivalent. Most languages avoid the use of a verb expressing ability because of the semantic incompatibilities we have just referred to. A notable exception is the Spanish which retains the idea, though places the translation 'puede hacer' in inverted commas to indicate that this expression doesn't really fit the bill in Spanish.

'Can Do' statements (English)

Especificaciones de capacidad lingüística ('puede hacer') (Spanish)

Kann-Beschreibungen, Kompetenzbeschreibungen (or Fähigkeitsbeschreibungen) (German)

Indicazioni de capacitá (Italian)

Descritores de capacidades (Portuguese)

Capacités de faire (French)

This is something of a digression, but it does throw some light on the difficulty of establishing compatible systems which are mutually comprehensible and could thus be used to establish comparable difficulty levels across languages.

If we look back at the two grammatical examples above, the performance descriptors, or 'Can Do' statements, which relate these grammatical structures to functional categories might be:

(Type 3 conditions – see Example 1 above)
'Shows the ability to discuss hypotheses and unfulfilled conditionality' or *'I can speculate about causes, consequences and hypothetical situations'* (DIALANG B2 level descriptor – CEFR p. 232)

and

(Verb 'to be' – see Example 2 above)
'Can describe him/herself, what s/he does, where s/he lives' (CEFR p. 59 – A1 level descriptor).

We have observed that there exists potential disagreement about the level of difficulty attributed to the grammar which operationalises these descriptors and that this difficulty varies with the language concerned.

Here is another example at another (A1) level:

'*Can ask people for things and give people things*' (CEFR p. 80 A1 level 'Can Do' statement).

'*Es capaz de pedirle a alguien alguna cosa, y viceversa*' MCER p. 80 (Spanish translation of the above).

Example 3
- Could you give me the book, please?
- Pourriez-vous me donner le livre, s'il vous plaît?
- ¿Me podrías dar el libro por favor?
- Дайте мне, пожалуйста книгу.
- أعطيني الكتاب من فضلك

Are these exponents at the same level of difficulty regardless of the language? It would appear that they are not. The English uses a past tense modal with SV inversion, infinitive without to and an indirect object pronoun. The French sentence similarly employs a conditional tense in interrogative form with SV inversion and indirect object pronoun. This contrasts sharply with the Russian and Arabic which require only imperative forms of the verb with an indirect object, rendering the latter forms undoubtedly easier to learn.

The exponents of '*Asking for and giving directions*' (A2) display similar incongruence:

Example 4
- Könnten Sie mir bitte sagen, wie ich zum Goethe-Institut komme.
- Scusi, mi può indicare la strada per l'università?
- Could you tell me how to get to the GI, please.
- Pour aller à l'Institut Goethe, s'il vous plait ?
- Как можно пройти в институт, пожалуйста?
- ¿Como llego al Instituto Goethe, por favor?

It seems that, at least at the lower CEFR levels, where specific lexico-grammatical factors can often be directly associated with descriptors of communicative function, these descriptors (and 'Can Do' statements) have to be individually tailored to suit the context and language of the test; i.e., the difficulty attributable to these lower level lexico-grammatical exponents has a tendency to vary from language to language. This state of affairs appears to issue a call for the development of new sets of language-specific band descriptors, which take into account discrepancies in the levels of lexico-grammatical complexity associable with specific communicative functions in different languages.

The cognitive dimension

The cognitive dimension refers to the different cognitive processing requirements of task types and test formats and attempts are currently being made to relate various features of these processes to CEFR levels. Insofar as it is possible to separate cognitive load or cognitive processing out from the linguistic elements of the construct, this is an important consideration. Clearly (thinking back to the Sapir-Whorfian hypothesis (see Carroll 1956)) there can be no language without cognition and no cognition without language, so this is a vital area which merits attention. Certainly, the type of cognitive processing or the cognitive load inherent in any task is going to have an influence on task difficulty and it is important to ascertain whether this is a source of measurement error or part of the test construct. It is fairly safe to assume that simpler tasks at the lower end of the scale will tend to have a lower cognitive load than higher level tasks. In tests of production there is a progression from the 'reproduction and reorganisation of known information' to the 'generation of new ideas', sometimes referred to as 'knowledge transformation' (Weir 2005, Weigle 2002). Clearly, these elements are supra-linguistic and certainly not language specific. There is an advantage in this, in that associating difficulty with cognitive processing allows us to compare test difficulties across language better than examining grammatical, notional or functional elements which are more likely to be language specific. We can identify high and low cognitive load in test tasks irrespective of the language of the test and associate this with a CEFR level. One could argue that if you are measuring cognition then this distracts from the measurement of language proficiency and therefore poses a threat to construct validity. We would argue, however, that the two are inextricably related and that more complex cognitive processing is associated with higher order linguistic processing skills and it is impossible to measure one without acknowledging the existence of the other.

However, no research has yet managed to convincingly associate, by more than anecdotal means, the cognitive processing associated with particular task types to task difficulty.

The statistical (psychometric) method

Classical test analysis, Rasch anchoring and scale construction

How can statistical analysis of test data help us resolve these issues? Linguistically speaking, it can't. But what these methods of analysis can do is give us information about the degree of difficulty a candidate is having in answering a specific task or question, which can confirm or refute subjective human judgements made about difficulty levels, i.e. standards fixing procedures.

Statistical methods enable us to look at the way test candidates respond to tasks/items by analysing response data with relatively simple tools. To an extent, this avoids the issue of having to answer all the questions posed by the foregoing discussion. It is an interim solution until cross-language studies in comparative morpho-syntax and comparative pragmatics provide us with solutions. Analysis of candidate responses enables us to create a scale of measurement which we can then apply to ALL language tests regardless of the language concerned.

Classical test theory and the candidate-centred approach

Traditionally, the concept of difficulty is expressed in terms of *p*-values for given samples. A *p*-value (facility value) is simply the proportion of the candidates in a given sample who respond correctly to a question, or item. Thus, a *p*-value of 0.5 for a given item means that half of the candidates have responded correctly. This informs us how the items within the test are working, but is only really the first step in deciding at which level the item is functioning, and a very preliminary one. The information it gives us is sample dependent; that is, the facility values, discrimination indices, etc. provided by CTT methods relate only to the response data under review and cannot really be generalised to other test admissions or other populations of test takers, even of the same test.

What is important about this is that the level of facility within a given sample is determined by the analysis of response data within a specific learner context. The learners, in giving their answers, are defining task and item difficulty in their terms, which is important information. Learners know, intrinsically at least, how difficult a task is better than the test producers, so it is critical that systems for the determination of task or test level take candidate response information into consideration.

Most software programs for the analysis of test data using classical means provide a frequency distribution of test scores. With a reasonably reliable measure and a large enough sample of candidates, the distribution of scores is likely to be more or less normal. In order to compare test score distributions in respect of the relative difficulty of the associated tests, these distributions need to be mapped onto a measurement scale. The resulting (idealised) distribution curves of six tests at six different levels mapped on to such a scale should look something like Figure 2.

As can be seen from Figure 2, this is basically a norm-referencing exercise which places a population of candidates along a scale extending from minimal proficiency to very high proficiency. The very low and the very high scores (complete beginner to highly competent user) are less difficult to comprehend and quantify. What is difficult linguistically is dividing up the levels in between – what is now being referred to by means of the unfortunate term 'partial competence'(everyone's competence in every language they know is,

Figure 2: Score distributions of six tests at six levels mapped onto a measurement scale

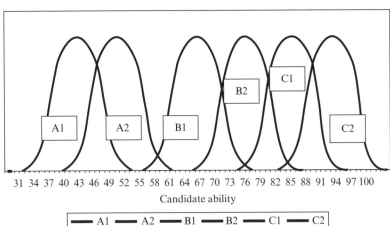

of course, partial). To an extent, these internal subdivisions are arbitrary, though there is a case to be made that the higher level subdivisions should be more compact, because it is more difficult to progress through the higher levels than it is through the lower ones. Following the model established by Cambridge ESOL, this is what has been done when creating the scales for ALTE exams (see Appendix 2).

Stability of the scale and consistency in its application can been achieved by means of Rasch (one parameter) anchoring procedures. These procedures can establish the definitive difficulty of a dichotomously scored test item by comparing response data from that item with response data acquired from an anchor test, administered along with the real test and consisting of items of pre-established, known difficulty. The difficulty of a test or a task can then be determined by calculating the mean difficulty of the items it comprises. Rasch analysis, unlike Classical Test Theory methods, allows us to establish the difficulty of a test task or item in a way which is not specific to the candidates in the response data sample, but representative of a broader population. If a lower intermediate set of candidates and an advanced set of candidates take the same test, then the difficulty of the items as calculated by Rasch IRT methods will be the same, provided that correct anchoring techniques are used. This would not be the case when using CTT. With CTT the facility values of the test items would be totally different for these two sets of candidates, reflecting the difference in candidate proficiency. Using response data from our tests and Rasch anchoring techniques it is possible to create a measurement scale which is universal, in that it attributes difficulty values to tests, tasks and individual items which do not change with the level of the candidates taking the test; in other words, difficulty values which are not sample dependent. Tests which have been calibrated in this way can then be mapped onto a scale with established cut scores, specified in logits, or a scale derived from them (such as the Cambridge/ALTE scale), as demonstrated in Figure 3. The ogives in this figure are test characteristic curves representing each of the six CEFR levels, starting with A1 on the left and progressing through to C2 on the right.

Figure 4 shows two of these test characteristic curves specifically for an A2 Waystage test and a B1 Threshold. The cut score (cut-off candidate ability) between A1 and A2 in this model is established as the point where a candidate with a true ability of 45 on the scale (-1.6 logits) would score 50% on the test; i.e., there would be a 0.5 probability of the candidate scoring 50%. If the test were constructed to be slightly easier, then the passing grade would have to be raised proportionately.

Figure 3: Possible test difficulty ogives mapped onto a Rasch logit scale Difficulty/ability indices for CEFR levels A1 to C2

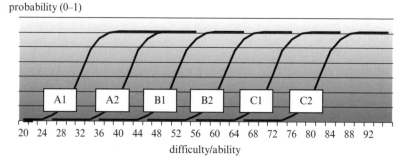

Figure 4: Test difficulty ogives for two tests at two CEFR levels (A2 and B1) mapped onto a Rasch logit scale

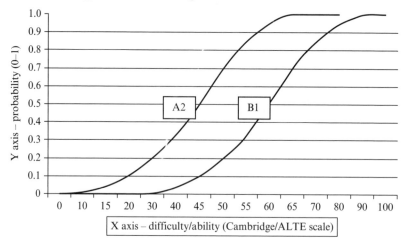

Appendix 2 shows the difficulty/ability indices associated with each CEFR level as it is being applied to all of the tests in this project.

It should be emphasised that this kind of analysis does not, of course, describe the linguistic or qualitative features of the test in any way. No statistical procedure is able to do this and in order for the tests to be interpretable and useful to stakeholders, clearly the data provided by statistical analysis has to be associated with an understanding of the knowledge, competences and skills which constitute the language proficiency supposedly reflected in the test scores. Therein lies the challenge.

References and further reading

ALTE (2001) *Principles of Good Practice for ALTE Examinations*, available online: <http://www.alte.org/quality_assurance/index.cfm>

ALTE (2004) *Minimum Standards for Establishing Quality Profiles in ALTE Examinations*, Mimeograph.

ALTE (2005) *The ALTE Code of Practice and Quality Management Systems*, available online: <http://www.alte.org/quality_assurance/index.cfm>

Béacco, J C (2005) *Description des niveaux de référence pour les langues nationales et régionales : Projet de guide de réalisation. Version provisoire,* Université de Lisbonne: CAPLE / Council of Europe.

Carroll, J B (Ed.) (1956) *Language, Thought and Reality: selected writings of Benjamin Lee Whorf,* Cambridge, MA.

Coste, D, Courtillon, J, Ferenczi, V, Martins-Baltar, M, Papo, E (1987) *Un Niveau Seuil,* Paris: Hatier-Didier.

Council of Europe (2001) *Common European Framework of Reference for Languages: Learning, teaching, assessment*, Cambridge: Cambridge University Press.

Council of Europe (2003) *Preliminary Pilot Version of the Manual for Relating Language Examinations to the Common European Framework of Reference for Languages: learning, teaching, assessment*, Strasbourg: Council of Europe, available online: <http://www.coe.int/T/DG4/Linguistic/Default_en.asp>

Council of Europe (2004) *Reference Supplement to the Preliminary Pilot Version of the Manual for Relating Language Examinations to the Common European Framework of Reference for Languages: learning, teaching, assessment.* Strasbourg: Council of Europe, available online: <http://www.coe.int/T/DG4/Linguistic/Default_en.asp>

Council of Europe (2006) *Relating Language Examinations to the Common European Framework of Reference: Learning, teaching, assessment. Reading and Listening Items and Tasks.* Strasbourg: Council of Europe, available online: <http://www.coe.int/T/DG4/Linguistic/Default_en.asp>

Glaboniat, M, Müller, M, Schmitz, H, and Rusch, P (2002) *Profile Deutsch,* Munich: Langenscheidt Verlag.

Van Ek, J A and Trim, J L M (1990a) *Threshold 1990,* Cambridge: Cambridge University Press.

Van Ek, J A and Trim, J L M (1990b) *Waystage 1990,* Cambridge: Cambridge University Press.

Van Ek, J A and Trim, J L M (1990c) *Vantage,* Cambridge: Cambridge University Press.

Weigle, S C (2002) *Assessing Writing,* Cambridge: Cambridge University Press.

Weir, C J (2005) *Language Testing and Validation: an Evidence-Based Approach,* Basingstoke: Palgrave Macmillan.

Appendix 1: Minimum standards for establishing quality profiles in ALTE examinations

1	Test Construction	Ensure that your examination is based on a theoretical construct, e.g. on a model of communicative competence.
2		Ensure that you can describe the purpose and context of use of the examination, and the population for which the examination is appropriate.
3		Ensure that you provide criteria for selection and training of test constructors and that expert judgement is involved in test construction, and in the review and revision of the examinations.
4		Ensure that parallel examinations are comparable across different administrations in terms of content, stability, consistency and grade boundaries.
5		Ensure that if you make a claim that your examination is linked to an external reference system (e.g. Common European Framework), then you can provide evidence of alignment to this system.

6	Administration & Logistics	Ensure that all centres are selected to administer your examination according to clear, transparent, established procedures, and have access to regulations about how to do so.
7		Ensure that examination papers are delivered in excellent condition and by secure means of transport to the authorised examination centres, that your examination administration system provides for secure and traceable handling of all examination documents, and that confidentiality of all system procedures can be guaranteed.
8		Ensure that your examination administration system has appropriate support systems (e.g. phone hotline, web services etc.).

9		Ensure that you adequately protect the security and confidentiality of results and certificates, and data relating to them, in line with current data protection legislation, and that candidates are informed of their rights to access this data.
10		Ensure that your examination system provides support for candidates with special needs.

11	Marking & Grading	Ensure that marking is sufficiently accurate and reliable for purpose and type of examination.
12		Ensure that you can document and explain how marking is carried out and reliability estimated, and how data regarding achievement of raters of writing and speaking performances is collected and analysed.

13	Test Analysis	Ensure that you collect and analyse data on an adequate and representative sample of candidates and can be confident that their achievement is a result of the skills measured in the examination and not influenced by factors like L1, country of origin, gender, age and ethnic origin.
14		Ensure that item-level data (e.g. for computing the difficulty, discrimination, reliability and standard errors of measurement of the examination) is collected from an adequate sample of candidates and analysed.

15	Communication with Stakeholders	Ensure that your examination administration system communicates the results of the examinations to candidates and to examination centres (e.g. schools) promptly and clearly.
16		Ensure that you provide information to stakeholders on the appropriate context, purpose and use of the examination, on its content, and on the overall reliability of the results of the examination.
17		Ensure that you provide suitable information to stakeholders to help them interpret results and use them appropriately.

Appendix 2: Target difficulties for ALTE exams in scaled logits

ALTE level	CEFR level	CEFR threshold score (cut score) *	Test (Portuguese)	Test (English)	Test (German)	Test (Spanish)	Test (Italian)
	A1 Breakthrough	33 (−3)			Start Deutsch 1		
1	A2 Waystage	45 (−1.6)	CIPLE	KET	Start Deutsch 2		CELI1
2	B1 Threshold	58 (−0.2)	DEPLE	PET	Zertifikat Deutsch	DELE Inicial	CELI2
3	B2 Vantage	67 (0.8)	DIPLE	FCE		DELE Intermedio	CELI3
4	C1 Effective Operational Proficiency	76 (1.8)	DAPLE	CAE	Zentrale Mittelstufenprüfung		CELI4
5	C2 Mastery	84 (2.6)	DUPLE	CPE	Zentrale Oberstufenprüfung	DELE Superior	CELI5

* Common Scale
95% of items should fall within 10 scale points of target difficulty level

Section Two
Assuring Quality

8 A socio-cognitive approach to writing test validation

Cyril J Weir – Centre for Research in English Language Learning and Assessment, University of Bedfordshire
Stuart Shaw – Cambridge ESOL (Cambridge Assessment)

Introduction

Examination boards are increasingly being required by their own governments and by European authorities to demonstrate that the language ability constructs they are attempting to measure are well grounded in the examinations they offer. Furthermore, examination boards in Europe are now being encouraged to map their examinations onto the Common European Framework of Reference (CEFR) (Council of Europe 2001) despite some reservations within the testing community as to the suitability of this instrument for practical test development and comparability purposes.

Weir (2005) argues that the CEFR in its present form is not sufficiently comprehensive, coherent or transparent for uncritical use in language testing. For example, the descriptor scales take insufficient account of how variation in terms of *contextual parameters* (i.e. specific features of the writing task or context) may affect test performance; differing contextual parameters can lead to the raising or lowering of the level of difficulty involved in carrying out the target writing activity represented by a 'Can Do' statement, e.g. 'can write short, simple formulaic notes'. In addition, a test's *cognitive validity*, which is a function of the cognitive processing involved in carrying out a writing activity, must also be explicitly addressed by any specification on which a test is based. Failure to explicate such contextual and cognitive validity parameters, i.e. an inability to comprehensively define the construct to be tested, vitiates current attempts to use the CEFR as the basis for developing comparable test forms within and across languages and levels, and hampers attempts to link separate assessments particularly through social moderation by expert judges.

Weir feels that the CEFR is best seen not as a prescriptive device but as a heuristic one, which can be refined and developed by language testers to better meet their needs. For this particular constituency its current limitations mean that comparisons based on the illustrative scales alone might prove to be misleading given the insufficient attention paid in these scales to issues of validity. The CEFR as presently constituted does not enable us to say with any degree of precision or confidence whether or not tests are comparable, nor does it equip us to develop comparable tests. Instead, a more explicit test validation framework is required which better enables examination providers to furnish comprehensive evidence in support of any claims about the sound theoretical basis of their tests.

Examination boards and other institutions offering high-stakes tests need to demonstrate and share how they are seeking to meet the demands of validity in their tests and, more specifically, how they actually operationalise criterial distinctions between the tests they offer at different levels on the proficiency continuum. This paper reports briefly on the background to Cambridge ESOL's work in articulating their approach to assessment in the skill area of writing. The perceived benefits of a clearly articulated theoretical and practical position for assessing writing skills in the context of Cambridge ESOL tests are essentially twofold:

- *Within Cambridge ESOL* – it will deepen understanding of the current theoretical basis upon which Cambridge ESOL tests different levels of language proficiency across its range of test products, and will inform current and future test development projects in the light of this analysis. It will thereby enhance the development of equivalent test forms and tasks.

- *Beyond Cambridge ESOL* – it will communicate in the public domain the theoretical basis for the tests and provide a more clearly understood rationale for the way in which Cambridge ESOL operationalises this in its tests. It will provide a framework for others interested in validating their own examinations and thereby offer a more principled basis for comparison of language examinations across the proficiency range than is currently available.

The work builds on Cambridge ESOL's traditional approach to validating tests namely the VRIP approach where the concern is with Validity, Reliability, Impact and Practicality (see Weir and Milanovic 2003, Chapter 2). It explores how the socio-cognitive validity framework described in Weir's *Language Testing and Validation: an evidence-based approach* (2005a) might contribute to an enhanced validation framework for use with Cambridge examinations. Weir's approach covers much of the same ground as VRIP but it attempts to show how its constituent parts interact with each other. In addition it conceptualises the validation process in a *temporal frame* thereby identifying the various types of validity evidence that need to be collected at each stage in the test development, monitoring and evaluation cycle. Within each constituent part of the validation framework criterial individual parameters for distinguishing between adjacent proficiency levels are also identified.

ESOL test development and validation

In Cambridge ESOL's existing approach to validation the four essential qualities of test or examination usefulness, collectively known by the acronym VRIP, have been identified as aspects of a test that need to be addressed in establishing fitness for purpose. Cambridge ESOL examinations are designed around these four essential qualities, their successful validation being dependent upon all the VRIP features being dealt with adequately and completely.

Before the development or revision of a Cambridge ESOL examination can be undertaken, a VRIP-based checklist must be constructed and a prioritised list of validation projects agreed and implemented. The necessary information which enables such a checklist to be compiled is collected through a process of successive cycles of consultation and trialling. Transparent and specific validation plans in the form of VRIP checklists are now used to ensure that all aspects of VRIP are appropriately accounted for a particular test thus corroborating any claims made about the usefulness of the test. The gathering of evidence, in the form of data collection, constitutes a principal consideration in the model based approach and provides the evidence to support the 'validity argument'.

The Cambridge ESOL approach to test validation is, however, an evolving one following on from the seminal work of Messick (1989) at the onset of the 1980s. In a recent position paper, Saville (2002) argues that '*In order to develop a "Cambridge ESOL validity argument", our test development model needs to be underpinned by theories (related to the VRIP features), in order to combine the test development process with necessary evidence*' (Saville 2002:2). Weir (2005a) provides a theoretical socio-cognitive framework for an evidence-based validity approach which accommodates and strengthens the existing VRIP approach.

The focus in this paper is on Weir's socio-cognitive model which is ostensibly concerned with specifying and inter-relating focus areas for the validation process rather than with how the validation case should be argued *per se*. We would emphasise that related approaches such as those advocated by Toulmin (1958), Kane (1992), Mislevy, Steinberg and Almond (2000), and Bachman (2004) are also under serious consideration in the development of a comprehensive approach to validation and the reporting of such at Cambridge ESOL. Of particular interest in this future development of our institutional approach to validation are:

• evidence-centred assessment design
• 'interpretive argument' logic.

Validity of Cambridge ESOL writing tasks

Work undertaken by Shaw and Weir (2007) offers a perspective on the central issues involved in the testing of writing in Cambridge ESOL examinations. Their work follows the conceptualisation of performance suggested by Weir (2005a). A diagrammatic overview of the socio-cognitive framework is reproduced below as Figure 1.

Figure 1: Components and framework for conceptualising writing test performance (Weir 2005a)

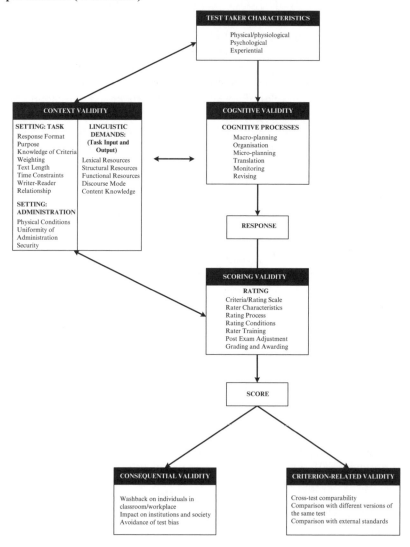

The framework is socio-cognitive in that the abilities to be tested are mental constructs which are latent and within the brain of the test taker (the cognitive dimension); and the use of language in performing tasks is viewed as a social rather than purely linguistic phenomenon (the contextual dimension). It represents a unified approach to establishing the overall validity of the test. The pictorial representation is intended to depict how the various validity components (and different types of validity evidence) fit together both temporally and conceptually. 'The arrows indicate the principal direction(s) of any hypothesized relationships: what has an effect on what, and the timeline runs from top to bottom: before the test is finalized, then administered and finally what happens after the test event' (Weir 2005a:43). Conceptualising validity in terms of temporal sequencing is of value as it offers a plan of what should be happening in relation to validation and when it should be happening.

The model comprises both *a priori* (before-the-test event) validation components of context and cognitive validity and *a posteriori* (after-the-test event) components of scoring validity, consequential validity and criterion-related validity. 'The more comprehensive the approach to validation, the more evidence collected on each of the components of this framework, the more secure we can be in our claims for the validity of a test. The higher the stakes of the test the stricter the demands we might make in respect of all of these' (Weir 2005a:47).

A number of critical questions can be addressed in applying this socio-cognitive validation framework to Cambridge ESOL examinations across the proficiency spectrum:

- How are the physical/physiological, psychological and experiential characteristics of candidates catered for by this test? (focus on the Test taker)
- Are the cognitive processes required to complete the test tasks appropriate? (focus on Cognitive validity)
- Are the characteristics of the test tasks and their administration appropriate and fair to the candidates who are taking them? (focus on Context validity)
- How far can we depend on the scores which result from the test? (focus on Scoring validity)
- What effects do the test and test scores have on various stakeholders? (focus on Consequential validity)
- What external evidence is there outside of the test scores themselves that the test is fair? (focus on Criterion-related validity)

These are precisely the sorts of critical questions that anyone intending to take a particular test or to use scores from that test would be advised to ask of the test developers in order to be confident that the nature and quality of the test matches up to their requirements.

The **Test Taker** box connects directly to the cognitive and context validity boxes because these individual characteristics will directly impact on the way the individuals process the test task set up by the context validity box. Obviously, the tasks themselves will also be constructed with the overall test population and the target use situation clearly in mind as well as with concern for their cognitive validity. Physical/physiological characteristics (individuals may have special needs that must be accommodated such as partial sightedness or dyslexia), Psychological characteristics (a test taker's interest or motivation may affect the way a task is managed or other factors such as preferred learning styles or personality type may have an influence on performance), and Experiential characteristics (the degree of a test taker's familiarity with a particular test may affect the way the task is managed) all have the potential to affect test performance.

The term content validity was traditionally used to refer to the content coverage of the task. **Context Validity** is preferred here as a more inclusive superordinate which signals the need to consider the discoursal, social and cultural contexts as well as the linguistic parameters under which the task is performed (its operations and conditions).

As a general principle it can be argued that language tests should place the same requirements on test takers as language does in non-test 'real-life' situations. Bachman and Palmer (1996:23) describe a task as being relatively authentic ' . . . whose characteristics correspond to those of the Target Language Use (TLU) domain tasks' and define authenticity as 'the degree of correspondence of the characteristics of a given language test task to the features of a TLU task' (1996:23). Following Bachman and Palmer (1996), in the Cambridge Suite of examinations authenticity is considered to have two characteristics. Firstly, *interactional* authenticity (see section on cognitive validity below), which is a feature of the engagement of the test taker's cognitive capacities in performing the test, and secondly, *situational* authenticity (context validity in our terms) which attempts to take into account the situational requirements of candidates. Cambridge ESOL adopts an approach which recognises the importance of both situational and interactional authenticity.

Context validity in the case of writing tasks relates to the particular performance conditions under which the operations required for task fulfilment are performed (such as purpose of the task, time available, length, specified addressee, known marking criteria and the linguistic and discoursal demands inherent in the successful performance of the task) together with the actual examination conditions resulting from the administrative setting (Weir 2005a:19).

Cognitive Validity involves collecting *a priori* evidence through piloting and trialling before the test event, e.g. through verbal reports from test takers on the cognitive processing activated by the test task and *a posteriori* evidence involving statistical analysis of scores following test administration. Language test constructors should be aware of the established theory relating to the language processing that underpins the variety of operations in real-life language use.

Scoring Validity is linked directly to both context and cognitive validity and is employed as a superordinate term for all aspects of reliability. Scoring validity accounts for the extent to which test scores are based on appropriate criteria, exhibit consensual agreement in their marking, are free as possible from measurement error, stable over time, consistent in terms of their content sampling and engender confidence as reliable decision making indicators.

Weir (2005a:35) points out that for cognitive and context validity, knowing what the test is measuring is crucial. There is a further type of validity which we might term **Criterion-Related Validity** where knowing exactly what a test measures is not so crucial. This is a predominantly quantitative and *a posteriori* concept, concerned with the extent to which test scores correlate with a suitable external criterion of performance (see Anastasia 1988:145, Messick 1989:16) with established properties.

A test is said to have criterion-related validity if a relationship can be demonstrated between test scores and some external criterion which is believed to be a measure of the same ability. Information on criterion-relatedness is also used in determining how well a test predicts future behaviour (ALTE 1998). Criterion-related validity naturally subdivides into two forms: concurrent and predictive. Concurrent validity seeks a '*criterion which we believe is also an indicator of the ability being tested*' (Bachman 1990:248) and involves the comparison of the test scores with some other measure for the same candidates taken at roughly the same time as the test. This other measure may consist of scores from some other tests, or candidates' self-assessments of their language abilities, or ratings of the candidate by teachers, subject specialists, or other informants (Alderson, Clapham and Wall 1995). Predictive validity entails the comparison of test scores with some other measure for the same candidates taken some time after the test has been given (Alderson et al 1995).

Messick (1989:18) argues that 'For a fully unified view of validity, it must . . . be recognised that the appropriateness, meaningfulness, and usefulness of score based inferences depend as well on the social consequences of the testing. Therefore social values and social consequences cannot be ignored in considerations of validity.' **Consequential Validity** relates to the way in which the implementation of a test can affect the interpretability of test scores; the practical consequences of the introduction of a test (McNamara 2000). 'Testers' argues Shohamy (1993:37) '*must begin to examine the consequences of the tests they develop . . . often . . . they do not find it necessary to observe the actual use of the test*'.

Weir (2005a) provides a comprehensive treatment of these key elements within the validation framework.

Although for descriptive purposes the various elements of the model are presented as being independent of each other, there is a 'symbiotic' relationship between context validity, cognitive validity and scoring validity, which together constitute what is frequently referred to as construct validity. Decisions taken with regard to parameters in terms of task context will impact on the processing that takes place in task completion. Likewise scoring criteria where made known to candidates in advance will similarly affect executive processing in task planning and completion. The scoring criteria in writing are an important part of the construct as defined by context and processing as they describe the level of performance that is required. Particularly at the upper levels of writing ability it is the quality of the performance that enables distinctions to be made between levels (Hawkey and Barker 2004). Additionally criterion-related validity represents evidence of the value or worth of a test, and both will impact on the test (in terms of design, tasks etc.) and on the test taker. The interactions between and especially within these different aspects of validity may well eventually offer us further insights into more closely defining different levels of task difficulty. However, given our current limited knowledge of these effects, the separability of the various aspects of validity is maintained as they offer the reader a descriptive route through the model and, more importantly, a clear and systematic perspective on the literature.

Importance and relevance to Cambridge ESOL

It is important that test developers provide a clear explication of the ability constructs which underpin the tests they offer in the public domain; such an explication is increasingly necessary if claims about the validity of test score interpretation and use are to be supported both logically and with empirical evidence.

Shaw and Weir (2007) propose a comprehensive test validation framework which adopts a socio-cognitive perspective in terms of its underlying theory and which conceptualises validity as a unitary concept; at the same time the framework embraces six core components which reflect the practical nature and quality of an actual testing event. They suggest that an understanding and analysis of the framework and its components in relation to specific tests can assist test developers to more effectively operationalise their tests, especially in relation to criterial distinctions across test levels. In their current research they apply the validation framework and its components to a set of actual tests produced by Cambridge, taking as its focus the construct of writing ability.

Research in the area of writing is already providing valuable insights, for example, into the cognitive processing that appears to be taking place at the various levels in the Cambridge Main Suite examinations and the ways in which Cambridge Main Suite writing tests operationalise various contextual variables. Of particular interest here is the variation of parameters across tasks intended for test takers at different levels of ability.

The research is also offering insights into a range of key ESOL personnel helping to:

- describe Cambridge ESOL's approach in skills assessment across levels and how this sits with theoretical context
- train subject officers in skills assessment
- provide rationale/guidance on specific issues, such as rubric design
- develop item writer guidelines, ensuring coherence and preventing drift over time
- inform internal ESOL working groups such as the Exams Modifications group and the skills-focused groups and identify areas in need of attention according to the framework
- tag items for the computer in terms of features likely to distinguish between levels
- inform the Languages Ladder (Asset) project
- link exams to the CEFR
- inform content of ALTE Handbook/guidelines.

Conclusion

The issue of what a particular level of language ability means is critical for all aspects of language learning. Exam boards and other institutions offering high-stakes tests need to demonstrate and share how they are seeking to meet the demands of context, cognitive, scoring, criterion-related and consequential validity. In relation to these they need to be explicit as to how they in fact operationalise criterial distinctions between levels in their tests in terms of various parameters related to these. The research undertaken by Shaw and Weir (2007) marks the first attempt by any examination board to do this. Future research needs to investigate whether the parameters explored either singly or in configuration can help better ground the distinctions in proficiency represented by levels in Cambridge ESOL examinations.

References

Alderson, J C, Clapham, C and Wall, D (1995) *Language Test Construction and Evaluation*, Cambridge: Cambridge University Press.

ALTE Members (1998) *Multilingual Glossary of Language Testing Terms*, Cambridge: UCLES/Cambridge University Press.

Anastasia, A (1988) Psychological Testing (6th edition), New York: Macmillan.

Bachman, L F (1990) *Fundamental Considerations in Language Testing*, Oxford: Oxford University Press.

Bachman, L F (2004) Building and supporting a case for test utilization, paper presented at the Language Testing Research Colloquium, March 2004, Temecula, Ca.

Bachman, L F and Palmer, A S (1996) *Language Testing in Practice*, Oxford: Oxford University Press.

Council of Europe (2001) *Common European Framework of Reference for Languages: Learning, teaching, assessment,* Cambridge: Cambridge University Press.

Hawkey, R and Barker, F (2004) Developing a common scale for the assessment of writing, *Assessing Writing* 9, 122–159.

Kane, M T (1992) An argument-based approach to validity, *Psychological Bulletin* 112, 527–535.

McNamara, T F (2000) *Language Testing*, Oxford: Oxford University Press.

Messick, S A (1989) Validity, in Linn, R L (Ed.) *Educational Measurement* (3rd edition), New York: Macmillan, 13–103.

Mislevy R J, Steinberg, L S and Almond R G (2000) On the structure of educational assessments, *Measurement: Interdisciplinary Research and Perspectives* 1, 3–62.

Saville, N (2002) The test development process for CELS, *Research Notes* 9, 8–10.

Shaw, S D and Weir, C J (2007) *Examining Writing: Research and practice in assessing second language writing*, Cambridge: UCLES/Cambridge University Press.

Shohamy, E (1993) *The Power of Tests – The Impact of Language Tests on Teaching and Learning*, Washington, DC: NFLC Occasional Papers.

Toulmin, S E (1958) *The Uses of Argument*, Cambridge: Cambridge University Press.

Weir, C J (2005) Limitations of the Council of Europe's framework of Reference (CEFR) in developing comparable examinations and tests, *Language Testing* 22, 281–300.

Weir, C J (2005a) *Language Testing and Validation: An Evidence-Based Approach*, Basingstoke: Palgrave Macmillan.

Weir, C J and Milanovic, M (Eds) (2003) *Continuity and Innovation: Revising the Cambridge Proficiency in English Examination 1913–2002*, Cambridge: UCLES/Cambridge University Press.

9 Assuring the quality of TestDaF examinations: a psychometric modeling approach

Thomas Eckes
TestDaF Institute, Germany

The Test of German as a Foreign Language (*Test Deutsch als Fremdsprache*, TestDaF) is a high-stakes test designed for foreign students applying for entry to an institution of higher education in Germany. Because of its relevance to far-reaching educational decisions affecting many individuals' lives, ensuring a high psychometric quality of this measure of German language proficiency is of utmost importance.

The linguistic conceptualisation underlying this test, its origin, format, and structure have been described in detail elsewhere (Althaus 2004, Eckes, Ellis, Kalnberzina, Pižorn, Springer, Szollas and Tsagari 2005; Grotjahn 2004; see also www.testdaf.de). Therefore, the focus in this paper is on the methodological approach adopted in order to render the TestDaF a high-quality measurement instrument. I will give special attention to the productive sections (in particular Writing), and will show how many-facet Rasch measurement provides an appropriate close-up view of how the rater-mediated performance assessment system functions.

First, I will briefly summarise basic features of the TestDaF. Subsequently, I will discuss the evaluation cycle, which is at the heart of the quality assurance process. Then, I will outline the conceptual–psychometric model on which the analysis of the language performance assessments in the TestDaF Writing and Speaking sections is based. Examples drawn from a typical TestDaF examination serve to illustrate this approach. Finally, I will address the issue of rater variability as apparent in TestDaF and other high-stakes language and non-language examinations.

The TestDaF at a glance

The TestDaF measures the four language skills in separate sections. Examinee performance in each section is related to one of three levels of language proficiency in the form of band descriptions; these levels (*TestDaF-*

Niveaustufen, TestDaF levels, or TDNs for short) are TDN 3, TDN 4, and TDN 5. The TDNs are intended to cover the Council of Europe's (2001) Lower Vantage Level (B2.1) to Higher Effective Operational Proficiency (C1.2); that is, the test measures German language proficiency at an intermediate to high level. There is no differentiation among lower proficiency levels; it is just noted that the TDN 3 level has not yet been achieved (below TDN 3).

The TestDaF is officially recognised as a language entry exam for students from abroad. Examinees who have achieved at least TDN 4 in each section are eligible for admission to a German institution of higher education (see Eckes et al 2005).

The Reading and Listening sections measure the examinees' ability to understand, and respond adequately to, texts relevant to academic life presented in writing or orally, respectively. Various types of tasks and items are used, including a matching task, multiple-choice questions, and forced-choice items of the type 'yes/no/no relevant information in the text' for reading, and short-answer and true/false questions for listening.

The Writing and Speaking sections are performance-based instruments. Writing is designed to assess the examinees' ability to produce a coherent and well-structured text on a given topic taken from the academic context. Likewise, Speaking taps the examinees' ability to communicate appropriately in typical situations of university life.

In Spring 2001, the TestDaF was administered worldwide for the first time. Until the end of 2007, more than 61,000 students had taken this test. In the same period, the total count of test centres actively involved in test administration went up to more than 380, with test centres located in 78 foreign countries throughout the world and in Germany. The number of test administrations increased from two exams in 2001 to seven exams in 2005 (including two separate exams in the People's Republic of China); in 2006, one more test date was added to the set of worldwide administrations. Table 1 portrays the growth of the TestDaF candidature, as well as the number of test centres and test countries from 2001 to 2007.

Table 1: Growth of TestDaF candidature, test centres, and test countries

Year	Test Takers	Test Centres	Test Countries
2001	1,190	81	34
2002	3,582	154	48
2003	7,498	211	65
2004	8,982	261	70
2005	11,052	275	72
2006	13,554	309	74
2007	15,389	318	75

The TestDaF evaluation cycle

With each new set of tasks and items, a comprehensive evaluation starts that is based on both quantitative and qualitative methods. The basic process is schematically depicted in Figure 1.

Figure 1: The TestDaF evaluation cycle

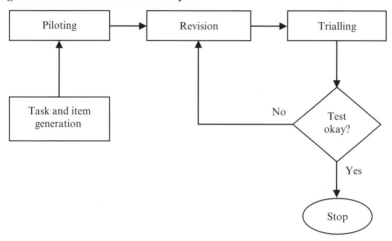

Item writers generating TestDaF tasks and items have a strong professional background as teachers and/or examiners in German as a foreign language. Also, item writers are specially trained in the requirements of the overall test design, the specific format of the test section they write items for, and the intended difficulty level of tasks and items typically included in that section. Each item written is reviewed by test developers at the TestDaF Institute before being considered further.

Since the TestDaF measures language ability required for beginning study at an institution of higher education in Germany, content and tasks are closely related to academic, scientific, and study-relevant topics. Item writers receive detailed guidance (i.e., test specifications, thorough vetting) designed to make sure that they produce tasks and items that elicit language use relevant to, and characteristic of, this specific context. Test specifications are issued for each of the four skills separately, distinguishing between various language use domains (personal, public, educational), communicative situations (e.g., locations, persons, cognitive operations), as well as content and task types.

The underlying test construct draws on Bachman and Palmer's (1996; see also Bachman 1990) model of communicative language ability. More specifically, for each language skill the following areas of language knowledge are taken into account: grammatical knowledge (not assessed separately, but indirectly addressed in each of the TestDaF sections), textual knowledge (coherence/cohesion, rhetorical functions, conversational organisation), functional knowledge (ideational, manipulative, heuristic functions), and socio-linguistic knowledge (registers, idiomatic expressions, cultural references). In addition, TestDaF tasks are intended to tap into areas of strategic competence (goal setting, assessment, planning).

After completion of the item writing and reviewing process, test tasks and items are assembled to form a pilot test version. In the *piloting stage* of the evaluation cycle, this test version is administered to relatively small samples of speakers of other languages (some 60 to 80 participants) and native speakers of German (some 20 to 40 participants). Participants' responses to test tasks and items are examined quantitatively, based on classical item analysis (item difficulty, item discrimination, test score distribution, Cronbach's coefficient alpha, and the like) and qualitatively, taking into account test taker feedback as provided on a questionnaire regarding task and item difficulty, the timing of the test, the comprehensibility of the test rubric, and so on. Qualitative feedback is also gathered from test administrators and raters scoring examinee responses in the productive test sections.

The quantitative and qualitative analyses of the piloting data regularly lead to a revision of those parts of the test that proved to be problematic in some respect or other. For example, in the Reading and Listening sections a revision is indicated when item facility is too high or too low for speakers of other languages, or too low for native speakers of German.

When the revision is completed, the *trialling stage* follows. In this stage, only speakers of other languages are considered (minimum $N=200$). The sample of participants is deliberately chosen so as to represent the population of examinees the TestDaF is designed for. Typically, participants are either attending German language courses as part of a preparatory study programme in Germany or planning to study at a German university while still in their home country. All examinees take part on a voluntary basis.

In addition to the four test sections, trialling participants have to complete a C-test, that is, a gap-filling test which measures general language proficiency (see Eckes & Grotjahn 2006a). This test consists of a small number of authentic texts with 20 gaps each. The C-test appears right after Reading (and before Listening) and is included for test-equating purposes; that is, this C-test is used as an anchor test (see Eckes & Grotjahn 2006b).

Analysis of the trialling data is primarily based on item response theory (Bond & Fox 2007, Eckes 2003, Embretson & Reise 2000, Wilson 2005). Specifically, a Rasch measurement approach is adopted to provide a fine-grained analysis of the psychometric quality of the test. Due to the heterogeneous nature of the response formats involved in the trial test, three kinds of Rasch models are applied.

1. Responses to the Reading and Listening items are scored true or false. Hence, the dichotomous Rasch model (Rasch 1960/1980, Wright and Masters 1982) is used to analyse this data. The Rasch analysis yields item difficulty and examinee proficiency measures, including estimates of each measure's precision, separation and fit statistics for items and examinees, including estimates of the examinee separation reliability (corresponding to Cronbach's Alpha). In addition, this analysis allows the examination of differential item functioning (DIF).

2. Generally, gaps within a given C-test text have to be locally dependent to a significant degree (see, e.g., Klein-Braley 1996). Thus, C-test texts are construed as super-items, item bundles, or testlets (see, e.g., Wainer, Bradlow & Wang 2007, Wilson & Adams 1995), with item values corresponding to the number of gaps filled in correctly; that is, each text represents a polytomous item. In the present case, each item could take on values between 0 and 20. In separate studies comparing the suitability of various polytomous Rasch models for analysing C-test data (Eckes 2006, 2007), the rating scale model (Andrich 1978) proved to work well. Therefore, C-test data is analysed by means of Andrich's model.

3. Examinees' Writing and Speaking performance is scored by trained raters. Hence, the many-facet Rasch model (Linacre 1989, Linacre and Wright 2002) is applied to yield the information required. In addition to providing linear measures of examinee proficiency and criteria or task difficulty, the many-facet Rasch model provides measures of rater severity and corrects the examinee proficiency estimates for this source of construct-irrelevant variance in the ratings. Moreover, the model allows the study of differential facet functioning (DFF), such as the dependency of rater severity measures on examinee gender (see, for in-depth discussions of this Rasch modelling approach to TestDaF Writing and Speaking sections, Eckes 2003, 2004, 2005a, 2005b).

Rasch analyses in cases 1 and 2 are carried out using the WINSTEPS computer program (Linacre 2005b). Many-facet Rasch measurement, case 3 above, is carried out using the FACETS computer program (Linacre 2005a). The relationships between the different sources of trialling data and the various measurement approaches employed in this stage are summarised in Figure 2. With the exception of the rating scale Rasch analysis of C-test data (as noted before, C-tests are administered in trialling exams only), these Rasch analyses are performed in an analogous fashion after each and every TestDaF examination (see the exemplary analysis below).

Figure 2: TestDaF sections, C-test (anchor test), and Rasch models used in the analysis of data from trialling examinations (DIF = differential item functioning, DFF = differential facet functioning)

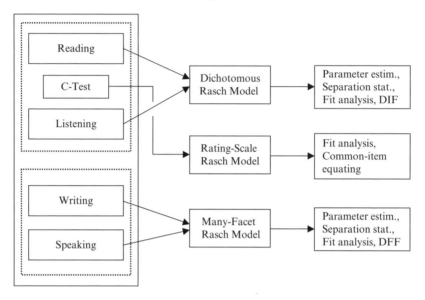

A conceptual model of language performance assessments

The evaluation of language performance assessments in TestDaF Writing and Speaking sections rests on a conceptual model of the factors that typically influence ratings of examinee performance (Eckes 2005a). Figure 3 depicts important factors and their mutual relationships. Of course, the factors shown do not encompass all that may happen in a particular rating session. The rating process is undoubtedly far more complex and dynamic in nature than can be summarised in a diagram like this, and the factors coming into play are multifarious at any given moment. Yet, I believe the following outline is of some heuristic value to a focused, psychometric analysis of rating data.

The middle part of the diagram outlines factors immediately impinging on performance assessments. These factors, also called *proximal* factors, include the construct to be measured (i.e., an examinee's language ability), and several factors that are basically irrelevant to the construct and thus contribute to construct-irrelevant variance in the ratings in Messick's (1989, 1995) sense of the term: (a) rater effects, such as the tendency to award unduly harsh or lenient scores, central tendency, and halo effects, (b)

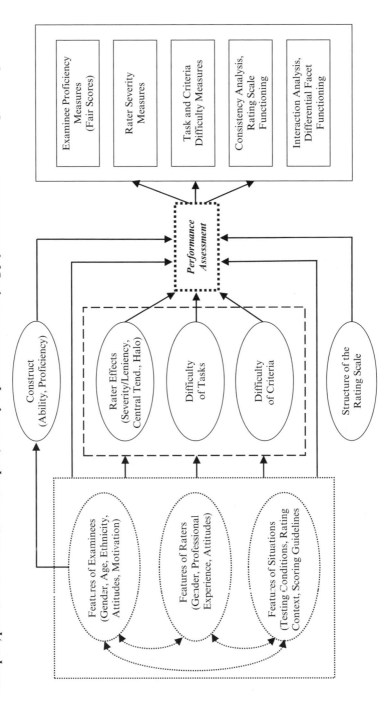

Figure 3: A conceptual framework of factors impinging on performance assessments. The diagram shows distal factors in the left-hand part, proximal factors in the middle part, and key aspects of the underlying psychometric model in the right-hand part.

variability in the difficulty of the tasks presented to examinees, (c) variability in the difficulty of scoring criteria, and, finally, (d) variability in the structure of the rating scale used (between or within raters, tasks, or criteria).

The left-hand side of Figure 3 shows three categories of *distal* variables that exert additional influence on the ratings, albeit usually in a more indirect and diffuse way: (a) features of examinees (e.g., examinee gender or ethnicity), (b) features of raters (e.g., gender or professional background), and (c) features of the situation, that is, features of the testing or the rating context (e.g., test setting, rater workload, applicability of the scoring rubric). Some of these distal factors may interact with one another and may also interact with some of the proximal factors, such as when examinee gender interacts with rater severity or when raters' degree of professional experience interacts with their interpretation and use of scoring criteria.

A psychometric model of language performance assessments

On the right-hand side, the diagram portrays how the conceptual model relates to the functions of a suitably chosen psychometric model. Instead of taking the performance assessments at face value, a psychometric model needs to be employed that takes as many factors (proximal or distal) as possible into account in order to provide a detailed look at the quality of the ratings.

The TestDaF quality assurance process utilises the many-facet Rasch measurement model (MFRM or *facets* model; Linacre 1989, Linacre & Wright 2002). This model extends the basic Rasch model (Fischer 2007, Rasch 1960/1980) to incorporate more variables (or 'facets') than the two that are typically included in a paper-and-pencil testing situation (i.e., examinees and items). In an analysis of data from a performance assessment, the model allows consideration of additional facets of that setting that may be of particular interest, such as raters and tasks. Within each facet, each element (i.e., each individual examinee, rater, item, or task) is represented by a parameter. These parameters denote distinct attributes of the facets involved, such as proficiency (for examinees), severity (for raters), and difficulty (for items or tasks).

A MFRM analysis provides useful group-level as well as individual-level diagnostic information about how the various facets and the various elements within each facet, respectively, are functioning. At the individual level, for each element of each facet, the analysis yields a measure (a logit estimate of the calibration), a standard error (the precision of that logit estimate), and fit indices (information about how well the data associated with a particular element agrees with model expectations). Group-level statistical indicators include separation statistics (information about how well the elements within a facet are differentiated along the logit scale), fixed-effect chi-square tests (tests of the hypothesis that elements within a facet form a homogeneous set of measures), and summary fit statistics (e.g., indices of global model–data fit; see, for a detailed discussion of individual- and group-level statistical indicators, Eckes 2005a, Engelhard 2002, Myford & Wolfe 2003, 2004).

Once the parameters of the model are estimated, interaction effects, such as the interaction between raters and examinees or between raters and tasks, can be detected by examining the standardised residuals (i.e., standardised differences between the observed and expected ratings). An *interaction analysis* (or *bias analysis*) may identify unusual interaction patterns among various facet elements, particularly those patterns that suggest consistent deviations from what is expected on the basis of the model.

Many-facet Rasch analysis of the TestDaF writing performance assessment

In this section, I illustrate how the many-facet Rasch analysis can be employed to yield insight into the functioning of the TestDaF rater-mediated system of performance assessment. The database is provided by ratings of examinee performance on the Writing section of a TestDaF examination that took place early in 2005.

Writing task

In the first part of this section, charts, tables, or diagrams are provided along with a short introductory text, and the examinee is asked to describe the relevant information. Specific points to be dealt with are stated in the rubric. In the second part, the examinee has to consider different positions on an aspect of the topic and write a well-structured argument. The input consists of short statements, questions, or quotes. As before, aspects to be dealt with in the argumentation are stated in the rubric. The time allowed is 60 minutes.

Examinees

The Writing section was administered to 1,677 participants (967 females, 710 males). Participants' mean age was 24.79 years ($SD=5.09$); 87.5% of participants were aged between 18 and 30 years.

There were 160 TestDaF test centres involved in this administration (54 centres in Germany, 106 centres in 34 foreign countries). In terms of the number of examinees, the following five national groups ranked highest (percentage in parentheses): Bulgaria (9.9%), Russia (9.5%), Turkey (7.7%), Poland (7.5%), and the People's Republic of China (6.2%).

Raters

Twenty-nine raters participated in the scoring of examinees' writing performance. Raters were all experienced teachers and specialists in the field of German as a foreign language, and were systematically trained and monitored to comply with scoring guidelines.

Procedure

Ratings of examinees' essays were carried out according to a detailed catalogue of performance aspects comprising nine criteria. The criteria were: fluency, train of thought, and structure (subsumed under the category 'global impression'), completeness, description, and argumentation ('treatment of the task'), and syntax, vocabulary, and correctness ('linguistic realisation'). On each criterion, examinee performance was scored using the 4-point TDN scale (with categories *below TDN 3*, *TDN 3*, *TDN 4*, *TDN 5*). Each examinee performance was scored by a single rater. Twenty-five raters scored 63 essays, the remaining four raters scored between 43 and 47 essays.

In general, a minimal scoring design, such as the one employed here, calls for measures to satisfy the precondition of connectivity of the resulting sparse data matrix. That is, all raters, examinees, and criteria need to be connected in the design such that they can be placed in a common frame of reference. It is only through such a linking that appropriate comparisons between facets, and between elements within each facet, can be made (Engelhard & Myford 2003, Linacre & Wright 2002). To generate a connective data matrix in the present case, each rater had to provide scorings for the same set of three essays, in addition to his or her normal workload. The additional essays, representing the range of TDN levels, had been preselected from a larger set of essays written by examinees in a previous trialling of the respective writing task.

Data analysis

I analysed the rating data by means of the computer program FACETS (Version 3.57; Linacre 2005a). The program used the ratings that raters awarded to examinees to estimate individual examinee proficiencies, rater severities, criteria difficulties, and scale category difficulties. FACETS calibrates the examinees, raters, criteria, and the rating scale onto the same equal-interval scale (i.e., the logit scale), creating a single frame of reference for interpreting the results of the analysis.

Results

Global model fit. Overall data–model fit can be assessed by examining the responses that are unexpected given the assumptions of the model. According to Linacre (2005a), satisfactory model fit is indicated when about 5% or less of (absolute) standardised residuals are equal or greater than 2, and about 1% or less of (absolute) standardised residuals are equal or greater than 3.

There were 15,821 valid responses (i.e. responses used for estimation of model parameters) included in the analysis. Of these, 673 responses (or 4.3%) were associated with (absolute) standardised residuals equal or greater than 2, and 84 responses (or 0.5%) were associated with (absolute) standardised residuals equal or greater than 3. These findings indicated satisfactory model fit. Below I present further statistics that are suited to assess the fit of the data to the Rasch model in specific parts of the measurement system (e.g. rater fit statistics).

Calibration of examinees, raters and criteria and tasks. Figure 4 displays the variable map representing the calibrations of the examinees, raters, criteria, and the four-point TDN rating scale as raters used it to score examinee essays on each criterion. Table 2 provides various summary statistics from the FACETS analysis for the three facets.

Table 2: Summary statistics for the many-facet Rasch analysis

Statistics	Examinees[a]	Raters	Criteria
Mean measure	0.41	0.00	0.00
Mean *SE*	0.61	0.08	0.04
Chi-square	19,025.8**	2,127.3**	1,155.6**
df	1,613	28	8
Separation index	5.07	11.73	15.39
Separation reliability	.93	.99	.99

Note: [a] Examinees with non-extreme scores only.

** $p < .01$

As can be seen, the variability across raters in their level of severity was substantial. The rater severity measures showed a 2.70-logit spread, which was more than a fifth (22.0%) of the logit spread observed for examinee proficiency measures (12.25 logits). Thus, despite all efforts at achieving high rater agreement during extensive training sessions, the rater severity measures were far from being homogeneous. This was consistently revealed by separation statistics: (a) the fixed chi-square value was highly significant, indicating that at least two raters did not share the same parameter (after allowing for measurement error), (b) the rater separation index showed that within the present group of raters there were about 12 statistically distinct strata of severity, and (c) the reliability of rater separation attested to a very high rater disagreement.

Rater fit. In the present analysis, rater fit refers to the extent to which a given rater is associated with unexpected ratings, summarised over examinees and criteria. FACETS reports two mean-square statistics indicating data–model fit

Figure 4: Variable map from the FACETS analysis of TestDaF writing performance data. Each star in the second column represents 10 examinees, and a dot represents fewer than 10 examinees. The horizontal dashed lines in column 5 indicate the category threshold measures.

Logit	Examinee High	Rater Severe	Criterion Difficult	TDN Scale (TDN 5)
7	.			
6	. .			
5	*. **. **.			
4	***. ***. ****.			
3	****. ******. *****			---
2	******. ********.			
1	********. *********. *********. ********.	26 16 21 04 11 12 27 29 03 08 24	argumentation description correctness	TDN 4
0	******. ********. ********.	01 05 06 13 18 20 22 14 15 19 23 02 10 28	fluency vocabulary train of thought completeness syntax structure	---
−1	*******. *******. ******	09 17 25 07		TDN 3
−2	*****. ****. ****.			
−3	**. ***. **.			---
−4	. *.			
−5	. .			
−6	. .			
	Low	Lenient	Easy	(below 3)

for each rater, *rater infit* and *rater outfit*. Whereas the infit statistic is sensitive to an accumulation of unexpected ratings, the outfit statistic is sensitive to individual unexpected ratings. Both statistics have an expected value of 1 and can range from 0 to infinity (Linacre 2002, Myford & Wolfe 2003).

Raters with fit values greater than 1 show more variation than expected in their ratings; data provided by these raters tends to *misfit* (or *underfit*) the model. By contrast, raters with fit values less than 1 show less variation than expected in their ratings; data provided by these raters tends to *overfit* the model. As a rule of thumb, Linacre (2002) suggested using 0.50 as a lower-control limit and 1.50 as an upper-control limit for infit and outfit mean-square statistics.[1] Other researchers suggested using a narrower range defined by a lower-control limit of 0.70 (or 0.75) and an upper-control limit of 1.30 (see, e.g., Bond & Fox 2007, McNamara 1996). In any case, it should be noted that the variance of infit and outfit values, respectively, is affected by sample size; that is, the larger the sample size is, the smaller the infit or outfit variance will be (Wang & Chen 2005).

Table 3 presents the frequencies of rater fit values falling into the overfit, acceptable fit, or misfit categories, using either a narrow or a wide range of upper- and lower-control limits. There were two raters showing overfit when the fit diagnosis was based on the narrow fit range. One rater fell into the misfit category irrespective of the fit range used; this rater (severity=0.95 logits, $SE = 0.08$) had an infit value of 1.61 and an outfit value of 1.56. For the most part, then, raters were internally consistent and used the TDN rating scale appropriately.

Table 3: Frequencies of rater mean-square fit statistics

Fit range	Infit	Outfit
Narrow		
fit < 0.70 (overfit)	2	2
0.70 ≤ fit ≥ 1.30	26	26
fit > 1.30 (misfit)	1	1
Wide		
fit < 0.50 (overfit)	0	0
0.50 ≤ fit ≤ 1.50	28	28
fit > 1.50 (misfit)	1	1

Note: Infit and outfit are mean-square fit statistics.

Psychometric dimensionality of the ratings. Indices of fit were also used to address the issue of possible psychometric multidimensionality (Henning 1992; McNamara 1996). The question asked was whether ratings on one criterion followed a pattern that was markedly different from ratings on the others, indicating that examinee scores related to different dimensions, or whether the ratings on one criterion corresponded well to ratings on the other criteria, indicating unidimensionality of the data. The fit statistics provided by the FACETS analysis are depicted in Table 4.

With a few exceptions, fit indices stayed well within even narrow quality control limits of 0.70 and 1.30. Only the infit and outfit values for the

Table 4: Measures and fit statistics of scoring criteria

Category	Criterion	Measure	SE	Infit	Outfit
Global impression	Fluency	−0.13	0.04	0.75	0.75
	Train of thought	−0.24	0.04	0.83	0.82
	Structure	−0.58	0.04	1.10	1.11
Treatment of the task	Completeness	−0.39	0.04	1.48	1.54
	Description	0.83	0.04	1.28	1.32
	Argumentation	0.58	0.04	1.19	1.14
Linguistic realisation	Syntax	−0.55	0.04	0.77	0.75
	Vocabulary	−0.02	0.04	0.74	0.72
	Correctness	0.51	0.04	0.87	0.87

Note: Measure = Difficulty in logits. *SE* = Standard error. Infit and outfit are mean-square statistics.

completeness criterion were a bit off that range. Overall then, these findings support the assumption of unidimensionality within the set of scoring criteria.

TDN rating scale

Another issue of importance concerns the functioning of the TDN rating scale that the raters employed to evaluate examinees' essays. To examine whether the four scale categories on the TDN scale were appropriately ordered, various statistical indicators can be used. In this study, I looked at (a) the category thresholds, which denote the point at which the probability curves of two adjacent rating scale categories cross (these thresholds should advance monotonically with rating scale categories), (b) the average examinee proficiency measure by rating scale category (these averages should also advance monotonically with categories), and (c) the outfit mean-square statistic for each rating category (this statistic should not exceed 2.0; see, for a detailed account of these and other indicators, Linacre 2004). Table 5 summarises the findings of this analysis.

Table 5: Functioning of the TDN rating scale

Category	Freq. %	Threshold	Average Measure	Outfit
below TDN 3	12%	–	−2.77	1.0
TDN 3	32%	−2.76	−0.80	1.0
TDN 4	36%	0.05	1.11	1.0
TDN 5	19%	2.71	3.05	1.0

Note: Threshold is the category threshold measure (in logits). Average measure is the average examinee proficiency measure (in logits) per rating category. Outfit is a mean-square statistic.

As Table 5 shows, there was a clear progression of scale category thresholds from –2.76 logits (i.e., the threshold between categories *below TDN 3* and *TDN 3*) to 2.71 logits (i.e., the threshold between categories *TDN 4* and *TDN 5*). Similarly, average measures of examinees increased as the rating categories increased, and these increases were nearly uniform (i.e., 1.94, + or – 0.03). Finally, the outfit mean-square statistics were all equal to the expected value of 1.0. Taken together, these findings strongly confirm that the 4-point TDN rating scale functioned as intended.

The rater variability issue

Since the advent of sophisticated analytical tools for the analysis of rating data, in particular since the development of generalisability theory (see, e.g., Brennan 2001, Cronbach, Gleser, Nanda & Rajaratnam 1972) and many-facet Rasch measurement (Linacre 1989, Linacre & Wright 2002), attention has been increasingly devoted to the issue of rater variability. The basic questions are: (a) do raters differ in the way they rate examinee performance, (b) if raters differ, how large are these differences, and (c) can rater training enable raters to function interchangeably?

Ideally, raters would function interchangeably; that is, it would make no difference at all which raters were selected from a larger group of raters to evaluate a particular examinee's performance. According to this view, when the data indicates that raters violate the ideal, systematic rater training would enable them to get sufficiently close to it.

Research into rater behaviour conducted since the early 1990s, however, has repeatedly demonstrated substantial degrees of *between-rater variability*, for example, variability in the severity or leniency of ratings awarded to examinees (see, e.g., Bachman, Lynch & Mason 1995, Engelhard 1994, Lynch & McNamara 1998). Moreover, rater training proved to be unlikely to significantly reduce between-rater differences in rating behaviour (Barrett 2001, Lumley & McNamara 1995, Weigle 1998).

Table 6 presents an overview of rater variability studies that adopted the many-facet Rasch measurement approach. Though by no means intended as a complete survey of extant research on this topic, the studies listed in the table demonstrate a striking consistency of results across diverse assessment domains.

Studies in the language domain, be it studies dealing with writing or speaking proficiency, as well as studies in non-language domains suggest the same general conclusion: the reliability of rater separation is noticeably above what is desired, given the ideal outlined above; that is, not a single study yielded evidence in favour of interchangeability of raters (note that this ideal situation would be indicated by a separation reliability close to 0.0).

Table 6: Rater variability as evidenced in many-facet Rasch measurement studies

Study	Assessment	Number of raters	Separation reliability
	Studies of writing proficiency		
Eckes (2005b)	TestDaF Writing Section	29	.98
Engelhard (1994)	Eighth Grade Writing Test	15	.87
Engelhard & Myford (2003)	Advanced Placement ELC	605	.71
Kondo-Brown (2002)	Japanese L2 Writing	3	.98
Weigle (1998)	ESLPE Composition	16	.94
	Studies of speaking proficiency		
Bachman, Lynch, & Mason (1995)[a]	Spanish (LAAS)	15	.92
Eckes (2005b)	TestDaF Speaking Section	31	.98
Lumley & McNamara (1995)	OET Speaking Section	13	.89
Lynch & McNamara (1998)	Speaking Skills Module (access:)	4	1.0
	Studies in non-language domains		
Eckes (2006a)	Physical attractiveness	20	.71
Lunz & Linacre (1998)	Job performance	31	.92
Lunz & Linacre (1998)	Product quality	43	.89
Lunz & Stahl (1993)	Medical oral exam	56	.85
Lunz, Wright, & Linacre (1990)	Histology certification exam	18	.95

Note: TestDaF = Test Deutsch als Fremdsprache. ELC = English Literature and Composition. ESLPE = English as a Second Language Placement Examination. LAAS = Language Ability Assessment System. OET = Occupational English Test.
[a] In this study no homogeneity statistic (chi-square test, fixed effects; see Linacre 2005, Myford & Wolfe, 2003) was reported; all other studies reported significant chi-square statistics ($p < .05$), attesting to substantial degrees of rater variability. Interchangeability of raters would be indicated by a separation reliability close to 0.0.

Reviewing the implications that these pronounced differences in rater severity/leniency have for rater training, McNamara (1996) recommended '. . . to accept that the most appropriate aim of rater training is to make raters internally consistent so as to make statistical modelling of their characteristics possible, but beyond this to accept variability in stable rater characteristics as a fact of life, which must be compensated for in some way . . . ' (McNamara 1996:127).

With respect to the TestDaF, several measures are routinely taken to diminish the degree of unwanted rater variability at the training stage. Thus, raters are trained on the basis of a detailed list of carefully devised scoring guidelines, they are certified to participate in the actual scoring sessions upon fulfilment of strict selection criteria, and they are monitored as to their compliance with scoring specifications on a regular basis. Yet, as mentioned previously, such training and monitoring procedures have only very limited chances to lower rater variability to any satisfactory degree.

Well-designed rater training can nonetheless be highly effective in terms of increasing *within-rater consistency*. That is, training can (and should) encourage individual raters to keep to their tendency to award more severe or lenient scores than others across examinees, criteria, tasks, and other facets involved (Stahl & Lunz 1996).

Given that raters demonstrate sufficiently high degrees of internal consistency, one way to compensate for rater differences in severity/leniency is to use *adjusted scores*, or *fair scores*, computed on the basis of many-facet Rasch model parameter estimates. An examinee's fair score (also called *fair average*, see Linacre 2005a) is defined as the expected rating for that examinee obtained from a rater with level of severity equal to zero, that is, from a rater with average severity (see, for a discussion of this statistical adjustment procedure, Eckes 2005b, Engelhard & Myford 2003).

Summary and conclusions

In the present paper, I discussed major steps in the complex process of assuring the quality of TestDaF examinations. The basic design of this process rests on the premise that, as a large-scale language test that is routinely used to make high-stakes educational decisions, the TestDaF needs to accord with common scientific standards of test construction, evaluation, and administration. At the heart of the TestDaF quality assurance process is the evaluation cycle, the building blocks of which are test generation, piloting, and trialling.

Based on a conceptual framework of some of the most important factors coming into play when language performance is examined through rater-mediated assessment, my focus in this paper was on the productive sections of the TestDaF, in particular the Writing section. Through exemplary analyses of rating data taken from a typical TestDaF examination, I investigated the psychometric quality of the ratings provided by 29 raters on the writing performance of 1,677 examinees. The main findings can be summarised as follows:

1. The many-facet Rasch measurement model proved to be a highly suitable approach to a fine-grained analysis and evaluation of the Writing performance ratings.

2. The performance ratings allowed separation of the group of examinees into a sufficiently large number of statistically distinct levels of language proficiency. There were about five such levels, which was one level more than the number of TestDaF levels used to characterise examinees'

performance. That is, the overall level of precision of the examinee proficiency estimates was satisfactorily high.

3. The nine scoring criteria worked together in constructing a single summary measure of writing proficiency; that is, this set of criteria proved to be unidimensional.

4. The TDN rating scale functioned as a 4-point scale, with scale categories appropriately ordered and clearly distinguishable.

5. Overall, the raters were internally consistent. Yet, they strongly differed in the severity/leniency with which they scored examinee performance.

In light of the marked differences in rater severity found in this analysis as well as in related research conducted in language and non-language domains, one of the questions that arises refers to the factors that are responsible for these differences. Potential sources of rater variability include raters' professional background (e.g. years spent as a teacher/examiner in the field of German as a foreign language), interpretation of scoring criteria (e.g. the differential importance attached to criteria), scoring styles (i.e. cognitive, reading/listening, or decision-making styles), and many others.

A major focus of earlier research dealing with rater variability was on the expertise effect; for example, researchers compared expert vs. lay raters, raters differing in professional background, or raters differing in scoring proficiency. Thus, significant differences between raters were found in (a) the weighting of performance features (Chalhoub-Deville 1995, Lumley 2002), (b) the perception as well as the application of assessment criteria (Brown 1995, Meiron & Schick 2000, Schoonen, Vergeer, & Eiting 1997), and (c) the use of general vs. specific performance features (Wolfe, Kao, & Ranney 1998).

In my own research, I recently examined *rater types*, that is, classes of raters that are characterised by distinctive patterns of attaching importance to routinely used scoring criteria. Using a cluster-analytic methodology, I identified a small set of rater types, each with a different focus on a subset of scoring criteria (Eckes 2008). Some types even evidenced complementary ways of attaching importance to criteria. For example, raters forming one large cluster focused on criteria referring to the treatment of the task and to linguistic realisation, whereas raters forming another large cluster focused on criteria referring to global impression. Research along these lines may eventually provide deeper insight into the intricate nature of rater variability.

Acknowledgements

I would like to thank my colleagues at the TestDaF Institute for many stimulating discussions on various issues revolving around the TestDaF quality assurance process. Special thanks go to Gabriele Kecker for thoughtful comments on an earlier version of this chapter.

Note

1 According to Linacre (2002), *outfit* values falling outside the 0.5–1.5 fit range are less of a threat to measurement than exceedingly large (or small) *infit* values. Moreover, *misfit* is generally deemed to be more problematic than *overfit* (Myford & Wolfe 2003).

References

Althaus, H J (2004) Der TestDaF [The TestDaF], in DAAD (Ed.), *Die internationale Hochschule: Ein Handbuch für Politik und Praxis* [The international university: A handbook for politics and practice] (Vol. 8, pp. 80–87). Bielefeld, Germany: Bertelsmann.

Andrich, D (1978) A rating formulation for ordered response categories, *Psychometrika* 43, 561–573.

Bachman, L F (1990) *Fundamental considerations in language testing*, Oxford: Oxford University Press.

Bachman, L F, and Palmer, A S (1996) Language testing in practice: *Designing and developing useful language tests*, Oxford: Oxford University Press.

Bachman, L F, Lynch, B K, and Mason, M (1995) Investigating variability in tasks and rater judgements in a performance test of foreign language speaking, *Language Testing* 12, 238–257.

Barrett, S (2001) The impact of training on rater variability, *International Education Journal* 2, 49–58.

Bond, T G and Fox, C M (2007) *Applying the Rasch model: Fundamental measurement in the human sciences* (2nd edition), Mahwah, NJ: Erlbaum.

Brennan, R L (2001) *Generalizability theory*, New York: Springer.

Brown, A (1995) The effect of rater variables in the development of an occupation-specific language performance test, *Language Testing* 12, 1–15.

Chalhoub-Deville, M (1995) Deriving oral assessments scales across different tests and rater groups, *Language Testing* 12, 17–33.

Council of Europe (2001) *Common European framework of reference for languages: Learning, teaching, assessment*, Cambridge: Cambridge University Press.

Cronbach, L J, Gleser, G C, Nanda, H, and Rajaratnam, N (1972) *The dependability of behavioral measurements: Theory of generalizability for scores and profiles*, New York: Wiley.

Eckes, T (2003) Qualitätssicherung beim TestDaF: Konzepte, Methoden, Ergebnisse [Quality assurance for TestDaF: Concepts, methods, results], *Fremdsprachen und Hochschule* 69, 43–68.

Eckes, T (2004) Facetten des Sprachtestens: Strenge und Konsistenz in der Beurteilung sprachlicher Leistungen [Facets of language testing: Severity and consistency in language performance assessments], in Wolff, A, Ostermann, T and Chlosta, C (Eds) *Integration durch Sprache* [Integration through language], Regensburg, Germany: FaDaF, 485–518.

Eckes, T (2005a) Evaluation von Beurteilungen: Psychometrische Qualitätssicherung mit dem Multifacetten-Rasch-Modell [Evaluation of ratings: Psychometric quality assurance via many-facet Rasch measurement], *Zeitschrift für Psychologie* 213, 77–96.

Eckes, T (2005b) Examining rater effects in TestDaF writing and speaking performance assessments: A many-facet Rasch analysis, *Language Assessment Quarterly* 2, 197–221.

Eckes, T (2006a) Multifacetten-Rasch-Analyse von Personenbeurteilungen [Many-facet Rasch analysis of person judgments], *Zeitschrift für Sozialpsychologie* 37, 185–195.

Eckes, T (2006b) Rasch-Modelle zur C-Test-Skalierung [Rasch models for C-tests], in Grotjahn, R. (Ed.) *Der C-Test: Theorie, Empirie, Anwendungen/The C-test: Theory, empirical research, applications*, Frankfurt: Lang, 1–44.

Eckes, T (2007) Konstruktion und Analyse von C-Tests mit Ratingskalen-Rasch-Modellen [Construction and analysis of C-tests with rating-scale Rasch models], *Diagnostica* 53, 68–82.

Eckes, T (2008) Rater types in writing performance assessments: A classification approach to rater variability, *Language Testing* 25, 155–185.

Eckes, T, Ellis, M, Kalnberzina, V, Pižorn, K, Springer, C, Szollás, K and Tsagari, C (2005) Progress and problems in reforming public language examinations in Europe: Cameos from the Baltic States, Greece, Hungary, Poland, Slovenia, France, and Germany, *Language Testing* 22, 355–377.

Eckes, T and Grotjahn, R (2006a) A closer look at the construct validity of C-tests, *Language Testing* 23, 290–325.

Eckes, T and Grotjahn, R (2006b) C-Tests als Anker für TestDaF: Rasch-Analysen mit dem kontinuierlichen Ratingskalen-Modell [C-tests as anchor for TestDaF: Rasch analyses using the continuous rating scale model], in Grotjahn, R (Ed.) *Der C-Test: Theorie, Empirie, Anwendungen/The C-test: Theory, empirical research, applications*, Frankfurt: Lang, 167–193.

Embretson, S E and Reise, S P (2000) *Item response theory for psychologists*, Mahwah, NJ: Erlbaum.

Engelhard, G Jr (1994) Examining rater errors in the assessment of written composition with a many-faceted Rasch model, *Journal of Educational Measurement* 31, 93–112.

Engelhard, G Jr (2002) Monitoring raters in performance assessments, in Tindal, G and Haladyna, T M (Eds), *Large-scale assessment programs for all students: Validity, technical adequacy, and implementation*, Mahwah, NJ: Erlbaum, 261–287.

Engelhard, G Jr and Myford, C M (2003) *Monitoring faculty consultant performance in the Advanced Placement English Literature and Composition Program with a many-faceted Rasch model* (College Board Research Report No. 2003–1), New York: College Entrance Examination Board.

Fischer, G H (2007) Rasch models, in Rao C R and Sinharay, S (Eds) *Psychometrics (Handbook of statistics)*, Amsterdam: Elsevier, 515–585.

Grotjahn, R (2004) TestDaF: Theoretical basis and empirical research in Milanovic, M and Weir, C J (Eds) *European language testing in a global context: Proceedings of the ALTE Barcelona Conference July 2001*, Cambridge, UK: UCLES/Cambridge University Press, 189–203.

Henning, G (1992) Dimensionality and construct validity of language tests, *Language Testing* 9, 1–11.

Klein-Braley, C (1996) Towards a theory of C-Test processing, in Grotjahn R (Ed.) *Der C-Test: Theoretische Grundlagen und praktische Anwendungen*, Bochum, Germany: Brockmeyer, 23–94.

Kondo-Brown, K (2002) A FACETS analysis of rater bias in measuring Japanese second language writing performance, *Language Testing* 19, 3–31.

Linacre, J M (1989) *Many-facet Rasch measurement*, Chicago: MESA Press.

Linacre, J M (2002) What do infit and outfit, mean-square and standardized mean? *Rasch Measurement Transactions* 16, 878.

Linacre, J M (2004) Optimizing rating scale category effectiveness, in Smith, E V and Smith R M (Eds) *Introduction to Rasch measurement*, Maple Grove, MN: JAM Press, 258–278.

Linacre, J M (2005a) *A user's guide to FACETS: Rasch-model computer programs* [Software manual], Chicago: Winsteps.com.

Linacre, J M (2005b) *A user's guide to WINSTEPS-MINISTEP: Rasch-model computer programs.* [Software manual], Chicago: Winsteps.com.

Linacre, J M and Wright, B D (2002) Construction of measures from many-facet data, *Journal of Applied Measurement* 3, 484–509.

Lumley, T (2002) Assessment criteria in a large-scale writing test: What do they really mean to the raters? *Language Testing* 19, 246–276.

Lumley, T and McNamara, T F (1995) Rater characteristics and rater bias: Implications for training. *Language Testing* 12, 54–71.

Lunz, M E and Linacre, J M (1998) Measurement designs using multifacet Rasch modelling, in Marcoulides, G A (Ed.) *Modern methods for business research*, Mahwah, NJ: Erlbaum, 47–77.

Lunz, M E and Stahl, J A (1993) The effect of rater severity on person ability measure: A Rasch model analysis, *American Journal of Occupational Therapy* 47, 311–317.

Lunz, M E and Wright, B D (1997) Latent trait models for performance examinations, in Rost, J and Langeheine, R (Eds.) *Applications of latent trait and latent class models in the social sciences*, Münster, Germany: Waxmann, 80–88.

Lunz, M E, Wright, B D and Linacre, J M (1990) Measuring the impact of judge severity on examination scores, *Applied Measurement in Education* 3, 331–345.

Lynch, B K and McNamara, T F (1998) Using G-theory and many-facet Rasch measurement in the development of performance assessments of the ESL speaking skills of immigrants, *Language Testing* 15, 158–180.

McNamara, T F (1996) *Measuring second language performance*, London: Longman.

Meiron, B E and Schick, L S (2000) Ratings, raters and test performance: An exploratory study, in Kunnan, A J (Ed.) *Fairness and validation in language assessment*, Cambridge: UCLES/Cambridge University Press, 153–174.

Messick, S (1989) Validity, in Linn, R L (Ed.) *Educational measurement* (3rd edition), New York: Macmillan, 13–103.

Messick, S (1995) Validity of psychological assessment: Validation of inferences from persons' responses and performances as scientific inquiry into score meaning, *American Psychologist* 50, 741–749.

Myford, C M and Wolfe, E W (2003) Detecting and measuring rater effects using many-facet Rasch measurement: Part I, *Journal of Applied Measurement* 4, 386–422.

Myford, C M and Wolfe, E W (2004), Detecting and measuring rater effects using many-facet Rasch measurement: Part II, *Journal of Applied Measurement* 5, 189–227.

Rasch, G (1980) *Probabilistic models for some intelligence and attainment tests*, Chicago: University of Chicago Press.

Schoonen, R, Vergeer, M and Eiting, M (1997) The assessment of writing ability: Expert readers versus lay readers, *Language Testing* 14, 157–184.

Wainer, H, Bradlow, E T and Wang, X (2007) *Testlet response theory and its applications*, Cambridge: Cambridge University Press.

Wang, W C and Chen, C T (2005) Item parameter recovery, standard error estimates, and fit statistics of the WINSTEPS program for the family of Rasch models, *Educational and Psychological Measurement* 65, 376–404.

Weigle, S C (1998) Using FACETS to model rater training effects, *Language Testing* 15, 263–287.

Wilson, M (2005) *Constructing measures: An item response modeling approach*, Mahwah, NJ: Erlbaum.

Wilson, M and Adams, R J (1995) Rasch models for item bundles, *Psychometrika* 60, 181–198.

Wolfe, E W (2004) Identifying rater effects using latent trait models, *Psychology Science* 46, 35–51.

Wolfe, E W, Kao, C W and Ranney, M (1998) Cognitive differences in proficient and nonproficient essay scorers, *Written Communication* 15, 465–492.

10 Problems affecting the use of raw scores: a comparison of raw scores and FACETS' Fair Average scores

David Coniam
The Chinese University of Hong Kong

Abstract

This paper examines the effect on the grades assigned to test takers either directly through the use of raters' raw scores, or through the use of scores obtained through the use of a statistical method of analysis such as multi-faceted Rasch measurement (MFRM). Using data from a Hong Kong oral examination, the current study examines how test takers' grades differ by comparing the results of grades from 'lenient' raters as against those of 'severe' raters on the two systems for assigning grades – raw band scores and MFRM-derived scores. Examination of the results of a pair of raters who exhibited the greatest range of severity in their rating of the same set of test takers indicates that the use of raw scores may produce widely different results from those obtained via MFRM. In the case of the more lenient rater, 54% of this rater's test takers would have received a significantly higher grade on the basis of raw scores. In contrast, in the case of the more severe rater, only 8% of test takers would have received a significantly higher grade while 8% would have received a significantly *lower* grade. As band scales will be used extensively in the Hong Kong public examinations system from 2007 onwards, the paper concludes with a call for attention to be given to the manner in which test takers' final grades may be derived from assessors' raw scores.

Introduction

The study in this paper examines the use of raw scores – obtained from raters on an oral test for Grade 11 test takers in Hong Kong. This study addresses an issue discussed by Weir (2005; see also Weir and Shaw in this volume) on the notion of scoring validity. In a closing comment in his address at the 2005 ALTE Conference, concerning the use of raw scores being a very imperfect measure of test taker ability, Weir stated to the effect that '. . . if FACETS is not being used in the evaluation of writing tests, I would want to know why not!'.

With one major exception (see Note 1), rating scales have never been a feature of the assessment scene in Hong Kong, where test takers are evaluated on holistic, norm-referenced scales during tests of spoken and written proficiency. Hong Kong is, however, about to undergo drastic changes to the English language elements of the examination system in 2007 (SCOLAR 2003) through the adoption of a standards-referenced, rather than a norm-referenced, approach to assessment, with scales and descriptors being adopted for rating test taker performance in English language examinations.

In Hong Kong English language examinations, results emerge directly from raters' raw scores. While these may be adjusted for mean and standard deviation on the basis of correlations with other papers, essentially, the result is the raw score. The potential for raw scores to provide accurate information about test takers has long been questioned. McNamara (1996:118), for example, states: 'It is clear that raw scores may be an unreliable guide to ability'. Likewise Eckes (2005), an ALTE 2005 presenter, in his discussion of quality control over the German TestDaF test, elaborated on the value of FACETS in analysing test takers' performance on the Speaking and Writing components of the TestDaF test (see previous paper in this volume).

Raters and raw scores

The problems associated with the use of raw scores are not, of course, new, and have been discussed by many researchers. McNamara (1996:122) presents a cogent discussion of some of the problems associated with the use of raw scores. Referring to studies by Linacre (1989) and Diederich, French and Carlton (1961), he illustrates the variability in raw scores awarded to test takers. In Diederich et al, French and Carlton's work, where 300 papers at a US university were graded by a number of raters, 94% of these papers received at least seven grades (on a 9-point scale).

There are many reasons why test takers' eventual raw scores may result in a wide range. McNamara (1996), for example, attributes some of the variability in raters' assessment to a range of causes: rater (mis)interpretation of the rating scales and descriptors, rater freshness (or tiredness), and interpersonal factors (albeit unintentional) where raters respond positively or negatively to certain gender, race, or personality types. Research conducted by Hamp-Lyons (1989) suggested that raters responded to cultural differences in writing, which was, in part, attributable to their own cultural and experiential background. Vann, Lorenz and Meyer (1991) relayed raters' responses to their sex as well as the academic discipline they were from. Vaughan (1991) illustrated how raters' reactions to different language features resulted in different grades being awarded to essays.

Hamp-Lyons (1991) discusses the effect the task, or prompt, may have on the piece of writing produced. Weigle (2002) discusses the different rating scales used (content, organisation etc.) which direct raters in their assessment and the effect these have on a grade awarded. Other factors Weigle (2002) mentions as possibly intruding are contextual factors such as the time of day of the rating sessions, whether rating is conducted individually or in groups and the type of training given to raters.

McNamara (1996) suggests that the above-mentioned issues (which may affect test taker performance) are *facets*, which can (or indeed should) be taken into account, and be modelled when assessing test takers in performance tests. This is especially the case with the latter type of test, where many more factors need to be considered unlike, for example, when a test consists of discrete multiple-choice test items. With fixed-response test items – for which a limited set of answers are possible – there are likely to be few extraneous factors to be taken account of.

To examine this issue of raw scores, and how test takers' grades compare when rated by a severe as opposed to a lenient rater, data was extracted from a study conducted on a Hong Kong secondary school's Grade 11 mock public oral examination in March 2004.

The Hong Kong school and examination system

Hong Kong's model of education practice, although currently undergoing substantial revisions, is modelled on the old British system. There are six years of primary school, and secondary school operates on a 5+2 model with students being banded, or streamed, on entry to secondary school. There are three broad bands of ability, with each band covering approximately 33% of the student ability range.

Hong Kong's major public examination for all school students is the Hong Kong Certificate of Education (HKCE) examination. This is taken at the end of Secondary 5 (Grade 11), with a yearly candidature for English language in the region of 100,000. There are four papers in the HKCE – Reading; Writing; Integrated Reading, Writing and Listening; and an Oral test. The HKCE Oral constitutes an example of a 'weak' performance test (see e.g., McNamara's (1996:44)); i.e., a task which resembles a real-world task, but one nonetheless where the focus is on the language generated rather than on the accomplishment of the task itself. The Oral lasts about 10 minutes per test taker and consists of two parts.

The first part of the test consists of a 'role play' exercise where a test taker has to obtain information from one examiner and then relay that information to the other examiner.

The second part consists of a group interaction/discussion between four test takers. Test takers are provided with a prompt and given 2 minutes' preparation time to think about the task, and what they are going to say. Test takers may take the points suggested in the prompt as a starting point, but are not constrained by these points. After 6 minutes of discussion have elapsed, the discussion is brought to a halt and that is the end of the Oral part of the HKCE test. Figure 1 (taken from the 2002 HKCE examination) presents a typical prompt.

Figure 1: 2002 HKCE Oral examination, Part 2: Group discussion

Your school is planning to have a special day to welcome new exchange students from overseas. Your group is helping to plan the day. You may want to talk about:

* Suitable activities
* Information to give the new exchange students about the school
* How to decorate the school
* How to get other students involved
* Anything else you think is important

Both parts of the HKCE Oral test are assessed independently by two examiners, and are – currently – pattern-marked on a single norm-referenced 7-point scale, with raters having to adhere quite closely to a specified pattern. Having to conform to a pattern mitigates, to an extent, the issue of severity/leniency since there are only so many high or low grades a rater may award. This will change, however, in 2007 when rating scales are adopted and raters are not constrained to a pattern.

The research design

In order to provide a limited but focused perspective, discussion will centre on the group discussion task. This is the less structured and, hence, more subjective of the two tasks. It is hypothesised that if divergence between raters is to become apparent, it would be more likely to emerge in the more subjective part of the test, rather than in the role play part, which is restricted through a set of fairly constrained questions and answers.

Subjects

Subjects were the entire Secondary 5 (Grade 11, age 16) cohort of a local average ability girls' school. There were five classes, a total of 181 test takers who were taking the exam as their mock examination, held at the end of March, before the live examination in June.

Raters

Raters (N=18) were English language teaching majors in their fourth and final year of a B.Ed. programme in ELT from a local university. They therefore had an appreciation and understanding of the English language capabilities of Hong Kong secondary students having been through the system themselves and having had a number of teaching practicum attachments to schools during their university course.

To prepare for the assessment sessions, raters were first trained and standardised. After having familiarised themselves thoroughly with the scales and descriptors, raters attended a half-day session of training and standardisation where they watched and rated a number of videotaped recordings of Grade 11 students taking previous HKCE oral tests. Finally, 16 of the 18 raters were randomly assigned to eight paired groups. The remaining two raters served as checkmarkers, providing 'data contact points' for FACETS (see below).

Assessment sessions usually lasted half a day, with a pair of raters typically assessing five or six groups of test takers (around 24 test takers).

Input prompts

The materials used were drawn from a past paper – the 2002 HKCE Oral. Seven different sets of material were used (along the lines of Figure 1 above), on the basis of advice from the HKEAA as to which prompts had worked well from feedback from raters who had used them. Arrangements had been made so that students would not have been exposed to any of these prompts before the oral test in the current study. Different sets of materials were used so that test takers might not pass on any of the content of the different oral tests to their classmates.

Assessment criteria

Four sub-scales and descriptors were used in the group discussion part of the test. These sub-scales were adapted from a validated test, the *ICAO* (International Civil Aviation Organization, 2003) language proficiency requirements, since the ICAO scales include generally accepted scales such as *Pronunciation*, *Vocabulary*, *Grammar* and *Interaction*.

The sub-scales each had six levels, ranging from 1 (indicating weakness) to 6 (indicating good ability).

Data analysis

A comparison of two composite scores was conducted. One score was produced simply as the total average band score obtained from the four raw sub-scale scores. The second score was obtained through multi-faceted Rasch measurement (MFRM), and involves the Fair Average score generated by the multi-faceted Rasch analysis computer program FACETS (Linacre 1994).

In MFRM, the measurement scale is derived by application of the Rasch model such that various phenomena – rater severity–leniency levels, rating scale difficulty, test taker ability, for example – can be modelled, allowing different features to be examined and their effects controlled. Rater behaviour was therefore conducted using a three-faceted model – raters, test takers and materials. While the focus of the study is on the rater, the different input prompt materials are a facet in the equation since the easiness/difficulty of the materials themselves will consequently have a bearing on the final band computed for each test taker.

The Fair Average score produced by FACETS involves converting the logit measure back onto the original rating scale metric. While Linacre (1997:550) notes that 'exact computation of the rating scale characteristic curve is arduous and error-prone', the Fair Average score does render the output more easily interpretable by end-users. Since it is presented in the format of the input sub-scale scores, it can be directly compared with the raters' raw scores.

Results and discussion

The analysis in this section centres, as mentioned, around the group discussion part of the Oral test, with discussion consisting of an examination of the differences between test taker scores using the two different methods of arriving at a final score, i.e., the average raw score of the four band scales compared with the Fair Average score provided by FACETS. Results are presented for one pair of raters only: the pair of raters who showed the widest degree of divergence in terms of leniency/severity between each other.

Table 1 presents the results for the raters derived through MFRM. In this Table, Column 3 presents the infit mean square statistic, which describes model fit – for which acceptable practical limits of fit have been stated as 0.5 for the lower limit and 1.5 for the upper limit (see Lunz and Stahl 1990, Weigle 1998 for a discussion of limits of fit).

Of the 16 raters, 14 were within acceptable degrees of fit on both parts of the test. Two fell outside acceptable limits, however, with an infit mean square above 1.5. The analysis was therefore run again, with these two raters omitted. (The data in Table 1 presents the reworked data, i.e., with the

Table 1: Raters' results

Measure (logits)	Model error	Infit mean square	Rater	Comment
+0.34	0.13	1.0	81	most severe rater
+0.21	0.13	1.1	41	
−0.25	0.13	0.7	21	
−0.31	**0.13**	**1.2**	**71**	**paired with rater 72 – tendency to severity**
−0.63	0.13	1.1	42	
−0.92	0.13	0.7	22	
−1.03	0.14	1.0	32	
−1.20	0.13	0.7	11	
−1.24	0.13	1.0	62	
−1.33	0.13	1.1	31	
−1.51	0.13	0.9	12	
−1.72	**0.13**	**1.5**	**72**	**paired with rater 71 – tendency to leniency**
−2.11	0.13	1.1	61	
−3.41	0.13	0.8	51	most lenient rater
−1.08	0.13	1.0	Mean	
0.94	0.00	0.2	S.D.	

RMSE 0.13 Adj S.D. 0.93 Separation 7.13 Reliability 0.98

Fixed (all same) chi-square: 738.2 d.f.: 13 significance: .00

misfitting raters omitted.) The fit statistics for the data above therefore indicate that the raters' judgements can be taken as being sufficiently reliable for the purposes of the current study.

Looking at Column 1 (measure logits), it can be seen that the raters show quite a spread of leniency, extending from the most severe rater at 0.34 logits (Rater 81), to the most lenient (Rater 51) at −3.41. While the range of rater severity is wide, the reliability of 0.98 indicates that raters are being reliably separated into different levels of severity.

An analysis of the data will now be presented with regard to test takers' overall band awarded compared with the Fair Average score. The analysis presented is based on the pair of raters who rated the same test takers and who showed the widest severity differential; these were Rater 71, with a measure of −0.31, and her partner Rater 72, with a more lenient measure of −1.72 logits. Their results are presented in bold type in Table 1 above.

In Table 2 below, Column 2 contains the Fair Average score generated by FACETS. Two sets of data are provided for Raters 71 and 72. The first column for each rater contains the rater's average raw band score from the four rating sub-scales; the second column presents the difference between the Fair Average score and the average raw band score. A positive figure in a rater's second column indicates that the test taker would have received a higher (i.e., more lenient) score from that rater. A negative figure indicates a lower score, a more severe rating.

Table 2: Paired raters 71 and 72 (N=24)

Test taker	Fair average (FA)	Rater 71 (tendency to severity)		Rater 72 (tendency to leniency)	
		Average raw band score	Raw score minus FA	Average raw band score	Raw score minus FA
5407	3.1	3.3	+0.20	3.5	+0.20
5113	3.3	3.5	+0.20	3.3	.00
5231	3.0	3.5	+0.50	3.0	.00
5340	2.9	3.0	+0.10	3.0	+0.10
5535	2.7	2.3	−0.40	3.0	+0.30
5103	3.4	2.8	−0.60	3.8	+0.40
5337	3.1	2.8	−0.30	3.5	+0.40
5218	2.9	2.8	−0.10	3.3	+0.40
5219	2.9	3.3	+0.40	3.3	+0.40
5342	2.6	3.0	+0.40	3.0	+0.40
5536	4.0	3.3	−0.70	4.5	+0.50
5338	3.3	3.0	−0.30	3.8	+0.50
5408	2.8	2.5	−0.30	3.3	+0.50
5107	2.8	2.8	.00	3.3	+0.50
5532	2.8	2.8	.00	3.3	+0.50
5230	1.7	2.0	+0.30	2.3	+0.60
5112	4.3	4.3	.00	5.0	+0.70
5111	3.0	3.0	.00	3.8	+0.80
5220	3.2	3.5	+0.30	4.0	+0.80
5533	2.9	3.0	+0.10	3.8	+0.90
5534	3.1	3.8	+0.70	4.0	+0.90
5109	2.7	3.0	+0.30	3.8	+1.10
5531	3.3	3.0	−0.30	3.5	+0.20
5221	3.3	3.5	+0.20	4.5	+1.20

As can be seen from Table 2, the tendency to 'severity' or 'leniency' is confirmed in the results that test takers would have received from individual raters. Comparing the raw score against the Fair Average scores, it can be seen that with Rater 71, 12 (50%) of her test takers would have received a lower grade, 4 (16%) the same grade and 8 (32%) a higher grade. In contrast, only 2 (8%) of Rater 72's test takers would have received a lower grade, whereas 20 (83%) would have received a higher grade. Two test takers (8%) would have received the same grade.

I would now like to explore further the extent to which the variation apparent in Table 2 above might be significant in determining a test taker's score.

As mentioned (see Note 1), band scales are only used on one test in Hong Kong – the English language teachers' Language Proficiency Assessment of Teachers (LPAT). On the test components that comprise the English language teachers' LPAT, test takers must reach level 3 of the 5-point scale on every scale, although they are permitted a 2.5 on *one* scale and still awarded a

Table 3: Summary of Fair Average scores versus raw average band scores

Leniency/Severity picture	Rater 71 (→ severity)	Rater 72 (→ leniency)
More lenient by half a band or more	**2**	**13**
More lenient by less than half a band	10	9
Same score	4	2
More severe by less than half a band	6	0
More severe by half a band or more	**2**	**0**
Total number of ratings	24	24
More lenient cases (total)	12 (50%)	22 (92%)
More severe cases (total)	8 (33%)	0 (0%)
More lenient cases (> 0.5 band)	2 (8%)	13 (54%)
More severe cases (> 0.5 band)	2 (8%)	0 (0%)

Pass (HKEAA 2001). Obtaining two 2.5 level scores, or indeed any level 2 or lower score, results in an automatic failure grade being awarded on the LPAT.

Further justification for half a band on the Hong Kong LPAT being taken as a determinant of 'notable difference' lies in the fact that the standard error of measurement (SEM) for the LPAT Speaking Test is approximately half a band (HKEAA, personal communication). This is very comparable to the SEM for the Speaking component of IELTS, where, for the IELTS 2003 examination, the SEM was stated to be 0.46 of a band (IELTS 2004).

Table 3 provides a summary of the differences between the Fair Average scores produced by MFRM and those produced from the two raters' average raw band scores. The cells in Table 3 (in bold font) indicate whether the grade arrived at between the two methods of analysis differs by half a band or more.

As can be seen from Table 3, if a score difference of less than half a band lies within acceptable bounds, 20 of Rater 71's test takers and 12 of Rater 72's test takers would have received a grade using MFRM that would not have affected their score on a test such as the LPAT. In the case of the rest of the test takers scored by Rater 72, however, (the more lenient rater), 13 test takers (54%) would have been rated more than half a band higher. Rater 71 had two test takers (8%) who would have received a higher score by half a band, and two test takers (8%) who would have received a score lower by half a band.

The implications of the differences between the two systems of rating are apparent: if a test taker were rated by a lenient rater such as Rater 72 as opposed to a severe rater such as Rater 71, the use of raw scores means that one test taker might 'pass' the test while the other might well 'fail'. This issue has been discussed in the context of the Hong Kong LPAT (see Coniam and Falvey 2001) where simple raw scores are used to determine a final grade, and where one half-band score did in fact result in failure.

Although the data has not been presented, it will be appreciated that a comparison of the most severe rater overall in Table 1 (Rater 81) versus the most lenient rater (Rater 51) results in an even more extreme picture of who would have received higher, or lower, grades.

Conclusion

The study described in this paper has examined the use of raw scores in the application of scales and descriptors to an oral test, where four test takers engage in a group discussion. The study has illustrated how the use of raw scores and scores derived through multi-faceted Rasch measurement (MFRM) produce substantially different results. The grades of two raters who assessed the same set of test takers were markedly different when the two methods of analysis were contrasted. Fifty-four per cent of the most lenient rater's test takers would have received a grade higher by half a band when this rater's raw scores were compared with MFRM-derived scores, with no test taker receiving a grade lower by half a band or more. In contrast, while only 8% of the most severe rater's test takers would have received a grade higher by half a band, 8% would also have received a grade lower by half a band.

Given the results discussed in the current paper, as Hong Kong moves towards adopting the use of scales and descriptors in rating test takers in its English language examinations when a standards-referenced approach to assessment is adopted in 2007, this issue of raw scores and consequent disparity of results through rater severity is one which merits substantial consideration.

Further, while the current study has focused on the assessment of English in English language examinations, the use of raw band scales will extend far beyond English language alone and will eventually be used in Hong Kong for many school subjects. The concerns raised in this study have potentially wider currency therefore than solely with respect to English language as an examined subject. Returning to Weir's concerns for scoring validity (2005), and the problems inherent to the use of raw scores, it is crucial that steps be taken to either complement the reliability of raw scores, or to explore viable alternatives for determining test results. Bennett & Taylor (2004), for example, discuss a mixed-mode method in the context of the Australian New South Wales Higher School Certificate. On this exam, test taker marks are aligned with a standards-referenced performance scale by the application of a structured multi-stage Angoff-based standards-setting procedure (involving teams of experienced teacher-judges who determine the raw scores that correspond best to each performance band).

The discussion in the current paper has a number of limitations. For one thing, the study was an experimental one where specially trained student teachers – rather than experienced raters – performed the rating. The set of scales and descriptors used (albeit a validated set) was also not Hong Kong-based. It was not possible, however, to use a Hong Kong set of scales and descriptors since none will be available until 2007, when a standards-referenced approach to assessment is adopted. Further, the discussion of the data sample discussed has been purposely limited to a single pair of raters – those who exhibited the most variation. What would be very revealing would be a more extensive study – conducted with the introduction of standards-referencing in 2007 in which scores were calculated for all possible combinations of raters rating all test takers using logit values. This would then provide a more systematic account of how much raw scores diverge from MFRM-derived scores.

Note

1. The one exception where scales and descriptors are currently used in a Hong Kong English language examination is the Language Proficiency Assessment of Teachers (LPAT) test for English language teachers (Government of the Hong Kong Special Administrative Region 2000). The test consists of five papers. Of these, Speaking, Writing and the Classroom Language Assessment test (a performance test conducted in a teacher's live classroom) are rated using scales and descriptors, with raw marks determining the final score. On the Speaking, Writing and the Classroom Language Assessment test components, LPAT test takers must reach level 3 of the 5-point scale on every scale, although they are permitted a 2.5 on *one* scale and still awarded a Pass (HKEAA 2001). Obtaining any level 2 score results in an automatic failure grade being awarded.

References

Arkoudis, S and O'Loughlin, K (2004) Tensions between validity and outcomes: teacher assessment of written work of recently arrived immigrant ESL students, *Language Testing* 21, 284–304.

Bennett, J and Taylor, C (2004) Is assessment for learning in a high stakes environment a reasonable expectation? Third Conference for the Association of the Commonwealth, Examination and Accreditation Bodies, Fiji, FIJI 8 – 12 March 2004, available at <http://www.spbea.org.fj/aceab_conference. html>

Brown, A (1995) The effect of rater variables in the development of an occupation-specific language performance test, *Language Testing* 12, 1–15.

Coniam, D and Falvey, P (1999) The English language benchmarking initiative: A validation study of the Classroom Language Assessment component, *Asia Pacific Journal of Language in Education* 2, 1 35.

Coniam, D and Falvey, P (2002) Does student language ability affect the assessment of teacher language ability? *Journal of Personnel Evaluation in Education*, 16, 269–285.

Coniam, D and Falvey, P (2001) Awarding passes in the Language Proficiency Assessment of English Language Teachers: Different methods, varying outcomes, Education Journal 29, 23–35.

Diederich, P B, French, J W, and Carlton, S T (1961) *Factors in the judgment of writing quality*, Princeton, NJ: Educational Testing Service.

Eckes, T (2005) Assuring the quality of TestDaF examinations, paper presented at the ALTE Second International Conference Berlin 19–21 May 2005.

Government of the Hong Kong Special Administrative Region (2000) *Language Benchmark Assessment for Teachers – English Language: Syllabus Specifications, Explanatory Notes, Specimen Questions with Suggested Answers, Scales and Descriptors*, Hong Kong: Government Printer.

Hamp-Lyons, L (1989) Second language writing: assessment issues, in Kroll, B (Ed.) *Second language writing*, Cambridge: Cambridge University Press.

Hamp-Lyons, L (1991) Pre-text: task-related influences on the writer, in Hamp-Lyons, L (Ed.) *Assessing second language writing in academic contexts*, Norwood, NJ: Ablex, 87–107.

International Civil Aviation Organization (ICAO) (2003) ICAO language proficiency rating scale, available at <http://www.miair.us/icao/scale.doc.pdf.>

International English Language Testing System (IELTS) (2004) Test performance 2003, available at: <http://www.ielts.org/teachersandresearchers/analysisoftestdata/article173.aspx.>

Linacre J M (1997) Communicating Examinee Measures as Expected Ratings, Rasch Measurement Transactions 11, 1: 550–551, available at <http://www.rasch.org/rmt/rmt111m.htm.>

Linacre, J M (1989) *Many-faceted Rasch Measurement*, Chicago: MESA Press.

Linacre, J M (1994) *FACETS: Rasch Measurement Computer Program*, Chicago: MESA Press.

Lunz, M E and Stahl, JA (1990) Judge consistency and severity across grading periods, *Evaluation and the Health Profession* 13, 425–444.

McNamara, T (1996) *Measuring second language performance*, New York: Longman.

SCOLAR (2003) *Action Plan to Raise Language Standards in Hong Kong*, Hong Kong: Government Printer.

Vann, R, Lorenz, F and Meyer, D (1991)Error gravity: Faculty responses to errors in the written discourse of nonnative speakers of English, in Hamp-Lyons, L (Ed.) *Assessing second language writing in academic contexts*, Norwood, NJ: Ablex, 181–195.

Vaughan, C (1991) Holistic assessment: What goes on in the writer's mind? in Hamp-Lyons, L (Ed.) *Assessing second language writing in academic contexts*,. Norwood, NJ: Ablex, 111–125.

Weigle, S C (1998) Using FACETS to model rater training effects, *Language Testing* 15, 263–287.

Weigle, S C (2002) *Assessing Writing*, Cambridge: Cambridge University Press.

Weir, C J (2005) A socio-cognitive approach to test validation, plenary paper presented at the ALTE Second International Conference Berlin 19–21 May 2005.

11 Testing teaching knowledge: developing a quality instrument to support professional development

University of Cambridge ESOL Examinations

Introduction

Cambridge ESOL has long been a major provider of high quality, internationally recognised awards for English language teachers. Many teachers have gained entrance to the ELT profession following successful completion of Cambridge Certificate in English Language Teaching to Adults (CELTA) courses, and thousands more have progressed to senior positions after passing the Cambridge Diploma in English Language Teaching to Adults (DELTA).

In recent years there has been large-scale educational reform in many countries across the world. English is now being taught much earlier in the curriculum. Consequently, many more English language teachers are needed, and many teachers of other subjects now find themselves needing to teach English. The existing Cambridge ESOL teaching awards require lengthy and/or intensive preparation courses, which, for practical reasons, may not be so attractive to many of this new generation of English language teachers. The high level of English language proficiency required by the existing awards might also be a barrier for some. In order to fulfil our mission of providing *'language learners and teachers in a wide variety of situations with access to a range of high quality international exams, tests and teaching awards, which will help them to achieve their life goals and have a positive impact on their learning and professional development experience'* (www. CambridgeESOL.org/about_us), it became clear that Cambridge ESOL needed to develop an alternative framework of teaching awards, and that this should cater more closely to the needs of teachers of English in a wide range of contexts around the world. Hence, the development of the Teaching Knowledge Test (TKT).

TKT and the Cambridge ESOL test development model

The development of TKT followed the Cambridge ESOL model of test development.[1] The model provides a rational and transparent basis for planning, managing, and auditing exams; links to professional standards (e.g. APA Standards 1999; the ALTE Code of Practice 1994, and other ALTE standards 2001, 2002); combines both theoretical and practical dimensions; and is iterative and cyclical.

In general, the development of a new exam starts with a perceived need that is derived from an appraisal of the intended context of use and the relationship of the new exam to any existing products or areas of expertise. Once the need is defined, planning starts to establish a clear picture of who the potential candidates are likely to be and who the users of the test results will be. Initial specifications are then drafted, sample materials written and reactions sought. This is followed by a trialling phase where concrete views and significant evidence are collected to demonstrate test usefulness. Based on the trialling results, modifications take place, test specifications reach their final form, test materials are written, and test papers are constructed. Once the exam goes live, results are monitored across a number of years, regular stakeholder feedback is gathered, and instrumental research is conducted to investigate various aspects of candidate and examiner performance to see what improvement might be needed.

With regards to TKT, in 2002 Cambridge ESOL sent out questionnaires to various teacher training institutions worldwide in order to elicit reactions to the development of a new test for teachers which would be quite different in format and concept from the existing Cambridge ESOL teaching awards. Considerable interest was expressed, which in turn led to a series of visits by Cambridge ESOL's Development Managers to countries throughout Latin America, East Asia, the Middle East and Europe. Potential partner organisations were identified and regular meetings took place both in Cambridge and overseas. This process of consultation continued up to the first half of 2004, and enabled Cambridge ESOL to develop TKT in such a way that is relevant to teachers working in different educational sectors in a wide range of countries.

In 2003 a working group, consisting of Cambridge ESOL staff and external consultants with considerable experience in teacher education and test development, was established. The group met regularly to elaborate the TKT syllabus and produce materials. This was an iterative process, with each version of the syllabus being sent out for review by teacher development professionals who have experience of working in the countries where interest in TKT has been expressed. Revisions to the syllabus were made, and materials writers were commissioned to produce test items to cover the revised syllabus. At various points in the development cycle, test materials were field tested in key countries. Further revisions, consultation and trialling followed until the development team was confident that the product met the needs of all the interested parties, and that it would be possible to achieve dependable coverage of the syllabus areas in the construction of live test versions.

The following section describes how teaching knowledge has been defined and operationalised in TKT.

TKT construct definition and operationalisation

The construct

During the planning and design phases of TKT, several questions arose over the nature of the teaching knowledge we are attempting to measure, and how this knowledge could be defined. When employers recruit teachers for a certain classroom, what do they expect these teachers to know? To find answers to these queries, a review of the literature was conducted focusing on models of teaching knowledge.

The literature survey revealed that Shulman (1986), Grossman (1990), and Day & Conklin (1992) share similar views as to key components of teaching knowledge. These are best summarised in Tsui & Nicholson (1999) as follows:

- *Subject matter knowledge*, i.e., knowledge of the concepts and terminology of a subject discipline; the understanding of the facts, concepts, substantive and syntactic structures of a subject discipline.
- *General pedagogic knowledge*, i.e., knowledge of general principles (strategies, beliefs and practices) of teaching and learning which are applicable across subject disciplines.
- *Pedagogic content knowledge*, i.e., specialised knowledge of how to represent content/subject matter knowledge in diverse ways that students can understand (e.g. through examples, analogies).
- *Knowledge of context*, i.e., knowledge of social, cultural and institutional contexts in which teaching and learning takes place.

The literature review also showed a movement from conceiving teaching knowledge as focusing on the conceptual and analytical to one that is conceptualised in terms of its situated and experiential nature. This movement derives from work by Schon (1983) whose conception of professional knowledge was of 'knowing in action'. He proposed that practitioners who find themselves in situations that are ill-defined, messy and full of uncertainties (e.g. the classroom) make sense of these through reference to experience, trial and error, intuition and muddling through. He also proposed that this kind of knowledge is developed through reflection, i.e., looking at a problem or phenomenon after or during action, and from that arriving at a new understanding. Schon's conceptualisation of teaching knowledge focuses on the practitioner 'knowing' in a given situation. It has been very influential in EFL, and teacher education in particular. It emphasises the role of context and raises the question of what role conceptual or analytical knowledge plays in 'knowing in action'. Similarly, Freeman and Johnson (1998:397) argue that:

> . . . the core of the new knowledge-base must focus on the activity of teaching itself, it should centre on the teacher who does it, the contexts in which it is done, and the pedagogy by which it is done. Moreover this knowledge base should include forms of knowledge representation that document teacher learning within the social, cultural and institutional contexts in which it occurs.

They see a risk that through teacher education, language educators may encourage teacher-learners to substitute received knowledge for knowing in action. Context becomes the location in which and the means through which learning to teach takes place.

In focusing more on conceptual knowledge rather than on knowledge in action, TKT may risk being seen as recreating the 1970s view of teacher education in which a teacher in training was considered to need to learn subject knowledge and methodology and then apply these in the classroom. This view failed to recognise (a) that the what and the how of teaching are often inseparable and (b) what the teachers bring to their learning and the role of context in shaping and developing teaching knowledge.

However, Wallace (1991:15) suggests that conceptual knowledge makes up received knowledge which feeds into practice. This is illustrated in his model below:

Figure 1: Reflective model for teacher education

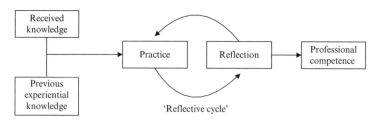

More recently, Tsui (2003:65) places conceptual knowledge in teachers' personal conceptions of teaching and learning. She says:

. . . teachers' personal conceptions of teaching and learning play a very important part in their management of teaching and learning. These personal conceptions are influenced by their personal life experiences, their learning experience, their teaching experience, their academic background as well as the opportunities for professional development, including professional courses.

We can therefore situate Grossman's (1990) categories and the construct of TKT within this wider understanding of teaching knowledge. The starting point for TKT development was a perceived need for an accessible and flexible tool that is relevant to an international candidature – a need that is not fully met by existing teaching awards which are lengthy and have a compulsory course component and/or compulsory teaching practice. Hence, the decision for TKT to be objective in format, modular in structure, and with no practical component. This design precludes the assessment of context which will vary from place to place and belong to that place. While TKT does not cater for 'knowing in action', it could be argued that it is not a course in teacher education and is not therefore concerned with modes of knowledge acquisition. Teacher education courses designed round the support of knowing in action are also likely to be resource hungry and therefore not offer an option open to many teacher education contexts. Through its suggestions for use of an unassessed portfolio, TKT does however recognise the value of and encourage reflection as an input to knowledge. Courses run for candidates wishing to take TKT may usefully choose to teach towards it by giving recognition in their course design to context and reflection, and perhaps be encouraged to do so.

To sum up, TKT covers three teaching knowledge areas, namely, subject knowledge, pedagogical knowledge, and pedagogical content knowledge. TKT does not assess knowledge of teaching context. This area is most appropriately assessed through teaching practice which forms part of the assessment of other existing teaching awards.

Test candidature

TKT is suitable for teachers of English and is intended for an international audience. Candidates taking TKT will normally have some experience of teaching English to speakers of other languages. TKT may also be taken by pre-service teachers, teachers who wish to refresh their teaching knowledge, or teachers who are moving to teaching English after teaching another subject.

To access TKT, teachers need a level of English of at least Level B1 of the Council of Europe's Common European Framework of Reference for

Languages (CEFR). TKT candidates are expected to be familiar with language relating to the practice of ELT.

Test format and delivery

TKT consists of three free-standing modules. The modules can be taken together in one examination session or separately, in any order, over three sessions. There is no aggregate score for candidates taking more than one module and candidates receive a certificate for each module that is taken.

TKT is task based and has a range of objective task types. As TKT tests candidates' knowledge of teaching rather than their proficiency in the English language or their performance in classroom situations, candidates are not required to listen, speak, or produce extended writing when taking TKT. Supporting materials include the TKT Glossary of ELT terms, the TKT Handbook and sample materials for each module. TKT candidates also have access to an electronic portfolio where they can maintain a record of their professional development and reflections on their teaching. Through this resource, candidates are encouraged to become reflective practitioners by analysing their teaching and how this impacts on their students' learning.

Module description

The testing syllabus for TKT has theoretical, practical and management strands, and covers universal aspects of what a successful teacher of English needs to know. The syllabus areas also apply to Cambridge ESOL's other teaching awards such as CELTA, DELTA and the In-Service Certificate in English Language Teaching (ICELT), but at TKT level teachers do not need to demonstrate such a wide and deep understanding of these. TKT is a test of professional knowledge about the teaching of English to speakers of other languages. This knowledge includes concepts related to language and language use, and the background to and practice of language learning and teaching. Below is a description of the focus of each module.

Module 1: Language and background to language learning and teaching
This module tests candidates' knowledge of terms and concepts common in English language teaching. It also focuses on the factors underpinning the learning of English and knowledge of the range and functions of the pedagogic choices the teacher has at their disposal to cater for these learning factors.

Module 2: Lesson planning and use of resources for language teaching
This module focuses on what teachers consider and do while planning their teaching of a lesson or series of lessons. Teaching in this context is intended also to refer to assessment. It focuses too on the linguistic and methodologi-

cal reference resources that are available to guide teachers in their lesson planning as well as on the range and function of materials and teaching aids that teachers could consider making use of in their lessons.

Module 3: Managing the teaching and learning process
This module tests candidates' knowledge of what happens in the classroom in terms of the language used by the teacher or learners, the roles the teacher can fulfil and the ways in which the teacher can manage and exploit classroom events and interaction.

In this section, we have discussed how teaching knowledge has been defined and operationalised in TKT in terms of test format and delivery, supporting materials, reporting of results and module focus. The subsequent section discusses how we have attempted to achieve quality assurance through field trialling, standard setting and continuous validation activities.

TKT and quality assurance

Field trials

During the development phase of TKT, test materials were trialled over an 18 month period. Local Education Authorities, Ministry Departments, State and Private Universities, and British Council Institutes in several countries in Latin America, Asia and Europe participated in the trials.

The main trialling stage took place between May and July 2004, and attracted over 1,000 participants. The sample was representative of the target candidature for TKT, consisting of both in-service and pre-service teachers, working with different age groups and with a range of teaching experience. Several instruments were used during the trials. In addition to full versions of all three TKT modules, a language test was used to enable us to gauge the extent to which candidate performance on TKT might be affected by language proficiency. The content of the language test reflected CEFR levels from A2 (KET) to C2 (CPE). Questionnaires were administered to key stakeholders and all participating teachers in order to gather feedback on the examination. In order to link performances to test taker characteristics, candidate information sheets were administered which enabled data collection on affecting variables such as age, gender, teaching experience, etc.

The following are the major findings from the field trials:

* *Reliability*. The trialled versions achieved high reliability figures of 0.9 with average facility values ranging from 0.72 to 0.81.
* *Language Proficiency*. The higher the candidates performed on the language test, the higher their performance was on TKT modules.

A paired sample t-test was used to show if significant differences occurred across modules. Significant differences occurred for PET and FCE level candidates in their performances on Modules 1 and 2 and 1 and 3 with the higher performance being on Module 1. More importantly, however, language proficiency did not appear to be an impeding factor. For example, candidates at CEFR A2 level (KET) scored 54%, 43% and 52% of the available total marks on Modules 1, 2 and 3 respectively. Candidates at CEFR B1 level (PET) scored 62.5%, 55% and 59% of the available total marks on Modules 1, 2 and 3 respectively.

- *Age.* There did not seem to be a pattern showing that performance on the Modules was affected by age. It was not possible, for example, to generalise that candidates at the higher end of the age scale perform better than those at the lower end of the scale or vice versa. To conclude, age did not seem to be a factor affecting performance.

- *Teaching Experience.* Years of teaching experience were grouped as follows: (a) 1 or less, (b) 2–5, (c) 6–10, (d) 11 or more. Candidates who had one or fewer years of experience performed significantly differently from candidates who had two years of experience and above on one module only (Module 1).

- *Stakeholder Feedback.* TKT appeared to be well received by test takers and end users. Positive feedback was received in terms of TKT content coverage, appropriacy, interest and relevance to local contexts. Potential candidates perceived sitting for an exam such as TKT to be a learning experience in itself. They welcomed the chance to reflect on their teaching practice and teaching knowledge. For example, a trainee teacher said: '*As a student and future teacher of English, I consider that we must be aware of the implications and responsibilities of our professional work. Tests like these are excellent to begin creating such awareness*'. A novice teacher in a primary state school said: '*Sometimes we overlook these aspects of our teaching, you got us to consciously brood upon them for a while. Thank you for giving us the opportunity to take the test. In my opinion, these kind of examinations are paramount to teaching and education as well*'. An experienced teacher in a state school said '*I think this test should be taken by all teachers of English. It's useful to polish our knowledge of English and covers different areas. Interesting, enjoyable and worth doing!*'

Standard setting

An exploratory standard setting activity was conducted to inform the reporting of results and the grading stage of TKT. A rich assembly of 10 judges with expertise in teacher training, rater-training, setting performance criteria, and language testing participated in the activity. Judges were asked to go through each module, answer each item and provide a rating on a 4-point difficulty scale with 1 being the easiest and 4 being the most difficult. Convergence and divergence between the ratings were discussed and a rationale for divergence was provided. Before deciding on a score range for each band, a comparison was made between the judges' ratings and IRT item statistics available from the aforementioned trials.

The activity proved to be very beneficial: in providing insights into item writing as far as the interaction between task format and content difficulty is concerned; in further refining candidates' profiles at each of the four bands; and in providing distinctive descriptors of knowledge of TKT content areas at each band.

Continuous validation activities

Cambridge ESOL continues to engage in a programme of research and validation activities in relation to TKT. Plans for continual improvement include studies monitoring or investigating:

a. the interaction between language level and test performance
b. the role of specialised professional knowledge and test performance
c. the executive processes and resources employed when answering test items
d. the impact on teacher training courses
e. the adaptation of TKT to another language.

Such validation activities are required to ensure that satisfactory standards are met in line with the established principles of good testing practice, covering validity, reliability, impact and practicality.

In this section, we have discussed how we attempted to achieve quality assurance as far as TKT is concerned. A logical follow-on from this section is a description of how Cambridge ESOL attempts to gather validity evidence as part of its commitment to provide quality products.

An evidence-based validity framework

The Cambridge ESOL model discussed earlier requires that adequate data is captured, stored, analysed and interpreted so that suitable evidence can be provided to stakeholders to support claims relating to the usefulness of the test for its intended purposes. This evidence is built up during the test design and development phases and continues to be collected as ongoing validation activities when the test is operational.

Figure 2 below illustrates a framework for building the validity argument.[2] It draws on the work of Messick (1994), Kane (1992), Kunnan (2004) and Bachman (2004) and is based on collaborative work in 2003–04 between the Research and Validation Group of Cambridge ESOL and the Centre for Research in Testing, Evaluation and Curriculum, University of Surrey Roehampton.

The underlying approach in this framework is socio-cognitive, in that:

- The abilities to be tested are mental constructs which are latent and within the brain of the test taker (the cognitive dimension).

- The interpretation and use of test results are social phenomena. The use of the test results in society can bring about intended and unintended consequences – both in educational and wider contexts.

Figure 2: A framework for building the validity argument

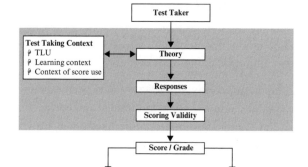

Weir (2005:48–49) developed key questions that are directly related to the above framework. He argues that test developers and users should address these questions when evaluating a test:

- Test Taker. *'How are the physical, psychological and experiential characteristics of test takers addressed?'*
- Test Taking Context. *'Are the contextual characteristics of the test task and its administration situationally fair to the test takers?'*
- Theory. *'Are the cognitive processes required to complete the tasks interactionally authentic?'*
- Scoring Validity. *'How far can we depend on the scores on the test?'*
- Consequential Validity. *'What impact does the test have on its various stakeholders?'*
- Criterion on related Validity. *'What external evidence is there that the test is doing a good job?'*

Conclusion

In spring 2005, Cambridge ESOL launched its new Teaching Knowledge Test (TKT) which offers teachers of English a stepping stone in their professional development journey, and could allow them to access higher-level teaching qualifications. This paper provides an account of how TKT was conceived, developed, and validated prior to its launch. It presents quality assurance procedures followed during TKT development, trialling, and live administration phases. The paper ends with a brief overview of a framework for gathering validity evidence.

Notes

1 Cambridge ESOL's well established set of test development procedures are fully described by Saville in chapter 2 of Weir & Milanovic 2003.
2 For a detailed discussion of the framework, see Weir 2005.

References

American Educational Research Association, American Psychological Association, & National Council on Measurement in Education (1999) *Standards for educational and psychological testing,* Washington, DC: Author.

Association of Language Testers in Europe (ALTE) (1994) *ALTE Code of Practice.*

Association of Language Testers in Europe (ALTE) (2001) *Principles of Good Practice.*

Association of Language Testers in Europe (ALTE) (2002) *ALTE Quality Management Checklists.*

Bachman, L F (2004) Building and supporting a case for test utilization, paper presented at Language Testing Research Colloquium, March 2004, Temecula, Ca.

Day, R R and Conklin, G (1992) The knowledge base in ESL/EFL teacher Education, paper presented at the 1992 TESOL Conference, Vancouver, Canada.

Freeman, D and Johnson, K (1998) Reconceptualizing the knowledge-base of language teacher education, *TESOL Quarterly* 32 (3).

Grossman, P (1990) *The Making of a Teacher,* New York: Teachers' College Press.

Kane, M T (1992) An argument-based approach to validity, *Psychological Bulletin* 112, 527–535.

Kunnan, A J (2004) Test Fairness, in Weir, C J and Milanovic, M (Eds) *European Language Testing in a Global Context,* Cambridge: UCLES/Cambridge University Press, 27–48.

Messick, S (1994) The interplay of evidence and consequences in the validation of performance assessments, *Educational Researcher,* 32, 13–23.

Saville, N (2003) The process of test development and revision within UCLES EFL, in Weir, C and Milanovic, M (2003) *Continuity and Innovation: Revising the Cambridge Proficiency in English Examination 1913–2002,* Cambridge: UCLES/Cambridge University Press, 57–120.

Schon, D A (1983) *The Reflective Practitioner*, London: Basic Books.

Shulman, L (1986) Those who understand knowledge growth in teaching, *Educational Researcher* 15 (2).

Tsui A (2003) *Understanding Expertise in Teaching*, Cambridge: Cambridge University Press.

Tsui, A and Nicholson, S (1999) A hypermedia database and English as a second language teaching knowledge enrichment, *Journal of Information Technology for Teacher Education* 8 (2).

Wallace, M (1991) *Training Foreign Language Teachers*, Cambridge: Cambridge University Press.

Weir, C J (2005) *Language Testing & Validation: An evidence-based approach*, Basingstoke: Palgrave Macmillan.

Weir, C J and Milanovic, M (2003) *Continuity and Innovation: Revising the Cambridge Proficiency in English Examination 1913–2002*, Cambridge: UCLES/Cambridge University Press.

12 The CERCLU project for certifying language competence in Italian university language centres

Maurizio Gotti – Università di Bergamo
Carol Taylor Torsello – Università di Padova

Abstract

In view of the recent university reform in Italy, the need has emerged to establish a system of certification valid in all Italian university language centres which would have full European recognition. Under the auspices of AICLU, the Italian Association of University Language Centres, the testing system known as CERCLU has been developed, in connection with similar initiatives launched by other members of the European Confederation of Language Centres in Higher Education, CERCLES.

CERCLU does not duplicate already existing certifications, as it tests two intermediate levels of language competence, B1 and B2 of the Common European Framework of Reference, in English and Italian, while reflecting the specific interests and needs of students in a university context.

The paper provides a description of the project and of the test as it stands today. The criteria followed in the creation of the tests are illustrated and the validation process is discussed. The modules of the tests for each skill are described and some samples are shown and commented upon. Problems relating to item weighting and evaluation are dealt with, as are some questions concerning the computer implementation of the tests. Finally, considerations regarding the future development of CERCLU are presented.

Background

The Italian university system has recently undergone an important reform, set in motion by a Ministerial decree (n. 509) of 1999. This reform has made knowledge of a second EU language compulsory for all students. They must show proof of possessing such knowledge in order to obtain the initial university *laurea* degree, which, under the new system, is typically achieved at the end of three years of study. The universities are obliged to ascertain that each student has the required language competence. The type and level of competence required and the means of evaluation to be applied have, however, been left to be established locally.

The result is that many faculties and degree courses are now, for the first time, facing the problem of whether or not, and to what degree, their students actually know a foreign language. They are also beginning to ask questions about the appropriate types of language competence that should be required, and about how to test them and what external certifications might be honoured.

In view of the national reform of 1999, the Italian Association of University Language Centres (AICLU) decided to set up a working-commission to prepare its own system for testing and certifying students' language competence in relation to the Common European Framework of Reference for Languages (CEFR), and gave it the name CERCLU (Gotti 2002, Taylor Torsello 2001). Language Centre Directors from the universities of Padua, Bergamo, Bologna, Siena, Cagliari, Verona, Trieste, Rome 3 and the Rome Institute for Motor Sciences were on this commission, and began work immediately. Of course one of the first problems they had to face was funding. At their request, each of these nine universities provided some initial money for the project. This made it possible to apply for and receive funding within the Italian Ministry's plan for internationalisation of the university system, which co-finances, on a 50–50 basis, important projects proposed by universities which contribute to the internationalisation of the system and involve at least one partner university of another country. Our partner university from outside Italy in the internationalisation project was Plymouth.

The more recent CampusOne programme for Italian universities, since it included foreign language certification as a prominent initiative, gave us another opportunity to bring resources to the project, as well as providing it with national recognition through CRUI – the Conference of Italian University Rectors. Those university language centres which were involved in developing the CERCLU project and included it in their programme for providing language certification had their projects approved and received funding. This was indeed an important recognition for CERCLU and for AICLU, and has brought our national association into close contact with CRUI, initiating a phase of positive co-operation for language-related matters which we see as extremely important for the future.

Description of the project

The aim of the CERCLU project is to make available to the member university language centres a system of assessing and certifying levels of proficiency in foreign languages, including Italian as a foreign language, which is particularly suitable to their needs. Indeed, English is the language studied by most students and required by most degree courses, and Italian must constantly be tested for the students on exchange programmes from other countries. The levels to be certified are those established by the CEFR as Level B1 (Threshold Level) and Level B2 (Vantage) (Council of Europe 1998, 2001a, 2001b), as these are the levels most commonly required throughout Italian universities in the various degree courses. CERCLU, in fact, caters for the specific needs of students in Italian universities, which also means that the texts, topics, and activities are chosen on the basis of their relevance to such students and to their situations. Furthermore, some differentiation is introduced between tests according to the disciplinary macro-area of the candidate: humanities, social sciences and physical sciences.

The CERCLU group wanted to create a criterion-referenced test – that is, one whose reference points are a set of common standards for well defined skills (Bachman 1990:72–76, Brown & Hudson 2002:10, Council of Europe 2001b:184, Lynch & Davidson 1997:263–274) rather than a norm-referenced assessment, where students are ranked in relation to their peers. This was seen as necessary to grant transparency and transferability of the results. The widely recognised standards of the CEFR seemed most suited for this purpose.

The CERCLU tests have been created in such a way as to achieve:

a) a constant typology of valid test-input (texts and related comprehension questions)
b) rapid administration
c) a limited-in-time testing process
d) computer assisted assessment
e) automatic interpretation of performance
f) automatic marking except for the productive skills
g) criterion-based and standardised interpretation and evaluation of productive performance.

A database of validated testing items has been created to be used, following established protocols, to create the tests to be administered in the individual centres. These protocols have been based on the models provided in Bachman & Palmer (1996), adapted to the situation of Italian university language teaching. Each item has a score, so that the candidates examined can be given clear information about their position relative to the level of the test they have taken. For both of the levels available, modules have been created corresponding to the four communicative skills (reading, writing, listening and speaking), and these can be evaluated separately. The choice to make it possible to use the modules separately as well as in combination derives from the specific reality of Italian universities, where skills are not always required at the same level. Clearly, however, the CERCLU certification will be awarded only on the basis of the results on all four skills, whereas scores can be supplied, for institutional purposes, on the individual modules.

From constructs to prototype

After an initial stage (2000–01) of research on testing and certification and of general planning of the action to be undertaken, the AICLU pilot group devised a set of constructs and created a complete, working prototype test for B1 and B2 levels both for English and Italian. Since the goal was a practical, flexible instrument able to measure the achievement of university students in English and Italian as foreign languages in relation to the communicative language abilities described in the CEFR statements for Levels B1 and B2, care was taken to give the tests the following characteristics:

a) They are task-based: that is, students are asked to perform tasks that reflect real-life situations, particularly of the domain of university life; they make use of authentic texts and aim at authenticity in the tasks.

b) They are modular: that is, the parts (or sub-tests) related to the four skills can be used singly or in the required combinations.

c) They are individualised: that is, options are made available relating to three major disciplinary domains.

d) They are web-based, computer administered, and, to the extent that this is possible, corrected automatically.

The first concern of the CERCLU project researchers was to construct tests tailored to the needs of their specific situation (Alderson, Clapham & Wall 1995:11–12, Bachman & Palmer 1996:88). The construct definition needed to specify the input (text types and related expected responses), and the relationship between the input and the observable product which is the candidate's response. These would then need to be kept constant in the realisation of each prototype by all the test writers, whose task would be to create a tool with which to measure the candidates' ability to do certain things in English or in Italian. The things the candidates would be asked to do needed to be specified for each level, and needed to reflect authentic behaviours which language users perform in real contexts. As a consequence, the first task was to list specific language functions particularly relevant to a student studying in a university where English or Italian is the language in which courses are taught. The next task was to determine the exam format to adopt in order to assess language competences and measure degrees of mastery in language activities specific to a university context. Subsequently, parameters which would make the different degrees of language mastery emerge clearly had to be identified.

For both levels, B1 and B2, the distinction into sub-tests linked to the four abilities – reading, listening, writing, speaking – has been maintained, so of course the authentic texts proposed have been distinguished by level. This has involved aspects of the texts themselves, such as their length and the index of frequency of words used in them, and also of the items, such as the number of alternatives for the answers. Beyond these surface features, the complexity of the elaboration process required of the candidates for giving their answers has been taken into account (Brown & Hudson 2002:216), as is foreseen in the CEFR descriptors (Council of Europe 2001a:65–72). A further differentiating criterion was the distinction between degrees of formality: in the productive tasks, the informal register required in the students' communication with their peers as opposed to the more formal register required in tasks involving interaction with non-peers is seen as contributing to the distinction between Levels B1 and B2.

Our method of operation was that of transforming the CEFR statements into a construct of language input and expected response for both levels and both languages (Taylor Torsello & Ambroso 2004:120–133). Once the types of input and output had been determined, the AICLU pilot group produced the prototype tests, taking into consideration the number and type of questions to present to candidates in order to have a significant sample of their level for each ability, the time to allow the candidates to perform each task, and the relative weight to give the various tasks and the modules for the four abilities.

The tests, with the exception of the oral production tests, were digitised and administered using the web-based software QuestionMark Perception. In order to insert the CERCLU tests into the software, several problems had to be overcome, such as limiting to two the number of times candidates could activate the 'play' function in a listening test, and making simultaneously available on screen the text and the question to be answered in reading tests (Castello 2004). Clear instructions had to be provided for each test, each module, and each new question type. A 'help' button was also activated at various points throughout the tests. The software's 'explanation questions' were used for giving instructions. Multiple-choice questions predominate in the reading and listening parts of the tests. In the listening modules, answers go from True or False to choices among three or among four options. Multiple choice has also been used to allow the candidates to choose the subject area for the domain-related parts of the test.

We experimented with both drop-down lists and multiple-choice questions with radio buttons, opting finally for the latter. The function 'Drag and drop' is also used for reading tests, although sparingly, due to the time and effort required to prepare good drag and drop questions. Essay, or open-ended questions, are used to test the candidates' ability in written production. The Essay grader facility in Perception allows the markers to review all these open answers and score them, but the scoring must be done by human markers, albeit with careful reference to the criteria charts.

The software made it possible to mark responses automatically for all the items in the listening and reading modules. Detailed procedural decisions had to be taken regarding the modules testing the productive skills, so as to be able to score them as objectively as possible. The oral production module required decisions regarding the testing procedure, to be translated into precise instructions. These of course went beyond the obvious ones requiring the contemporary presence of an interlocutor and an observer and the tape recording of the candidate's oral performance. The following carefully defined and weighted parameters were set for both B1 and B2 levels and included on the examiners' scoring tables:

Oral production:

- phonology: phonological control
- grammar and lexis: grammatical control and accuracy; lexical control and range
- discourse: discourse management
- flexibility and interaction: socio-linguistic appropriateness, flexibility, and interactive ability.

Written production:

- lexical resources
- grammar
- cohesion and organisation
- task fulfilment (content and register)
- spelling and punctuation.

Since the students who sat the CERCLU exams during the experimentation phases required information about their level, the pilot group decided that the percentage on each module indicating success in terms of actually being a B1 or a B2 in the language tested would be 60%, which became the pass mark. It was also decided that, in case a student reached the average score of 60% for the whole test, but with one or more individual modules below this, the CERCLU certification would not be granted. To be certified as B1 or B2, the candidate would have to pass on all four modules. The total number of points for each of the test parts in the reading and listening modules corresponds to the number of possible right answers, since these are machine-corrected. The writing and speaking modules, on the other hand, are scored directly in percentages by the assessors, who consider the performance as a whole, giving points on the basis of the parameters listed above, and of overall task fulfilment. Since each ability is considered equally important, the points given to reading and listening had to be turned into percentages in order to be weighted equally with writing and speaking. The analysis of the results of the first phase of experimentation allowed us to refine some initial choices made.

Duration and phases of the project

The project is an ongoing one that will require development, adaptation, and upkeep for all the time of its existence. However, the time anticipated for bringing it into operation was four years.

In the first year (September 2000–August 2001), information about the various systems of certification in use in Europe was acquired. A detailed bibliography on testing and systems of certifying language competence was elaborated. A website was created for the materials collected and the documents produced by the group. The software (QuestionMark Perception) was selected for the writing, storage and retrieval of test items, for the production of tests according to the agreed protocols and for the analysis of the statistics relating to the results. The objectives related to the European B1/B2 levels and to the target language use domains and text types were closely examined, and the test constructs were defined.

In the second year (September 2001–August 2002), the design statement was elaborated and the elements necessary to consider an item adequate for a particular level and a particular objective were defined. The protocols for the creation of the tests were detailed. The hardware and software for the management of the database of items and of the tests themselves were prepared. Meetings were organised with our first non-Italian partner, Plymouth University, to discuss the project and recognition of the certification. The prototypes were prepared and trials were run using groups of students carefully selected for level on the basis of other tests. To identify the students to whom CERCLU B1 and CERCLU B2 should be administered, other tests were used: for English, the *Oxford Quick Placement Test,* and for Italian the tests created and used locally (in Bologna, Padua and Roma Tre University Language Centres) to place Erasmus students in the various courses. In this experimentation 59 candidates took the B1 English test, 32 took the test for B2 English, 30 took B1 Italian and 35 took B2 Italian. The tables of parameters, with relative points for scoring, which were used for evaluating candidate performance on the productive skills, and the instructions given to the oral examiners, were also trialled and modified on the basis of the results. The performances of candidates on the productive tests provided authentic examples to be inserted as notes in the tables of parameters to help future assessors.

In the third year (September 2002–August 2003), and on the basis of the results to date, the prototypes, the oral examination, and the tables for evaluation were modified where necessary, including the elimination or replacement of unsuitable items. A further calibration was performed, using the tests of the Association of Language Testers in Europe (ALTE) as control tests for the corresponding levels of the CERCLU candidates, and specifically, PET and FCE for English and CELI 2 and CELI 3 for Italian. This time the sample included 172 candidates who completed the trialling doing the CERCLU B1 English test, 135 doing the CERCLU B2 English test, 85 doing the CERCLU B1 Italian test, and 62 doing the CERCLU B2 Italian test. The results of this experimentation were sufficiently positive to allow us to use the prototype, with only very minor modifications, as the basis for the creation of an initial database of test items, to be stored in the QuestionMark Perception server located at the language centre in Padua. In September 2002 the project was presented at the CERCLES Conference in Paris (Taylor Torsello & Ambroso 2004) and in June 2003 it was presented at the AICLU Conference in Trieste (Gotti & Taylor Torsello 2005).

During the fourth year (September 2003–August 2004) the validation process was completed. The validation phase provided excellent results. For each kind of test the degree of correlation between each single part and the overall test was calculated, obtaining in general very satisfactory results (between 0.828 and 0.642). This confirmed the well-balanced structure of the various tests. The average scores obtained in the CERCLU tests were also compared to the ones obtained in the ALTE tests and showed a correlation rate (average rxy=0.654). The results obtained were in general fairly homogenous, thus confirming the high degree of correlation between the tests deriving from the various systems.

The test-prototypes and the methods and results of their validation were examined in detail by Prof. Charles Alderson from Lancaster University, who discussed them with the CERCLU team in October 2003. Some changes have been made in the tests on the basis of Professor Alderson's comments. In particular, pull-down lists have been replaced by radio-button multiple-choice items, an answering machine item formerly used in the B2 oral production test has been replaced by a peer-interaction item, and both oral tests have been shortened (B1 to 11 minutes and B2 to 13 minutes). A further phase of trialling was implemented. As new tests were created and added to the database, they were calibrated against the previous ones. At the same time, the process of negotiating the recognition of the certification at an international level continued. The above-mentioned phases of the project are being reported on analytically in a book to be published in Italy (Evangelisti, Gotti & Taylor Torsello, forthcoming).

Relationship between the CERCLU project and Italian university language teaching

Although the university language centres involved in this project are structures for innovative language teaching, with technological support, this testing project does not contain a teaching component. However, the nine universities involved in the project have certainly been influenced in their language teaching by the attention that work on the CERCLU project, and the administration of the CERCLU tests to students, has concentrated on the Common European Framework of Reference Levels B1 and B2 and the kind of operational competences in reading, writing, listening and speaking which these entail. Less directly, all the AICLU member universities' language programmes have probably been influenced to some extent by the attention that has been given in the national association to the CERCLU project.

As far as the role the CERCLU tests can play in the university language programmes is concerned, it must be recalled that it is a characteristic of the tests in point that they are based on standards set by an external organisation, in this case the Council of Europe. This characteristic makes the tests suitable for three uses in particular:

1. Evaluating students of different origins for purposes of placement, acceptance, and assignment of credits.
2. Evaluating the quality of language teaching in the universities, in those cases in which the proficiency of students who have already attended courses is measured.
3. Assigning certification with a clear reference to competencies identified by an international institution, for purposes of mobility or as a credential in the curriculum for purposes of employment or career advancement.

At the end of the project it is intended to evaluate CERCLU's penetration and impact. CERCLU's contribution in applying that part of the university reform concerned with students' proficiency in language will also be evaluated. Finally, decisions will be taken on how to go about turning the CERCLU project into a system with an ever-increasing databank of items, and one which can be made use of on a wide scale and can function on an independent and permanent basis.

Perspectives for CERCLU

CERCLU has made significant steps since the idea was first conceived in 1999. But there is still a lot of work to be done. The CERCLU group must now undertake an intensive training campaign. The project will need, for both languages, qualified teams of item writers for all parts of the tests, of examiners and evaluators for oral production, and of correctors/evaluators for written production. Indeed, the training process will have to be an ongoing part of the project from now on (Council of Europe Language Policy Division 2003:65–88). A permanent editing committee must be set up, with fixed procedures for checking and revising the tests produced by the item writers (Alderson, Clapham & Wall 1995:223–28). Benchmarking of the test samples to use as models in this task will be important (Council of Europe Language Policy Division 2003:87–89). The number of testees involved in Italian university contexts makes it essential that the database be large, so a very dynamic production system must be established. Finally, a certification system is a formidable enterprise to administer and manage, and cannot remain within the confines of the research interests of a group of university professors who are also language centre directors. Nonetheless, the language centres involved in the pilot project, on the basis of the database available and the staff members involved in the project plus some support personnel it has been possible to train, are ready to administer the CERCLU tests to small groups of students. They will issue the corresponding B1 and B2 certificates in Italian to students involved in the Socrates/Erasmus exchanges, and in English to students enrolled in degree courses involved in experimentations requiring language certifications. As the databank of test items grows and the certification system is consolidated, more and more Erasmus/Socrates exchange students visiting Italy will return to their countries with a CERCLU certification of B1 or B2 level in the Italian language, and more and more students from Italy will arrive in European universities with a CERCLU certificate as proof that they are Level B1 or B2 in English.

Although at present the certification system is limited to English and Italian, it is hoped that in the future it will be possible to extend it to other languages. The fact of basing the levels of testing and certification on the European parameters makes it possible to insert the CERCLU tests into a system of recognition along with tests created in other countries for which the same parameters (based on the Council of Europe levels) are adopted. The CERCLU certification issued by Italian language centres is meant to be recognised by language centre members of the European Confederation of Language Centres in Higher Education (CERCLES) in other European countries. The CERCLU project has, in fact, been developed in Italy in close connection with analogous projects developed by other members of CERCLES, and agreements are being negotiated whereby the national associations will promote recognition of CERCLU certification, and also of certification developed by other CERCLES members which are similarly based closely on the descriptors of the CEF.

With CERCLU, an important step toward the internationalisation of the Italian university system has been taken, which should contribute to greater mobility within Europe. It is hoped that European funding might be acquired for the further development of the project. The initial recognition agreement signed with a small number of UK universities has been seen as an anticipation of wider recognition within Europe, to be obtained especially thanks to the network of language centres created by CERCLES, and to the positive interaction between the national associations of language centres. Among the types of inter-association collaboration envisaged, two promising possibilities are:

1. Agreements for reciprocal recognition of CEFR-based certification systems produced and endorsed by national associations.
2. Agreements for development of the CERCLU system in a European project that would permit the rapid expansion of the data bank for English and Italian and the extension of the system to cover other European languages.

This project thus marks the beginning of a process of internationalisation in university language testing which, it is hoped, will be further strengthened by adding new agreements with partners in other countries.

References

Alderson, J C, Clapham, C and Wall, D (1995) *Language Test Construction and Evaluation*, Cambridge: Cambridge University Press.

Bachman, L F (1990) *Fundamental Issues in Language Testing*, Oxford: Oxford University Press.

Bachman, L F and Palmer, A S (1996) *Language Testing in Practice*, Oxford: Oxford University Press.

Brown, J D and Hudson, T (2002) *Criterion-referenced Language Testing*, Cambridge, Cambridge University Press.

Castello, E (2004) Experience with web-based testing software for the CERCLU project and other purposes, in Satchell, R and Chenik, N (Eds) *University Language Centres: Forging the Learning Environments of the Future*, Paris: CERCLES, 135–142.

Council of Europe (1998) *Threshold*, Cambridge: Cambridge University Press.

Council of Europe (2001a) *Vantage*, Cambridge: Cambridge University Press.

Council of Europe (2001b) *Common European Framework of Reference for Languages: Learning, Teaching, Assessment,* Cambridge: Cambridge University Press.

Council of Europe Language Policy Division (2003) *Relating Language Examinations to the Common European Framework of Reference for Languages: Learning, Teaching, Assessment (CEF) – Manual: Preliminary Pilot Version* (Council of Europe Document DGIV/EDU/LANG (2003) 5), Strasbourg: Council of Europe.

Evangelisti, P, Gotti, M and Taylor Torsello, C (forthcoming) *Il Progetto CERCLU per la certificazione delle competenze linguistiche nei centri linguistici universitari.*

Gotti, M (2002) La valutazione delle competenze linguistiche in un'ottica europea: il Progetto CERCLU, in Taylor Torsello, C, Catricalà, M and Morley, J (Eds) *Anno europeo delle lingue: proposte della nuova università italiana*, Siena: Terre de Sienne editrice, 27–40.

Gotti, M and Taylor Torsello, C (2005) Il Progetto CERCLU: *Work in progress* e primi risultati, in Taylor, C, Taylor Torsello, C and Gotti, M (Eds) *I centri linguistici: approcci, progetti e strumenti per l'apprendimento e la valutazione,* Trieste: Centro linguistico di Ateneo, XV-XXXVII.

Lynch, B K and Davidson, F (1997) Criterion Referenced Testing, in Clapham, C and Corson, D (Eds) *Encyclopedia of Language and Education,* Volume 7: *Language Testing and Assessment,* Dordrecht: Kluwer Academic Publishers, 263–274.

Taylor Torsello, C (2001) La Certificazione delle competenze linguistiche, *Universitas,* 79, 26–29.

Taylor Torsello, C and Ambroso, S (2004) The CERCLU Project for Certifying Language Competence in Italian University Language Centres, in Satchell, R and Chenik, N (Eds) *University Language Centres: Forging the Learning Environments of the Future,* Paris: CERCLES, 119–133.

13 An impact study of a high-stakes test (IELTS): lessons for test validation and linguistic diversity

Roger Hawkey
Consultant in testing to Cambridge ESOL

Abstract

The article reports on some of the findings of a 3-phase worldwide impact study of the IELTS test as they relate to the themes of the ALTE Berlin International Conference, namely test quality and diversity. The study used validated questionnaires, face-to-face interviews or focus groups, and classroom observation to collect qualitative and quantitative data and opinions on IELTS from test takers (pre- and post-test), preparation course teachers and receiving institution test administrators.

Cited findings relevant to test quality and test taker diversity cover perceptions of test fairness; test anxiety and motivation; test difficulty, and differential validity, that is how fair IELTS is to a diversity of test takers.

Introduction

There are messages from an impact study of a high-stakes language test, the International English Language Testing System (IELTS), that relate to the title and themes of the ALTE Berlin 2005 International Conference, *Language Assessment in a Multilingual Context: Attaining standards, sustaining diversity*.

IELTS, now taken by almost a million candidates each year at more than 300 centres in well over 100 countries, is a clear example of language assessment in a multilingual context. The test's high stakes require its strict validation, which must be pursued through rigorous research, including the study of impact. The two key Berlin Conference constructs, quality and diversity, were, according to conference publicity, to be 'explored through avenues such as the quality of examinations and codes of practice, the testing of language for specific purposes, the testing of young learners, IT and Distance Learning as well as looking at the research on impact and various state certification projects'. The study described in this article is an example of 'the research of impact' as a part of an investigation of 'the quality of examinations'.

Impact and washback

Alderson (2004:ix) notes that 'washback and the impact of tests more generally has become a major area of study within educational research'. The IELTS study investigates the *impact* and the *washback* of the test. Both concepts are complex, as are the relationships between them.

Weiss (1998) sees 'impact' as the effects of educational programmes on the larger community, the impact concerned being positive or negative, planned or unplanned, short and long term (Kirkpatrick 1998, Varghese 1998). In the fields of language teaching and testing, it is the relationships between impact and 'washback' that are a common focus of discussion. Hawkey (2006:8) suggests that the current practice is to 'use "washback" to cover influences of language tests or programmes on language learners and teachers, language learning and teaching processes (including materials) and outcomes' and 'to use "impact" to cover influences of language tests or programmes on stakeholders other than language learners, teachers'.

So impact has a broader meaning than washback, and may be seen, quite logically, as *including* it. Green (2003:6) in fact notes how Bachman and Palmer (1996:30), McNamara (1996, 2000), Hamp-Lyons (1998) and Shohamy (2001) place washback 'within the scope of impact'. Bachman and Palmer (1996) actually refer to matters of test use and social impact as *'macro'* issues of impact, while washback takes place at the 'micro' level of participants, mainly learners and teachers. Messick (1989) sees *consequential validity* as crucial in the validation of tests, to investigate whether their effects on a range of stakeholders are appropriate. Weir (2005) suggests that consequential validity, as investigated through studies of the impact and washback that tests have on various stakeholders, involves demonstrating that: 'bias has been avoided, and the test has beneficial effects on learning and teaching, and on society, individuals and institutions'.

Weir's reference here to the avoidance of bias is a matter of *differential validity* and is relevant to the discussion below of the fairness of IELTS to a diverse range of test takers, a theme of the ALTE Berlin Conference, of course, and of this article. *Differential validity* is achieved through efforts to try to ensure that the 'test is not biased or offensive with regard to race, sex, native language, ethnic origin, geographic region or other factors' (Rudner 1994:3). Weir (2005) notes that steps taken during test development, validation, standardisation and documentation 'may include evaluating items for offensiveness and cultural dependency, using statistics to identify differential item difficulty, and examining the predictive validity for different groups'. This notwithstanding, it is important to remember Bachman's (1990:278) *caveat* that group differences must be treated with some caution as they may be an indication of differences in actual language ability rather than an indication of bias.

Impact studies involve a broad potential set of people affected by a test or a programme. Such people are normally called 'stakeholders' 'because they have a direct or indirect interest (stake) in a program or its evaluation' (Weiss 1998:337). Even though it is a narrower term, tending to refer to a narrower stakeholder constituency, washback is still a complex concept. Wall and Alderson's (1993) well-known 15 washback hypotheses suggest a test's potential influence on: the teacher; the learner; what and how teachers teach, and learners learn; the rate and sequence of learning; and attitudes to teaching and learning methods.

Both impact and washback are difficult to specify in cause and effect terms. Green (2003:18) refers to 'a wide variety of moderating variables interacting with test influences', Watanabe (2004:19) to the process of washback 'mediated by numerous factors'. This important constraint on drawing clearcut conclusions about impact and washback is also acknowledged by Wall and Alderson (1993), as by Shohamy, Donitsa-Schmidt and Ferman (1996).

The IELTS test

The Academic or General Training modules are selected by IELTS candidates according to their need for an English language qualification for academic studies or for immigration, training and employment qualification purposes in English-speaking countries. A candidate's IELTS score is reported as a profile of his/her ability to use English. Scores on each of the four skills modules (Listening, Academic or General Training Reading, Academic or General Training Writing, and Speaking) are averaged into an overall IELTS band score. Performance on the test, which is not a 'level-based test . . . but is designed to stretch across a much broader proficiency continuum' (Taylor 2004:2) is assessed in terms of a scale of bands from 1 to 9, Band 1, for example, describing a non-user of the language (*Essentially has no ability to use the language beyond possibly a few isolated words*), Band 9 an expert user (*Has fully operational command of the language: appropriate, accurate and fluent with complete understanding*), both these descriptions are taken from the IELTS Handbook 2005:4. The specification of IELTS bands as cut-off levels for candidates for particular academic, professional, vocational or entry purposes is the responsibility of the test users rather than the test owners.

Taylor (2004:2) notes that 'test users frequently ask how IELTS scores "map" on to the Main Suite and other examinations produced by Cambridge

ESOL, as well as the Common European Framework of Reference (CEFR) published by the Council of Europe'. As Taylor warns (2004:2–3), 'the different design, purpose and format of the examinations makes it very difficult to give exact comparisons across tests and test scores'. She nevertheless cites evidence from the ALTE 'Can Do' project (e.g. Jones and Hirtzel 2001) and the Cambridge ESOL Common Scale for Writing project (e.g. Hawkey and Barker 2004) to suggest 'the IELTS band scores we would expect to be achieved at a particular CEFR Level'. Table 1 summarises the comparative levels:

Table 1: Indicative IELTS band scores, CEFR and Main Suite exam levels

IELTS band scores	CEFR levels	Main Suite exams
7.5 +	C2	CPE
6.5–7	C1	CAE
5–6	B2	FCE
3.5–4.5	B1	PET
3	A2	KET

IELTS impact study in context

The IELTS impact study described in this article is an action in Cambridge ESOL's continuous and iterative examination research, development and validation systems. Saville (2003:73–76) notes that Cambridge ESOL must 'be able to monitor and investigate the educational impact that examinations have within their contexts of use'. Procedures are thus needed 'to collect information that allows impact to be examined', such procedures to include: 'collecting data on: candidate profiles, exam result users and purposes; test preparation courses; public and participant perceptions of the exam'.

Cambridge ESOL has thus, since the mid-1990s, developed 'a systematic approach to investigating impact'. The system, which includes 'procedures to monitor the impact of IELTS as part of the next revision cycle', is an example of 'the continuous, formative, test consultation and validation programme pursued by UCLES' (2003:76). Shaw and Weir (2007:228) note Cambridge ESOL pre- and post-test validation efforts 'to establish evidence of the context and cognitive validity of test tasks to try and ensure that no potential sources of bias are allowed to interfere with measurement'. Central to this is the candidate biodata as collected using the Candidate Information Sheet (CIS), which gathers, at the time of the test, information on age, gender, nationality, first language etc. for research purposes, included as baseline data for later comparison with IELTS scores.

Much of the responsibility for the monitoring, research and revision activities for IELTS is taken by the Cambridge ESOL Research & Validation Group. The Group provides quality assurance services for the validity, reliability, impact and practicality (VRIP) of Cambridge ESOL exams, including IELTS. The validation operations include: statistical analyses of candidate scores, test task and item validation, and test writing and speaking corpus analysis. The Group's remit includes:

- routine operational analyses for exam production, conduct, marking/grading, and post-exam evaluation
- instrumental research involving small-scale projects to inform the operational activities
- research projects involving longer-term assessment objectives relevant to broader objectives and future developments.

Such routine and non-routine longer term research on IELTS is supported by the two other partners in the IELTS test, IDP: IELTS Australia and the British Council through the IELTS Joint-funded Research Program, which calls for proposals and designates funds for suitable shorter-term IELTS research projects. The Program is managed by a Joint Research Committee, which agrees annual research priorities and oversees the tendering process. The 10 rounds since the Program's inception in 1995 have included research projects with a focus on: IELTS impact, monitoring or evaluation; IELTS skill modules (reading, listening, writing, speaking); stakeholders (including candidates, examiners, receiving institutions); IELTS preparation courses, and candidates' future target language-related needs.

Cambridge ESOL is constantly reviewing its test systems. Current moves towards a revised model for test validation and use aim to take account of relevant recent theoretical developments, including:

- Weir's socio-cognitive framework for the validation of language tests (Weir 2005), with validity as the superordinate construct, and cognitive, context, scoring, consequential and criterion-related validities as hyponyms
- the 'standards approach to validation' of Chapelle, Enwright & Jameson (2004), which directs validation researchers to gather the types of evidence required 'to evaluate the intended interpretation of test scores', by 'developing a set of propositions that support the proposed interpretations (AERA/APA/NCME 1999: 9)'
- the work of Mislevy, Steinberg & Almond on evidence-centred assessment design (ECD), described by Saville (June 2004) as 'a way of introducing greater systematicity in the design and development' of language tests

- the *interpretive argument* of Kane (1992) and Kane, Crooks and Cohen (1999), which insists on clarity of argumentation, coherence of argument, and plausibility of assumptions
- the method of Toulmin (2003), analysing an argument into its different parts (for example, *claim, reasons,* and *evidence*) to make judgements on how well the different parts work together.

The study of IELTS impact: structure, approaches and participation

Structure

The study of the impact on a wide range of stakeholders of a high-stakes international, gate-keeping, full-ability range test such as the IELTS (see Hawkey 2006 for a full account of the IELTS study) has implications for both ALTE Berlin Conference themes, *attaining standards* and *sustaining diversity*. The aim of the IELTS study was to investigate, as part of a continuous test validation process, the impact of IELTS on test takers, language teachers, language learning, teaching and materials, and on other test users, to help ensure that the test remains as valid, effective and ethical as possible. The study was structured in three phases.

- In Phase One, Cambridge ESOL commissioned Charles Alderson and his research team at Lancaster University (see Alderson and Banerjee 1996, Banerjee 1996, Bonkowski 1996, Herington 1996, Horak 1996, Winetroube 1997 and Yue 1997) to develop data collection instruments and pilot them locally.
- In Phase Two, these instruments were trialled on larger international participant groups similar to the target populations for the study. The trial data was analysed for instrument validation, revision and rationalisation by Cambridge ESOL Research & Validation Group staff and outside consultants (see, for example, Gardiner 1999, Green 2007, Hawkey 2006, Kunnan 1999, Milanovic and Saville 1996 and Purpura 1996).
- Phase Three of the IELTS impact study saw data collection and analysis for the study.

Approach and participation

The IELTS impact study used both qualitative and quantitative research approaches from various points along the *continua* in Figure 1 (adapted from Lazaraton 2001, after Larsen-Freeman and Long 1991). The asterisks in

Figure 1: Continua of research approaches

Quantitative Research			Qualitative Research
controlled	---------------------	------------------*--	naturalistic
experimental	---------------------	------------------*--	observational
objective	--------------------	*---------------------	subjective
inferential	---------------------	--*------------------	descriptive
outcome-oriented	------------*-------	----------------------	process-oriented
particularistic	---------------------	--*------------------	holistic
'hard', 'replicable' data	---------------------	-*-------------------	'rich', 'deep' data

Figure 1 indicate a balance between quantitative and qualitative approaches in the impact study, though with a slight overall tendency towards the qualitative.

Useful research lessons were learned about the differences between the validation of data collection instruments and the validation of tests. During Phase Two of the study, the data collection instruments were subjected to a range of validating measures, including: *descriptive analyses* (mean, standard deviation, skew, kurtosis, frequency); *factor analysis; convergent – divergent* and *multi-trait, multi-method validation; brainstorming, expert opinion and review.*

Phase Three of the IELTS impact study saw the administration of the following revised data collection instruments:

- a modular IELTS test taker questionnaire course (completed by 572 pre- or post-IELTS candidates) seeking information on background, as well as language learning and testing experience, strategies, attitudes
- a teacher questionnaire (completed by 83 IELTS preparation course teachers), covering background, views on IELTS, experience of IELTS-preparation programmes
- an instrument for the evaluation of books used to prepare students for IELTS (completed by 45 evaluators)
- an IELTS-preparation lesson observation analysis instrument (used in the analysis of 12 observed and video-recorded lessons).

To enhance and triangulate questionnaire data from student and teacher participants, 120 students, 21 teachers and 15 receiving institution administrators participated in face-to-face interviews and focus groups as part of the study.

IELTS test takers from all world regions prominent in the actual IELTS test taker population (see Table 2) completed the impact study student questionnaires in 2002. There was a reasonable match across 97% of the two populations, though with a particular imbalance in South Asia candidate representation.

Table 2: Comparison of IELTS impact study and IELTS candidate regions

World Region	Impact study participant %	IELTS 2002 candidate %
(CSA) Central and Southern Africa	2	2
(EAP) East Asia Pacific	73	61
Central and Eastern Europe	3	3
Central and South America	1	1
Middle East and North Africa	1	4
North America and Mexico	1	1
South Asia	8	21
Western Europe	8	4
Total	97	97

The gender balance of the study population reversed the actual IELTS current male (55%):female (45%) percentages, but participant ages, socio-linguistic histories, fields of study and educational levels reflected the overall IELTS population quite well. The IELTS test band scores of impact study candidates who had taken the test were close to the global averages. The focus of the study was on IELTS Academic rather than General Training candidates.

Findings relevant to attaining standards and sustaining diversity

The impact study *findings* cited in this article are selected for their relevance to ALTE Berlin Conference themes. They by no means cover the whole IELTS impact study research area (see Hawkey 2006). Data concerning IELTS washback on preparation courses are not, for example, presented in this article (but see Green 2007).

Test fairness and difficulty

On the key validation question of *test fairness*, impact study participants who had already taken IELTS were asked whether they thought IELTS a fair way to test their proficiency in English. Table 3 below summarises the responses (of the 190 post-IELTS test takers concerned) to this question and to the follow-up question asking for their reasons.

The 72%:28% division on perceived test fairness may be considered a positive response, especially if, as is useful practice when developing questionnaire items, one attempts to *predict* the response of test takers in general to

Table 3: IELTS takers' perceptions of the fairness of the test

Do you think IELTS is a fair way to test your proficiency in English? (N=190)		
	YES	72%
	NO	28%
If No, why not?		
1	opposition to all tests	
2	pressure, especially of time	
3	topics	
4	rating of writing and speaking	
5	no grammar test	

such a question. When the issue of test fairness is pursued further in the post-test taker questionnaire, the most frequent specific objection to the test is, interestingly and revealingly, *opposition to all tests.* This is explained, in participants' open responses, with arguments such as:

- *'Any test is unfair as they're tested for a day while they have done a lot before'*
- *'It is a test – some students can get a good mark in the test but are not able to use it in real life'*
- *'It just depends on one test'*
- *'I usually cannot perform well on exam day'*
- *'Because sometimes it depends on your fate'.*

There is an interesting reminder in these comments for the test provider. There is no such thing as a test universally accepted as completely fair.

Responses from the 83 participating preparation course teachers were sought on a related matter. The teacher questionnaire item on whether the overall IELTS band scores of their students appeared to fairly represent the teachers' own perceptions of the English language proficiency levels of the students concerned indicated that 70% of the scores were in accordance with the teachers' expectations.

Table 4 below summarises related data from the impact study post-test taker questionnaires on factors candidates considered most affected their IELTS performance.

Table 5 suggests that IELTS candidates and IELTS preparation course teachers have closely similar perceptions of the relative difficulties of the IELTS *skills modules.*

Table 4: Factors affecting post-IELTS candidate performance (%)

Time pressure	40%
Unfamiliarity of topics	21%
Difficulty of questions	15%
Fear of tests	13%
Difficulty of language	9%

Table 5: Student and teacher perceptions of IELTS module difficulty

Most difficult IELTS Module? (%)		
	Students	Teachers
Reading	49%	45%
Writing	24%	26%
Listening	18%	20%
Speaking	9%	9%

In terms of construct, context and even differential validity, these two findings, that time was perceived as such a prominent factor in test performance and that the Reading module appeared so significantly the most difficult, warranted further investigation.

Table 6 pursues through further quantitative analysis relationships between perceived skill difficulty and other factors affecting candidate test performance.

Table 6: Relationships between perceived skill difficulty and other factors perceived as affecting candidate test performance

	Difficulty of language	Difficulty of questions	Unfamiliarity of topics	Time	Fear of tests	Others	Total
Listening	4	7	6	16	4	1	38
Reading	13	20	28	51	14	2	128
Writing	10	10	19	26	8	0	73
Speaking	2	4	6	9	3	1	25

Table 6 confirms that time pressure was the dominant factor for candidates rating the IELTS Reading module as the most difficult.

To seek further data on the validity of this important finding, relevant points from the impact study face-to-face data were examined, collected from visits to a selection of the 40 study centres involved in the study. A frequently expressed view in the impact study interviews and focus groups was that it is, by definition, difficult to test reading and writing skills directly in ways that relate them directly to actual academic reading and writing activities in the target language domain of, for example, university courses. These tend to involve long, multi-sourced texts, handled receptively and productively, and heavy in reference and statistics. This language use is difficult to replicate in a normal, time-constrained test context.

Test anxiety

Learner and teacher views on the question of *test anxiety* is a frequent concern in the study of high-stakes test impact, and sometimes considered a particular negative impact of high-stakes tests. IELTS test taker and preparation course teacher views on the matter compare interestingly, as the response summaries in Table 7 indicate.

Table 7: Candidate and teacher views of IELTS test anxiety and motivation

Candidates	*Do you worry about taking the IELTS test?*
Very much	41%
Quite a lot	31%
A little	19%
Very little	9%
Teachers	*Does the IELTS test cause stress for your students?*
Yes	53%
No	33%
Don't know	14%
Teachers	*Does the IELTS motivate your students?*
Yes	84%
No	10%
Don't know	6%

The table suggests that 72% of the candidates were *very much* or *quite a lot* worried about the test, which, like the similar figure cited above for test fairness, may be seen as a predictable rather than an exceptional proportion. Rather fewer of the preparation course *teachers* see IELTS as causing their students *stress* but 84% see the test as a source of *motivation* for the students. The stress:motivation balance is clearly an interesting high-stakes test washback issue.

Diversity

As suggested above, IELTS is designed to produce scores, for use by receiving institutions, organisations or countries, for test takers of diverse proficiency levels. As also discussed above, such a high-stakes test should also achieve differential validity through measures to avoid test bias in terms of factors such as gender, ethnic origin, first language and region.

In response to a post-IELTS candidate questionnaire item on whether the test is *appropriate for all nationalities/cultures,* 73% of the respondents answered positively. Most of the negative responses referred to learning approaches implied by the test, which may have been unfamiliar to some candidates, though they may well reflect the realities of academic life in the target countries concerned. From the 156 related face-to-face comments from impact study students and teachers, only the following few were related to diversity issues:

- occasional inappropriate test content such as questions on family to refugee candidates
- target culture bias of IELTS topics and materials
- non-European language speaker disadvantages re Latin-based vocabulary
- some IELTS-related micro-skills, e.g. the rhetoric of arguing one's opinions, unfamiliar to some candidates.

Both teachers and students, however, recognised that most such matters needed to be prepared for, given that they are intrinsic to the international education challenge facing candidates.

Conclusion

The general impression of the IELTS test created by the findings of the study is of a test:

- recognised as a competitive, high-stakes, four skills, communicative task-based test
- seen as mainly fair, though hard, especially in terms of time pressures
- assessing mainly appropriate target-domain content and micro-skills
- constantly reconsidering relationships such as those between target and test *reading* and *writing* tasks
- crucially maintaining *continuous* test validation activities, including through impact studies.

From the analyses of the qualitative and quantitative data collected, hypotheses will be developed on many aspects of IELTS impact. Findings and recommendations that are felt to need further enquiry will be compared with related IELTS research or receive it in a possible Phase Four of the impact study. The impact study is described in detail with a full analysis of data and findings in Hawkey (2006).

References

Alderson, J and J Banerjee (1996) How might Impact study instruments be validated? Paper commissioned by the University of Cambridge Local Examinations Syndicate as part of the IELTS Impact Study.

Bachman, L and A Palmer (1996) *Language Testing in Practice*, Oxford: Oxford University Press.

Banerjee, J (1996) The Design of the Classroom Observation Instruments, internal report, Cambridge: UCLES.

Bonkowski, F (1996) *Instrument for the Assessment of Teaching Materials,* unpublished MA assignment, Lancaster University.

British Council, IDP IELTS Australia, University of Cambridge ESOL Examinations. 2003: *Annual Review.*

Chapelle, C, Enwright, M and Jamieson, J (2004) Issues in developing a TOEFL validity argument, draft paper presented at LTRC, California, March 2004.

Gardiner, K (1999) Analysis of IELTS impact test-taker background questionnaire. UCLES IELTS EFL Validation Report .

Green, A (2003) Test impact and English for academic purposes: a comparative study in backwash between IELTS preparation and university pre-sessional courses. Unpublished PhD thesis, University of Roehampton.

Green, A (2007) *IELTS Washback in Context: preparation for academic writing in higher education.* Cambridge: UCLES/Cambridge University Press.

Hamp-Lyons, L (2000) Social, professional and individual responsibility in language testing. *System* 28, 579–591.

Hawkey, R (2004) *An IELTS Impact Study: Implementation and some early findings. Research Notes, 15.* Cambridge: Cambridge ESOL.

Hawkey, R (2006) *Impact Theory and Practice: studies of the IELTS and Progetto Lingue 2000* Cambridge: UCLES/Cambridge University Press.

Hawkey, R and F Barker (2004) Developing a common scale for the assessment of writing. *Assessing Writing*, 9 (2), 122–159.

Herington, R (1996) Test-taking strategies and second language proficiency: Is there a relationship? Unpublished MA Dissertation, Lancaster University.

Horak, T (1996) IELTS Impact Study Project, unpublished MA assignment, Lancaster University.

Jones, N and M Hirtzel (2001) Appendix D, ALTE Can Do Statements, in the CEFR for Languages: Learning, Teaching, Assessment. Council of Europe, Cambridge: CUP.

Kirkpatrick, D (1998) *Another look at Evaluating Training Programs*, American Society for Training & Development

Larsen-Freeman, D and M Long (1991) *An Introduction to Second Language Acquisition Research*, London: Longman.

Lazaraton, A (2001) Qualitative research methods in language test development and Validation, in Milanovic and Weir (eds) *European Language Testing in a Global Context: proceedings of the ALTE Barcelona Conference July 2001.* Cambridge: UCLES/Cambridge University Press.

Milanovic, M and N Saville (1996) Considering the Impact of Cambridge EFL Examinations, internal report, Cambridge: UCLES.

Mislevy, R, S, Steinberg, L and Almond, R (2002), Design and analysis in task-based language assessment, *Language Assessment* 19, 477–496.

Kunnan, A (2000) IELTS impact study project. Report prepared for UCLES.

Purpura, J (1996) 'What is the relationship between students' learning strategies and their performance on language tests?' Unpublished paper given at UCLES Seminar, Cambridge, June 1996.

Rudner, L (1994) Questions to ask when evaluating tests. *Practical Assessment, Research & Evaluation, 4(2)*.

Saville, N and R Hawkey (2004) A study of the impact of the International English Language Testing System, with special reference to its washback on classroom materials, in Cheng, L, Watanabe, Y and Curtis, A (eds): *Concept and method in washback studies: the influence of language testing on teaching and learning*. Mahwah, New Jersey: Lawrence Erlbaum Associates, Inc.

Shaw, S and C Weir (2007*) Examining Writing; Research and practice in assessing second language writing*. Cambridge: UCLES/Cambridge University Press.

Shohamy, E. Donitsa-Schmidt S. and I. Ferman. 1996: Test impact revisited: Washback effect over time. *Language Testing, 13*, 298–317.

Taylor, L (2004) IELTS, Cambridge ESOL examinations and the CEFR. *Research Notes* 18.

Varghese, N (1998) Evaluation vs. impact studies in V McKay and C Treffgarne (1998) *Evaluating Impact, Proceedings of the Forum on Impact Studies* (24–25 September 1998), Department for International Development Educational Papers, Serial No. 35

Wall, D and C Alderson (1993) Examining Washback: the Sri Lankan Impact Study, *Language Testing* 10, 41–70.

Weir, C J (2005) *Language Testing and Validation: an evidence-based approach*. Palgrave Macmillan: Basingstoke.

Weiss, C (1998) *Evaluation*, New Jersey: Prentice Hall.

Winetroube, S (1997) The design of the teachers' attitude questionnaire. Internal report, Cambridge: UCLES.

Yue, W (1997) An investigation of textbook materials designed to prepare students for the IELTS test: a study of washback, unpublished MA dissertation, Lancaster University.

14 Towards a model of test evaluation: using the Test Fairness and the Test Context Frameworks

Antony John Kunnan

California State University, Los Angeles

Abstract

Evaluation of tests and testing practice – referred to narrowly as test review – is typically conducted with minimal analyses. In the mid-20th century, test reviews were focused on two test qualities – reliability and validity, and this narrow focus continues in many parts of the world. In a paper presented at the first ALTE meeting in Barcelona in 2001, I proposed a Test Fairness Framework (Kunnan 2004) that expands the traditional concept of test review to include validity, absence of bias, access, administration, and social consequences. While this framework provides a micro framework to analyse a test in terms of test fairness, it does not take into account the wider context in which the test is operating. In this paper, I expand the Test Fairness Framework (TFF) by proposing a complementary macro framework called the Test Context Framework (TCF) to analyse the wider context in which a test functions. I believe the two frameworks, the micro and the macro, when used together, will offer a comprehensive model for evaluation of tests and testing practice.

Introduction

Test evaluation has become a primary concern to language testing professionals today, but it may be a somewhat recent preoccupation in the history of testing itself. Perhaps this is so because of the egalitarian view that tests were considered beneficial to society as they helped ensure equal opportunity for education and employment and attacked the prior system of privilege and patronage. For this reason, tests have unfortunately been seen in many parts of the world as infallible. But everyone who has taken a test knows that tests are not perfect and that tests and testing practices need to be evaluated too.

The first explicit, documented mention of a test quality was in the 19th century after competitive examinations became entrenched in the UK. According to Spolsky (1995) in 1858 a committee for the Oxford examinations 'worked with the examiners to ensure the general *consistency* of the examination as a whole' (p. 20). According to Stigler (1986), Edgeworth articulated the notion of *consistency (or reliability)* in his papers on error and chance much later, influenced by Galton's anthropometric laboratory for studying physical characteristics. As testing became more popular in the later decades of the 19th century and early 20th century, modern measurement theory developed techniques including correlation and factor analysis. These statistical procedures became the primary evaluative procedures for test development and test evaluation. In modern language assessment, test evaluation has clearly derived from this tradition of statistical procedures (and quantitative methods). In recent years, however, there has been interest in using qualitative methods and the concept of fairness too has specifically emerged, but a framework that includes these methods and concepts has not been debated.

In this paper, influenced by the work of Messick on test validation, and based on work from ethics and philosophy, I first present a test fairness framework that broadens the scope of traditional test evaluation in Part 1, and then I present a test context framework that further broadens the context of testing practice in Part 2.

Part 1: The Test Fairness Framework[1]

Early approaches to test evaluation

Many testing professionals hold the view that testing research has always focused on issues of fairness (and related matters like bias, justice and equality) within the framework of test evaluation through the concepts of validity and reliability. A closer examination of this view should clarify whether this is an acceptable idea. Influenced by the work in statistics and measurement and the *Standards* (actually recommendations for educational and psychological tests and manuals of the American Psychological Association (APA) (1954)), Lado (1961) was the first author in modern language assessment to write about test evaluation in terms of validity (in terms of face validity, validity by content, validation of the conditions required to answer the test items, and empirical validation in terms of concurrent and criterion-based validation) and reliability. Later, Davies (1968) presented a scheme for determining validities listing five types of validities: face, content, construct, predictive and concurrent and Harris (1969) urged test writers to establish characteristics of a good test by examining tests in terms of content, empirical (predictive and concurrent), and face.

The *Standards* were reworked during later years (APA 1966, 1974) and the interrelatedness of the three different aspects of validity (content, criterion-related and construct validities) was recognised in the 1974 version. This trinitarian doctrine of content, criterion-related and construct validity continued to dominate the field. In 1985, the *Standards* were reworked again titled 'Standards for educational and psychological testing' (instead of *Standards for tests*). This new reworking included Messick's unified and expanded conceptual framework of validity that was fully articulated in Messick (1989) with attention to values and social consequences of tests.

The 'Test Usefulness' approach

The 1990s brought a new approach to test evaluation. Translating Messick's conceptual framework, Bachman and Palmer (1996) articulated their ideas regarding test evaluation qualities: 'the most important consideration in designing and developing a language test is the use for which it is intended, so that the most important quality of a test is its usefulness' (p. 17). They expressed their notion thus: 'Usefulness = Reliability + Construct Validity + Authenticity + Interactiveness + Impact + Practicality' (p. 18). This representation of test usefulness, they asserted, 'can be described as a function of several different qualities, all of which contribute in unique but interrelated ways to the overall usefulness of a given test' (p.18).

Test evaluation in practice

Another way of noting which test evaluation qualities were important to researchers is to examine the research they carried out. For example, researchers at Educational Testing Service, Princeton, examined the tests of English (TOEFL, TSE, TWE, CBT and IBT among others) in about 100 reports. The areas of enquiry include test validation, test information, examinee performance, test use, test construction, test implementation, test reliability, and applied technology (ETS 1997).[2] University of Cambridge ESOL Examinations which administers many EFL tests examined their tests (FCE, CPE and the IELTS among others) but judging from published reports (IELTS 1999), the range of studies is also limited to investigations of test reliability, validity and authenticity (although recently research has been conducted on washback and impact (Hawkey 2006, Wall 2005)).[3][4] The English Language Institute, University of Michigan, Ann Arbor, which administers many EFL tests, produced a technical manual in support of the Michigan English Language Assessment Battery.[5] This manual includes discussions on validity and reliability using quantitative methods.[6]

The many editions of the *Mental Measurement Yearbook* and the Volume of *Test Critiques* include a few reviews of language tests. Most of them uniformly discuss validity and reliability and differential item functioning and bias.[7] The *Reviews of English Language Proficiency Tests* (Alderson, Krahnke and Stansfield 1987) and the *ESOL Tests and Testing* (Stoynoff and Chapelle 2005) are the only compilation of reviews of English language proficiency tests available. Here too the reviews follow the set pattern of discussing reliability and validity and justifying test use. There is no direct reference to test fairness. More recently, the journals *Language Testing* and *Language Assessment Quarterly* have started to carry language test reviews with some attention to fairness although not all reviewers discuss fairness in their reviews.

Early test bias studies

While these general studies and reviews do not typically focus on the concept of fairness, a separate interest in developing culture and bias-free tests developed in educational testing. These studies began with the narrow focus on test and item bias studies and then developed into the technical literature now known as DIF (Differential Item Functioning) studies.[8] Early landmark studies examined prediction of grades for Black and White college students, differential validity of employment tests by race, and fair selection models. Similarly, in language testing research in the last two decades, differences in test performance in terms of gender, academic major, and native language and culture have been examined the most. In summary, while some researchers are interested in test bias, the approach is fragmentary at best as all tests are not evaluated using a uniform concept of fairness.

Ethics in language testing

A language test ethic has been slow to develop over the last 100 years. Spolsky (1995) convincingly argued that from the 1910s to the 1960s, social, economic and political concerns among key language testing professionals in the US (mainly at the Ford Foundation, the College Board, and Educational Testing Service, Princeton) and the UK (mainly at the University of Cambridge Local Examinations Syndicate [UCLES]) dominated boardroom meetings and decisions. A language test ethic was not evident in this period although ethical theories of different persuasions had been in existence for several centuries.

Davies (1977) was the first to make an interesting suggestion for 'test virtues' that could be considered the first suggestion of ethical concerns in language testing.

Except for Davies' 'test virtues' of reliability and validity, there has been no mention of test ethics. In the last two decades, ethical concerns emerged sporadically in language assessment. Spolsky (1981) argued that tests should be labelled like drugs 'Use with care'. Stevenson (1981) urged language testers to adhere to test development standards that are internationally accepted for all educational and psychological measures. Canale (1988) suggested a naturalistic–ethical approach to language testing, emphasising that language testers should be responsible for ethical use of the information they collect. Stansfield (1993) argued that professional standards and a code of practice are ways to bring about ethical behaviour among testers. Alderson, Clapham and Wall (1995) reviewed principles and standards but concluded that 'language testing still lacks any agreed standards by which language tests can be evaluated, compared or selected' (p. 259).

In the last few years, momentum has gathered through publications such as the special issue of *Language Testing* and of *Language Assessment Quarterly* guest-edited by Davies (1997a, 2004). The International Language Testing Association (ILTA) published a report of the Task Force on Testing Standards (1995) which was followed by ILTA's Code of Ethics (2000) that lays out some broad guidance of how professionals should conduct themselves. However, these documents are general explorations of applied ethics without specific application of ethical methods that can be applied to test evaluation.

Recently, Hamp-Lyons (1997b) posed the following question (with slight modification) 'What is the principle against which the ethicality of a test is to be judged?' (p. 326). Corson (1997), broadly addressing applied linguists, makes a case for the development of a framework of ethical principles by considering three principles: the principle of equal treatment, the principle of respect for persons, and the principle of benefit maximisation. In addition to the above ideas, we also need answers to other questions such as: What qualities should a language test have to be considered an ethically fair test? What qualities should a language testing practice have to be considered one with fairness or right conduct? What qualities should a code of ethics or a code of practice include so that its professionals follow ethical practice?

Defining fairness

The notion of test fairness has developed in many ways that the many positions may appear contradictory. One useful way of understanding the many points of view is to examine recent documents that have brought this to the forefront: the Code of Fair Testing Practices in Education (1988, *Code* for short) from the Joint Committee on Testing Practices in Washington, DC and the AERA, APA and the NCME's Standards (1999, *Standards* for short) for educational and psychological testing.

The *Code* approach

The *Code* (1988) presents standards for educational test developers and users in four areas: developing and selecting tests, interpreting scores, striving for fairness and informing test takers. Specifically, the *Code* provides practical guidelines to test developers and test users as to how to strive for fairness. Keeping these guidelines in mind, standards for implementation and acceptability for the qualities are discussed here. Here is the excerpt from Section C, *Striving for Fairness* divided into two parts, one for test developers and one for test users:

> **Test developers** should strive to make tests that are as fair as possible for test takers of different races, gender, ethnic backgrounds, or handicapping conditions . . . (and) **Test users** should select tests that have been developed in ways that attempt to make them as fair as possible for test takers of different races, gender, ethnic backgrounds, or handicapping conditions (*Code* 1988, p. 4–5).

The *Standards* approach

In the recent *Standards* (1999), in the chapter titled, 'Fairness in testing and test use', the authors state by way of background that the 'concern for fairness in testing is pervasive, and the treatment accorded the topic here cannot do justice to the complex issues involved'. The authors outline four principal ways in which the term is used:

> The first two characterizations . . . relate fairness to *absence of bias* and to *equitable treatment of all examinees* in the testing process. There is broad consensus that tests should be free from bias . . . and that all examinees should be treated fairly in the testing process itself (e.g., afforded the same or comparable procedures in testing, test scoring, and use of scores). The third characterization of test fairness addresses the *equality of testing outcomes* for examinee subgroups defined by race, ethnicity, gender, disability, or other characteristics. The idea that fairness requires equality in overall passing rates for different groups has been almost entirely repudiated in the professional testing literature. A more widely accepted view would hold that examinees of equal standing with respect to the construct the test is intended to measure should on average earn the same test score, irrespective of group membership . . . The fourth definition of fairness relates to *equity in opportunity to learn* the material covered in an achievement test. There would be general agreement that adequate opportunity to learn is clearly relevant to some uses and interpretations of achievement tests and clearly irrelevant to others, although disagreement might arise as to the relevance of opportunity to learn to test fairness in some specific situations (*Standards* 1999, p. 74; emphasis added).

Further, the document discusses two other main points: bias associated with test content and response processes and fairness in selection and prediction. Based on these, the document goes on to formulate 12 Standards for fairness.

Based on these ideas, four characteristics of fairness that are the most critical to fair assessment practices emerge. They are: comparable or equitable treatment in the testing process; comparability or equality in outcomes of learning and opportunity to learn; absence of bias in test content, language and response patterns; and comparability in selection. It is these characteristics that form the backbone of the framework that I propose below.

The Test Fairness Framework

I present an ethics-inspired rationale for the Test Fairness Framework (TFF) with a set of principles and sub-principles. The two general principles of justice[9] and beneficence and sub-principles are articulated as follows:

Principle 1: *The Principle of Justice*: A test ought to be fair to all test takers, that is, there is a presumption of treating every person with equal respect.[10]

Sub-principle 1: A test ought to have comparable construct validity in terms of its test-score interpretation for all test takers.

Sub-principle 2: A test ought not to be biased against any test taker groups, in particular by assessing construct-irrelevant matters.

Principle 2: *The Principle of Beneficence*: A test ought to bring about good in society, that is, it should not be harmful or detrimental to society.

Sub-principle 1: A test ought to promote good in society by providing test score information and social impacts that are beneficial to society.

Sub-principle 2: A test ought not to inflict harm by providing test-score information or social impacts that are inaccurate or misleading.

The TFF views fairness in terms of the whole system of a testing practice not just the test itself. Therefore, multiple facets of fairness that includes multiple test uses (for intended and unintended purposes), multiple stakeholders in the testing process (test takers, test users, teachers and employers), and multiple steps in the test development process (test design, development, administration and use) are implicated. Thus the TFF has five main qualities: validity, absence of bias, access, administration, and social consequences. Figure 1 presents the TFF within the circle of tests and testing practice where validity is at the centre of the framework and the other qualities with their distinct roles overlapping validity. The TFF is operationalised and presented in Table 1 which presents the TFF as a linear list with the main quality and the main focus of each of the qualities. Although Table 1 clearly lists the main qualities and their main focus, this representation does not do justice to the idea of how the qualities interact and overlap as Figure 1 implies.

1. Validity: Validity of a test score interpretation can be used as part of the TFF when the following evidence is collected:

a. *Content representativeness or coverage evidence:* This type of evidence (sometimes simply described as *content validity*) refers to the adequacy with which the test items, tasks, topics, and language dialect represents the test domain.

Table 1: Test Fairness Framework (Kunnan 2004)

Main Quality	Main Focus of Analysis
1. Validity	
Content representativeness & relevance	Representativeness of items, tasks, topics
Construct or theory-based validity	Construct/underlying trait
Criterion-related validity	Score comparison with external criteria
Reliability	Internal consistency, inter-rater, and alternate forms
2. Absence of bias	
Offensive content or language	Content and language of population groups
Language	Dialect, register & style use
Disparate impact	Differential Item Functioning
Standard setting	Standard setting and selection decisions
3. Access	
Educational	Opportunity to learn
Financial	Cost and affordability
Geographical	Location and distance
Personal	Accommodations
Equipment and conditions	Familiarity of equipment and conditions
4. Administration	
Physical setting	Physical settings
Uniformity and security	Administration and security procedures
5. Social consequences	
Washback	Impact on instruction and learning
Remedies	Re-scoring/evaluation

Figure 1: The Test Fairness Framework

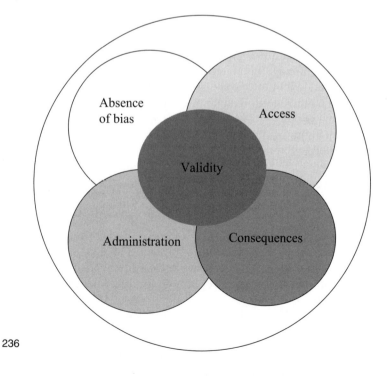

b. *Construct or theory-based validity evidence:* This type of evidence (sometimes described as *construct validity*) refers to the adequacy with which the test items, tasks, topics, and language dialect represents the construct or theory or underlying trait that is measured in a test.

c. *Criterion-related validity evidence:* This type of evidence (sometimes described as *criterion validity*) refers to whether the test scores under consideration meet criterion variables such as school or college grades and on-the-job ratings or some other relevant variable.

d. *Reliability:* This type of evidence refers to the reliability or consistency of test scores in terms of consistency of scores among different testing occasions (described as *stability* evidence), among two or more different forms of a test (*alternate form* evidence), among two or more raters (*inter-rater* evidence), and in the way test items measuring a construct function (*internal consistency* evidence).

2. Absence of bias: Absence of bias in a test can be used as part of the TFF when the following evidence is collected:

a. *Content or language:* This type of bias refers to content or language or dialect that is offensive or biased to test takers from different backgrounds. Examples include content or language stereotypes of group members and overt or implied slurs or insults (based on gender, race and ethnicity, religion, age, native language, national origin and sexual orientation); or choice of dialect that is biased to test takers.

b. *Disparate impact:* This type of bias refers to different performances and resulting outcomes by test takers from different group memberships. Such group differences (as defined by salient test taker characteristics such as gender, race and ethnicity, religion, age, native language, national origin and sexual orientation) on test tasks and sub-tests should be examined for Differential Item/Test Functioning (DIF/DTF).[11] In addition, a differential validity analysis should be conducted in order to examine whether a test predicts success better for one group than for another.

c. *Standard setting:* In terms of standard setting, test scores should be examined in terms of the criterion measure and selection decisions. Test developers and score users need to be confident that the appropriate measure and statistically sound and unbiased selection models are in use.[12] These analyses should indicate to test developers and score users that group differences are related to the abilities that are being assessed and not to construct-irrelevant factors.

3. Access: Access of a test can be used as part of the TFF when the following evidence is collected:

a. *Educational access:* This refers to whether a test is accessible to test takers in terms of *opportunity to learn* the content and to become familiar with the types of tasks and cognitive demands.

b. *Financial access:* This refers to whether a test is financially *affordable* to test takers.

c. *Geographical access:* This refers to whether a test site is accessible in terms of distance to test takers.

d. *Personal* access: Here refers to whether a test offers certified test takers with physical and learning disabilities with appropriate test accommodations. The 1999 *Standards* and the *Code* (1988) call for accommodation in order that test takers who are disabled are not denied access to tests that can be offered without compromising the construct being measured.

e. *Conditions or equipment access:* This refers to whether test takers are familiar with test taking equipment (such as computers), procedures (such as reading a map) and conditions (such as using planning time).

4. Administration: Administration of a test can be used as part of the TFF when the following evidence is collected:

a. *Physical conditions:* This refers to appropriate conditions for test administration such as optimum light, temperature and facilities as relevant for administering tests.

b. *Uniformity:* This refers to uniformity in test administration exactly as required so that there is uniformity and consistency across test sites and equivalent forms, and that test manuals or instructions specify such requirements. Examples include uniformity in test length, materials and any other conditions (for example, planning or no-planning time for oral and written responses) so that test takers (except those receiving accommodations due to disability) receive the test under the same conditions.

c. *Test security:* This refers to issues of breach of security of test materials or test administration. Examples include fraud, misrepresentation, cheating, and plagiarism.

5. Social consequences: The social consequences of a test can be used as part of the Test Fairness Framework when evidence regarding the following needs to be collected:

a. *Washback:* This refers to the effect of a test on instructional practices, such as teaching, materials, learning, test taking strategies, etc.

b. *Remedies:* This refers to remedies offered to test takers to reverse the detrimental consequences of a test such as re-scoring and re-evaluation of test responses, and legal remedies for high-stakes tests. The key fairness questions here are whether the social consequences of a test and/or the testing practices are able to contribute to societal equity or not and whether there are any pernicious effects due to a particular test or testing programme.[13]

In summary, the TFF is best served when evidence from the five test fairness qualities (validity, absence of bias, access, administration and social consequences) working together are collected and used in a defensible argument. Further, the Test Fairness Framework meets the guidelines of fairness in assessment contained in the recent *Code* (1988) and the *Standards* (1999). Finally, it is expected that the TFF can be used in a unified manner so that a fairness argument like the validity argument proposed by Kane (1992) and utilisation and use arguments proposed by Bachman (2005) can be used in defending tests.

Part 2: The Test Context Framework

Most individuals who have been required to take language tests know that tests are part of the socio-political set up of a community. Yet, language testing is characterised as a field that is primarily concerned with the psychometric qualities of tests and one in which test developers/researchers ignore the socio-economic-political issues that are critically part of tests and testing practice. It is not that these perspectives have not been known earlier. In fact, about two decades ago, Cronbach (1984) pointed out that 'testing abilities have always been intended as an impartial way to perform a political function – that of determining who gets what' (p. 5). Bachman (1990) too succinctly stated that 'tests are not developed and used in a value-free psychometric test-tube; they are virtually always intended to serve the needs of an educational system or of society at large' (p. 279).

Examining the intentions and social benefits of language testing in the 20th century, Spolsky's (1995) pioneering and eye-opening treatise entitled *Measured Words* was critical of the whole enterprise. He also called for a different approach to understanding the motivations and impact of tests. It is only by taking full account of the institutional or political context that one can appreciate how the psychometric controversies have distracted attention from more serious social (or anti-social) motivations and impact, (p. 1).

This part of the paper follows these researchers in spirit. I propose that a Test Context Framework (TCF) would be necessary to examine tests and testing practice from a wide context in order to more fully determine whether and how these tests are beneficial or detrimental to society. The wide 'context', constructed from reflection and research in the last two decades, includes the political and economic, the educational, social and cultural, the technological and infrastructure, and the legal and ethical.

Opening up the 'Context'

In the late 1980s, Messick (1989) revolutionised test validity discussions by arguing for a unified view of validity. Specifically, he asserted that validity should be considered as a unified concept (in contrast to the three traditional validity types: content validity, predictive and concurrent criterion-related validity, and construct validity developed and applied in earlier decades) with a super-ordinate role for construct validity. In this view of validity, Messick also explicitly advanced a critical role for value implications and social consequences, particularly evaluation of intended and unintended social consequences of test interpretation and use, as part of test validity. This was the first time that values implications and social consequences were brought from the backroom (where test developers had conveniently ignored them) and included as part of test validity. This view has now been instantiated in the 1999 *Standards* (AERA, APA, NCME 1999). The examination of the social value of tests as well as their unanticipated consequences or side effects, especially if such effects were traceable to sources of invalidity of test score interpretation, received support from this view. Many researchers welcomed this significant development as a possible sign of a new beginning in a hitherto psychometrically driven field and such discussions are widespread today. Messick's view of test validity also triggered the re-working of the role of test reliability and has led many researchers to argue that test reliability evidence should be used as evidence that contributes to validity of score interpretation (Chapelle 1999, Kunnan 2000).

The Test Context Framework

The Test Context Framework (TCF) refers mainly to the collection of traditions, histories, customs, and academic and professional practices, and social and political institutions of a community. This collection can then be identified loosely as the political and economic, the educational, social and cultural, the technological and infrastructure, and the legal and ethical contexts of a community in which a test operates as shown in Figure 2 below.[14]

Other contexts that may also play a role in a community but which are not explicitly shown in Figure 2 include race and ethnicity, gender, class, caste, religion, sexual orientation, entertainment, etc. As shown in the figure, the main contexts surround, overlap and enmesh each other and it is into this milieu that a test is thrust when it is commissioned. But in reality, it is likely that one or two contexts may overlap fully or only be tangentially involved. Much depends on the how and why a test is commissioned, developed, administered, scored, reported, researched, and used by the community in which the test operates. Moreover, the main contexts need not be always configured in the manner shown. In particular communities, depend-

Figure 2: The Test Context Framework

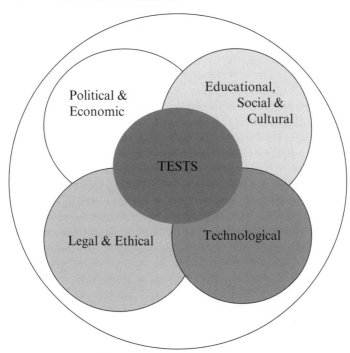

ing on the local situation, the main contexts of interests could be social and political or economic and technological, or legal and political, etc. This conceptualization also implies that we need to use this wider context in debating and evaluating tests and testing practice but does not exclude any of the technical aspects of language testing practice, such as the qualities outline in the TFF.

The political and economic context

The political and economic context of language assessment has not been – until very recently – overtly acknowledged, and relative silence on this front has contributed to the notion that language testing is an apolitical discipline (see McNamara 1998, Shohamy 2001, Spolsky 1995, for notable exceptions). An examination of school-level testing and testing for immigration and citizenship will be discussed along these lines.

The politicisation of school-level testing

In the US, there has recently been a huge growth in publications and public discussions on school-level standardised testing, so much so that electoral campaigns and platforms have become a key stage for such debates.[15] Elected officials (such as the president, state governors, mayors and school superintendents) often take the first opportunity to underscore their desire to impose standardised testing on schools in their jurisdiction in the guise of public accountability.

Large-scale standardised testing is now the main component that drives the concept of public school accountability. This is largely because until recently most schools did not require tests for grade-level promotion or high-school graduation. Instead, schools depended on teacher grades for courses and students were promoted to the next grade automatically. College-bound students took additional courses and standardised tests such as the SAT (formerly known as the Scholastic Aptitude Test) for admission to colleges and universities. The official accountability argument goes as follows: if parents knew how well their children were doing, then educators, policy makers and the public would know how well their schools were doing. Financial incentives would then be offered to schools that have met or exceeded their goals or punitive action would be taken against schools that do poorly.

US President Bush's education agenda added negatively to this state of affairs when he signed the 'No Child Left Behind' (NCLB) Act of 2001 which requires all States to introduce testing in science, mathematics and (English language) reading for Grades 3 to 8. It is based on four basic principles: stronger accountability for results, increased flexibility and local control, expanded options for parents, and an emphasis on teaching methods that have been proven to work. In terms of increased accountability, the Act requires States to implement statewide accountability systems covering all public schools and students on State standards in reading and mathematics, annual testing for all students in Grades 3–8, and annual statewide progress objectives ensuring that all groups of students reach proficiency within 12 years. Results of such tests are required to be broken out by poverty, race, ethnicity, disability, and limited English proficiency to ensure that no group is left behind. School districts and schools that fail to make adequate yearly progress (AYP) toward statewide proficiency goals will be, over time, subject to improvement, corrective action, and restructuring measures. Schools that meet or exceed AYP objectives or close achievement gaps will be eligible for State Academic Achievement Awards. This overtly stated goal masks the Bush Administration's related concept of awarding parents tuition fees (known as the School Voucher Program) if they choose to remove their children from failing public schools and place them in private schools.[16] A detailed analysis of the legislation and the testing practices that have been put in place needs to be conducted.

Testing for immigration and citizenship: political and economic gate-keeping

Political and economic interests have been at the centre of gate-keeping in the high-stakes arena of immigration and citizenship. In most countries, language abilities (in the official language of the country) have been required of potential immigrants. Often, the overt goal of assessing language proficiency and the associated intention of providing free language instruction is not the real reason for the testing policy. The real objective may be 'racial exclusion', as in the case of the dictation test in Australia and in the case of intelligence tests in the US in the early 20th century.

In the case of Australia, language tests were used as part of the immigration requirement as early as 1901 as part of the 'White Australia' policy. The first test was a dictation test in a European language (or any 'prescribed language') to a potential immigrant in such a way that the immigrant (if not from the British Isles) could be excluded. As a result of rigorous application of this policy from 1902 to 1946, only 125,000 members of 'the alien races' (Asians and 'coloured') were admitted to the country. In 1956, the dictation test given in any European language was changed to an English dictation test. In the 1990s, first the ACCESS and then the STEP tests were introduced to assess English language proficiency of professionals prior to registration or immigration or those seeking permanent residence. However, standard setting was influenced by immigration policy that was intended to be benign but sometimes indefensible in practice.

Rather similarly, in the US, the use of literacy tests for voting rights and intelligence tests for immigration in the 1920s had a 'racial exclusion' objective. The earliest language testing was the English Competence examination prepared by the College Entrance Examination Board in 1930, which also had a similar goal. According to Spolsky (1995), this test was intended to deal with a loophole in the Immigration Act of 1924: 'Carl Brigham gave evidence in Congress on the deleterious effects of permitting non-Nordic immigrants to "contaminate the American gene pool"' (p. 55). Similarly, detailed examinations of the political and economical contexts of gate-keeping need to be conducted. See Kunnan (2007, 2008) for papers on testing citizenship and the US Naturalization Test.

The educational, social and cultural context

Standardised language tests are common in the educational, social, and cultural contexts. They are used for a variety of educational and career-related purposes that include competency, admission, and employment. Key concerns that have been raised about these tests are primarily regarding their educational and social consequence: test bias and washback.

Standardised tests and accountability

In keeping with the accountability concept, the state of California introduced the California High School Exit Examination in English from 2003–04. According to the State Education Code, the purpose of the CAHSEE is to ensure that students who graduate from high school can demonstrate grade-level competency in the state content standards for reading, writing, and mathematics. The exam has two parts, English-language arts and mathematics, and students must pass both portions of the test to receive their high school diploma, beginning in the 2006 school year. While the independent evaluation of the test reports that the test development, administration, scoring and reporting is flawless, the report documents through one table that teachers spent 45 hours on test preparation and in one short paragraph that a small DIF study was conducted for Hispanic test takers.[17]

In 1998, anticipating the national accountability concept, California introduced a standardised test (Stanford 9) that assesses students from Grades 2 to 11 in a variety of subjects including English reading and writing, mathematics and science. The impact of this test has generally been negative particularly in terms of washback: teacher anecdotes have indicated that they have to 'teach to the test' for about two months prior to the test and that the curriculum has in general become 'test-driven' with less time devoted to activities that are not part of the test. Further, there have been complaints that the test is not aligned to the stated curriculum, a clear problem of content representativeness/coverage. This is a result of many factors including the situation that different school districts have slightly different curricula and different timelines for completion of topics, units, and concepts. It is clear therefore that more systematic washback studies need to be conducted although the limitations and dangerous consequences of such standardised tests have been regularly raised.[18] The value of these high-stakes educational tests to California society depends on construct validity, and the absence of bias and positive washback of the tests on instruction.

The technology and infrastructure context

The importance of this context has become clearer in the last decade than ever before due to the rapid use of high technology in testing such as computers and the internet. A key concern with the use of technology often articulated is whether test takers have access to and knowledge of the technology necessary for success on a test.

In low technology use areas, where machine scoring has replaced human scoring, it is likely that this is coupled with the promotion of multiple-choice test items and the use of machine-scorable cards that enable machine scoring (such as most US based tests). While recording responses to test items on a machine-scorable card might be easy for test takers who are used to this format, test takers who are not used to it might find it rather confusing and unnecessarily tricky from two points of view: the use of multiple choices for each test item and the recording of responses. Thus, it is critical that test developers are aware of how familiar test-taking groups (in their targeted population) are with multiple-choice test items and whether they are able to record their responses.

Similarly, in the case of tape-mediated tests (such as the *Test of Spoken English* or the *Simulated Oral Proficiency Tests*), talking into an audio-tape recorder in response to an unseen voice that asks for responses is another problematic test format. Test takers who are unfamiliar with this format will have difficulty dealing with it (especially starting and completing responses within the time allocated for each response). Further, from a social and cultural point of view, it may seem inappropriate to particular test-taking groups to talk into a tape recorder, especially in tests that claim to assess communicative language ability.

In high technology use areas, computers may be used in all aspects of test development, administration, scoring and reporting. In test administrations using computers (such as the *Computer-based TOEFL*), a test taker would receive test items on the computer screen that have been either based on item difficulty and person ability estimates (if the test section is a *computer-adaptive test*) or based on a set order of items (as in a *computer-based test* or a paper-and-pencil test). Either way, the test taker would need to have the requisite computer keyboarding and mouse movement skills (clicking, scrolling, highlighting, etc.) in order to read the test items and to record the answers. This calls into question the issue of test access if the test is required of test takers in places where such computer skills and computer-based tests are relatively new or non-existent.

For example, the administrators of the Computer-based TOEFL (which replaced the paper-and-pencil TOEFL) had to deal with this issue as the test is offered worldwide, including places in which high technology use is new or non-existent. As the test administrators were aware of the test access issue, a computer-familiarity study of potential TOEFL test takers was conducted prior to launching the test (Taylor, Jamieson, Eignor and Kirsch 1998). This study enabled the test administrators to be confident that most test takers who might take the Computer-based TOEFL have sufficient familiarity with keyboarding and mouse skills and that those who do not could benefit from a free tutorial that test takers could take prior to taking the test. This solution is acceptable for test takers who come forward to take the tutorial and the test, but it would not be sufficient if the very thought of having to take a computer-familiarity tutorial and computer-based test inhibited a sizeable number of test takers in a particular area from taking the test. This example shows how the use of high technology has to be understood and managed in areas where such technology may not be commonplace among test takers.

The legal and ethical context

Test takers and test score users need a remedial procedure whenever a test is shown to be in violation of established practice or a regulation. For example, if there are problems with any aspect of a test or if any existing regulations have been violated that have a direct impact on test takers, remedial measures should be available to test takers or any affected persons or agencies. Further, if decisions made on test scores that are in doubt can be reversed as in non-high stakes tests, then any of the following remedial measures might satisfy affected test takers: re-scoring, re-totalling, or re-taking of the test for free or a small fee. In cases when decisions are not easily reversible or test takers are affected adversely, legal action may be the only recourse.

Legal framework in the US

In the United States, legal frameworks based on the Constitution, federal civil rights statutes and judicial decisions apply to standardised tests (including language tests) in educational, licensure, employment and professional arenas. Test score interpretations and decisions based on scores can be challenged on three grounds by test takers or interested parties. They are:

The discrimination challenge: In terms of the discrimination challenge, three types of claims can be made to a court. 1. A test is intentionally discriminating against test takers (who are a particular class of people) on the basis of race, colour, national origin or gender. This challenge is based on the equal protection clause in the 14th Amendment of the US Constitution that forbids public employers from engaging in acts of discrimination. 2. A test preserves the effects of prior discrimination. 3. A disparate impact claim. This claim can be made when different test taker groups receive different scores (such as female and male or from different race/ethnic groups). State and public school agencies that receive federal funding are prohibited from discriminating against students based on federal statutes.[19]

The due process challenge: High-stakes tests that are not found to be discriminating against protected classes may still be illegal under the due process provision of the 5th and 14th Amendments of the US Constitution. The claims under this provision may be either that the test takers did not receive sufficient advance notice or adequate notice of the test or that the test takers did not receive instruction on the test knowledge and skills (also known as curricular validity). In terms of the adequate notice provision, test score users or similar agencies are expected to provide adequate notice. This has been interpreted by courts to mean anywhere between one to four years of advance notice before a test becomes effective, so that the test takers have adequate opportunity to learn the relevant knowledge or skills. In terms of curricular validity, there have been disagreements as to how educational agencies can demonstrate what students have been taught. Some argue that the formal written school or district curriculum can be used to match the knowledge and skills measured in the test. Others argue that it is not the formal written curriculum that should be used to check curricular validity but the instructional curriculum of the classroom. Test researchers too have made the same argument: they prefer to examine whether test takers have had the 'opportunity to learn' the knowledge and skills in the classroom rather then merely matching test knowledge and skills with a formal written curriculum.

Accommodations for test takers with disabilities: Test accommodations for test takers with disabilities were given a major push in the form of three pieces of legislation as part of a political and social agenda: Section 504 of the Rehabilitation Act of 1973, the Americans with Disability Act (ADA) of 1990, and the Individuals with Disabilities Educational Act (IDEA) of 1991 and 1997. Of these, the ADA of 1990 prohibits not only discrimination against individuals with disabilities but also relates to the opportunities for individuals to obtain employment and education.[20]

In the various rulings, courts have not provided clear directions on many critical matters like test accommodations (such as extended time). Pitoniak and Royer (2001) state, 'the results of these cases do not present a consistent picture, owing to courts' struggling with both how to determine whether a learning disability exists and what that disability means in terms of the affected individual's rights' (p. 63). In summary, as legal challenges in testing are relatively new, court opinions do not offer clear directions as to how to proceed with many matters, including how to avoid discriminatory testing practice, how to identify individuals with disabilities, or what test accommodations are appropriate for different physical and learning disabilities.[21] Similar statutes and legislation in other parts of the world could be used to find remedies for test takers.

In summary, the TCF can be used to examine the wider context of testing and testing practice so that stakeholders are made aware of the rationale and different contexts in which a test has to operate and serve. This paper also explicitly puts forward the notion that tests are best understood when a wider interdisciplinary perspective is used in debating and evaluating tests and testing practice. As Spolsky (1995) asserts, 'in the study of fields like language testing and teaching, scholars need to be ready to draw not just on the obvious theoretical disciplines that underpin applied linguistics, such as the various language sciences and education, but also on fields like economics, political science, and sociology that furnish methods of investigating the context in which language and education exist'(p. 3).

Conclusion

In the two parts, two complementary frameworks, the TFF and the TCF were presented and discussed briefly. It is suggested that test agencies and institutions such as universities that develop large scale standardised tests will benefit from the use of the two frameworks in test evaluation. This could be an internal or an external evaluation in which evidence for or against a test is marshalled and then an argument either defending or rejecting a test will be made using Bachman's (2005) test utilisation and use argument structure.

Notes

1 Only a brief exposition of this framework is presented here due to space constraints. For a full exposition, see Kunnan (2004) in Milanovic & Weir (2004).

2 See this document for a full listing of titles and abstracts of research studies from 1960 to 1996 for TOEFL as well as other tests such as SAT, GRE, LSAT and GMAT.

3 FCE stands for First Certificate in English, CPE for Certificate of Proficiency in English and IELTS for International English Language Testing System.

4 Another organisation, the Association of Language Testers in Europe (ALTE), of which UCLES is a member, has a *Code of Practice* that closely resembles the Code of Fair Testing Practices in Education (1988). However, there are no published test evaluation reports that systematically apply the *Code*.

5 The MELAB stands for the Michigan English Language Assessment Battery.

6 Recent reviews in *Language Testing* of the MELAB, the TSE, the APIEL and the TOEFL CBT have begun to discuss fairness (in a limited way) along with traditional qualities such as validity and reliability.

7 This uniformity is probably also due to the way in which MMY editors prefer to conceptualise and organise reviews under headings, such as description, features, development, administration, validity, reliability and summary.

8 For DIF methodology, see Holland & Wainer (1993) and Camilli & Shepard (1994).

9 See Rawls' (1971) *A Theory of Justice* for a clear position of why it is necessary to have an effective sense of justice in a well-ordered society.

10 These principles are articulated in such a way that they complement each other and if there is a situation when the two principles are in conflict, Principle 1 (The Principle of Justice) will have overriding authority. Further, the sub-principles are only explications of the principles and do not have any authority on their own.

11 There is substantial literature that is relevant to bias and DIF in language testing.

12 For standard setting, the concept and practice, see numerous papers in Cizek (2001).

13 In the US, Title VII of the Civil Rights Act of 1964 provides remedies for persons who feel they are discriminated against due to their gender, race/ethnicity, native language, national origin, and so on. The Family and

Education Rights and Privacy Act of 1974 provides for the right to inspect records such as tests and the right to privacy limiting official school records only to those who have legitimate educational needs. The Individuals with Disabilities Education Amendments Act of 1991 and the Rehabilitation Act of 1973 provides for the right to parental involvement and the right to fairness in testing. Finally, the Americans with Disabilities Act of 1990 provides for the right to accommodated testing. These Acts have been used broadly to challenge tests and testing practices in court.

14 Only a brief exposition of this framework is presented here due to space constraints. For a full exposition, see Kunnan (2005) in Hinkel (2005).

15 Most of the examples in this paper are from the US as this is where the author works but this does not mean that the 'Wider Context' perspective promoted in the paper is restricted to the US. This framework could be used for evaluation of tests and testing practice of any community.

16 Most commentators read private schools to mean faith-based (meaning, religious and Christian schools) which is very much in line with the Republican President Bush's agenda.

17 See website for HUMRRO's (2002) independent evaluation of the CAHSEE: www.cde.ca.gov/statetests/cahsee/eval/2002/2002humrro.html retrieved on 1/25/2003.

18 The FairTest: The National Center for Fair and Open Testing at the following website has many arguments on these lines: www.fairtest.org

19 This is a uniquely American legal provision due to legal (for example, slavery) and illegal discrimination of several groups of people (Native Americans, African Americans, Hispanic Americans and Asian Americans) practised for centuries in the country.

20 Similar laws are on the books in the UK, the European Union, and India.

21 See Bersoff (1981) and Fulcher & Bamford (1986) for legal challenges that are possible in the US and UK. Also, see Kunnan (2000) for a list of court cases related to testing in the US and Lippi-Green (1997) for court cases related to employment-related language use and discrimination.

References

Alderson, J C, Krahnke, K and Stansfield, C (1987) (Eds) *Reviews of English Language Proficiency Tests*, Washington, DC: TESOL.

American Psychological Association (1954) Technical Recommendations for Psychological Tests and Diagnostic Techniques, Washington, DC: Author.

American Psychological Association (1966) *Standards for Educational and Psychological Tests and Manuals*, Washington, DC: Author.

American Psychological Association (1974) *Standards for Educational and Psychological Tests*, Washington, DC: Author.

American Psychological Association (1985) *Standards for Educational and Psychological Testing*, Washington, DC: Author.

American Educational Research Association, American Psychological Association, National Council for Measurement in Education (1999) *Standards for Educational and Psychological Testing*, Washington, DC: Author.

Angoff, W (1988) Validity: an evolving concept, in Wainer, H and Braun, H (Eds), *Test Validity*, Hillsdale, NJ: Lawrence Erlbaum Associates, 19–32.

Bachman, L F (1990) *Fundamental considerations in language testing*, Oxford: Oxford University Press.

Bachman, L F and A S Palmer (1996) *Language testing in practice*, Oxford: Oxford University Press.

Bersoff, D (1981) Testing and the law, *American Psychologist* 36, 1047–1056.

Canale, M (1988) The measurement of communicative competence, *Annual Review of Applied Linguistics* 8, 67–84.

Chapelle, C (1999) Validity in language assessment, *Annual Review of Applied Linguistics* 19.

Code of Fair Testing Practices in Education (1988) Washington, DC: Joint Committee on Testing Practices. Author.

Corson, D (1997) Critical realism: an emancipatory philosophy for applied linguistics? *Applied Linguistics* 18, 166–188.

Cronbach, L (1980) Validity on parole: How can we go straight? New directions for testing and measurement: Measuring achievement over a decade. Proceedings of the 1979 ETS Invitational Conference, San Francisco: Jossey-Bass, 99–108.

Davidson, F and Lynch, B (2001) *Testcraft*, New Haven, CT: Yale University Press.

Davies, A (1997a) (Guest Ed.) Ethics in language testing, *Language Testing* 14.

Davies, A (1997b) Demands of being professional in language testing, *Language Testing* 14, 328–339.

Fulcher, G and Bamford, R (1996) I didn't get the grade I need: Where's my solicitor? *System* 24, 437–448.

Hamp-Lyons, L (1997a) Washback, impact and validity: ethical concerns, *Language Testing* 14, 295–303.

Hamp-Lyons, L (1997) Ethics in language testing, in Clapham, C and Corson, D (Eds) *Language Testing and Assessment, Encyclopedia of Language and Education*, Vol 7, Dordrecht: Kluwer, 323–333.

Hawkey, R (2006) *Impact Theory and Practice: Studies of the IELTS test and Progetto Lingue 2000*, Cambridge: Cambridge University Press.

Hawthorne, L (1997) The political dimension of English language testing in Australia. *Language Testing* 14, 248–260.

Heubert, J and Hauser, R (Eds) (1999) *High Stakes: Testing for tracking, promotion, and graduation*, Washington, DC: National Academy Press.

International Language Testing Association (1995) *Task Force on Testing Standards*.

International Language Testing Association (2000) *Code of Ethics*.

Joint Committee on Testing Practices (1988) *Code of Fair Testing Practices in Education*.

Kane, M (1992) An argument-based approach to validity, *Psychological Bulletin* 112, 527–535.

Kunnan, A J (1990) DIF in native language and gender groups in an ESL placement test, *TESOL Quarterly* 24, 741–746.

Kunnan, A J (1995) *Test taker characteristics and test performance: A structural modeling approach*, Cambridge: UCLES/Cambridge University Press.

Kunnan, A J (1998) Approaches to validation, in Kunnan, A J (Ed.) *Validation in language assessment*, Mahwah, NJ: Erlbaum, 1–14.

Kunnan, A J (2000) Fairness and justice for all, in Kunnan, A J (Ed.), *Fairness and validation in language assessment*, Cambridge: UCLES/Cambridge University Press, 1–13.

Kunnan, A J (2004) Test fairness, in Milanovic, M and Weir, C J (Eds) *European Language Testing in a Global Context*, Cambridge: UCLES/Cambridge University Press, 27–48.

Kunnan, A J (2005) Language assessment from a wider context, in Hinkel, E (Ed.) *Handbook of research in second language teaching and learning*, Mahwah, NJ: Erlbaum, 779–794.

Kunnan, A J (2007) The redesign of the US Naturalization Test: set up to fail? Paper presented at the Language Testing Research Colloquium, Barcelona, Spain.

Kunnan, A J (2008) American Citizenship and the Testing for Citizenship, paper presented at the American Association of Applied Linguistics Conference, Washington DC, US.

Lado, R (1961) *Language Testing*, London: Longman.

Linn, R, Baker, E and Betebenner, D (2002) Accountability systems: implications of requirements of the No Child Left Behind Act of 2001, *Educational Researcher* 31, 3–16.

Messick, S (1989) Validity, in Linn, R (Ed.) *Educational measurement* (3rd edition), New York: Macmillan, 13–103.

McNamara, T (1998) Policy and social considerations in language testing, *Annual Review of Applied Linguistic* 18, 304–319.

Pitoniak, M and Royer, J (2001) Testing accommodations for examinees with disabilities: A review of psychometric, legal and social policy issues, *Review of Educational Research* 71, 53–104.

Read, J (2001) The policy context for English testing for immigrants, in Elder, C, Brown, A, Grove, E, Hill, K, Iwashita, N, Lumley, T, McNamara, T and O'Loughlin, K (Eds), *Experimenting with uncertainty: Essays in honor of Alan Davies*, Cambridge: UCLES/Cambridge University Press, 191–199.

Shohamy, E (2001) *The power of tests*, London: Longman.

Spolsky, B (1995) *Measured Words*. Oxford, UK: Oxford University Press.

Spolsky, B (1981) Some ethical questions about language testing, in Klein-Braley, C and Stevenson, D (Eds) *Practice and problems in language testing*, Frankfurt: Verlag Peter Lang, 5–21.

Spolsky, B (1997) The ethics of gatekeeping tests: what have we learned in a hundred years? *Language Testing* 14, 242–247.

Stansfield, C (1993) Ethics, standards and professionalism in language testing, *Issues in applied linguistics* 4, 189–206.

Stigler, S (1986) *The history of statistics*, Cambridge, MA: The Belknap Press of Harvard University Press.

Taylor, C, Jamieson, J, Eignor, D and Kirsch, I (1998) The relationship between computer familiarity and performance on computer-based *TOEFL tests tasks, TOEFL Research Report No. 61*, Princeton, NJ: Educational Testing Research.

University of Michigan English Language Institute (1996) *MELAB Technical Manual*, Ann Arbor, MI: University of Michigan Press.

Wall, D (2005) *The Impact of High-stakes Testing on Classroom Teaching: A case study using insights from testing and innovation theory*. Cambridge: UCLES/Cambridge University Press.

Zeidner, M (1986) Are English language aptitude tests biased towards culturally different minority groups? Some Israeli findings, *Language Testing* 3, 80–95.

Zeidner, M (1987) A comparison of ethnic, sex and age biases in the predictive validity of English language aptitude tests: some Israeli data, *Language Testing* 4, 55–71.

Section Three
Sustaining Diversity

15 Language assessment and citizenship: European policy perspective

Joseph Sheils
Language Policy Division, Council of Europe[1]

Introduction

The Council of Europe was pleased to be associated with ALTE's initiative to organise a Forum at the ALTE Conference in Berlin on the relation between language and citizenship. This was a priority issue that was closely linked to the Council's actions in the political and social domains to promote participatory democratic citizenship and social cohesion.

Accordingly, in the first part of this paper I will briefly outline the wider socio-political context which guides the Council of Europe's policy on social integration and citizenship, and link this to the European Year of Citizenship through Education which the Council declared for 2005. In the second part, I will address the language policy dimension, which of course is strongly influenced by the political and social context.

I will summarise Council of Europe language policy and point to a number of our European Conventions that are relevant to language provision for integration and citizenship purposes. Then I will briefly highlight some common issues in member states concerning language provision and testing for residence or citizenship purposes.

Finally, I will look at how the Council's recent work around the Common European Framework of Reference for Languages can be of assistance in our efforts to address some of these issues.

The socio-political context – What are the priorities of the Council of Europe?

The Council of Europe, since its inception over 50 years ago, has been centrally concerned with human rights, democracy and the rule of law. These fundamental values, and its constant concern with respect for diversity and social cohesion, are guiding principles in the actions of the Council of Europe.

On 16 and 17 May 2005, the Third Summit of Heads of State and Government of the Council of Europe's 46 member states took place in Warsaw, and in the Summit Declaration Europe's leaders committed themselves, *inter alia*, to ensuring that our cultural diversity becomes a source of mutual enrichment, to the protection of the rights of national minorities and the free movement of persons. They went on to state:

> . . . In order to develop understanding and trust among Europeans, we will promote human contacts and exchange good practices regarding free movement of persons on the continent, with the aim of building a Europe without dividing lines . . . We are determined to build cohesive societies by ensuring fair access to social rights, fighting exclusion and protecting vulnerable social groups. [2]

> We acknowledge the importance of the European Social Charter in this area and support current efforts to increase its impact on the framing of our social policies. We are resolved to strengthen the cohesion of our societies in their social, educational, health and cultural dimensions.

This high level political Declaration was to be followed up in an Action Plan, agreed at the Summit, and which has considerable implications for our work on minorities and immigrants. I shall return to this later.

The question of migration has steadily grown in importance in the work of the Council of Europe as governments have come to acknowledge that Europe has become a region of immigration, and the final destination of many who have immigrated.

The 7th Conference of European Ministers responsible for migration affairs in 2002 addressed the challenges in connection with integration policies and with migration management and ways of dealing with them in Council of Europe member states. The Ministers recalled that the economic, social, cultural and political integration of migrants lawfully residing in European countries is a factor of social cohesion of the host state, and that countries should ensure a commitment to their full integration based on the mutual obligations of migrants and the receiving society.

The Ministers undertook to implement induction programmes for newcomers and to actively encourage immigrants to learn the language of the receiving country.

European Year of Education through Citizenship

The European Year of Education through Citizenship declared by the Council of Europe for 2005 offered a particular opportunity to focus on the integration and social and political rights and responsibilities of immigrants and minorities.

The promotion of the necessary political and personal attitudes for integrated and cohesive societies was a fundamental aim of the Year. Its programme of activities, which included the ALTE Berlin Forum, was intended to highlight the importance of raising awareness, in formal and informal education programmes, of the need to respect diversity and avoid discrimination of any kind, and the need to value difference rather than perceiving it as a problem. It aimed to strengthen social cohesion through respect of fundamental social rights and solidarity with vulnerable groups. The Year was particularly concerned with promoting participation – active socially responsible involvement in society and in decision-making processes, as a right and a responsibility for all.

Respect of diversity, non-discrimination, participation and cohesion have clear implications for language policies – policies which value the languages of all the members of society; policies that equally ensure the full integration and equal participation of all through support for their efforts to develop the necessary communication skills in the language of the society in which they reside.

Turning now to the language dimension, what are the main goals of Council of Europe language policy?

Council of Europe language policy

The Council of Europe aims to promote:

- plurilingualism
- linguistic diversity
- mutual understanding
- democratic citizenship
- social cohesion.

Plurilingualism: All are entitled to develop a degree of communicative ability in a number of languages over their lifetime in accordance with their needs; plurilingualism refers to the full linguistic repertoire of the individual, including their mother tongue or first language; individuals may learn or acquire different languages for various purposes at different points in their lives. Therefore, their plurilingual repertoire is a dynamic one, and may be composed of different kinds of competence and differing levels of proficiency in those languages.

Linguistic diversity: In our multilingual Europe all languages are equally valuable modes of communication and expressions of identity; the right of minorities to use and to learn their language is protected in Council of Europe Conventions and therefore language rights are part of human rights.

Mutual understanding: The opportunity to learn the languages of others is an essential condition for intercultural communication and acceptance of cultural differences. Intercultural competence is a key component of plurilingualism which includes openness to and acceptance of the languages and practices of others.

Democratic citizenship: The exercise of democracy and participation in social processes in multilingual societies depends on the plurilingual competence of individuals. They need to be supported in their efforts to become plurilingual in ways that are appropriate to the area they live in and to develop a shared feeling of belonging and of shared democratic citizenship. This is clearly of particular relevance for immigrants and minorities.

Social cohesion: Equality of opportunity for personal development, education, employment, mobility, access to information and cultural enrichment depends on access to language learning throughout life. Lifelong learning should support the development of proficiency in the official language of the country of residence where necessary, as well as in the languages of others in order to avoid the danger of marginalisation.

Council of Europe Conventions and Recommendations

What do Council of Europe Conventions and Recommendations say about languages, and in particular about learning the official language(s) of member states?

The European Convention on Human Rights and Fundamental Freedoms contains provisions concerning non-discrimination on grounds of, among others, language. Two other key Council of Europe Conventions provide specifically for the protection of language-related rights. The Framework Convention for the Protection of National Minorities guarantees the right to learn and use one's mother tongue in specific circumstances. It should be noted that this right is without prejudice to learning the official language. The European Charter for Regional or Minority Languages is not concerned with the rights of language users as such but with the protection of languages as part of our cultural heritage. It is concerned with languages traditionally spoken on the territory.

Two other Conventions, with reference to immigrants, explicitly make provision for developing skills in the language of the receiving country; they make no reference to language tests.

The *European Convention on the Legal Status of Migrant Workers* (1997) includes provision for teaching the language of the receiving state to migrant workers and their families: 'To promote access to general and vocational schools and to vocational training, the receiving state shall facilitate the teaching of its language, or if there are several, one of its languages to migrant workers and members of their families'.

The *European Social Charter* (1961/1996), an instrument mentioned explicitly by Europe's leaders at the May 2005 Summit, has a broadly similar provision in Article 11: 'To promote and facilitate the teaching of the national language of the receiving state or, if there are several, one of these languages, to migrant workers and members of their families'.

The Parliamentary Assembly of the Council of Europe recommended that integration programmes for recently arrived immigrants should be voluntary and should include 'language tuition, information on the way of life and customs of the host society' (Recommendation 1625 (2003)).

With reference to the *European Convention on Nationality*, the situation of immigrants and national minorities is of course quite different, even if many of the issues that now arise in relation to language for citizenship purposes are broadly similar.

The democratic and demographic changes in Europe, brought about in particular by state succession which occurred in central and eastern Europe since 1989, led the Council of Europe to elaborate the European Convention on Nationality. One of its aims is to guarantee that the procedures governing application for nationality are just, fair and open to appeal.

The Convention itself does not refer to language requirements directly but the Explanatory Report to the Convention notes that a common criterion is the requirement of knowledge of the national language in order to be naturalised. It might be inferred from this that there is an obligation for language tests for nationality or citizenship purposes equally to reflect just, fair procedures that are open to appeal.

Some common issues

As the conference literature outlining the aims of the ALTE Berlin Forum indicated, the conditions for obtaining residence or citizenship increasingly, although not everywhere, require evidence of proficiency in the state language.

The situation seems to vary enormously, and is well documented for six northern and western European countries in a report of a meeting on language and the integration of adult immigrants organised in 2004 by the French Ministry responsible for employment, labour and social cohesion, the Ministry responsible for culture and communications, and the *Délégation générale à la langue française et aux langues de France.*

The meeting, held at the CIEP in Sevres, Paris, noted the considerable differences in approach to language provision and, where this exists, to testing for residence or citizenship purposes.

There is an alarming difference in the levels of proficiency required – ranging from A1 to B1 or even B2 (oral) of the CEFR. This is an area where our work on how to interpret the Framework levels has been valuable, and I will return to this shortly.

There are of course considerable differences among immigrants in terms of education background and some countries make special provision to take account of such differences, including illiteracy among immigrants.

In some cases language learning is obligatory, perhaps as part of an 'integration contract', or it may be voluntary and left to the individual to decide. It may be part of a wider programme of integration, or perhaps vocational training, or quite separate. The number of hours of tuition can vary considerably, as can the cost – it may be free or subsidised.

The administrative responsibilities may be centralised or delegated locally. Teaching may be provided by specially trained professionals or left to market forces with or without quality assurance mechanisms.

There may or may not be a language test, and no doubt the approach to testing may vary.

High-stake situations concerning language skills require a degree of transparency and guarantee of fairness that legal frameworks on their own do not necessarily ensure. An organisation such as ALTE clearly can play an important role in ensuring a professional approach to testing for citizenship – and indeed some of its members (Cambridge ESOL and CITO) have in the past assisted the Council of Europe in this area during its co-operation programme concerning language requirements for citizenship in some states in central and eastern Europe.

Common European Framework of Reference for Languages

I will now look at the potential contribution of recent work in Strasbourg around the Common European Framework of Reference for Languages in addressing the problem of levels for residence or citizenship.

It is hardly necessary to recall its huge impact on learning, teaching and assessment. The ALTE Berlin Conference itself was a good illustration of this impact with several key presentations, including the plenary on Saturday by Brian North whose work was central to the Framework's development; up to 20 conference contributions linked to the CEFR in one way or another.

The Framework has been translated into over 30 languages. It is widely used in education systems as a basis for curricula and examinations, and inspires textbooks and teacher training. It is becoming increasingly clear to us that the Framework is also very influential in the field of examinations and certification across Europe, and indeed well beyond Europe. Its reference levels have been incorporated into certain European Union initiatives, most recently in *Europass,* a framework for the transparency of vocational qualifications and experiences launched earlier in 2005. We have started to carry out a survey of the uses of the CEFR in different institutions in order to attempt to assess more clearly the extent and manner of its use.

Interpreting the CEFR levels

As language testers everywhere have become interested in the use of the Framework, we have responded to what we consider to be an obligation to try to ensure that the common reference levels are interpreted consistently and in a comparable manner in different contexts. As Brian North has pointed out, the wording of even very thoroughly developed descriptors defining relatively concrete, salient features at each level can still be interpreted in a slightly different way by different individuals. We have to avoid the danger that the many different users in our member states, dealing with a range of different languages and working in a variety of contexts, might create varying interpretations that would run counter to the original aim of a common reference framework. This problem was succinctly expressed in the question posed by Charles Alderson 'How do I know that my B1 is the same as your B1?'

We need to ensure, as best we can, therefore, that claims made about the levels of examinations in relation to the Framework are reliable because they are based on appropriate and transparent linking procedures. The Council of Europe initially examined this question at a seminar in Helsinki in July 2002, and the seminar led to the setting up of a project to produce a Manual in draft form entitled *Relating language examinations to the Common European Framework of Reference for Languages.* Thanks to the dedicated work of an authoring group under the leadership of Brian North, with Neus Figueras, Sauli Takala, Piet van Avermaet (representing ALTE), and Norman Verhelst, the first version of the Manual has undergone piloting. It proposes a methodology for linking examinations to the CEFR in three phases:

1. Specification: of coverage, profiled in relation to the CEFR.
2. Standardisation: of interpretation, using calibrated illustrative samples of performances and test items to facilitate a consistent interpretation of the common reference levels.
3. Empirical validation: checking that exam results relate to CEFR levels as intended.

Support material

Illustrative reference materials to accompany the manual have been prepared. This includes videos/DVDs with calibrated illustrative samples of oral performance, and CD-ROMs with calibrated illustrative test items for listening and reading, and calibrated samples of written performances. These can be used in training for the standardisation phase, so as to ensure that the reference levels are made concrete and more easily interpreted in a consistent manner by testers, and indeed teacher trainers and teachers who may be interested.

Illustrative reference material of this kind is available for oral performances for English (Eurocentres and Cambridge ESOL) and French (CIEP and Eurocentres) and a benchmarking conference for German was organised in autumn 2005 by the Goethe-Insititut. Similar plans were made for the Spanish (Instituto Cervantes) and Italian (Perugia). The version of the CD-ROM contains reading and listening items for English, French, German, Italian and Spanish. A similar CD-ROM for writing tasks and written performance was planned in 2005 for English, French, German, Spanish and Italian (under the co-ordination of Nick Saville).

There are also CEFR-related classification grids. Many will be familiar with the grid for listening and reading items from a project funded by the Netherlands (Dutch CEFR Construct Project Group), and a grid for writing tasks has been elaborated as a further development of the work carried out by ALTE in the 1990s. These grids can provide the detailed specification for test developers that is not, and of course was never intended to be, included in the Framework itself.

I take this opportunity to record the gratitude of the Language Policy Division of the Council of Europe to those who have generously offered us the use of their material and who have, at some cost, produced video material for the project. It is not possible to mention all the examination bodies and institutes, but most are members of ALTE. The Association and Eurocentres are key contributors. Both have consultative status with the Council of Europe and we appreciate their very active involvement in that capacity. We gratefully acknowledge also the contribution of material from the EC-funded DIALANG project and from Finland.

A *Reference Supplement to the Preliminary Pilot version of the Manual* has also been published which aims to provide users of the Manual with additional information to help them in their efforts to relate their certificates and diplomas to the Framework. It contains quantitative and qualitative considerations in relating these to the CEFR and also different approaches in standard setting.

We invite any institution or individual interested in joining this pilot project to consult the information on the website where you can register, or to contact the Secretariat in Strasbourg who can give you more information directly. Of course, in the interests of linguistic diversity, we hope to see an even greater range of languages covered, and we welcome expressions of interest from anyone who might wish to develop calibrated oral performances or calibrated test items for new languages. We can supply a guide for the production of oral performances, based on our recent successful experience of this process for the French language with the CIEP and Eurocentres.

Language-specific level descriptions

Another relevant initiative concerns the elaboration of CEFR-based detailed language-specific descriptions for a range of languages – typically referred to as 'Reference Level Descriptions'.

The pioneer was Profile Deutsch with four levels initially and now C1 and C2. Levels B2 and A1 have been developed for French and others are in preparation. Work is under way for Greek (four levels completed), Portuguese, Italian, Georgian, Serbian, and planning is under way for English (in the form of the English Profile project) and for Spanish. These detailed linguistic specifications will be very useful for course planning and assessment, and the Language Policy Division will be pleased to hear from institutions that may be interested in joining this project. Guidelines are available on the website or from the Secretariat in Strasbourg. I believe that these tools are a valuable language-specific complement to the generic nature of the CEFR, not least in relation to planning teaching and testing, where this is obligatory, for residence and citizenship purposes, and in some cases are being used for that purpose.

European Language Portfolio

The ongoing work around the *European Language Portfolio* is also relevant. A preliminary bank of validated descriptors drawn selectively from different portfolios is available on the ELP website and this will be expanded over time. Electronic portfolios are now under development in several contexts, and ALTE-EAQUALS has developed and piloted a model – the first electronic ELP – which is being submitted for accreditation to the European Validation Committee in Strasbourg.

Among the 64 portfolios validated by Strasbourg so far, several are designed specifically for use by both young and adult immigrants, to guide and support their efforts to learn the language of the receiving country for residence and occupational purposes, while also giving recognition to the other languages in their plurilingual repertoire – including of course their mother tongue. The ELP provides a valuable tool for supporting immigrants and acknowledging their plurilingualism in a way that a test can never do.

We consider this work around the Framework, and relevant initiatives by others, as contributing to the CEFR toolkit, which both enriches the Framework and supports its implementation in accordance with the spirit in which it was designed.

Conclusion

I began with a reference to the Summit of Heads of State and Government of the member states of the Council of Europe held in May 2005, and I conclude with a further reference to this highly significant event which set out our future priorities.

The leaders adopted an *Action Plan* laying down the principal tasks for the Council in the coming years. Among these, and of direct relevance to the theme of the ALTE Berlin Forum, they identified *nationality* law in all its aspects, including the *promotion of the acquisition of citizenship*, as a focus point of the Council of Europe.

They reaffirmed their commitment to building a Europe without dividing lines, and in order to ensure social cohesion the Council of Europe will step up its work in the social policy field on the basis of the European Social Charter and other relevant instruments. There is a particular concern with the protection of vulnerable groups.

The Heads of State and Government stated that the Council of Europe will build on the European Year of Education through Citizenship and on its work on language learning.

They also recalled the importance of enhancing the participation of NGOs in the Council of Europe's activities as an essential element of civil society's contribution to the transparency and accountability of democratic government.

In that spirit I look forward to close co-operation with ALTE and other relevant partners in our future work on language for residence or citizenship purposes. This was taken a step further in September 2005 in co-operation with the French authorities whom I have mentioned earlier, and who once again invited the representatives of a number of other countries to a meeting at the CIEP, Paris.

The Language Policy Division finalised a new medium-term project for approval by the Steering Committee for Education in autumn 2005, and languages and citizenship have been identified as a key element in this project. We look forward to providing a platform for European co-operation in this area, and to working closely with all concerned.

Further information:
Language Policy Division website: www.coe.int/lang
European Language Portfolio website: www.coe.int/portfolio

Notes

1 The views expressed in this article are those of the author and do not commit the Council of Europe.
2 Based on the communiqué of the 112th Ministerial Session (May 2003): 'We agree that promoting human contacts and free movement of Europeans on the continent constitutes an aim which would contribute to building a Europe without dividing lines.'

16 Language testing for migration and citizenship: contexts and issues

Nick Saville
University of Cambridge ESOL Examinations, UK
Piet van Avermaet
Centre for Diversity and Learning, University of Ghent, Belgium

Introduction

The Council of Europe declared 2005 as the European Year of Citizenship through Education. One of the aims of the Year was to support democratic citizenship and participation in order to promote social cohesion, intercultural understanding and respect for diversity and human rights. In that context, the Council of Europe (Language Policy Division, Strasbourg) and ALTE set up a 1-day Forum at the second international ALTE Conference in Berlin. The Forum focused on the political and ethical issues involved in defining and assessing the language proficiency required for citizenship and for the active participation of newcomers to a country in its social, occupational and democratic processes. The event aimed to contribute to the discussion on the purpose of language assessment for citizenship throughout a wider Europe by organising a debate with key stakeholders such as politicians, policy makers and language testers and test developers. This paper describes the background to the growing role played by language proficiency testing in migration and citizenship policy and it discusses some of the contexts, practices and issues that were explored during the 2005 Forum.

Historical, social and political background

The 20th century was characterised by the mass movement of people across national and international borders, especially for migration purposes. Graddol (2006) observes that by 2000 the total number of international migrants had reached 175 million, or 3% of the world's population; people migration has continued to increase in the early years of the 21st century and it is unlikely that this trend will change in the short or longer term.

Factors underlying the movement of people on this scale are many and varied, but they are much the same as they have been over the past century; they include access to international education, international business operations, and more recently mass tourism, as well as economic migration and the search for asylum or safe haven. Recent economic and socio-political developments such as globalisation, the breakdown of the former Soviet Union, and the extension of the European Union have accelerated the growth in people movement over the past 10 years, especially in relation to migration into Western European countries. At the same time, Europe is undergoing a process of economic and political unification, and both of these processes are having an effect on the different nation states across Europe. Some fear that such processes will have a negative effect, not only on a country's economic and political structures but also on its culture and language. This fear is reflected in concerns expressed about the social cohesion of the nation, its identity, and its cultural and linguistic heritage. Questions are raised such as: *What unifies the nation? What is needed for being a citizen of a nation state?* Others raise questions from a less emotional, less rhetorical, more functional perspective. Governments search for policies and practices that will, hopefully, ensure the social cohesion of a country or a region. Language proficiency and societal knowledge are often seen as key elements within these policies and, as a result, instruments are developed to measure the language proficiency and societal knowledge of potential 'citizens' or 'new' immigrants. Whatever the underlying factors, the large-scale movement of people invariably has complex linguistic and socio-cultural implications, not only for them as individuals but also for the societies they leave behind or those to which they relocate.

It is perhaps worth noting also that nowadays migration is no longer necessarily a process whereby people simply leave place A and start a new life in place B. Migration has become much more 'fluid' than that. People often move from one place to another, stay there for some time and then go on to yet another place. For example, political refugees or asylum seekers are likely to enter one of the European member states, stay there for some time, and then move on to another country, either within Europe or elsewhere in the world, e.g. the US or Canada. Similarly, increased access to air and other forms of international travel has led to changes in the processes of economic migration. Polish welders, for example, can take a cheap flight on Monday morning from Krakow to Brussels; they work in the construction business in Brussels till Friday and then fly back to Krakow that same day to spend the weekend with the family in Krakow. Polish women working in the cleaning business in different parts of Germany arrive by bus on Monday at the start of the working week and return to their family on Friday. These new 'types' of migration can place considerable pressure on Europe and its nation states in relation to concepts like social cohesion, integration, citizenship, identity, culture and language.

Citizenship, identity and language

Not surprisingly, notions of citizenship, and the role of identity and language within citizenship, have assumed an increasingly high profile, especially within the European context. Some defining of terms may be helpful here. *Citizenship* is generally regarded as a universal concept, with cosmopolitan citizenship being based on principles of equality, freedom of speech, respect for democracy, human rights, non-discrimination, etc. Citizenship is most commonly experienced at the local, regional and national level though it can also exist at a supranational level such as Europe (Starkey 2002). *Identity* is generally regarded as concerned with who or what a particular person is; it consists of different elements depending on circumstances, context and other factors. Identity can be shaped by where we live, whom we meet, our income, our temperament, age, symbolic capital, etc. When one of these parameters changes, our identity can change; we recognise that these parameters change constantly, hence Pinxten and Venstraete's assertion that 'Every identity is temporary' (Pinxten and Verstraete 1998). *Language* is generally recognised as a system of human expression by means of words, signs, movements, pictures, graphs, etc. which can be used to express meaning or feelings.

For some years now a shift has been taking place in many European countries towards more rigorous conditions for those seeking to apply for citizenship. One of the new (or renewed) conditions for obtaining citizenship is language proficiency. In some countries those applying for citizenship are asked to provide evidence that they have attained a certain level of proficiency in the official language (or one of the official languages) of the country. More and more frequently language tests are being used for this purpose. However, the socio-political contexts in which these conditions have been instituted and language tests developed differ widely. The grounds for stipulating language as a requirement for citizenship, for example, in Slovenia or Latvia may differ from the justification in the Netherlands or Germany. At the same time, it is interesting to examine the rationale in other countries, such as Belgium, for not stipulating language and a language test as one of the conditions for attaining citizenship. The motivation for countries in Europe (who promote the multicultural and multilingual richness of Europe) to have language and language tests as a condition for obtaining citizenship is a matter for debate. To what extent is knowing the language of a country a token of integration and a prerequisite for being a citizen?

Re-examining some commonly held assumptions

It is a commonly held view that immigrants have no language tools to function successfully in a country or region; in order to be able to function satisfactorily in society they need to know or learn the national language. Though this might seem a reasonable view at first glance, it is founded upon three somewhat questionable assumptions: that knowing the national or standard language increases opportunities for work, education and upward social mobility; that only the standard language guarantees these opportunities; and that the standard language is the only efficient and necessary means of communication. Each of these three assumptions is worth examining in more depth.

Assumption 1: Knowing the language increases opportunities for work, education and upward social mobility.
In fact, knowing the standard language does not by definition solve the 'problems' of immigrants. Immigrants are often on the receiving end of a systemic structural discrimination, and their language use is an effect of that rather than a cause. As long as socio-economic marginalisation continues, the access to the standard language (status language) is likely to remain restricted. As long as the poor performances of immigrant children at school are the outcome of systematic and structural factors, upward social mobility and access to the standard language (which often go hand in hand) will remain restricted.

Assumption 2: Only the standard language guarantees these opportunities and the standard language is the only efficient and necessary means of communication.
In reality of course, all European countries are multilingual. The language of schooling is in most countries the national standard language(s). At the same time linguistic varieties abound in the workplace, in schools, in the street and in the media. For example, teachers in Flanders often use another variant of the Dutch standard language in the playground. People being interviewed on British television channels often use a dialect or a regional variant of the English language. For more and more of their academic and professional work Europeans need English or French. In our daily social life we make use of other languages and/or language varieties on a regular basis: through the internet, in different communication modes used in newspapers and magazines. Participation in society and opportunities for the increase of social upward mobility presupposes plurilinguality for all, including the standard language. So this needs to be reflected in education, teaching and assessment for all, not just for migrants.

Assumption 3: Immigrants have no language tools to function successfully in a country or region.

The truth is that immigrants are often plurilingual. They master many languages and language varieties, often including the standard language. Indeed they often master more languages than the average 'Flemish' or 'English' person. This functional plurilinguality enables them to 'integrate' in their neighbourhood, contrary to the political and/or media discourse which suggests 'they don't speak "the language", so they are not "integrated" or don't want to become so'. For example, a Turkish immigrant who has lived for more than 30 years in Flanders may speak Turkish with family and friends, some Arabic at the mosque, and even a bit of French he learned at school; in Brussels he can use some Dutch to function at work and some Ghent dialect to do some shopping. In a multilingual society languages fulfil multiple functions and there are different options to choose from: standard languages; regional minority languages; dialects; and immigrant languages.

The position of the Council of Europe

Education for democratic citizenship has become a key element in the integration of migrants in different European countries. Language tuition and tuition in cultural and societal knowledge of the nation play an important role in this. Language learning in Europe can be contextualised within the declaration on Education for Democratic Citizenship (1999) adopted by the Committee of Ministers of the Council of Europe, which states that the purposes of education for democratic citizenship are:

- to equip men and women to play an active part in public life and to shape, in a responsible way, their own destiny and that of society
- to instil a culture of human rights
- to prepare people to live in a multicultural society and to deal with difference knowledgeably, sensibly, tolerantly and morally
- to strengthen social cohesion, mutual understanding and solidarity.

The Committee of Ministers of the Council of Europe, in its Recommendation Rec (2002) 12 on education for democratic citizenship, recommends that 'all public and private, official and non-governmental, professional and voluntary actors [be involved] in designing, implementing and monitoring policies on education for democratic citizenship.' It is perhaps ironic, however, that it is primarily newly arriving immigrants who are perceived as needing to be 'educated for democratic citizenship'. One might argue that preparation for living in a multicultural society is needed as much by the so-called 'original inhabitants' of the 'host country' as by the immigrant population.

The Council of Europe's concern for the social inclusion and active participation of migrants in society is reflected, for example, in the provisions for language tuition for migrants contained in the European Convention on the Legal Status of Migrant Workers and the European Social Charter. At the same time, the European Convention on Human Rights (ECHR) and the Universal Declaration of Human Rights (UDHR) both enshrine the linguistic and other rights of minorities. For example, Article 10 of the ECHR states that people in Europe have the right to speak, broadcast and publish in any language, so long the content is respectful of the rights, privacy and dignity of the others. Article 14 of the ECHR and Article 2 of the UDHR protects individuals against discrimination in their entitlement to rights such as language use. Conventions and Declarations such as these can provide language testing professionals with important reference points when they are asked by policy makers and governments to be involved in the development of an assessment instrument with high ethical consequences e.g. admission to the country, citizenship, etc.

Clearly, it is important to address and reflect upon the philosophical and ethical issues raised so far when considering the role of language tests for migration and citizenship purposes. This becomes especially important for professional language testers involved in test development for citizenship and migration purposes since it touches directly upon the ethics of testing and the quality of test development. The second part of this paper considers in more detail the minimum standards that might need to be in place for the appropriate use of language proficiency tests linked to migration policy and practice.

The role of language tests in migration and citizenship

The use of language tests in conjunction with the movement of people is nothing new. For example, tests like the Cambridge examinations (and similar tests in other European languages) have always provided achievable learning goals and meaningful accreditation for those who want to study or work abroad, or those who enjoy being international travellers and tourists. Some tests, like IELTS, have been used for many years by educational institutions for international study/training purposes; more recently they have been used for registration and licensing purposes by professional bodies dealing with international applicants in domains such as the health professions and government agencies.

The large-scale adoption of language tests by governments and nation states for decision-making regarding the admission of newcomers to their countries and the granting of citizenship is a more recent phenomenon. The language testing community finds itself being drawn increasingly into discussions about the role of language tests in the management of migration and decisions about citizenship. The use of language tests, sometimes in conjunction with tests of cultural knowledge, to determine whether an individual should be granted formal citizenship is a sensitive issue, sometimes hotly debated. Indeed it has been the source of vigorous and ongoing debate within the language testing and assessment community for some years now.

As a body of specialists in language testing and assessment, the Association of Language Testers in Europe (ALTE) has been seeking to make a significant contribution to this debate at both national and international levels with view to ensuring that where language tests and their outcomes are used for purposes of migration or citizenship this is done in an appropriate and ethical way. ALTE's status as an international non-governmental organisation (INGO) for the Council of Europe[1] makes it especially well-placed to contribute to this debate. In 2002 ALTE established a working group to co-ordinate these activities and members of this group have been working closely with the Council of Europe and with relevant government departments in their own countries. Cambridge ESOL, for example, maintains an active interest in the educational and socio-political issues associated with migration and citizenship in the UK context, since these touch directly upon language and education as well as culture and identity in British society today. As the British government seeks to develop and implement appropriate policies for managing migration in the UK context, exams like the ESOL Skills for Life suite introduced in 2005 are likely to play a growing role.

The joint *Language Testing and Citizenship Forum* at the 2005 ALTE Conference, set up by the Council of Europe and ALTE, aimed to contribute to the discussion on the purpose of language assessment for citizenship throughout a wider Europe by organising a debate with key stakeholders such as politicians, policy makers and test developers. Keynote presentations were given by the Council of Europe (see Sheils in this volume) and by Dr Rita Sussmuth, Member of the Global Commission on International Migration. Case studies from various European countries were presented, including Slovenia, Germany, Latvia, UK, France and the Netherlands, offering information and insights on policy and practice in specific European contexts. Acknowledged academic specialists in the field – Prof Elana Shohamy and Prof Antony Kunnan – chaired a debate. Through the keynote talks, the case studies, and the debate between presenters and audience, a number of questions were addressed:

Why should proficiency in 'national' languages be a requirement for obtaining citizenship and a prerequisite for integration and social cohesion?

Can a tension be observed between European policies and national policies?

How should language proficiency be measured? At what level? What is the rationale behind determining a level of language proficiency for citizenship purposes?

What is good practice and good ethical behaviour for professional language testers?

What should a professional test developer do in order to make language tests for citizenship as ethical as possible?

How can a European organisation of professional language testers like ALTE contribute to such a process?

One direct outcome of the *Language Testing and Citizenship Forum* at the Berlin 2005 Conference was the production of an information leaflet by the Council of Europe's Language Policy Division in co-operation with ALTE. The leaflet aims to inform interested parties of some of the key issues to be taken into account when considering the use of language tests for migration and citizenship purposes.

As an increasing number of European countries introduce or formalise their requirements for migration and citizenship purposes, more and more national governments are adopting language tests or other formal assessment procedures. Where language tests are used, and given the wide-ranging consequences of using such tests in high-stakes contexts, it is important for all test developers and policy makers to follow established Codes of Practice to ensure that all aspects of the assessment process are of high quality and that all stakeholders are treated fairly. Professional test developers can assist policy makers in ensuring that suitable language tests are chosen and, where necessary, new tests are constructed, used and reported appropriately for these purposes; their contribution should address both the ethical and technical issues that can arise.

International Codes of Practice and Standards

The outcomes of language tests which are used for migration or citizenship purposes have serious consequences and affect the lives of the test takers. Whereas high-quality tests and appropriate uses can facilitate the process of language learning and integration of the test takers within a multicultural society, poor-quality tests or inappropriate uses can endanger integration and may lead to social exclusion. Professional test developers thus have a responsibility in raising awareness of the implication of national policies for the development of valid and reliable tests, taking into account diverse purposes and contexts of use which can exist. Their expertise and experience can ensure that the needs of both the policy makers and test takers are fully taken into account. However, the responsibility for the appropriate selection, interpretation and use of tests is a shared one: the policy makers (often the test sponsors), the users of the results (employers, government officials, etc.) and the test takers themselves all need to play their part in striving for fairness. To do so they need to be kept adequately informed and to be consulted in appropriate ways.

The international Codes of Practice and Standards which have been developed to help ensure fairness in language-testing practices typically cover:

- test development and routine test construction
- test conduct and administration systems
- test marking, grading and issue of results (including certification)
- test analysis and validation procedures, including provision of evidence to back up claims made about the tests' validity and reliability.

Key issues to be addressed in developing assessment instruments

Questions of the following kind should be raised by those involved in planning and developing assessments, and well-reasoned answers supported by evidence of good practice need to be provided.

*What is **the purpose of the test** and how does this influence the level, the content, the administration and the use of results?*
It makes a difference whether a test is meant to motivate the learners (to help them use and improve their current competence in the target language), to ascertain whether their competence is sufficient for participation in well-defined social situations (for study or work), or to make decisions which affect their legal rights, such as their right to remain in the country or acquire citizenship. It is very important for the test takers to know the purpose, so that they can prepare accordingly. It is also necessary for other members of society to understand the intended purpose so that the results can be interpreted and used correctly.

*Which **level of language proficiency** is required in the target language for the stated purposes, and how does this relate to international level systems, such as the Common European Framework of Reference for Languages (CEFR) developed by the Council of Europe?*
An appropriate level of proficiency in the target language should be chosen to reflect the stated purpose of the test and use of the results. In building a rationale for this, the CEFR can be used to ensure transparency and coherence of these aims. Test development and validation procedures must be

employed to ensure that this level remains stable and consistent whenever the test is used.

*Who is responsible for the **administration of the tests** to ensure that professional standards of conduct are met?*
Standardised procedures are necessary for the accreditation of suitable test centres and the administration of the tests. There must be adequate provision of information and support systems for the test takers and other test users.

*What procedures are in place for **monitoring test outcomes**, including possible negative impacts, and what evidence is collected to **demonstrate fairness**, and that the test design and use does not lead to bias or unfair discrimination against some test takers?*
Data should be collected and analysed regularly to ensure that the test is valid and reliable and fulfils its intended purpose effectively, and to monitor for unintended consequences. Changes in the groups taking the test, as well as the effect of general changes in the contexts in which the test is being used, can only be detected and acted upon when there is a proper system of monitoring the results of the test for the various groups of test takers.

Conclusion

Work on issues relating to migration, citizenship and language assessment continues, building on work already completed in the ALTE context specifically in relation to the debate in France and Germany. For example, in 2006 ALTE representatives were invited to join an Ad Hoc Project Group which forms part of a mid-term Council of Europe project to look at Language, Migration and Social Cohesion. ALTE's contribution to the project was intended to provide advice and support to government departments and non-governmental organisations in their understanding and use of language assessment for migration and citizenship purposes. The ALTE group working on these issues met in Copenhagen in April 2006 and again at Sevres in May 2006 to discuss two specific contributions to the project: the development of a survey questionnaire and an extended information booklet which will elaborate on the information provided in the leaflet referred to above.

Note

1 The Council of Europe is an intergovernmental organisation whose principal aims are to: protect human rights, pluralist democracy and the rule of law; promote awareness of Europe's cultural identity and diversity; seek solutions to problems facing European society; help consolidate democratic stability in Europe; and promote unity in diversity. Founded in May 1949, the Council

of Europe now has 46 member states, including the 25 European Union states. Its permanent headquarters are in Strasbourg, France.

References and further reading

ALTE website: www.alte.org

Council of Europe website: www.coe.int

Council of Europe (2002) *Recommendation Rec (2002) 12 of the Committee of Ministers to member states on education for democratic citizenship*, available at <http://www.coe.int/T/e/Cultural_Co-operation/Education/E.D.C/ Documents_and_publications/By_Type/Adopted_texts/>

Graddol, D (2006) *English Next*, The British Council.

Starkey, H (2002) *Democratic Citizenship, Languages, Diversity and Human Rights*, Reference study for Language Policy Division, DGIV, Strasborg: Council of Europe.

Pinxten, R and Verstraete, G (1998) *Cultuur en Macht*, Antwerpen: Houteriet.

17

Language varieties and their implications for testing and assessment

Lynda Taylor
Consultant to University of Cambridge ESOL
Examinations

Abstract

This paper considers the issues that linguistic diversity raises for language test developers. Findings from a recent survey of perceptions, policy, and practice among European language test providers are presented and discussed. The paper concludes with suggestions on how testing agencies can adopt a principled and pragmatic approach to the issues – one which acknowledges and affirms linguistic diversity while at the same time maintaining essential standards of quality and fairness.

Introduction

The 2005 ALTE Conference took as its theme the impact of multilingualism on language assessment and focused on the challenge of setting common standards at the same time as sustaining linguistic diversity. Linguistic diversity can be considered from a variety of perspectives: for example, notions of multilingualism and multiculturalism across groups and within societies; notions of plurilingualism and pluriculturalism at the individual and personal level; and notions of cross-cultural and inter-cultural understanding within and between nations. Not surprisingly, references to all of these dimensions can be found in the Council of Europe's *Common European Framework of Reference for Languages: Learning, Teaching, Assessment* (2001) which is having an increasing influence on European policy-making in language teaching and learning.

Perhaps one of the most interesting perspectives to consider in relation to linguistic diversity is the issue of *language variation* within and across languages and linguistic communities. This paper begins by reviewing the general phenomenon of language variation and varieties, considering some of the implications it may have for language teaching, and especially for testing agencies. It goes on to describe a small-scale survey of perceptions, policy, and practice on language varieties among European language test providers in the context of the ALTE partnership. The paper concludes with a brief discussion of some possible principles for testing policy and practice which may help to address the issues raised by language variation.

The nature of language variation

The nature of language variation and evolution is a well-established and increasingly well-described phenomenon. In the case of English, for example, the worldwide spread of English over several centuries has led to the emergence of regionally based varieties – British, American, Australian English; more recently, so-called 'new Englishes' have emerged in certain regions – for example, Hong Kong, Singapore, and the European Union. The situation as it relates to English has been well documented over the past decade by many writers in the field (see for example, Brutt-Griffler 2002, Crystal 1995, 1997, Jenkins 2000, McArthur 1998, Trudgill and Hannah 1994 and many others). For a helpful and up-to-date overview of this field since the early 1980s, see Bolton (2004).

However, English is not the only European language to have experienced such linguistic evolution; other widely spoken languages in Europe can testify to a similar experience, though perhaps not on such a grand or global scale. For example, French, Spanish and Portuguese all have established or emerging varieties in different parts of the world such as Canada, Mexico, Brazil. Less widely spoken European languages experience a similar phenomenon; for them variety may be less wide-ranging geographically but there can still be debate at national and regional level about how closely a particular 'localised' variety of the language does or does not align with an accepted or acceptable national standard.

At the micro-level, language variation manifests itself in certain distinctive features: phonological, morphological and lexical, syntactic and orthographic; at a more macro-level, variation can also be seen in discoursal features (to do with rhetorical structure), and in pragmatic features (to do with the socio-cultural context of use). The function of language variation is well recognised within applied linguistics: it helps to support notions of identity, belonging to a community, or being a member of a particular fellowship. Identity may be regionally based and be reflected in a particular accent or dialect; or it may be more personally or group based, giving rise to what are sometimes referred to as 'idiolects' or 'sociolects'. Linguistic analysis has also identified variation across high and low forms of language (acrolects/mesolects/basilects), and in recent years we have learned much about the important variation which occurs between language in its *spoken* forms and language in its *written* forms.

The relationship between language varieties

How do we explain the relationship between the many different regionally based linguistic varieties which exist? In the case of English, applied linguists have made various attempts to model relationships between language varieties using analogies with biology or geography, and using metaphors such as a tree structure (Strevens 1980) or a wheel (McArthur 1992). Most famously, perhaps, Kachru defined 'world Englishes' as 'the functional and formal variations, divergent sociolinguistic contexts, ranges and varieties of English in creativity, and various types of acculturation in parts of the Western and non-Western world' (Kachru 1992:2). Kachru subdivided varieties of English into three categories or 'circles': *inner*, *outer* and *expanding*, with each circle relating to the notion of norms in a different way. He went on to describe some varieties as *norm providing* (e.g. English as a native language in the US, UK, Australia); some as *norm-developing* (e.g. English as a second language in India, Nigeria, Malaysia); and others as *norm-dependent* (e.g. English as a foreign language in China, Israel, Indonesia). With its focus on 'norms', Kachru's analysis has particular relevance for language teachers and testers.

The debate about world Englishes has often been a complex and controversial one. Most contributors to the debate agree on the rapid increase in the numbers of L2 speakers of English worldwide and the growth in world Englishes. In light of this, some have suggested that control or ownership of the English language is steadily expanding beyond the traditional L1 speaker communities who are largely white, Anglo-Saxon and Protestant (Kachru and Smith 1985, Strevens 1980); others have focused on the continuing necessity for some sort of internationally recognised standard (Quirk 1990). Some have warned of the dangers of 'linguistic imperialism' (Pennycook 1994, Phillipson 1992); others have discussed the relevance and usefulness of the traditional 'native speaker' model or norm (Davies 1991, 2003: Graddol, McArthur, Flack and Amey 1999); and there are those who predict we may be moving towards some sort of 'standard world English' which is neutral and non-political (Crystal 1997, McArthur 1998) or towards an international lingua franca English (Jenkins 2003, Seidlhofer 2001).

Language variation and implications for language teaching and testing

In recent years discourse and corpus linguistic techniques have given us increasingly sophisticated approaches to analysing language in use; as a result our description and understanding of the extent and nature of language variation have improved considerably; better description and increased understanding have led in turn to a greater awareness of the issues language variation can raise for the teaching and learning of language, and also for testing and assessment. One issue, for example, concerns the role of *standardisation* and the choice of *norms* – where do/should we get our norms and standards from, and why? Another issue concerns the notion of *prescriptivism* – does one variety have an inherently higher value than another, and should this variety be imposed as widely as possible for purposes of teaching and learning? The notion of dialects existing on a continuum, with some closer to one another than others (Crystal 1995), raises questions about precisely which dialects it is reasonable to expect a speaker to cope with: should it be only those dialects which are close to their own, or those at some distance? Analysis of spoken interaction has also highlighted the fascinating phenomenon of *accommodation*, i.e. the tendency for speakers to converge in the way they choose and use their words, to facilitate interaction or to obtain approval. Is this something we should teach language learners, and how do we deal with it in an assessment context?

For both the teacher and the tester, language variation raises practical issues about *what to teach* – in relation to pedagogy, materials and training, and *what to test* – in relation to the standards, norms, models and judgement criteria we adopt (Davies, Hamp-Lyons and Kemp 2003, Lowenberg 2000). The theoretical and practical decisions facing teachers and testers are made even more complicated by socio-political sensitivities about *whose* language should be the focus of our attention, as well as by the ever increasing rate of language change in today's fast-moving world in which the information and communications revolution continues to have such an impact. There are also many voices in the debate – each one with a particular point of view seeking to be heard and acknowledged; they include the voices of not only language teachers and testers, but also applied linguists, educational policy-makers, and language learners themselves (and even their parents). The topic of language varieties can be a sensitive one, precisely because it touches on issues of culture and personal identity; this is likely to be the case not just for English but for other languages too, particularly in the European context with its constantly shifting socio-political realities. It is perhaps significant that the 2005 annual conference of the British Association of Applied Linguistics (BAAL) took as its theme 'Language, Culture and Identity in Applied Linguistics'; the conference included a symposium which aimed to bring together specialists from applied linguistics, language pedagogy and language assessment to explore issues surrounding the concept of the 'native' and 'non-native' speaker and its relationship with language, culture and identity.

Those of us who are responsible for assessing language ability need to be able to account somehow for language variation within the model of linguistic or communicative competence underpinning our tests. We need to consider how language variation affects the validity, reliability, practicality and impact of the tests we offer. At the very least we need to keep our policy and practice on language variation under review and maintain a clear rationale for why we do what we do in relation to the inclusion, or non-inclusion, of more than one linguistic variety in our tests.

In the light of the ongoing world Englishes debate, Cambridge ESOL embarked on an internal review of its own policy and practice with regard to the English(es) used in our tests (see Taylor 2006 for some discussion of the issues); our internal discussion began from a review of documentation produced by several other international providers of English language proficiency tests to see what they said about their stimulus materials, test task design, assessment criteria, standard/norms, and rater training. The results showed a striking diversity of approach across different English language testing agencies with few test providers seeming to offer a clear rationale for their policy and practice (Taylor 2001, 2002). In 2004 the investigation was extended to take a broader perspective and consider the issues faced by assessment providers testing languages other than English. The ALTE partnership offered a unique opportunity to conduct a survey of current perceptions, policy and practice among a selection of European language testing agencies. At the time of writing, there are 28 members of ALTE – all European language testing agencies – representing 24 European languages, some more widely spoken than others. In addition, at least 16 further test providers have observer status within ALTE offering tests in at least six other European languages.

Methodology

The methodology used for this small-scale survey was relatively simple and involved a short, open questionnaire instrument with three parts:

- Part A captured background information
- Part B focused on language varieties – in terms of professional, personal and public perceptions
- Part C probed the impact of language varieties on testing policy and practice.

The questionnaire instrument was trialled with a small group of ALTE partners in November 2004; following this, no significant changes to the questionnaire were considered necessary. Questions 1 to 3 in Part A gathered background information such as name, organisation and language of interest, and the remaining 13 questions are listed below.

Part B:

Q4: Please list regional areas where the language you have identified is widely used.

Q5:   Do different 'varieties' of the language exist as a result of this internationalisation regionalisation? If so, please list them as you perceive them to exist.

Q6:   Do 'varieties' of the language also exist within country?

Q7:   How does this variation manifest itself?

Q8:   How does the general public tend to regard these within-country and international varieties?

Q9:   To what extent are language varieties reflected in the news media?

Q10:   Are any varieties considered to be 'more/less educated'? Or 'high/low prestige'?

Q11:   Are some varieties better 'codified' or described than others?

Q12:   Which language variety is generally used as a model for teaching and learning?

Part C:

Q13:   How would you describe the language variety/ies used in your organisation's tests?

Q14:   Do your tests reflect different language varieties in any way?

Q15:   How important/relevant is the notion of the 'native speaker' (NS) and the 'non-native' speaker (NNS) in your testing policy/practice?

Q16:   Are you aware of external pressures to reflect multiple language varieties in your tests?

For most of the questions some exemplification or indication of level of response expected was provided. (The full questionnaire is included as Appendix 1.)

The survey questionnaire was sent out electronically in February 2005 to 28 ALTE members and to 16 ALTE observers with an option to complete and return it either electronically or by post. A reminder invitation was sent (with a second copy of the questionnaire) in March 2005. In all, nine respondents completed and returned the questionnaire. Seven respondents were ALTE members and two were ALTE observers – representing eight languages overall: Basque, Czech, Dutch, English, French, German, Portuguese (x 2) and Welsh. Despite the limited return, this nevertheless made for an interesting sample. The set of eight included a mix of widely spoken and less widely spoken languages, some with international and others with intranational varieties; some languages had strong geopolitical support, others had less; some were stronger and others were weaker, depending on certain criteria, e.g. number of speakers, contextual relevance/use. As Gardner (2004) notes, number of speakers can be difficult to determine accurately and it may not always correlate with the actual use of a language or its state of health.

The original version of this paper presented at the ALTE Berlin conference in May 2005 reported on the analysis and results for the eight languages listed above. One additional completed questionnaire – for Italian – was received following the conference; although the information for Italian was not included in the original conference paper, it has been integrated into the analysis and is reflected in what follows.

Results and analysis

Even with only 10 respondents, there were discernible common threads in the questionnaire responses: all respondents commented on levels of linguistic variation – either internationally, or within national borders, or both (e.g. German, Czech, Basque), and all gave examples of types of variation for their languages which are included here for illustrative purposes.

Examples of lexical variation

French phrases for 'toss the salad' can include *remuer* or *tourner* or *tournebouler* or *fatiguer la salade*. The Welsh word used for 'milk' can be *llaeth* in the north of the country, or *llefrith* in the south. The German word for 'newsstand' would normally be *Kiosk* while in Austria *Trafik* would be more usual; similarly, German/Austrian variations exist for 'doctor's surgery' – *Arztpraxis* and *Ordination*.

Examples of syntactic variation

In German variation can occur in the use of complementary verb structures between northern and southern regions (*Ich bin gesessen/Ich habe gesessen*), and also in noun gender, e.g. *die Butter* (N) and *der Butter* (S). In Portuguese the standard form for 'Give me' would be *Da-me*, while in spoken Brazilian Portuguese *Me da* would be more common. Interestingly, for French it was reported that 'grammar rules are the same everywhere' – perhaps reflecting a particular view of language standardisation, epitomised by the existence of the national Académie Française.

Examples of phonological variation

Phonological variation – as expressed through regional dialects – is perhaps one of the most familiar and widespread aspects of language variation. Examples from Portuguese include the shift between northern and southern Portugal from /v/ to /b/ in the word *vaca* (cow), as well as the pronunciation of *dje* rather than *de* in Brazilian Portuguese in the word *cidade* (city). North German speakers tend to use a voiced [z] for *Sonne* (sun) while those in the south tend more to an unvoiced consonant [s]. For historical reasons, there is a long-established Welsh-speaking community in Patagonia, South America, and perhaps not surprisingly they are reputed to speak Welsh with a strong Spanish accent!

Examples from the Basque language illustrate well how lexical, syntactic and phonological variation can occur even within less widely spoken languages such as Basque and Welsh which each have fewer than one million speakers. Basque is spoken in parts of Southern France as well as in the Basque country and in northern Spain.

	Lexis	**Grammar**	**Pronunciation**
Western Basque (N Spain)	*Baltz* *Ondo*	*Joan jat*	*Jan* /j/, /x/ *Harri* /th/
Middle Basque (N Spain)	*Beltz* *Ongi*	*Joan zait*	*Jan* /x/ *Harri* /th/
Eastern Basque (S France)	*Beltz* *Untsa*	*Joan zaut*	*Jan* /j/ *Harri* /h/

Other common threads running through responses to Questions 4–12 – on professional, personal and public perceptions of language varieties – are discussed below.

Public perceptions of varieties

Many respondents pointed to the existence of 'dialects' or 'varieties' of a commonly shared national language, with variation largely determined along regional or geographical axes, i.e. a north/south/east/west divide. Some respondents pointed to intra-national 'languages', e.g. Frysian and Limburg within the Netherlands; Breton and Occitan within France. Some reported inter-national varieties, e.g. Portuguese in Portugal and Brazil; French in France and Canada.

Use of language varieties in public life and media

Respondents often noted the use of a common formal, written language but greater variation in the informal, largely spoken medium, where varieties are generally more accepted/acceptable; there is also a tendency to use 'standard' forms in the national media (newspapers, TV, etc.) and more variation in the local media. One respondent speculated that the growth of the media might be leading to the population becoming more accustomed to dialects, with communication across the dialect continuum becoming easier as a result.

The perceived status of varieties

Concern about high/low status of particular varieties was generally perceived as less of an issue in today's world, and there were few cases where it was felt certain varieties might be regarded as 'more/less educated'. Interestingly, there were three languages for which it was felt that 'northern' norms might be perceived by some as more 'correct' or 'prestige' – Welsh, German and Italian. Could this have something to do with economic success and socio-political influence in more northerly regions for some countries, in a similar way some centuries ago to the development of a standard English out of the socio-economic importance of southern England?

The degree of description or 'codification' of varieties

Most respondents reported the availability now of a wide range of dictionaries, grammar, textbooks and other language-related materials for regionally based language varieties, including extensive web-based information. The recent contribution of language corpora and corpus linguistics to this phenomenon was noted. There are, however, some regions of the world where it was felt certain varieties remain far less codified, e.g. Portuguese in Lusofone Africa; French in Senegal, Togo and Burundi.

The role of varieties in teaching/learning

In most cases some sort of 'standard' model was acknowledged for use in the teaching and learning context; in the case of Basque, this means 'unified Basque'. However, it was reported that the 'standard' model adopted may reflect the region concerned, i.e. for Portuguese whether the teaching/learning context was Europe or Brazil; whether it was Netherlands or Flanders for Dutch/Flemish; and whether it was north or south Wales for Welsh. In some cases the role and influence of national bodies were acknowledged, e.g. The Institute of Czech Language, the Académie Française. Several respondents noted the issues raised by the shift in language education away from the traditional focus on reading/writing towards a more communicative, spoken curriculum – a change which is more recent in some parts of Europe than in others.

Questions 13–16 of the questionnaire focused more closely on the perceived impact of language varieties on the policy and practice of language test providers.

- Question 13 – *How would you describe the language variety/ies used in your organisation's tests?*

Seven respondents made reference to the words 'standard', six to the term 'native speaker', and four referred to 'educated speaker'. Tests of the Basque language are based on 'unified Basque'.

- Question 14 – *Do your tests reflect different language varieties in any way?*

Some variation was reported for reading materials as a result of selecting texts from a range of authentic sources, e.g. texts in French from Québec, Belgium and African countries as well as from France. Listening materials appeared to contain greater levels of variation, mainly in terms of range of regional accents. One test provider reported including no regional varieties. Interestingly, separate variety-based versions were reported for some languages. For Welsh, for example, there exist North and South versions of the Entry and Foundation level tests, and the Intermediate level has two versions of the Listening dialogue; at the more advanced level, however, candidates are expected to be able to understand different Welsh dialects. It seems that in this suite of tests, at least, language variety is placed somewhere on a continuum of difficulty.

- Question 15 – *How important/relevant is the notion of the native-speaker/non-native-speaker in your testing policy/practice?*

Once again responses varied considerably as shown by the original comments below. Some respondents reported relying entirely on native speakers (NS) and not using non-native-speakers (NNS) at all.

> *'so far we have never used any NNS'*
> *'very important – we never employ NNS raters of written and spoken production'*
> *'we always use NS for oral components and written foreign language'*

Others reported using both NSs and NNSs but in differing roles:

> *'NNS raters of written/spoken production are employed in collaboration with NS'*
> *'only NS for test development, often NNS for administration (examiners)'*

Some comments focused more strongly on the level of language competence involved rather than on the origin of the speaker:

> *'there are some NNS used as raters, but these are experienced language tutors and highly fluent; these would generally not be employed as raters or interlocutors at the intermediate or advanced levels'*
> *'our sociolinguistic reality basically refers to the quality of the speaker, more than to the origin of the speaker'*

Views varied on the usefulness or otherwise of the NS as the criterion for success:

> *'the idealised NS is the criterion for success'*

> *'one of the main criteria for success is fitness for purpose/effectiveness of communication'*
>
> *'the notion of native speaker is best avoided when designing assessment criteria'*

- Question 16 – *Are you aware of external pressures to reflect multiple language varieties in your tests?*

This final question attempted to probe how far test providers might be sensitive to internal and/or external demands for them to accommodate language varieties in their tests. Once again responses varied:

> *'no'*
> *'not at the moment'*
> *'our test is not designed for language varieties'*
> *'yes, every day'*
> *'absolutely, particularly in the case of the minority languages'*
> *'yes, in advanced courses'*
> *'there is pressure from X and Y (two other countries) – however our colleagues would prefer standard L (name of language)*
> *'yes. . . course designers tend to want to reflect their own dialect. . . there has to be a compromise between dialects, classroom practice, and materials or tests which are published at national level'*

Discussion

The findings from this small-scale and somewhat preliminary study suggest that a number of general observations can be made. On the basis of this sample at least, there are clearly certain perceptions and elements of experience which are shared across a range of European test providers; however, there is also evidence of some diversity in attitude and approach. Any testing organisation's policy and practice will naturally be shaped by factors such as the context and purpose for a given test (i.e. where the test is being used, what/whom it is designed for, etc.). Issues of validity, reliability, impact and practicality play their part too, along with the notion of 'test usefulness' or 'fitness for purpose'; although the words 'equal access' and 'fairness' did not appear explicitly in the responses, there is some evidence that these too are considerations. At a more macro-level, historical and socio-political factors cannot be ignored either.

Clearly the challenge facing all language testers is the need to set and maintain common language standards for assessment purposes and at the same time acknowledge and reflect the reality of linguistic diversity. But how far do we have a principled approach to dealing with this in our policy and practice? Can we identify principles for good/best practice? And how might we want to see our policy/practice develop in the future as the languages we teach and test continue to evolve, and as new or established varieties assume an increased social, political or educational significance? There are three key areas in which it may be possible to articulate helpful guidelines for our test developers and perhaps communicate a more transparent position to the wider world: *selecting the test input; evaluating the test output; interlocutors and raters.*

When selecting test input, in terms of the content and linguistic features of reading and listening texts and the tasks designed around them, the guiding principles must be to do with clarifying the test purpose and the underlying construct. Our content sampling will ideally be as representative as it can be of the target language use (TLU) domain. This may have implications for the level of variation we can reasonably consider acceptable or desirable across different modes (spoken and written) or codes (informal and formal) as well as other types of variation such as accent. The notion of the 'main host language of communication' may be a helpful one to consider here. For example, in the case of IELTS, an international English proficiency test used to assess the language level needed for study, work or training in English-speaking environments, the test tasks are prepared by an international team of test writers drawn from the TLU context (i.e. UK, Australia, New Zealand); consequently test input, especially in the Listening test, reflects features of the English varieties used in the TLU domain. The design specification for any test will ideally draw on a linguistic description of the target language (including extent of variation) and be based on some sort of needs analysis (for an explicit model of test development see Chapter 2 of Weir and Milanovic 2003). This may be easier in situations where the TLU context is relatively easily defined, as in the case of IELTS. It can prove more difficult, however, where the TLU context is far broader and perhaps still awaiting description or codification, e.g. the use of English as a lingua franca between non-native English speakers anywhere in the world. A comprehensive linguistic description of EIL (English as an International Language) varieties remains some years off although progress is beginning to be made on the use of English in the European context through projects such as the Vienna–Oxford International Corpus of English (VOICE) (Seidlhofer 2001).

Accommodating variation within the test input is one aspect requiring careful thought; the standards against which we evaluate a candidate's output are another. What do we set as the criterion for success? How should we treat features of a candidate's written or spoken production (e.g. spelling/pronunciation) which may reflect a variety they have learned or grown up with? Once again, clarifying the test construct and purpose can help us here. We need to be clear about the focus of our assessment and the degree of precision we require. In the light of this, we may be prepared to accept differential standards for different modes of communication, e.g. greater flexibility in evaluating candidates' spoken language (where variation tends to be the norm) and more stringent requirements in written production (where conformity to a standard is more common and reasonable). At the very least we must ensure that our marking criteria (e.g. in relation to spelling requirements) are as transparent as possible not just for our raters, but also for test candidates; test takers are often aware of differences across language varieties and sometimes fear they will be penalised for using the 'wrong' lexical item or spelling convention. As one survey respondent noted in relation to tests of European and Brazilian Portuguese: *'candidates get worried and think the differences might result in them being marked down'*. This can be addressed through clear instructions on the test paper itself as well as by making publicly available the specified assessment criteria against which any task will be evaluated (see Bachman 1990, and Bachman and Palmer 1996, for useful discussion of the importance of clarity in task instructions).

A third key area is the question of who is best qualified to make judgements about standards? In language testing this raises the interesting question of whether NS or NNS examiners are better qualified to evaluate proficiency and it echoes the ongoing debate about the relative strengths and weaknesses of NS/NNS teachers. The reality must surely be that all interlocutors and raters – both NS and NNS – need to be suitably qualified, and to receive initial training and ongoing standardisation. Lowenberg (2000) has suggested that some awareness of potential divergence in norms across so-called native/non-native varieties should be an essential part of any rater's expertise whether or not they are a 'native speaker'. Norrish (1997) extends this recommendation to learners and teachers as well as examiners because of the way languages so often evolve – mixing and shifting in multilingual environments. Once again, it may help for testing agencies to be explicit as they can be about aspects of examiner recruitment, training and monitoring.

The main thrust of this paper is to suggest that as language testers we need to develop a principled and well thought out approach to our policy and practice in relation to linguistic diversity. Policy and practice need to be well articulated and transparent to both our internal and our external stakeholders; we need to be able to respond with clarity and confidence to the question: How do you address issues relating to linguistic diversity in your tests?

One might be tempted to ask why this matters. After all, generally speaking there is a high degree of uniformity across published texts in a common language, and any differences in standards are often restricted to a relatively small set of spelling and lexical variants. I would suggest that it does matter – for both philosophical and pragmatic reasons. One reason is that perceptions about the 'ownership' of a given language do change over time – largely because language is so closely linked with issues of socio-cultural identity, culture and power; we only need to look at the changed and changing face of Europe in our own time to know that this is true. Another reason is the rapid rate of language change today. This may be for demographic reasons – political unrest, economic deprivation and easier international travel are just a few of the factors which lead to the mass movement of language users; and the revolution in information and communications technology also plays an increasingly significant role in the changing linguistic landscape.

In the context of language education more specifically, we are seeing steady growth in the 'localisation' of language teaching and assessment: locally published syllabuses, curricula, and teaching materials, as well as the development of locally generated standards for teaching, learning and assessment, especially in certain parts of the world. There is also a growing focus on the teaching of oral communication skills (listening and speaking) and to some degree linguistic variation is most apparent in the oral mode. At the same time, we observe increasing 'globalisation' of educational and employment opportunities for which accessible international standards – both written and spoken – are needed.

It also matters because today, more than ever before, we have sophisticated tools to analyse and describe the nature of linguistic variation, for example through corpus-based studies of spoken and written language. Such advances make possible the study and codification of less widely spoken languages and linguistic varieties as well as just the 'big' languages. In time, findings from specialised corpora for varieties of English and of many other languages will inform approaches to language teaching and language testing.

Sound policy and practice on linguistic diversity matters for language testers because we need to be concerned with matters of content and construct validity, and we must pay due attention to the standards of language we use in our tests and the standards of quality we lay claim to. We cannot ignore the greater focus in today's world on matters of accountability and fairness which impact on professional and public attitudes to tests and test use; it is no accident that core themes at the 2005 ALTE conference included 'quality', 'ethics' and 'transparency'.

Conclusion

Language testing organisations are sometimes criticised for taking insufficient account of linguistic diversity in their testing practice, or for failing to take more of a lead in promoting recognition of language varieties (Jenkins 2006, Lowenberg 2000, Norrish 1997). Such criticism is understandable given the high-stakes role testing plays in so many parts of the world but it does not always readily acknowledge the complexities involved in dealing with linguistic variation in the testing/assessment context. Despite the centrality of the test taker in any assessment activity, it can be difficult to balance provision for individual/group variation across the test taker population against the requirement to adhere to professional standards of quality and fairness for all test takers. This becomes even more of a challenge when dealing with a large and/or highly heterogeneous test population, e.g. an international test candidature, or a population of test takers with a potential age range from 17 to 70.

Wherever it is feasible, appropriate and equitable to do so, there is no reason why language tests should not reflect aspects of linguistic diversity along the lines previously discussed in this paper. Although, as discussed above, this may be more difficult to achieve in large-scale formal, standardised assessment practice, alternative, individualised approaches to assessment may be able to recognise linguistic diversity more flexibly; one example of such an assessment instrument is the European Language Portfolio (ELP)[1] designed as a tool to promote plurilingualism and pluriculturalism.

There is also a potentially useful contribution to be made by language test providers such as the ALTE members in developing further our understanding of linguistic diversity. For example, work in the area of 'construct definition' may help shed light on theories of language ability and the role of linguistic variation within it. Testing organisations can also be directly involved in creating learner corpora of the languages for which they offer tests in order to provide a valuable research resource for investigating learner language; potential areas for study include the nature of the language proficiency continuum and the role of variation within it, as well as identifying where the boundary lies between language variety and learner interlanguage.

This paper has sought to explore some of the issues and challenges which language testing agencies face in relation to language varieties and their implications for testing and assessment. Although much of the debate over recent years has centred around the testing of English, hopefully this paper will enable the voices of language testers who test other European languages to be heard and will raise awareness more broadly within the ALTE language testing community and beyond. Gardner (2004) commended the ALTE partnership for its decision to pursue a policy of respect for the many languages represented within it and suggested that the association should make a public statement on its internal language policy as well as make explicit the positive features of its present practices. If ALTE chooses to act on this recommendation, hopefully the results of the survey reported here, and the discussion which accompanies them, can feed into that process. It is interesting to speculate what the results might be were the survey to be repeated in five or 10 years' time!

Postscript: I would like to express my sincere thanks and appreciation to those ALTE partners and observers who took the time and trouble to respond to the original survey questionnaire, and who therefore made possible the original presentation at the ALTE 2005 conference in Berlin and this follow-up paper.

Note

1 The European Language Portfolio (ELP) was developed and piloted from 1998–2000 by the Language Policy Division of the Council of Europe in Strasbourg. In collaboration with EAQUALS, ALTE has successfully developed an electronic version of the portfolio – eELP – which is freely available from the ALTE website www.alte.org

References and further reading

Bachman, L F (1990) *Fundamental Considerations in Language Testing,* Oxford: Oxford University Press.

Bachman, L F and Palmer, A S (1996) *Language Testing in Practice,* Oxford: Oxford University Press.

Bolton, K (2002) Hong Kong English: autonomy and creativity, in Bolton, K (Ed.) *Hong Kong English: autonomy and creativity*, Hong Kong: Hong Kong University Press, 1–25.

Bolton, K (2004) World Englishes, in Davies, D and Elder, C (Eds) *The Handbook of Applied Linguistics*, Oxford: Blackwell, 367–396.

Brutt-Griffler, J (2002) *World English,* Clevedon: Multilingual Matters Ltd.

Council of Europe (2001) *Common European Framework of Reference for Languages: learning, teaching, assessment*, Cambridge: Cambridge University Press.

Crystal, D (1995) *The Cambridge Encyclopedia of the English Language*, Cambridge: Cambridge University Press.

Crystal, D (1997) *English as a global language*, Cambridge: Cambridge University Press.

Davies, A (1991) *The native speaker in applied linguistics*, Edinburgh: Edinburgh University Press.

Davies, A (2003) *The native speaker – myth or reality,* Clevedon: Multilingual Matters Ltd.

Davies, A, Hamp-Lyons, L and Kemp, C (2003) Whose norms? International proficiency tests in English, *World Englishes* 22, Oxford: Blackwell Publishing Ltd, 571–584.

Gardner, N (2004) ALTE: A minority sociolinguistic perspective, paper given at the open day on 'Testing the less widely spoken languages' in the context of the ALTE Meeting in Bilbao, Spain, November 2004.

Graddol, D (1997) *The future of English?* London: The British Council.

Graddol, D, McArthur, T, Flack, D and Amey, J (1999) English around the world, in Graddol, D and Meinhof, U H (Eds) *English in a Changing World*, AILA Review 13. Jenkins, J (2000) *The Phonology of English as an International Language*, Oxford: Oxford University Press.

Jenkins, J (2003) *World Englishes: a resource book for students,* Routledge.

Jenkins, J (2006) The spread of EIL: a testing time for testers, *ELT Journal* 60, Oxford: Oxford University Press, 42–50.

Kachru, B B (1992) World Englishes: approaches, issues, resources, *Language Teaching* 25, 1–14.

Kachru, B B and Smith, L E (1985) Editorial, *World Englishes* 4, 209–212.

Lowenberg, P H (2000) Non-native varieties and issues of fairness in testing English as a world language, in Kunnan, A J (Ed.) *Fairness and validation in language assessment. Selected papers from the 19th LTRC, Orlando, Florida.* Cambridge: UCLES/Cambridge University Press, 43–59.

McArthur, T (1992) Models of English, *English Today* 32.

McArthur, T (1998) *The English Languages*, Cambridge: Cambridge University Press.

Norrish, J (1997) English or English? Attitudes, local varieties and English language teaching, *TESL-EJ*, Vol 3/1.

Pennycook, A (1994) *The cultural politics of English as an international language*, London: Longman.

Phillipson, R (1992) *Linguistic imperialism*, Oxford: Oxford University Press.

Quirk, R (1990) Language varieties and standard language, *English Today* 21, 3–21.

Seidlhofer, B (2001) Closing a conceptual gap: the case for a description of English as a lingua franca, *International Journal of Applied Linguistics* 11, 133–58.

Seidlhofer, B (2003) *A concept of international English and related issues: from 'Real English' to 'Realistic English'?* Strasbourg: Language Policy Division, Council of Europe.

Strevens, P (1980) *Teaching English as an International Language*, Oxford: Pergamon.

Taylor, L (2001) Assessing learners' English: but whose/which English(es)? paper presented at the UK Language Testing Forum in Nottingham, November 2001.

Taylor, L (2002) Assessing learners' English: but whose/which English(es)? *Research Notes* 10, University of Cambridge ESOL Examinations.

Taylor, L (2006) The changing landscape of English: implications for language assessment, *ELT Journal* 60, Oxford: Oxford University Press, 51–60.

Trudgill, P and Hannah, J (1994) *International English: a guide to varieties of standard English* (3rd edition), London: Edward Arnold.

Weir, C J and Milanovic, M (2003) *Continuity and Innovation: Revising the Cambridge Proficiency in English Examination 1913–2002*, Cambridge: UCLES/Cambridge University Press.

Appendix 1

This questionnaire is designed to elicit your comments on perceptions about language variety/ies in your context and the way these impact on your language testing policy and practice. The questions are deliberately designed to be open so that you can share your thoughts and views freely.

PART A – BACKGROUND

1 Your name(s): ....
   (if you are completing this questionnaire with a colleague/s, please include all names)

2 Name of your organisation/testing agency: ....

3 For which European language does your testing agency offer proficiency tests? *(e.g. French, Spanish, etc.)*

   ....

PART B – LANGUAGE VARIETIES: PROFESSIONAL/PERSONAL/ PUBLIC PERCEPTIONS

4 Please list regional areas where the language you have identified in 3 above is widely used. *(e.g. French in: France, Belgium, Switzerland, Canada, Algeria, etc.)*

5   Do different 'varieties' of the language exist as a result of this international regionalisation? If so, please <u>list</u> the different 'varieties' as you perceive them to exist.

i)   ....

ii)   ....

iii)   ....

Other (as many as you wish): ....

6   Do 'varieties' of the language also exist within country, i.e. inside national borders?
(e.g. varieties of French spoken in the north and south of France)

7   How does this variation manifest itself? Can you give one or two examples to show how vocabulary/grammar/pronunciation changes across language varieties – both within national borders, and across international borders?

8   How does the general public tend to regard these within-country and international varieties? *(e.g. as dialects of a commonly shared national language, or more as languages in their own right)*

9   To what extent are language varieties reflected in the news media (newspapers, TV, radio, etc.)?

10   Are any varieties considered to be 'more/less educated'? Or 'high/low prestige'? *(Give examples, if possible)*

11   Are some varieties better 'codified' or described than others? *(i.e. you can buy dictionaries and grammars for some varieties, but other varieties have no such reference publications – give examples if possible)*

12   Which language variety is generally used as a model for teaching and learning? *(i.e. it forms the basis for classroom teaching, it is the model found in teaching coursebooks, etc.)*

PART C– LANGUAGE VARIETIES: IMPACT ON TESTING POLICY/PRACTICE

13   How would you describe the language variety/ies used in your organisation's tests? *(e.g. 'standard', 'native-speaker', 'educated', etc.)*

14   Do your tests reflect different language varieties in any way? *(e.g. do some reading texts contain the grammar/vocabulary/spelling/etc. of different regional varieties? do listening materials sometimes reflect regional accents?)*

15   How important/relevant is the notion of the 'native speaker' (NS) and the 'non-native-speaker' (NNS) in your testing policy/practice? *(e.g. do your listening materials always reflect NS speech? is the idealised NS the criterion for success? do you ever employ NNS raters of written/spoken production?)*

16   Are you aware of external pressures to reflect multiple language varieties in your tests? *(e.g. from linguistic experts or minority language groups? are newer language varieties clamouring for attention? Give examples if possible)*

Thank you very much for completing this questionnaire. If you have any additional comments you would like to make, please write them on a separate sheet and return it with your completed questionnaire by **7 March 2005** at the latest.
Please return your completed questionnaire electronically to:
taylor.l@ucles.org.uk
If you have completed the questionnaire by hand, please return it to the following address:
Dr Lynda Taylor
Assistant Director – Research and Validation
University of Cambridge ESOL Examinations
1 Hills Road, Cambridge
CB1 2EU, UK

18 Non-native speakers as language assessors: recent research and implications for assessment practice

Anne Lazaraton
University of Minnesota

Introduction

Until recently, there has been an unquestioned assumption that the native speaker of a language (from herein, English, or a NS) is the best teacher of that language, the ideal model for language use, and the natural examiner or rater of English language ability. Likewise, the non-native speaker of English (NNS) was always a learner of English, who would be studied for his or her linguistic deviations from the native speaker norm, taught by native English-speaking teachers (NESTs), and have their English assessed by native speakers and according to NS norms. That is, NNSs were not seen as competent language users, always falling short, by definition, from the NS norm; as suitable English teachers (unless no NS teachers were available); as qualified language professionals (e.g., journal article authors); or as competent language testers, raters, and examiners.

This picture has changed drastically in the last decade, with an explosion of work on these taken-for-granted notions. The native speaker construct has come under fire for being vacuous, wrong, and/or discriminatory; non-native-English-speaking teachers (NNESTs) have found their own voice and are demanding a reexamination of the construct, which serves as a de facto rationale for discrimination in hiring; and those involved in language assessment have begun to ask not only what role NNSs should play in the testing process, but, resulting from insights from the World Englishes perspective, what language norms should be used in such assessments.

This paper covers each of these areas in turn – the native speaker construct; the NNEST; and the non-native examiner/rater of English – by considering both theoretical and empirical work on these topics. I conclude with a discussion of the implications of this body of work for current and future language assessment practice.

The native speaker construct

For many applied linguists, the native speaker construct can be traced to the work of Chomsky in the 1950s and 1960s on linguistic competence and the 'ideal speaker-hearer' of a language. However, the native speaker construct was evident in Bloomfield's work of the 1930s; in fact, Graddol (2001) points out that it is 'wrong, however, to think that the importance of native speakers began with Chomsky. Traditional dialectologists, as well as anthropologists, drew on similar ideas of "good speakers". . . since the European Renaissance, identities have been constructed according to a particular model of perfection: unified, singular, well-ordered' (p. 68).

As we know, Chomsky's (1965) theory of language was subsequently attacked – but not for his giving centre stage to the native speaker in various applied contexts: it was the competence aspect that was later modified by Hymes (1972), Canale and Swain (1980), and Bachman (1990), among others, to include the notion of communicative competence and its subparts. Even in these later models of language competence or ability the native speaker was still the target for use and the norm by which it would be judged. Chomsky was also taken to task by other linguists, as Paikeday (1985) reports from his mediated discussion with 40 linguists, philosophers, lexicologists, and psychologists. He concludes that the term 'native speaker' 'represents an ideal, a convenient fiction, or a shibboleth rather than a reality like Dick or Jane . . . I have no doubt that "native speaker" in the linguist's sense of arbiter of grammaticality and acceptability of language is quite dead' (Paikeday 1985:x).

Around 1990, a 'deconstruction' of the native speaker construct had begun, most prominently with the publication of Davies' *The Native Speaker in Applied Linguistics* (1991, but also taken up by Leung, Harris & Rampton 1997, Medgyes 1992, Phillipson 1992 and Rampton 1990). Davies' book examined the native speaker from the perspective of linguistic competence, socio-linguistic competence, psycholinguistic knowledge, intelligibility and the speech community; his updated version, *The Native Speaker: Myth and Reality* (2003) also analyses the native speaker in relation to globalisation and the ownership of English. Native speakers, according to Davies, embody the following characteristics:

1. L1 acquisition in childhood.
2. Intuitions about grammar.
3. A unique capacity to produce fluent, spontaneous discourse.
4. A unique capacity to write creatively.
5. A unique capacity to interpret and translate into the L1.

Others have added additional characteristics to such a list; Kamhi-Stein (2001) includes:

6. Primacy in order of acquisition.
7. The manner and environment of 6.
8. Acculturation by growing up in the speech community.
9. Dominance, frequency, and comfort of use.
10. Ethnicity.
11. Nationality/domicile.
12. Self-perceptions of linguistic identity.
13. Other-perceptions of linguistic membership and eligibility.
14. Monolinguality.

Yet, there seems to be agreement that such lists of characteristics may represent a form of overkill, in the sense that Cook (1999) describes: 'the indisputable element in the definition of *native speaker* is that a person is a native speaker of the language learnt first; the other characteristics are incidental, describing how well an individual uses the language' (p. 187). Or as Davies (2003) admits: on all but the first, non-native speakers can achieve the native speaker norm; 'all but 1) are "contingent issues"'.

In place of these features, Davies then proposes some 'flesh-and-blood or reality' ways in which one can be considered a native speaker:

1. By birth (or early childhood exposure).
2. By being an exceptional learner (i.e., native-like).
3. By being educated using the target-language medium (e.g., a lingua franca case).
4. By virtue of being a native user (e.g., a post-colonial case).
5. By long residence in the adopted country.

Yet, even these criteria have proved problematic. A reviewer of Davies' (2003) book found that although she 'fit into all five of Davies' "flesh-and-blood" definitions of a native speaker' she still did not identify herself as a native speaker, nor did speakers of standardised English accept her as one; she comments thus: '. . . this is a powerful illustration of the difficulty of pinning down exactly who a native speaker is and the psychological, sociological, and political factors involved in this definition' (Malabonga 2004:248).

Perhaps more damning, though, is the 'postmodern' critique of the native speaker construct, which rejects the biological basis for native speakerness in favour of what Rampton (1990) terms a 'social construction of identity'. In fact, Brutt-Griffler and Samimy (2001) conclude that 'nativeness constitutes a non-elective socially constructed identity rather than a linguistic category'

(p. 100). In this view, the native speaker is not only a myth, but a means by which non-native speakers are oppressed via what Amin (2001) terms nativism, which she defines as:

> The belief that the national culture is embodied in certain groups of people who were born in that country. It further refers to the belief that these native-born individuals are native speakers and that one born outside the country to parents speaking another language cannot attain native-speaker status (p. 104).

This 'oppressive ideology' (Mattix 2000) has its roots in a number of -isms, including, at least, racism and colonialism (and even finds its way into professional organisations, such as JALT; see Oda 1999).

Finally, insights from World Englishes scholarship certainly call into question the construct. Simply put, if there is no longer a single norm for standard English, it is pointless to talk about a native speaker of that target norm. Or, as Medgyes (1999) contends, 'So long as International English is a nonlinguistic entity, it is unteachable too. What is teachable is a large stock of native and non-native varieties of English' (p. 185).

Therefore, the native speaker construct has fallen out of favour with a number of applied linguists (but perhaps not Davies (2003), who states 'the denial of a special status for native speakers of English is surely ideological, belonging to an argument about the role of English in a world filled with World Englishes, where there are more ESL than L1 speakers of English' (p. 160); (see also Davies 2005 on these issues). As Graddol (2001) shows, this decline in the status of the native speaker is traceable to two factors: the decreasing number of Inner Circle native speakers of English relative to the number of English speakers in the Outer and Expanding Circles, that is, the increasing number of World English(es) speakers, and the changing ideological discourse about languages, competence, and identity.

The issue of the 'ownership of English' has been addressed in an insightful paper by Widdowson (1994). He asks, *Who are the custodians of English? What exactly is in their custody?* If, as he believes, 'grammars' express social identity, 'Standard English, then, is not simply a means of communication but the symbolic possession of a particular community, expressive of its identity, its conventions, and values. As such it needs to be carefully preserved, for to undermine standard English is to undermine what it stands for: the security of this community and its institutions' (p. 381). As such, 'what native speakers say is invested with both authenticity and authority' (p. 386). It follows, then, that native speaker language use is privileged, because 'authenticity can only be determined by insiders. Native speakers become the custodians and arbiters not only of proper English but of proper pedagogy as well' (p. 387).

It is this position that has attracted the attention of those who question whether native speakers still have the ultimate right to be ESL/EFL teachers and how the non-native-English-speaking teacher fits into this picture; this topic is taken up in the next section.

Non-native-English-speaking teachers

Briefly, it is notable that NNESTs have only recently found a voice within the TESOL profession (for example, see the Non-native English Speakers in TESOL Caucus website, http://nnest.mousssu.net; and the edited volumes by Braine [1999] and Kamhi-Stein [2004]), given that there are far many more NNESTs than NESTs – by some estimates, 80% of English language teaching professionals worldwide are NNESTs (McKay 2002).

According to Davies (2003), there are three perspectives on the NNEST. The first is what he calls the 'traditional foreigner perspective', which stresses both comparison and co-operation with NS teachers. A second perspective is 'the revisionist foreigner' (Davies 2003), in which the traditional NS model is abandoned. A final perspective postulated by Davies is 'the other native', which is critical, postcolonial, and protesting discrimination; authors such as Amin (2001), Braine (1999), Brutt-Griffler and Samimy (2001), Pennycook (1994), and Rampton (1990) exemplify this position. It is worth remembering that claims about NNESTs rest on mostly unquestioned assumptions about this identity. But we should be hesitant in assigning identities based on certain ethnographic or demographic characteristics participants bring to interaction. As the conversation analytic literature (see, for example, Wong & Olsher 2000) points out, any claim for the importance of a specific 'identity' in talk-in-interaction needs to be shown as being relevant to the participants, and it needs to be shown for any particular segment of talk. Identity is not omnirelevant for any interaction – the participants jointly and sequentially construct and reconstruct such identities in and through the talk. Even if language teachers are, in fact, NNESTs, we cannot claim that this particular identity (or any other, for that matter) is automatically relevant for the entire, or even part of the interaction in which the NNS takes part. In fact, it might be argued that while there are clearly 'nonnative features' of a teacher's or examiner's talk, they are not necessarily relevant as NNS talk.

These same arguments can be made to NNS as language assessors, the topic of the next section.

Non-native speakers and language assessment

It is notable that while a substantial body of work exists on non-native-English-speaking *teachers*, there is very little published work on the role of NNSs in language assessment. It is possible that as fundamental changes in language teaching and the role of language teachers takes place (due to the sorts of changes noted by Graddol [2001] mentioned earlier), there will be concomitant changes in language assessment practice. In any case, there are two relevant issues to consider: the first concerns the standards set for language input to and output from test takers (e.g., test bias and the role that World Englishes should take in language assessment; see Taylor 2002); the second revolves around the role of NNSs as examiners and/or raters. These are taken up in turn.

Bias is language assessment

According to Davies (2003), 'The question of which English(es) should be privileged on tests is particularly problematic and interesting in academic contexts where traditionally "standard" forms of English are the only ones accepted' (p. 177), since 'arguments about the purpose of assessment can be reduced to the issue of what to use as the criterion (or norm) for judgments' (p. 172).

On the one hand, Lowenberg (2002) claims that norms for Expanding Circle varieties of English are developing and language tests need to take these norms into account. The problem, as he sees it, is that 'examiners must try to distinguish deficiencies in the second language acquisition of English by these speakers (that is, errors) from varietal differences in the speakers' usage resulting from their having learned and used such non-native normative features' (p. 433). These 'non-native normative features' include for example, preposition use, phrasal verbs, and count vs. noncount nouns (see also McKay [2002] on this point).

On the other, one judgement study of various English proficiency tests (Davies, Hamp-Lyons & Kemp 2003) begins with the premise that international English tests are biased. However, the authors point out that the issue is not differential performance, but unfair differential performance. And, they claim that 'there is a remarkable dearth of empirical evidence to substantiate cries of language test bias' (p. 572). Although they do not deny that language variation exists, they feel that the important issue is what the role and status of local norms should be (and whether or not local raters are or are not applying these local norms to assessment). That is, 'if English proficiency tests are not to be localized, they must instead be based on a demonstrably common language core – language that can be shown to be shared by all the native varieties of English, and by curriculum/syllabus documents worldwide' (p. 573). At least for now, it is not clear what the actual differences are between Standard American English and its many variants, so integrating findings from the World Englishes perspective (or the English as a lingua franca position; see Seidlhofer [2005]) into language tests appears rather risky at the current time.

In response to Davies, Hamp-Lyons, & Kemp (2003), Brown (2003) attempts to further explicate the important terms that they use, including *bias, Englishes in testing,* and *English language proficiency*. One important point Brown raises is that there are at least eight 'Englishes' that might have an impact on a language test:

1. The English(es) of the test taker's local community.
2. The dominant English of the test taker (which may not be the same as the local community).
3. The English(es) of test content.
4. The English(es) of test proctors.
5. The English(es) of test scorers/ratings.
6. The English(es) of the decision target community.
7. The English(es) decision target purpose.
8. The English(es) of decision makers (p. 318).

Brown argues that there will be many instances where not all the Englishes will be the same, which may lead to 'shifting the bias'. Therefore, Brown poses 'the overriding question: What should drive test design? Should it be the characteristics of people taking the test, or should it be the purpose of the test and the decisions being made with it?'

One implication of the World Englishes perspective that cannot be overlooked, though, is the role that so-called native speakers should play in language assessment, if there are no longer clear-cut native speakers of English. In other words, should 'native speakers' (still) be the ultimate criterion group in language assessment? Hamilton, Lopes, McNamara, and Sheridan (1993) note that native speaker performance on language tests has been underresearched, and it appears increasingly tenuous to use the NS as a benchmark for ESL student performance. With reference to IELTS, they argue that even if 'the band scales for IELTS do not refer explicitly to native speaker performance . . . the native speaker makes a covert but unmistakable reappearance in the high band scale . . . it is clear that the native speaker "hovers" over IELTS' (p. 341). The results of their study on reading and writing subtests of the then-current IELTS revealed that NS performance was 'far from homogeneous' (p. 348). They conclude that 'it is clear that reference to the native speaker as some kind of ideal or benchmark in scalar descriptions of performance on performance tests is not valid' (p. 350).

McNamara (1996), following up on Hamilton et al takes issue with descriptions of 'native-like proficiency' in rating descriptors. McNamara maintains that even if performance by native speakers on tests like the TOEFL (which, by the way, he terms 'noncommunicative tests') is fairly homogeneous, that homogeneity evaporates on tests of reading and writing, where native speakers perform 'neither homogeneously nor homogeneously well' (p. 96).

As for testing pronunciation, Jenkins (2000) takes a number of existing EFL oral assessments to task for their reliance on the ambiguous concept of intelligibility. Jenkins asks, *Intelligible for whom?:* 'When interlocutors share the same L1, a stronger L1 accent is communicatively more effective than a less "obtrusive" one, and is therefore likely to be produced even in testing situations where it will lead to the candidates being awarded low marks for pronunciation' (p. 215). Thus, she believes that the more important question is 'Are speakers able to adjust their pronunciation appropriately to accommodate their interlocutors? . . . the level of understanding achieved by the assessors is irrelevant' (p. 213). This would mean that rating descriptors would need to be redesigned in terms of core English as an International Language (EIL) elements, not in terms of features of a 'NS accent', and in terms of the accommodations and mutual understanding achieved by the interlocutors, not the assessor's understanding of the talk produced.

This last point is taken up in detail in the recent Point – Counterpoint section of *ELT Journal.* Jenkins (2006) maintains that English language testing must adapt to recent notable changes in English language use as well as in the users of English, and suggests some ways this might be accomplished. In response, Taylor (2006) argues that a number of 'questionable assumptions' underlie Jenkins's assertions. These issues involve:

- the attitudes and expectations of learners and teachers
- the role of the native speaker model
- the focus on accuracy or 'correctness'
- the relationship between testing and teaching/learning
- the treatment of 'accommodation' in testing.

Taylor also elucidates how varieties of English are dealt with by examination boards in terms of test purpose, validity and reliability, and impact and practicality. She concludes that 'Over the next 10 or 20 years, emerging Englishes – including EIL – may well grow in status and take on a role as pedagogic and assessment models for English learners'.

NNS examiners and raters

Taylor (2002) suggests that a familiarity with World Englishes variation 'is an essential part of any rater's expertise'. For Taylor, this raises the question as to whether NS or NNS should be examiners and raters of language proficiency, in this case, for Cambridge ESOL assessments. In fact, she states that 'it is certainly not a requirement that a writing or oral examiner for our exams should be a "native speaker" of English; all examiners (both NS and NNS) are, of course, expected to meet minimum professional requirements in terms of their language competencies' (p. 20). Specific questions about NNS examiners posed by Taylor include:

> *How does the language competence of the examiner impact test delivery?*
> *How does the fact that the examiner and the candidate share an L1 impact test delivery?*
> *How does the observable behaviour of the NNS examiner resemble that of a comparable NS examiner in the assessment of similar candidates?*

To this, a fourth question could be added:

> *How are ratings distributed between NS and NNS examiners?*

Unfortunately, there is very little empirical work to guide us in answering these questions. In terms of *oral assessment*, Berwick and Ross (1996) report on the interview styles of a NS of English and a NS of Japanese with an eye towards understanding Oral Proficiency Interviews (OPIs) as rule-governed, cross-cultural encounters. Because examiners may be unaware of how their own cultural background is implicated in the sample of speech elicited, Berwick and Ross looked at various features of accommodation in the interviews. They found that the 'Japanese style' consists of authority through attention to form and 'instructional caretaking'; on the other hand, the American style is characterised by control through attention to content and reliance on candidate willingness to 'engage the issues'. That is, the *form* of response was critical for the Japanese as a Second Language (JSL) interviewers, while the *content* of response was the most salient for the English as a Second Language (ESL) interviewers.

Although Berwick and Ross do not take test taker behaviour into account, nor do they note that these deviations they found are only relevant for unscripted exams like the OPI, they conclude with some intriguing questions: 'Does this mean that we are headed towards a kind of chaotic approach to oral proficiency testing in which local norms for the organization and enforcement of oral behavior overturn the relative certainty a single protocol provides?' And 'how influential are cultural differences among interviewers, and what do we think we should do about them?' (p. 48).

Reeves and Richter (2004) report on training Chinese L1 raters to assign holistic ratings to speaking samples. This entailed promoting an understanding of communicative competence, and encouraging holistic scoring beyond grammar. Reeves and Richter found that beyond the 'universal challenges for rater training' (raters scoring too high or too low, or focusing too much on grammar), the NNS raters, who shared an L1 background with the candidates, found the speech samples more intelligible than NS raters did; that is, the degree of listener effort required was different than that of L1 English raters. The Chinese assessors also missed the holistic aspect of scoring. They suggest that NNS raters need a high level of English proficiency, and an awareness of the concepts of listener effort and holistic scoring. Nevertheless, the raters were able to listen differently after training with ETS LanguEdge software.

With respect to *writing* assessment, Weigle (2002) does not discuss non-native raters *per se* (nor do Fulcher [2003] or Luoma [2004] for speaking assessment), but she does discuss two rater variables that one would expect to be salient when considering the use of NNS raters. First, the attention paid by raters to various aspects of the text may vary, and second, various rater attributes are implicated in ratings of writing, such as composition teaching and rating experience, cultural background, rater training, specialist and content teacher knowledge vs. ESL teacher knowledge, and rater expectations. These variables have been found to be important in at least two empirical studies. Shi (2001) used 10 authentic writing samples and no predetermined evaluation criteria to elicit ratings by 23 native English speakers and 23 Chinese college writing teachers. Her results indicated that 'NES and NNS teachers gave similar scores to EFL students' writing . . . although the NES teachers attended more positively to content and language, whereas, NNS teachers attended more negatively to organization and length . . . the NNSs appeared to be more concerned with ideas and general organization . . . and NES teachers focused on intelligibility' (p. 316). One implication of this study is that EFL students may receive different directions or different emphases from the two types of teachers, so there needs to be co-operation between the two.

Finally, Hill (1997) studied how 13 NS Australian English and 10 NS Indonesian English classroom teachers rated the writing section responses of 100 candidates on the Indonesian English Proficiency Test. The raters were given a 6 point scale to use in assessing overall impression, content, vocabulary, cohesion and coherence, and linguistic features. They were told not to employ the 'native speaker' as a reference point, but to look for 'good models' for Indonesian English teachers. Her FACETS results indicated that the Australian native speaker raters were harsher; that the Indonesian raters were 'unconsciously applying a native speaker standard' (p. 285) (it was harder to get a rating of 6 from these NNS raters); and that the two groups demonstrated a different conception of 'what level of performance is "adequate" for the purposes of the test' (p. 285). Hill concludes that these NNS raters were no less suitable than NS raters, in that all but one of the Indonesian raters assessed the test output consistently (and it should be remembered that 'NS' raters from, even within, different English-speaking countries can vary in their scoring; see Chalhoub-Deville & Wigglesworth 2005).

Implications and recommendations

Several implications and recommendations for language assessment practice can be put forward from this literature review. One general implication (and one noted by Davies [2003]) is that language test developers need to focus on judgements of *language* rather than judgements of *identity* (if this is even possible). Although large-scale language tests may or may not be scrutinised for features of various Inner Circle varieties of English (so that British vocabulary is not tested on the TOEFL, for example), to my knowledge these tests have not, to date, been developed and/or validated with an eye towards avoiding bias against speakers or writers from Expanding and/or Outer Circle countries. For example, McKay (2002) offers evidence that English users from Singapore and India add plurals to mass nouns ('furnitures'), create new phrasal verbs ('cope up with') and come up with innovative lexical items ('bed spacers', 'prepone') not found in Standard English varieties. Jenkins (2000) makes a similar case for various features of EIL phonology. Therefore, testing organisations may want to consider looking at their exams to see how speech or writing production containing these Standard English 'errors' are dealt with. As Taylor (2004) recommends, corpus analysis provides a means by which 'language change' in a broad sense can be monitored.

A second related implication is that rating scales and descriptors for speaking and writing assessment might be checked for evidence of native speaker bias. If the NS construct is as poorly off as it seems to be at the present time, it may be worth deciding, theoretically and empirically, what a realistic target is for test takers.

Finally, it would behove large scale, international testing organisations to clearly articulate a position on the English(es) of language test input, the language standards by which spoken and written output are judged and why, and the role that NNS of English may play in administering and rating speaking and writing tests. Taylor (2005, see this volume) reports on a recent survey of nine European language test providers who responded to questions about linguistic diversity 'perceptions, policy, and practice in the ALTE context'. She suggests 'some principles for good practice', including:

- Selecting the input – clarifying test purpose, ensuring content representativeness.
- Evaluating the test output – defining test construct, acknowledging differential standards, making criteria transparent to all.
- Interlocutors and raters – suitably qualified and trained, ongoing standardization, the importance of 'linguistic awareness'.
- The need for a principled and well-conceived approach to policy/practice – one which is transparent and well-articulated.

Conclusion

I conclude with some thoughts from Jennifer Jenkins (2000), who has staked out a fairly extreme position on the role of NS and NNS in English language teaching, (and by extension, assessment):

> It will be interesting in years to come to see whether the term 'native' undergoes another change in connotation. In the days of empire, the natives were the indigenous populations and the term itself implied uncivilized, primitive, barbaric, even cannibalistic . . . With the spread of English around the globe, 'native' – in relation to English – has assumed newer, positive connotations. 'Native speakers' of English are assumed to be advanced (technologically), civilized, and educated. But as 'NSs' lose their linguistic advantage, with English being spoken as an International Language no less – and often a good deal more – effectively by 'NNSs' (preferably no longer labeled as such); and as bilingualism and multilingualism become the accepted world norm, and monolingualism the exception, perhaps the word 'native' will return to its pejorative usage. Only this time, the opposite group will be on the receiving end (p. 229).

References

Amin, N (2001) Nativism, the native speaker construct, and minority immigrant women teachers of English as a second language, *CATESOL Journal* 13, 89–107.

Bachman, L F (1990) *Fundamental considerations in language testing*, Oxford: Oxford University Press.

Berwick, R and Ross, S (1996) Cross-cultural pragmatics in oral proficiency interview Strategies, in Milanovic, M and Saville, N (Eds) *Performance testing, cognition and assessment: Selected papers from the 15th Language Testing Research Colloquium, Cambridge and Arnhem*, Cambridge: UCLES/Cambridge University Press, 34–54.

Bloomfield, L (1933) *Language,* New York: Holt, Rinehart.

Braine, G (Ed.) (1999) *Non-native educators in English language teaching,* Mahwah, NJ: Lawrence Erlbaum.

Brown, J D (2003) What do we mean by bias, Englishes, Englishes in testing, and English language proficiency? *World Englishes* 22, 317–319.

Brutt-Griffler, J and Samimy, K K (2001) Transcending the nativeness paradigm, *World Englishes* 20, 99–106.

Canale, M and Swain, M (1980) Theoretical bases of communicative approaches to second language teaching and testing, *Applied Linguistics* 1, 1–47.

Chalhoub-Deville, M and Wigglesworth, G (2005) Rater judgment and English language speaking proficiency, *World Englishes* 24, 383–391.

Chomsky, N (1965) *Aspects of the theory of syntax*, Cambridge, MA: MIT Press.

Cook, V (1999) Going beyond the native speaker in language teaching, *TESOL Quarterly* 33, 185–209.

Davies, A (1991) *The native speaker in applied linguistics*, Edinburgh: Edinburgh University Press.

Davies, A (2003) *The native speaker: Myth and reality*, Clevedon, UK: Multilingual Matters.

Davies, A (2005, September) *'Native' or 'non-native' speaker? A question of language, culture, or identity?* paper presented at the BAAL Conference, Bristol.

Davies, A, Hamp-Lyons, L and Kemp, C (2003) Whose norms? International proficiency tests in English, *World Englishes* 22, 571–584.

Fulcher, G (2003) *Testing second language speaking*, Harlow, UK: Pearson.

Graddol, D (2001) The decline of the native speaker, *AILA Review 13: English in a changing world*, 57–68.

Hamilton, J, Lopes, M, McNamara, T and Sheridan, E (1993) Rating scales and native speaker performance on a communicatively oriented EAP test, *Language Testing* 10, 337–353.

Hill, K (1997) Who should be the judge? The use of non-native speakers as raters on a test of English as an international language, in Huhta, A, Kohonen, V, Kurki-Suonio, K and Luoma, S (Eds), *Current developments and alternatives in language assessment: Proceedings of LTRC 1996*, Jyväskylä: University of Jyväskylä, 275–290.

Hymes, D H (1972) On communicative competence, in Pride, J B and Holmes, J (Eds), *Sociolinguistics*, Harmondsworth, UK: Penguin, 269–293.

Jenkins, J (2000) *The phonology of English as an international language*, Oxford: Oxford University Press.

Jenkins, J (2006) The spread of English as an International Language: A testing time for testers, *ELT Journal* 60, 42–50.

Kamhi-Stein, L D (2001) New voices in the classroom: Nonnative English-speaking professionals in the field of teaching English to speakers of other languages, *CATESOL Journal* 13, 47–51.

Kamhi-Stein, L D (Ed.) (2004) *Learning and teaching from experience: Perspectives on nonnative-English-speaking professionals*, Ann Arbor, MI: University of Michigan Press.

Leung, C, Harris, R and Rampton, B (1997) The idealized native speaker, reified ethnicities, and classroom realities, *TESOL Quarterly* 31, 543–560.

Lowenberg, P (2002) Assessing English proficiency in the Expanding Circle, *World Englishes* 21, 431–435.

Luoma, S (2004) *Assessing speaking*, Cambridge: Cambridge University Press.

Malabonga, V (2004) Review of *The native speaker: Myth and reality* (A Davies, 2003), *Language Testing* 21, 245–248.

Mattix, M (2000) Going further beyond the native speaker model: A remark concerning language models, *TESOL Quarterly* 34, 328–329.

McKay, S L (2002) *Teaching English as an international language*, Oxford: Oxford University Press.

McNamara, T (1996) *Measuring second language performance*, Essex, UK: Longman.

Medgyes, P (1992) Native or non-native: Who's worth more? *ELT Journal* 46, 340–349.

Medgyes, P (1999) Language training: A neglected area in teacher education, in Braine, G (Ed.) *Non-native educators in English language teaching*, Mahwah, NJ: Lawrence Erlbaum, 177–195.

Nonnative English Speakers in TESOL Caucus (NNEST) website, <http://nnest.moussu.net>.

Oda, M (1999) English only or English plus? The language(s) of EFL organizations, in Braine, G (Ed.) *Non-native educators in English language teaching*, Mahwah, NJ: Lawrence Erlbaum, 105–121.

Paikeday, T M (1985) *The native speaker is dead!* Toronto: Paikeday Publishing Inc.

Pennycook, A (1994) *The cultural politics of English as an international language,* London: Longman.

Phillipson, R (1992) *Linguistic imperialism,* Oxford: Oxford University Press.

Rampton, M B H (1990) Displacing the 'native speaker': Expertise, affiliation, and Inheritance, *ELT Journal* 44, 97–101.

Reeves, M and Richter, T (2004, March) LanguEdge™: Training nonnative speakers of English to perform holistic scoring, poster presentation, Language Testing Research Colloquium, Temecula, CA.

Seidlhofer, B (2005, September) *Native/non-native speaker variation – Insights from corpus studies of Lingua Franca English,* paper presented at BAAL Conference, Bristol.

Shi, L (2001) Native- and nonnative-speaking EFL teachers' evaluation of Chinese students' English writing, *Language Testing* 18, 303–325.

Taylor, L (2002, November) Assessing learners' English: but whose/which English? *Research Notes* 10, 18–20.

Taylor, L (2004) Testing times: Research directions and issues for Cambridge ESOL Examinations, *TESOL Quarterly* 38, 141–146.

Taylor, L (2005, May) *Linguistic diversity: Language varieties and their implications for testing and assessment*, paper presented at the ALTE Conference, Berlin.

Taylor, L (2006). The changing landscape of English: Implications for language assessment, *ELT Journal* 60, 51–60.

Weigle, S C (2002) *Assessing writing*, Cambridge: Cambridge University Press.

Widdowson, H G (1994) The ownership of English, *TESOL Quarterly* 28, 377–389.

Wong, J and Olsher, D (2000) Reflections on conversation analysis and nonnative speaker talk: An interview with Emanuel A. Schegloff, *Issues in Applied Linguistics* 11, 111–128.

19 Citizenship materials for ESOL learners in the UK

Helen Sunderland
LLU+
London South Bank University

Chris Taylor
National Institute of Adult Continuing Education
(NIACE)

This paper will describe the regulations for would-be citizens in the UK, and give some background to current citizenship initiatives. It will go on to report on a pilot programme on English language and citizenship and end with feedback from teachers and learners.

In August 2004, the Home Office posted new regulations for citizenship on its website. These specified that applicants would now have to give evidence to show they have 'sufficient knowledge' of the English language (or Welsh or Scottish Gaelic) in order to qualify for citizenship.

While the sudden posting of these regulations caused some consternation, they were not entirely unexpected. Immigration has been a hot issue in the UK for the last 10 years, with hostility in much of the press and public opinion. This hostility was further inflamed by riots in the north of England in summer 2001 and by the events of 11th September 2001. Though the argument was not accepted by everyone, public and government opinion made links between immigration and social disruption and even terrorism.

At the same time, the government was getting interested in the concept of education for citizenship. In 1998, the Qualifications and Curriculum Authority (QCA) published a report on the teaching of citizenship in schools[1] and in 2002 citizenship teaching became compulsory in secondary schools and recommended for primary schools.

In December 2001, the report of the summer riots[2] recommended the need to build social cohesion in areas of high immigration through an increased commitment to citizenship. As a result, the government published legislation[3] requiring United Kingdom residents seeking British citizenship to be tested to show 'a sufficient knowledge of English, Welsh or Scottish Gaelic', to have 'a sufficient knowledge about life in the United Kingdom' and to take a citizenship oath and a pledge at a civic ceremony. They also asked Sir Bernard Crick, an eminent political theorist and academic, to lead an advisory group on how this could be put into practice.

The government has accepted most of the recommendations of Sir Bernard Crick's Advisory Group[4] and the requirements for citizenship are as follows[5]:

Applicants whose English is at Entry 3 (B1 in the Common European Framework of Reference) and above must take a citizenship test. This will be an online test about life in the UK and is based on the handbook *Life in the UK: a Journey to Citizenship.*[6] They will not need to take a separate language test.

Applicants who have not yet reached Entry 3 in English will be able to meet the requirements for citizenship by successfully completing an ESOL with citizenship course. This is an English language course which uses learning materials incorporating information about life in the UK. (See below for information about the materials and the project which developed and piloted them.) Though not entirely clear from the Ministerial Statement, it seems that one of the key recommendations of the Advisory Group has been accepted.[7] That is, these learners will not have to reach Entry 3 in order to satisfy requirements for citizenship; they will only need to make progress in one level. So learners who come in with no English at all will need to pass a test at Entry 1 (A1 in the CEFR). This will ensure equal access to citizenship for learners who have had very little previous education, and have low levels of literacy in any language.

The ESOL with Citizenship Development Project

Introduction

The report of the Advisory Group outlined six broad categories which should make up the curriculum for would-be citizens. These are British national institutions, Britain as a diverse society, Knowing the law, Employment, Sources of help and information and Everyday needs. In February 2004, the Home Office and the Department for Education and Skills (DfES) asked NIACE and LLU+ at London South Bank University to produce a scoping paper to develop these six broad categories into a proposed scheme of work for ESOL citizenship and one for a standalone citizenship course. The authors of this report thus embarked on the management of what turned out to be a substantial project that is still continuing.

Phase 1 of the project was the outline of the citizenship curriculum and was produced for the end of March 2004. Phase 2 entailed drafting sample teaching resources to go with the outline curriculum. In Phase 3, the project worked with 18 different organisations to pilot the learning materials and make suggestions for improvement. Phase 4 ran concurrently, and provided familiarisation workshops in using and adapting the learning materials for their own learners. Over 800 ESOL teachers attended these workshops. The project is currently in Phase 5, and is revising the learning materials in the light of the feedback. Starting in September 2005, there are plans to publish the revised pack and run familiarisation workshops for approximately 1,000 more teachers as well as train teacher trainers all over the UK to deliver the workshops. Below, we give some more detail about each phase.

Phase 1 – Scoping Paper

From the six broad categories outlined by the Advisory Group (see above) the project drew up suggested course content under 12 key headings. Some of this detail is shown as an example under the relevant headings:

What is Citizenship?
Parliament

- Who is your MP?
- Contacting your MP
- Meeting your MP
- What can your MP do to help you?
- How does your MP deal with your problems?
- Petitions, local campaigns and demonstrations (ways of voicing dissent) c.f. NIACE pack Making a Difference
- Comparison with government in learners' countries (where appropriate)

The UK in Europe, the Commonwealth and the UN

- What the EU does
- Which countries are in the EU now
- What the Commonwealth does
- Britain's role in the Commonwealth
- Brief history of the Commonwealth and its legacy in Britain's multi cultural society
- Link to learners' own countries where appropriate, and other similar organisations, e.g. African Union
- What the UN does
- Britain's role in the UN

UK History and Geography
UK as a diverse society
Human Rights

- Concept
- Relevance to learners – experience of human rights in learners' former countries and expectations in the UK
- Amnesty International
- Medical Foundation
- The Human Rights Act, Articles and Protocols
- The 1951 Geneva Convention Relating to the Status of Refugees

Working in the UK
Health
Housing
Education
Community Engagement

- Helping in your child's school
- Other opportunities for voluntary work
- Mentoring
- Police committees
- Working for charities, etc.
- Faith communities/multi-faith councils
- Recording voluntary work as part of your CV

The law

Phase 2 – producing the learning materials

Once the content was agreed, the project started work on developing materials which would teach English language skills at Entry 1, 2 and 3 (CEFR A1, A2, and B1) through the context of citizenship and in particular the contexts that were identified in the Scoping Paper. These were drafted and put together into a learning materials pack over the summer of 2004. They include teachers' notes and are referenced to the national curriculum for ESOL.[8] The pack was published in a limited edition only, to be used in Phases 3 and 4, in both paper and electronic version.

Because good practice dictates that materials reflect the needs and interests of the learners and because of the huge potential scope of the curriculum content, the learning materials are examples only. Teachers are encouraged to use them as a basis to develop learning materials that have a very local focus and reflect the specific concerns of each group of learners. This is stressed both in the materials pack and the 1-day familiarisation workshops for teachers. The electronic version of the pack allows teachers to customise materials for their learners using Word.

Phase 3 – trialling the learning materials pack

NIACE and LLU+ piloted the ESOL citizenship learning materials pack with 18 ESOL providers in England. Providers from all around the country were asked to use the materials in ESOL courses and feed back on their relevance, accessibility and fitness for purpose in preparing ESOL learners for citizenship. Over 80 ESOL providers applied to take part, but as there was only room for 18 (approximately three in each of the nine government regions) the project tried to reflect the range. Pilot centres included further education colleges, vocational training organisations, sixth form centres, local authorities and smaller organisations from the voluntary sector.

Learners also reflected the range usually found in ESOL classes. The learners were working towards ESOL Entry 1 (18%), Entry 2 (33%) or Entry 3 (47%). They included asylum seekers (26%), refugees (24%), long-term immigrants (42%), and learners with prior educational experience to degree equivalence or with no formal qualifications and little school experience. Across the nine government office regions, 28% of learners in the pilot came from London and fewest (5%) from the Eastern Region. The vast majority of learners (97%) were taking an ESOL qualification and 77% reported they intended to apply for British citizenship.

A familiarisation workshop was developed and delivered for ESOL teachers participating in the pilot, to introduce them to the materials pack and generate ideas on how to use it effectively. The 1-day workshop content drew on existing good practice in ESOL provision and referred to the recommendations of the Advisory Group report (op cit). Each teacher received a copy of the pack. They spent the day navigating the pack, becoming familiar with the sections and adapting the learning materials. They also discussed the management of the pilot and support available to them. Teachers were encouraged to be 'developers' by contributing ideas and additional materials.

The pilots were encouraged to choose different sections of the learning materials pack so that, overall, all 12 sections were tried out. Section 1, *What is Citizenship?* was trialled with 78% of learners. The majority of teachers (54%) said they had not worked on this topic before.

It was intended that funding from the pilot project would buy teachers development time and space for reflective practice as well as meeting and evaluation time. Teachers needed time to familiarise themselves with the materials, adapt them for the group of learners and research and collect local resources. They were encouraged to invite outside speakers and make visits with learners.

A consultant was appointed to work with each provider, visiting the site at least three times during the pilot and meeting with the key contact, teachers and learners. The key contact provided feedback to the consultant. The project team met monthly to discuss the pilot progress and evaluate the effectiveness of the pack as a teaching and learning resource.

Evaluation tools were developed to capture a range of data. These included consultants' visit reports, teacher questionnaires, learner questionnaires, learner focus groups and interviews with teachers, managers and other key stakeholders. In total, 361 learner questionnaires and 36 teacher questionnaires were returned. Nineteen focus groups were held with learners. A pilot feedback day was held in March 2005 to gather responses from all providers and allow teachers to share their experiences of piloting the pack.

The general feedback on the learning materials pack was overwhelmingly positive. Teachers reported that the materials pack had introduced subject matter which was of interest to learners and it had been particularly successful with more controversial and less functional topics, like Human Rights. A consultant reported: 'I've observed some lessons where the materials have generated considerable interest and discussion. This has been true especially on those sections that deal with issues less frequently covered in ESOL lessons – Section 2 on Parliament and Section 6 on Human Rights.'

Teachers reported that most of the learning activities need to be adapted by the ESOL teacher. Though this is generally accepted to be good practice, some teachers found it too time consuming. Teachers also asked for some changes to be made. They found not enough materials for the younger learners (16–19 year olds), and rather too much emphasis on reading activities (usually the easiest way of getting over new information). In particular, there was a request for more listening activities and resources to reflect regional accents. Consultants observed that the materials pack worked very well at Entry 2 and Entry 3. However, particularly in the *What is Citizenship?* section there were some difficulties reported at all levels because of the use of abstract vocabulary and in general teachers asked for more materials at Entry 1 level. Those teachers working with Entry 1 classes had to adapt most materials to the appropriate level. Consultants also noticed that very few teachers printed out colour materials from the CD, instead photocopying colour photos on a black and white machine. This raised issues of resources available to teachers – even in 2005 it seems that few have access to colour photocopiers or printers. Most crucially, given that the aim is to teach English language skills within a citizenship context, both consultants and teachers reported getting confused about whether they were teaching ESOL or citizenship content. In other words, they found it difficult to be clear about whether the main aim is to improve learners' reading skills or to teach them information about how parliament works – and, given it should be the former, how to ensure that the language skill got the main emphasis. On the other hand, it could be argued that the essential thing is to engage learners' interests and the language skills will follow. And the citizenship content certainly seemed to engage learners' interests (see below).

Outside speakers were generally very popular. However, teachers felt the guest speakers needed to be language aware and able to communicate effectively at the appropriate level. Teachers invited a wide range of outside speakers including:

- a local historian
- a local councillor
- a doctor
- a drugs project worker
- a support worker for a deaf student
- a police officer
- the local MP
- the college principal
- a speaker on careers from Connexions
- a Jobcentre Plus adviser
- a speaker on domestic violence
- a former refugee now a British citizen.

Most of the ESOL providers (60%) said they had arranged visits as a result of the citizenship course and these proved equally popular with the learners. Outside speakers were popular with learners too. The majority of learners said they would welcome more visitors and speakers to the class and would enjoy more visits to historical sites. When asked in focus groups whom they would like to invite, learners suggested a local MP, local councillor, representatives from local services like hospitals, police or education providers, a union representative, a local charity, a DfES minister, David Beckham and Tony Blair!

In general, the feedback from the learners was even more positive than from the teachers. Issues of politeness aside (i.e. learners possibly wanting to feed back what they thought the consultants wanted to hear), learners appeared engaged and focused during the consultants' visits. In one focus group, a learner said the materials pack helped them to feel more connected with British society. A learner from Leicester College reported that the course was 'relevant to my life'. A selection of other comments is given below. We have not included any negative ones because we did not receive any.

'Because I live in the UK I should know about everything in this country, for example, citizenship is very important and I need passport and also about law & services.'
Sheffield College learner

'It has been very useful and helpful and I would recommend it to other students.' Tower Hamlets College learner

A learner from Hastings College said, *'I like to know places & traditions about GB. It really made me think more deeply about our society'.*

'We liked the team work. We learned about UK culture, everybody brings different ideas, we all mix, different religions & cultures.'
Learner from Apex, Leicester

Learners from Waltham Forest College said:
'This country is different to other countries – it is a mix – I like learning about this.'
'I like learn about England. These are very interesting for me. I like learning about different culture. I think – we live here, we must know about this country.'

A learner from Sheffield College said, *'Human rights was one of the sections I liked best because it helps me to know about the law and duty'.*

'I get interest with the human rights, especially a topic about slavery and discrimination. I would like to learn a lot more about British history. In my opinion all human beings should know their rights, it is very important.'
Thomas Danby College learner

One learner from Waltham Forest College said the Employment material was his favourite section of the pack:
'because I want a good job for the future.'
A learner from Newcastle College said: *'For me learning of citizenship, education, health and history is very good and then very interesting for me, I enjoyed myself because education is the key of life'.*

Croydon Continuing Education and Training Service (CETS) learners made positive comments in their returned questionnaires:
'I like section 11 because if you help in the community, they will help you in return.'

The role of mother tongue

The use of mother tongue and of bilingual resources is recommended in the pack but not all providers were able to use them. Some providers may not have the funding for resources such as interpreters or even bilingual dictionaries.

Other providers commented that it was difficult to use mother tongue effectively as classes were linguistically heterogeneous. A class of learners may include speakers of many languages and providing an interpreter for all of these may be unrealistic. Also, the usefulness of bilingual learning materials depends on learners being literate in their mother tongue. It was felt that the use of mother tongue was most appropriate in Entry 1 classes where learners shared the same first language. Bilingual ESOL teachers have specialist skills in this respect.

In the pilot, the Chinese ICT Open Learning Centre in Newcastle trialled the materials in imaginative ways using simultaneous translation and electronic whiteboard technology. The ESOL teacher was English, the support teacher bilingual and the group was a homogeneous Cantonese speaking group. The learners discussed the concepts in their own language then the support teacher provided the English/Cantonese translation on the whiteboard. At the end of each session a dual language vocabulary list was provided to each learner to take away.

The visiting consultant reported: 'The session was very interactive, with lots of conversation and contributions, and relating to learners' own history (e.g. Tudor period likened to Ming dynasty). The Interactive whiteboard was used to provide instant translations of difficult words from English into Cantonese.'

Some teachers remain to be convinced on the important role of mother tongue in the ESOL classroom. As ESOL learners become more diverse in one class, the advantages may not be immediately evident. However, the project managers and consultants are still keen to promote the idea of grouping learners together to discuss complex or abstract issues in their own language. This would be particularly valuable in Section One, for example, where learners need to discuss the concept of citizenship and distinguish subtle differences in cross cultural understanding of the term.

Dissemination Day

Over 150 learners, teachers, managers and consultants came together at the end of the project for a dissemination event. Appropriately enough for a project on citizenship, the event, which had been planned months in advance, was on the same day as the general election. Sir Bernard Crick introduced the day, and teachers and learners ran workshops to showcase the work they had done on the pilots. The enthusiasm of both teachers and learners was infectious. One learner, a refugee doctor, explained how learning about 'What our MP can do for you' had given him the idea of writing to his MP who wrote a letter on his behalf to the Home Office and organised a clinical placement for him at the local hospital.

Phase 4 – regional familiarisation workshops

At the same time as the pilot project, the Home Office, keen to get citizenship teaching started, asked for the draft pack to be disseminated more widely. A series of teacher familiarisation workshops was run during January and February 2005, to introduce the learning materials to ESOL teachers. A total of 20 trainers were recruited and trained to deliver the workshops in pairs.

In total, 961 ESOL teachers were trained in 29 workshops across the nine government office regions of England with one additional event in Scotland.

The events recruited well and trainers reported that participants were enthusiastic and engaged well with the activities. Response to the materials pack was generally positive. In some cases, the teachers' concerns around the current political situation and uncertainties around language testing took up a disproportionate amount of time. Because of the high degree of interest in and anxiety about the Citizenship Test, ESOL teachers wanted to be given detailed information on the Home Office language requirements for citizenship. Some delegates also wanted discussion on the ethical issues and the ESOL teacher's role in implementing government policy. The trainers felt they benefited from working in pairs in this respect, as they gave each other support and shared knowledge.

While some more experienced teachers said they could have done without the workshops, most teachers found the workshops very useful and reported that the workshops gave them confidence and an opportunity to try things out. Workshops were an opportunity to clarify the purpose of the pack and the regulations on language requirements for citizenship. Some teachers reported they would not have known where to source learning materials on Human Rights, for example. The sections on Health, Education and Housing were not essential in the same way as most ESOL teachers were accustomed to teaching these topics anyway.

One useful function of the workshops was that everyone had an opportunity to use the CD for accessing the recommended websites and for adapting learning materials. Part of the day was spent in small groups, while teachers wrote materials based on the pack then displayed them.

Phase 5 – revision of the pack and revised regional workshops

The revised pack will be published in September 2005. Local adjustments are being considered in Scotland, Wales and Northern Ireland. Further workshops will be run in the autumn of 2005, for approximately another 1,000 teachers throughout the UK. More trainers will be briefed so that the workshops can continue locally, across the UK, once the current round of nationally funded training is completed.

Conclusions

This was always a potentially controversial area of work, but proved popular with both teachers and learners in the end. Teachers, and ESOL teachers in particular, tend to be angry with the hostile way that immigration is handled in the British media and often feel they need to champion their learners against the government in issues of settlement and entitlements. Many were initially suspicious of the citizenship agenda, worrying that, through the English language requirements, they would become gatekeepers for the

Home Office. Others felt that the agenda of citizenship was in fact about cultural integration, and that it came with the intention of denying immigrants and refugees their own cultures.

However, most teachers we have worked with were won over, to a considerable extent because of the enthusiasm of their learners for the citizenship content. Teachers also welcomed the materials and ideas for activities. It seemed to us that they were also pleased to be able to take part in a project about curriculum development. In an education culture in which it sometimes feels that measuring and documenting takes priority over learning and teaching, it was a pleasure to work on the creative side of the education process.

The potential for future developments is limitless; for instance there is a need for more learning materials for teachers, materials for learners such as workbooks, tapes and videos and much more.

The current situation is not entirely clear yet, however. Also on the horizon are changes in the language requirements for settlement as well as citizenship. This has been flagged up in the Ministerial Statement and may bring further complications. The first application for citizenship using the Skills for Life ESOL qualifications has still to be submitted. When applications begin, the clarity of the regulations and the systems will be tested. Once they are established, it will probably be time for the next change.

Notes

1 QCA (1998) Education for citizenship and the teaching of democracy in schools; report of the advisory group on citizenship.
2 Community Cohesion: a report of the independent review team. (2001) Chaired by Ted Cantle, London: Home Office.
3 The Nationality, Immigration and Asylum Act (2002).
4 The New and the Old; the report of the 'Life in the United Kingdom' Advisory Group, London: Home Office (2003).
5 Written ministerial statement (15 June 2005) 'Tests of language and knowledge of life in the UK for new citizens' www.ind.homeoffice.gov.uk/ind/en/home/news/press_releases/ new_language_requirement.html.
6 Life in the United Kingdom; A Journey to Citizenship, (2004) London: HMSO.
7 Editor's note 2008 – this is the case.
8 Adult ESOL Core Curriculum, (2001) London: DIUS.

20 Best practice in writing assessment

Liz Hamp-Lyons
The University of Hong Kong

The first three generations

The first generation of writing assessment was what we would now call 'direct testing', that is, assessing a person's ability to write by requiring them to do some writing. This tradition continued for around two thousand years beginning in China and spreading through Europe and finally to the New World (Hamp-Lyons 2002). It was only in the 20th century, and in the USA, that the second generation began.

Indirect testing – multiple-choice testing, often (inaccurately) called 'objective' testing – was promoted as a more reliable and precise way of assessing writing, but was more realistically a solution to the problems of large-scale assessment that arose around the time of the second world war. US education has been fighting its way out of that blind alley since the late 1970s (White 1983). However, the British educational system, like most of those in Europe, was in the 1950s–1970s (and perhaps still is) considerably more elitist than the American, with only 5% of 18 year olds going on to higher education, there was no equivalent of 'freshman writing' in UK colleges and universities. The ability to write was taken for granted. In Britain, at the high school level, the traditional 'exam boards'such as the University of Cambridge Local Examinations Syndicate, the Oxford Delegacy, and others, which had been using much the same practices since the turn of the 20th century, were in general fairly content to continue using written exams.

The third generation of writing assessment is portfolio-based assessment, which has also been in existence for many years, notably in the arts, and in primary education more widely, but has become very popular in many areas of education since the 1980s, and increasingly in the 2000s. In English education around the world, portfolios in instruction and portfolio-based assessment have been seen as valuable tools for writing-to-learn as well as assessing the ability to write (Hamp-Lyons & Condon 2000).

Balance to the best

While there was undoubtedly good practice in all three of these 'generations' of writing assessment, there is still a feeling that we are trying to reconcile a philosophical and values dilemma between the demand for equality and the search for equity. The fairness equation means the search for a way of balancing opposing demands: the demand/expectation that standards exist, can be established, described and applied to all test takers 'equally' and the desire to ensure that assessments are 'equitable', that is, that they provide opportunities for different kinds of learners to demonstrate their diverse abilities. Equality means the same for everyone; yet in modern-day education we now believe that an 'equal' world can never be a 'fair' world. The decision of the world's richest countries to 'forgive' the debt of the least-developed countries reflects a growing understanding that equity and equality are not the same thing. It reflects a 21st century view of fairness, a view which I believe also needs to be a fundamental element of what I think of as fourth-generation assessment practice. Best practice in writing assessment in the 21st century must also move into the fourth generation.

A fourth generation is needed

In writing assessment, the first generation, the 'Old World' generation, focused on validity, on getting learners to write and then scoring it. The second generation was the 'New World' generation; it discovered reliability and with it came tests of 'writing' that did not require a person to write. The second generation is alive and fairly well in testing contexts all around the world[1], although writing researchers and teachers decry its negative influence on what and how students perceive literacy and ways of teaching and learning to write. The third generation disregarded reliability and privileged certain representations of language constructs, and has been seen (though often unjustly) by many as eschewing standards. As a result, it has become popular only in limited contexts and rarely exerts any systemic/political influence. A fourth generation is needed, but it must contribute to the development of writing assessments that can meet quality standards for assessment and at the same time bring us closer to balancing equity and equality.

Talking about standards of **quality** leads us to another kind of 'standard': the notion of standard language. In most countries the notion that there is a 'standard' form of the language is just that – a notion. Yet language tests by their nature seek to standardise their expectations, and this makes it difficult to flexibly assess and reward language performances that communicate clearly, even strongly, yet use non-standard language patterns. Writing assessment finds this particularly difficult because we assess writing using scales, which themselves are attempts to define standards by which writing is to be measured, and that inherently circumscribe the kinds of performances and the language domain features that can be accepted as meeting each level on the scale. On the other hand, writing assessments may offer the most fruitful context in which variation from standard language behaviour can be judged on its own merits, and thus may offer chances for balancing equity and equality that tests of other skills do not.

Yet another kind of standard relates to the 'standards movement', a term used to denote the determination to prescribe expected levels of student achievement. As Davison & McKay (2003) discuss, the term is often used by educational administrators as a form of guidance for parents to understand what healthy and comparable progress towards successful achievement in later years should look like for their child, and as a form of accountability to exhort schools to ensure that students reach these levels of performance. Davison & McKay (2003) point out that with this uneasy mix of prescriptive and descriptive uses, 'standard' in this sense easily becomes a management tool rather than an educational tool. In particular, my own experience shows me that there is a kind of fatal attraction about the whole notion of 'standards' – an entropic tendency that leads all assessment to seek the 'universal solution', the universal test with universal standards. The prescriptive rather easily overwhelms the descriptive.

A final meaning for the word 'standard' must be considered: a standard in the sense of a convention, of conformity to the typical. How easy our lives would be if all educational and employment contexts were the same, so that we could arrive at a 'one size fits all' test that would assess all learners equitably and equally well. To a considerable degree, this is the principle upon which 'standardised' testing depends. But all contexts and needs are not the same. Certainly it is true that there are large numbers of traditional learners of languages for general educational purposes; in many contexts, it may be wholly appropriate to assess progress or readiness, or achievement, using (narrowly defined) 'academic' assignments, interchangeable scoring criteria, and generalised reporting of performance standards. But that leaves aside nurses, doctors, accountants, airline pilots and ship navigators, peacekeepers, and others. How easy our lives would be if all learners were the same, with the same needs! But they are not. Not only are there learners who study and use English for, and need to be assessed on, specific purposes and academic purposes, it is also true that not all academic disciplines demand the same kinds of writing, the same amounts, the same standards of performance. It is equally true that even academic conventions are changing. In assessing language – any language, in any way – we are assessing a moving target.

Fortunately, it is also true that there are continual, if sometimes subtle, changes in what we know and what we can do when it comes to large-scale writing assessment. In what follows I consider the possibilities that are ahead of us for the fourth generation.

Toward the fourth generation

Being technological

The technical side of developments in writing assessment is the one that gets the most attention, with the advent and increasing application of automated essay scoring (Shermis & Burstein 2003). Computer-based/assisted writing assessment can be used for both large-scale assessment and for assessing distance learners – also a rapidly-growing group. Increasingly sophisticated software such as the *Intelligent Essay Assessor*, *Intellimetric* and *e-rater* are trained to identify ideal features of text and reward them, and also to analyse the scoring behaviours of human raters, find the underlying text features of essays at each level, and model computerised scores on these patterns. Claims have been made that the software can be trained to reward non-standard varieties of a language, and to score/reward different traits in a text differentially. But I have yet to read convincing research that this has been done; in fact, even if it can, it remains true that, as Sir Mike Tomlinson has said, 'the present educational culture seems only to value what we can measure, but the parts of education that we remember are those that excite us, that are unconventional and probably unmeasurable' (Tomlinson 2005). While teachers recognise and celebrate unconventional but highly effective writing, computer programs do not. Even when scoring the most conventional forms of writing, computers cannot be 'taught' to score reliably without substantial databanks of human ratings of each essay topic. This makes it, so far at least, expensive. Furthermore, when essay raters are asked to score essays online, they enter into a process that is distant, difficult, lonely and de-professionalising (Hamp-Lyons 2005). This is a dimension of writing assessment that offers great potential but has yet to achieve anything close to the status of 'good practice'.

Automated essay scoring has a particular problem when it comes to scoring the writing of non-native users of a language. Automated responses are built up from rules; rules are derived from either established 'rulebooks' that describe and legislate what is right and what is wrong; or from corpora of actual language use relevant to the context. The world we now live in has more multi-plurilingual contexts than it has monolingual or even bilingual ones. Multilingual Europe is a splendid case in point. But the same is true of the US, Canada and Australia/New Zealand. Asian and African countries have a preponderance of people who need to function in more than one language, using different languages for the home, education, and interaction with the power structure of their country. The case of English is supremely complex; the role of international 'standard' English is under consideration in many places, but particularly when a country or region possesses a recognised or emerging variety of English. Davies and Elder (2006) discuss several kinds of English as a lingua franca and describe 'ELF4', a (new) code used for interaction among NNSs, not Standard English and not based on Standard English. Some researchers would argue that post-colonial or World Englishes (Brutt-Griffler 2002, Kachru 1990) such as Indian English could be classified as a sub-set of ELF4. Lingua francas by their developing and ephemeral natures pose problems for all assessment, and automated scoring systems cannot yet respond appropriately to variations in language patterns; and to teach them to do so requires not only technical development but also some difficult socio-political decisions.

Being humanistic

In **first** language writing and writing assessment, great emphasis is put on the humanistic aspect; this is less foregrounded in **second** language writing and writing assessment. This may be explained by the origin of the teaching of writing to non-native writers in remedial (or, what the Americans call 'compensatory') education, with a focus on copying, on practising model sentences, filling gaps in sentences or very short texts, and working from model essays. Happily, these days there is much more 'leakage' between first and second language theory and practice. Second language writing scholars increasingly adopt approaches used in first language writing, while first language writing scholars accept that they need to study the second language writing literature and practice in order to help the tide of non-native speakers who have flowed into school, and increasingly higher education, classrooms in Britain, the USA, Canada and Australia in the past 20 years. However, it has taken much longer for second language writing assessment practices to start reflecting the humanistic elements of second language writing pedagogy and education theory.

Among the key principles that lead to and support humanistic writing assessment we can list:

- teaching and learning approaches and activities that foster learner independence
- the conscious awareness and valuing of differences among learners and test takers
- the recognition that individual learners' voices need to be nurtured if a student is to discover confidence in themselves and their expression of their knowledge and ideas in written form
- the deliberate explication and modelling of the 'standard' 'values' (i.e., the expectations that need to be met in the context of a specific writing assessment context)

- the importance of feedback in learning to write
- ensuring that learners/test takers have the opportunity to present a 'paper trail' of their learning and writing.

This last is an area where distinctions between classroom- or school-based assessment and large-scale formal tests and examination, are significant. Obviously, classroom and school contexts offer far more potential for humanistic forms of writing assessment. Sadly, however, in many schools the only way that teachers and systems seem to know for assessing students' writing is the formal exam – or worse still, the multiple-choice test. In a later section I will briefly describe how portfolio assessment can bring a humanistic dimension even to quite large assessment contexts.

Here, I will focus on one of the principles that starts from the first language field – feedback; and another that starts from the second language field – learner independence. I will then describe some of the key tools currently being employed and explored to expand the humanistic quality in writing assessments.

Focus on feedback

A key characteristic of humanistic assessment is the attention paid to students' roles in the assessment event; when writing assessment is humanistic, it works consciously to ensure that students understand what the assessment is about, what it looks like, how teachers and other 'judges' make their judgements, and most importantly, how learning to write well can lead to more successful writing on formal assessments. Feedback has been an important element in the teaching of writing to L1 writers for a long time, first as 'marking'or 'grading' with the use of written comments on texts (e.g. Murray 1978) and later through oral forms of feedback, notably the writing conference (e.g. Sperling 1990). While marking/grading continues to hold a tremendous attraction for second language writing teachers (despite studies that show it to be mainly ineffective), more recently different kinds of feedback that are more interactive, more humanistic and more nuanced have begun to play an important role in helping second language writers learn to write well, including self and peer assessment (Cheng & Warren 2005, Tsui & Ng 2000) as well as teacher feedback (Goldstein 2007, Hyland & Hyland 2007). I am a strong believer that if we train teachers to give feedback well, and students to be able to appreciate and take advantage of this feedback, we can also help students learn to perform better on writing assessments.

Learner independence

Learner independence is essential if teaching writing with feedback is to be successful. But independence within formal learning contexts depends on instruction: it does not come 'naturally'. It comes far less naturally when a person is learning in a language other than their own. Furthermore, most (English L2) teachers have themselves been through an education process that did not encourage independence, but was marked by a narrow curriculum, prescriptive behaviours, genres, standards; and a belief that 'the teacher is right'. From such a tradition, some teachers find it very difficult to be independent themselves, and much harder to encourage independent learning and thinking in their students. Independence is the ultimate humanist contribution a teacher can make to a student; every teacher wants every learner to be able to learn without them before they leave school/university. In Hong Kong, the establishment of self-access centres and independent learning programmes, made possible through special government grants to universities has made a positive contribution to helping students learn to be independent learners; some universities have within their resources a 'writing assistance programme' modelled on similar facilities in the US, where students can take a text at various stages in its development process and get advice on how to take it forward, revise it, edit it, etc. This funding has stimulated significant research into learner independence and self-access learning in Hong Kong and has contributed to growth in this field in other countries (e.g., Gardner & Miller 1999). Because writing is a language skill that must take place principally alone, it is inherently independent. Because it is a visible record, once completed it is a strong indicator of how well a person has done a task. Because writing tasks are, in the modern world, becoming more complex, and needs are becoming more differentiated, model-based and genre-based teaching has its limits. A good writer is an independent writer. Since it is truer now even than it was 25 years ago that 'writing is thinking', an independent writer has a good likelihood of also being an independent thinker.

In writing assessment, we do not yet have good instruments for assessing 'thinking', but there have been some encouraging moves in that direction, among them Topical Structure Analysis (TSA) (e.g. Connor & Farmer 1990 Education Resources Information Center (ERIC)), and formal argument as developed by Stephen Toulmin (1958); for a nice explanation of Toulmin's argument visit faculty pages at www.unl.edu/speech/comm109/Toulmin/layout.htm or www.winthrop.edu/wcenter/handoutsandlinks/toulmin.htm (both retrieved 5/11/05). There is also potential in primary trait theory (Faigley, Cherry, Jolliffe & Skinner 1985) and multiple trait theory (Hamp-Lyons 1991, Weigle 2002) to develop criteria and scales for assessing argument quality in writing.

Being socio-political

It is when we turn to this aspect of writing assessment (and indeed, any kind of assessment), that the tension between equality and equity becomes most evident. In the post-2001 world, the social, economic and political imperatives on governments and quasi-government agencies to use education and access to education as a political tool is growing stronger all the time. Wealthy, 'developed' countries are seeing more and more refugees, temporary workers, children of immigrants entering education from ghettoised language communities and 'economic refugees' trying to reverse the southern drift struggling to enter their countries. In these efforts, large-scale tests are a tool of discrimination – positive and negative. In 2003 the USA was using visa restrictions to keep out Muslims and Chinese for different reasons; in 2005 it significantly eased visa constraints on Chinese seeking to study, and offered 'sweeteners' such as the chance to work for a time. Why did it do this? Partly because the universities were suffering financially from the loss of essential international student income; and partly because of the political fallout from the intransigent attitude: as China becomes more powerful politically and economically on the world stage, it increasingly behoves the US to work on its friendship strategies. This puts test scores, including those from writing assessments, into wholly different relationships with test takers than directly proficiency- or competence-related. Similarly, after decades of extreme suspicion of the US, China now welcomes Americans learning Chinese and in summer 2005 many Chinese campuses were – literally – overrun with American students. Why is China now eagerly welcoming US (and other international) students? Principally for the foreign currency they bring in, as universities are made increasingly self-reliant for income; but also as part of a conscious attempt to win friends among the young, wealthy and intelligent – the future leaders of their countries, the future business leaders and politicians. There are no pure or simple motives on either side!

But there are many, many other contexts where political and economic considerations determine (language) assessment policy. Rarely is it the case that all comers have equal chances of success; to begin with, on major international tests the cost of taking the test is already a discriminating variable among people. Another significant factor is the ability to afford test preparation classes, which in some countries are considered essential to success. Test preparation schools in China claim to be able to 'crack' the TOEFL or the IELTS, and their writing classes tell people what the writing items will be, provide model answers, and drill paradigms and formulae for competently responding on any conceivable topic. Who can turn down such a tempting promise? Those who cannot afford it have no choice but to turn away. Equality? Yes, for the schools accept anyone. Equity? Not exactly. But then, equity is an ideal, rarely achieved. Nevertheless, we must always be aware of this ideal and aim for it. We see a growing awareness of this need in, for example, the increased provision of 'special accommodations' for learners with special needs such as deafness, blindness, dyslexia, and mobility limitations. In this case we see equity and not equality. But it is still difficult to work out how to manage an equitable writing assessment for females and males (research shows that females tend to score higher on written tests unless topics are specifically biased towards males) or black test takers (demographic data shows that on average black homes in the US have lower incomes, more children, fewer books, and a lower probability of a male parent present, than white or Asian homes; and research shows that black test takers score significantly lower on written tests than white or Asian test takers). These are socio-political issues, and much of the solution must lie in socio-political change; but professional ethics demands that we continuously try to learn as much as possible about the size and shape of the issues and provide whatever technical solutions are possible within our professional best practice . . . and this brings us to the final dimension of best practice in (writing) assessment – ethicality.

Being ethical

As is clear from the work of large language assessment agencies such as Cambridge ESOL and the ETS–TOEFL programme, the ethics of assessment are now prominent on the agenda when we consider 'best practice'. We must consider and try to solve such questions as: How do we ensure test takers' rights? How do we monitor our own conduct? Have we the right to do so? When there are disagreements, whose judgements *count* and whose rights take precedence? How do we ensure that the decisions made are the best possible decisions? How do we monitor the use to which our tests are put when they leave the doors or portals of the testing organisations which have developed them? Certainly these are all difficult questions, and I do not hold the answers. But I believe that being ethical means engagement with the issues and questions, and the conscious attempt to ensure that they are considered thoughtfully by all those who serve as assessment professionals.

As we consider what we now believe about being technological, humanistic, and socio-politically aware, and take all these into account in trying to move writing assessment further towards a modern-day ethical perspective, it becomes evident that humanistically and socially we must be able to recognise and support the abilities and needs of language learners; and that technological developments have given us tools to move in that direction.

In order to assess writing in ways that respond to the abilities and needs of language learners, assessments must be in at least some ways 'local'. By 'local' I mean more than the population taking the test: I mean it to refer to appropriate content and contexts, language forms, frequencies, and *perhaps* to criteria and standards. In observations of classes in test prep schools in China and the US, and in interviews with students in these classes, we have often heard teachers and students talking about the predictability of the writing topics/prompts; and in particular, their culturally loaded content. Test prep classes teach 'tips' for writing timed essays; but they also talk about the quirks of US or British/Australian culture, believing that knowing 'the right stuff' is a key component of success on these writing assessments. Of course a writer must have a message even if the test's target is the medium which expresses it. But – do we need to require test takers to master details of cultures other than their own, in order to succeed on a language test? Research (e.g. Hamp-Lyons 1989, Hamp-Lyons & Zhang 2001) indicates that raters react negatively to writing/writers who display lack of knowledge of (what they consider to be) basic culture. Writing assessments that draw on local cultural knowledge and traditions make an assessment more accessible to all students within that cultural milieu, and may therefore stimulate good writers to stretch to real self-expression, and weaker writers to feel comfortable enough to show the best they can do.

Adapting international tests to make content demands accessible to test takers at local levels places some demands on test development and validation; but these demands can be met with creativity, and can be assisted by full utilisation of the new technologies available to us such as online rating and semi-adaptive computer–human rating. What large-scale writing tests have not done until now, however, is to provide the nuanced assessment and reporting that would enable schools, colleges or programmes the level of detail that means each learner can be offered a range of placement options to suit their proficiency level and the areas where they are in particular need, and help programmes plan their teaching provision, including teachers with appropriate training and suitable materials, for every kind of learner. For writing assessments that really do enable such fine-grained decisions, we have to look for best practice at local levels; and yet unfortunately understanding of writing assessment development and educational use is still not well established. Until it is, we cannot have real best practice in operation for individual learners/test takers.

The feasibility and appropriacy of adapting writing assessments to local *linguistic* norms is still very much an open question; there are practical issues, but also humanistic as well as socio-political ones (Brown & Lumley 1998, Davies, Hamp-Lyons & Kemp 2003). As we are really only beginning to think through this question, the ethical dimensions of it are still not clear to me. However, if a decision is made that it is appropriate for a particular test to use local norms, we do now at least have the technological tools to support it: concordancing, frequency analyses, text structure analytic algorithms, and so on. In developing 'localised' writing assessments there may be greater problems around the development of and decisions about criteria and standards. Language learning practices and opportunities vary from context to context; it has by no means been established yet whether or not criteria and standards that are entirely appropriate in one context are equally appropriate or unrealistic in another (Broad 2003). Making those decisions must involve local experts of various kinds as well as specialists in writing assessment development. But that just makes the ethical issues harder: it doesn't excuse us from considering them.

We see, then, that there is still a very long way to go in writing assessment research and development before we reach best practice; and we can be forgiven for believing that in any case the notion of 'best practice' is a moving target, always out of reach. If knowledge in related areas expands, as it should, then indeed our target will and should be always just beyond our reach. But having goals to strive towards is what stimulates researchers, and many teachers, to remain fascinated by and committed to their profession.

Writing – assessment and instruction

The most critical aspect of best practice that we should be making major progress towards is the strengthening of the links between assessment and instruction (as detailed in particular by Huot 2002). Once again, this is best done by focusing on the local: large-scale, international tests have problems creating real, positive links to the classroom. However, developments in the last 20 years have made several interesting and promising new approaches possible, as described below.

Portfolio-based assessment

Of the newer approaches, portfolio-based assessment has been around the longest. Writing folders became common in the UK from the 1950s, and became part of the examination system in the 1970s in the GCE 'Mode 3'. In the US and Canada, portfolios were introduced in the 1970s and most research was done in the US. Using portfolios in writing assessment became widely known through the programme implemented by Belanoff and Elbow at SUNY Stony Brook (Elbow & Belanoff 1986) and rapidly became popular (Belanoff & Dickson 1991). Since then a great deal of development has been done to make portfolios as assessments well-understood, sufficiently reliable and underpinned by clear validity evidence, and theory supporting them as an assessment tool has been developed (Hamp-Lyons & Condon 2000). Portfolio assessment, when done well, offers best practice options to teachers and also provides the important added value of offering motivating, local professional development opportunities to teachers.

Web-based writing

Since the late 1980s, exciting developments have been taking place in uses of computer software to support the teaching of writing; the best-known early system was probably Daedalus, a set of software options that enabled teachers to provide students with guided prewriting and revision activities and to deliver these both over the internet asynchronously (i.e., not in real time) and in connected writing classrooms to individuals and 'warm' groups within a class in real time (synchronously). There are now a number of resources on the worldwide web to support writing teachers and learners; many universities in the US now have an OWL (online writing laboratory: for an example visit http://owl.english.purdue.edu), and most of these include resources for varied forms of writing assessment (for example: http://cwa.njit.edu/programs/esl/esl.htm or www.wsu.edu/~wassess). There are some signs of similar developments in the UK (for example 'Composer' at the University of Brighton) but many of them tend to be only for postgraduate students. In Hong Kong, where English exists in an uncertain relationship with Chinese, more attention has been paid to supporting undergraduate writing (see for example the Hong Kong University's http://ec.hku.hk/writing_turbocharger/ or the Hong Kong Polytechnic University's http://elc.polyu.edu.hk/WAP/).

School-based writing assessment

A new area that offers potential is the development of alternative assessment of English that puts formal assessment decisions in the hands of teachers. This has been common, of course, in universities, and in the early years of school, but in senior secondary schooling in many countries these decisions have been put into the hands of testing agencies such as State Boards in the US and exam boards in the UK. These bodies have often found it difficult to assess the language proficiency of non-native English speakers through exams designed with native users in mind. We would do well to look to Australia for models of good practice in this area, in particular the State of Queensland, where school-based assessment has gradually taken over at the high school exit point; and to the work of the Assessment Reform Group in Britain (http://www.ltscotland.org.uk/assess/about/keydocs.asp), particularly as it has been implemented in Scotland (www.ltscotland.org.uk). Although this work is still at an early stage, I believe it offers us great scope for further progress toward best practice in writing assessment.

Duties of professionals in (language) assessment

Assessment professionals have to take their expertise to the real world, by engaging with classroom teachers-as-assessors to ensure that best practice, if it exists, is not confined to professional organisations. This knowledge and skill should not be secret: rather the exact opposite. Test takers are best served when the fullest knowledge about what a test is, how it works, what its effects will or may be, what it looks like, how it is scored, who scores it, what values underlie its principles – when all this is made available to them, and to their teachers and where appropriate, their parents. This implies that academic language testers need to do more than theoretical research or experiments in semi-laboratory conditions with very small-scale low-stakes tests/assessment. They need to engage with testing agencies. They need to understand the practical conditions that determine the boundaries of innovation in assessment, and work with other interest groups to push out those boundaries. This of course is not only 'best practice' for writing assessment, but for all kinds of language assessment – and indeed, for all assessment.

Writing assessment as professional development

Although I have made this my last point, it is a very important one because it is an argument for added value in working towards best practice in writing assessment. Good writing assessments involve teachers as the key informants in making judgements about the quality of writing and the appropriacy of writing tasks, topics, criteria, and levels for their students. But this is a 2-way process, a win–win situation for assessment programmes and for teachers who participate. As Bill Condon and I found in each stage of writing assessment development we went through at the University of Michigan in the 1990s; as I found again doing similar work with less-experienced and qualified writing teachers at the University of Colorado in Denver (both of these discussed in Hamp-Lyons & Condon 2000); and as I am finding now in working with secondary English teachers in Hong Kong: participating in the *development* of assessment processes and instruments for *their own students* is a tremendous motivator and professional development tool for teachers. It may the best form of learning about teaching that we can offer. So – good practice in assessment can also be good practice in teacher professional development: and good value for money!

In conclusion

As this paper has indicated, we still have much to learn before we can claim to understand and be implementing 'best practice' in writing assessment. Nevertheless, there are some clear paths towards that goal, and some clear steps ahead of us on that journey. It may well be that we can expect only uneasy and temporary resolutions, but as keepers of the gates of educational opportunity, and as ethical educators, we need to ensure that we apply best practice principles to our work. And, since knowledge and values are always changing and developing, we need to keep up-to-date with new developments so that we will continue to ensure the best writing assessments current understanding can offer.

Note

1 For example, in the US, in 2005 the College Board has introduced a 'new' SAT (Scholastic Aptitude Test) that includes a test of 'writing' containing a 20-minute 'essay' and a multiple-choice 'test of writing'.)

References

Belanoff, P and Dickson, M (Eds) (1991) *Portfolios: Process and product,* Portsmouth NH: Boynton/Cook.

Broad, B (2003) *What we really value: Beyond rubrics in teaching and assessing writing,* Logan UT: Utah State University Press.

Brown, A and Lumley, T (1998) Linguistic and cultural norms in language testing: A case study, *Melbourne Papers in Language Testing* 7, 80–96.

Brutt-Griffler, J (2002) *World English: a study of its development*, Clevedon: Multilingual Matters.

Cheng, W and Warren, M (2005) Peer assessment of language proficiency, *Language Testing* 22, 93–121.

Connor, U and Farmer, M (1990) The teaching of topical structure analysis as a revision strategy for ESL writers, in Kroll, B (Ed.) *Second language writing: Research insights for the classroom,* New York: Cambridge University Press, 126–139.

Davies, A, Hamp-Lyons, L and Kemp, C (2003) Whose norms? International proficiency tests in English, *World Englishes* 22, 571–584.

Davison, C and McKay, P (2002) Counting and dis-counting learner group variation: English language and literacy standards in Australia, *Journal of Asian-Pacific Communication*, 12: 17–94.

Elbow, P and Belanoff, P (1986) Portfolios as a substitute for proficiency examinations, *College Composition and Communication* 37, 336–339.

Elder, C and Davies, A (2006) *Assessing English as a Lingua Franca*. Annual Review of Applied Linguistics, 26: 282–301.

Faigley, L, Cherry, R, Jolliffe, D and Skinner, A (1985) *Assessing Writers' Knowledge and Processes of Composing,* Norwood, NJ: Ablex.

Gardner, D and Miller, L (1999) *Establishing self-access,* Cambridge: Cambridge University Press.

Goldstein, L (2007) In search of the individual: The role of individual differences in second language conference, written, and online feedback and revision, in Hyland, K and Hyland, F (Eds) *Feedback in second language writing: Contexts and issues,* New York: Cambridge University Press.

Hamp-Lyons, L (2007) The impact of testing practices on teaching: ideologies and alternatives, in Cummins J and Davison, C (Eds) *Kluwer Handbook on English Language Teaching*.

Hamp-Lyons, L (2004) Automated Essay Scoring, Book Review in *Assessing Writing* 9.

Hamp-Lyons, L (1989) Raters respond to rhetoric in writing, in Dechert, H and Raupach, G (Eds) *Interlingual Processes*, Tubingen: Gunther Narr, 229–244.

Hamp-Lyons, L and Condon, W (2000) Assessing the portfolio: Principles for practice, theory and research, Cresskill NJ: Hampton Press.

Hamp-Lyons, L and Zhang, B (2001) World Englishes: Issues in and from academic writing assessment, in Flowerdew, J and Peacock, M (Eds), *English for Academic Purposes: Research Perspectives*, Cambridge UK: Cambridge University Press, 101–116.

Huot, B (2002) *(Re)articulating writing assessment*, Logan UT: Utah University State Press.

Hyland, F and Hyland, K (2007) Mitigation and miscommunication: constructing and interpreting teacher written feedback, in Hyland, K and Hyland, F (Eds) *Feedback in second language writing: Contexts and issues*, New York: Cambridge University Press.

Kachru, B (1990) *The Other Tongue* (2nd edition), Urbana and Chicago: University of Illinois Press.

McKay, P (2000) On ESL standards for school age learners, *Language Testing* 17, 185–214.

Murray, D (1978) Internal revision: A process of discovery, in Cooper C R and Odell, L (Eds) *Research on composing: Points of departure*, Urbana IL: NCTE, 85–103.

Shermis, M D and Burstein, J C (Eds) (2003) *Automated Essay Scoring*, Mahwah NJ: Lawrence Erlbaum Associates.

Sperling, M (1990) I want to talk to each of you: Collaboration and the teacher-student writing conference, *Research in the Teaching of English* 24, 279–321.

Tomlinson, M (2005) Radio interview, BBC 4, October 31 2005.

Toulmin, S (1958) *The Uses of Argument,* Cambridge: Cambridge University Press.

Tsui, A and Ng, M (2000) Do Secondary L2 Writers Benefit from Peer Comments? *Journal of Second Language Writing* 9.

Weigle, S (2002) *Assessing writing,* Cambridge: Cambridge University Press.

White, E M (1983) *Teaching and assessing writing,* San Francisco: Jossey-Bass.

Zhang, W X (1999) *The rhetorical patterns found in Chinese EFL student writers' examination essays in English and the influence of these patterns on rater response,* unpublished PhD dissertation, Hong Kong Polytechnical University.

Notes on the volume contributors

Piet van Avermaet is Director of the Centre for Diversity and Learning at the University of Ghent, Belgium. For many years he was the co-ordinator of the Certificate in Dutch as a Foreign Language (CNaVT). His expertise and research interests are: educational linguistics; multilingual and multicultural education; diversity and social inequality in education; sociolinguistics; and language testing.

Sibylle Bolton works as a Consultant for different organisations and has worked for many years at the Goethe-Institut headquarters in Munich, where she was responsible for revising the examinations of the Goethe-Institut and for developing new tests. She has also given seminars in test development to teachers of German in many countries.

David Coniam is a Professor in the Faculty of Education at The Chinese University of Hong Kong, where he is a teacher educator working with ESL teachers in Hong Kong secondary schools. His main publication and research interests are in language assessment, computational and corpus linguistics, and language teaching methodology.

Thomas Eckes is Deputy Director and Senior Research Scientist at the TestDaF Institute, Germany. He is in charge of the language testing methodology, research and validation unit. His research interests include: rater effects; many-facet Rasch measurement; polytomous IRT models; construct validity of C-tests; standard setting; computerised item-banking and internet-delivered testing.

Maurizio Gotti is Professor of English Linguistics and Director of the Language Centre at the University of Bergamo. From 1999–2001 he was President of the Italian Association of English Studies. From 2000–04 he was President of Cercles – European Confederation of language centres in Higher Education. He is a member of the Editorial Boards of national and international journals and edits the *Linguistic Insights* series for Peter Lang.

Liz Hamp-Lyons is Professor of English Language Assessment at the University of Bedfordshire. She holds Honorary Professorships at the University of Hong Kong, the University of Nottingham (UK), and

Shanghai Jiao Tong University (PRC). She is the Editor of *Assessing Writing* and of the *Journal of English for Academic Purposes.*

Peter Hardcastle works as an assessment advisor in the Middle East and has also worked at Cambridge ESOL as the Validation Officer for the Association of Language Testers in Europe (ALTE). He liaised with ALTE partners in Spain, Germany, Italy and Portugal and with the Council of Europe, establishing test equivalency among European language tests.

Johannes Hartig is currently working as a senior research fellow at the German Institute for International Educational Research in Frankfurt. He is an experienced teacher and has an extensive background in multivariate methodology including structural equation modelling, hierarchical linear modelling, and IRT scaling. His research interests include proficiency scaling in educational assessment, item context effects in questionnaires, personality theories, the use of the internet in psychological research, and evaluation of educational quality at universities.

Roger Hawkey has many years' of experience in English language teaching, teacher education, course design, and assessment projects in Africa, Asia and Europe. He is now a consultant on testing with Cambridge ESOL and a Senior Research Fellow at the University of Bedfordshire. He has published widely in applied linguistics, language teaching and testing.

Hanan Khalifa is a Principal Research & Validation Co-ordinator at University of Cambridge ESOL Examinations, specialising in reading assessment and the construct validation of language tests. Previously, she worked as a senior testing specialist with international development agencies on developing test batteries and item banks, ESP/EAP curriculum development, teacher training, programme evaluation and educational reform.

Antony John Kunnan is Professor of TESOL at California State University, Los Angeles where he teaches courses in language assessment. He is the author of many books, journal articles, and book chapters and has presented at ALTE conferences in Barcelona, Berlin, Budapest, Cambridge and Sofia. He is the Editor of *Language Assessment Quarterly*.

Anne Lazaraton is an Associate Professor of English as a Second Language at the University of Minnesota, where she teaches courses in ESL Methods, Language Analysis, Language Assessment, and Discourse Analysis. She is the author of *A Qualitative Approach to the Validation of Oral Language Tests*, Volume 14 in the *Studies in Language Testing* series (UCLES/Cambridge University Press 2002).

Waldemar Martyniuk is Assistant Professor of Applied Linguistics at the Jagiellonian University in Krakow, Poland. He is the author of textbooks, curricula, and testing materials for Polish as a foreign language and a visiting professor and lecturer at universities in Germany (Bochum, Giessen, Goettingen, Mainz, Muenster), Switzerland (Basel), and in the USA (Stanford University). In 2005–06 he was seconded to the Council of Europe, Language Policy Division (Strasbourg, France).

Marianne Mavel Ingénierie de la Statistique (2003) du CNAM, Centre National des Arts et Métiers à Paris, après avoir suivi une Maitrise de Sciences et Techniques d'Informatique et de Statistiques Appliquées aux Sciences de l'Homme. Elle est actuellement psychométricienne au CIEP, établissement public opérateur du ministère de l'Education Nationale pour la coopération internationale dans le service du TCF, Test de Connaissance du Français. Elle réalise des analyses psychométriques sur le test TCF: celles ci garantissent la qualité des items, caractéristiques des candidat (le sexe, la langue maternelle, etc . . .), et déterminent le niveau de difficulté des items (calibrage des items). Elle effectue des analyses statistiques pour d'autres services du CIEP et des expertises pour le Ministère des Affaires Etrangères.

Eli Moe works at the University of Bergen, Norway, developing and validating tests. She is involved both in developing tests in Norwegian for adult immigrants as well as tests in English for Norwegian school children. Eli Moe holds a Master's degree in Second Language Acquisition from the University of Bergen, 1996.

Montserrat Montagut holds a degree in Catalan Philology (University of Barcelona, 1996) and postgraduate courses in Lexicography (1997). Since 2001 she has worked as a language planner for the Catalan Government, updating Catalan language teaching programmes and tests and creating learning materials for virtual environments, as well as in the area of language assessment and translation.

Pilar Murtra holds a degree in Catalan Philology (University of Barcelona, 1985). Since 1997 she has been working as a language planner for the Catalan Government on the Catalan language certificates at Advanced and Higher Levels as well as in language assessment more broadly.

Guenter Nold is a member of DESI consortium (German-English-Student Assessment-International). His special research interests include: developing and assessing/testing language competences; testing and the CEFR; second language acquisition; language awareness; intercultural competence; and content and language integrated learning (CLIL).

Brian North is Head of Academic Development at Eurocentres, the educational foundation which teaches languages worldwide where they are spoken, and which has been an NGO consultant to the Council of Europe since 1986. Brian is co-author of the CEFR, developer of the CEFR levels and descriptor scales (his PhD) and co-ordinator of the authoring group that produced a manual for relating examinations to the CEFR. He is also currently Chair of EAQUALS (European Association for Quality Language Services), the accreditation scheme for language schools with over 100 members.

Francesca Pelliccia has an extensive background in language teaching. She has worked as a teacher of Italian in the Università per Stranieri di Perugia (Italy) and in University College Dublin (Ireland), and also as a teacher trainer in South America. She currently works as Examiner Trainer and Validation Officer for the Language Certification Centre (CVCL) of the University of Perugia for Foreigners.

Patrick Riba is currently responsible for the French certifications DELF and DALF at the Centre international d'études pédagogiques in France. He is also assistant lecturer at the University of Paris III, la Sorbonne. Previously Patrick has been manager of the Alliance Française of Maracaibo, Venezuela, pedagogical manager of the Alliance Francaise, Lima, Peru and linguistics attaché, French Embassy Peru. Patrick Riba has published in 'Le français dans le monde' and was in charge of the review 'Synergies Pérou', dedicated to the didactics of languages and cultures in 2003. He is currently collaborating in the elaboration of French referentials 'A1', 'A2' and 'B1'.

Henning Rossa held a research position in Applied Linguistics at the University of Dortmund from 2001–06. His research interests are the assessment of listening skills, construct validity and test takers' perspectives on task difficulty. He currently teaches EFL at a secondary school in Dortmund and is involved in teacher training courses and the development of a nationwide assessment programme.

Nick Saville is a Director at University of Cambridge ESOL Examinations and is responsible for planning and co-ordinating the work of the Research & Validation Group. He is the Cambridge ESOL representative in ALTE and has close involvement with other European initiatives, such as the Council of Europe's Common European Framework of Reference (CEFR) and related 'toolkit'. He is an Associate Editor of the journal *Language Assessment Quarterly*.

Stuart Shaw is the Principal Research Officer and Research Co-ordinator, Assessment Standards and Quality at Cambridge International

Examinations (CIE). Before leading a research team in the area of mainstream international examinations, he worked on a range of Cambridge ESOL products with specific responsibility for Writing. Particular interests include demonstrating how Cambridge Assessment seeks to meet the demands of validity in its tests.

Joseph Sheils is Head of the Department of Language Education and Policy at the Council of Europe. Current projects include reference standards for foreign/second languages and for the languages of instruction in education systems, national policy reviews, intercultural learning, teacher education and plurilingual curricula.

Helen Sunderland is Head of ESOL at LLU+, London South Bank University where she manages educational projects and teacher education programmes. Her special interests are dyslexia and ESOL and teaching basic literacy, and her publications include *Dyslexia and the Bilingual Learner and Teaching Basic Literacy to ESOL Learners*.

Chris Taylor works for the National Institute of Adult Continuing Education (NIACE). Chris led the ESOL citizenship project, funded by the UK Home Office, to develop the language learning materials for citizenship. She has extensive experience in the teaching and managing of basic skills and ESOL programmes, having worked in Bangladesh, Uganda, the Caribbean, USA, Malta and the Soviet Union.

Lynda Taylor is a Consultant to University of Cambridge ESOL Examinations and until July 2007 was Assistant Director of the Research & Validation Group, helping to co-ordinate the research and validation programme for Cambridge ESOL's language tests and teaching awards. She has extensive experience of the theoretical and practical issues involved in L2 testing and assessment, and has provided expert assistance for test development projects worldwide. She regularly writes and presents on the work of the Group and has edited several titles in the *Studies in Language Testing* series.

Carol Taylor Torsello is Professor of English Language and Linguistics in the Humanities Faculty, University of Padua, Italy. She is president of Cercles – European Confederation of Language Centres in Higher Education. Her research interests include systemic functional linguistics, text analysis, English language teaching and testing and e-learning.

Cyril J Weir holds the Powdrill Chair in English Language Acquisition at the University of Bedfordshire (UK) and is Guest Professor at Shanghai Jiao Tong University (PRC). He has taught short courses and carried out consultancies in language testing, evaluation and curriculum renewal in over 50 countries worldwide. He has published many books on language testing, including most recently *Language Testing and Validation: an evidence based approach* (2005) and *Examining Writing* (2007). He is also joint Series Editor of *Studies in Language Testing*. Current interests include academic literacy and test validation.

Presentations at the ALTE Conference Berlin, 2005

Ene Alas
Tallinn Pedagogical University, Estonia
Assessing academic writing

Richard J Alexander
Department of English Business Communication Wirtschaftsuniversität, Austria
Language and content integration in ESP tests and examinations: dilemmas or solutions?

Mardik Andonyan and Aspaziya Borisova
Sofia University, Bulgaria
Distance preparation system for the Standard Test of Bulgarian (STBFL)

Christine Anthonissen
Stellenbosch University, South Africa
On determining what counts while counting: correlating language testing with perceptions of testtakers

Karen Ashton
University of Cambridge ESOL Examinations, England, UK
Standardising speaking tests for The Languages Ladder: A case study across 3 languages and levels

Jennifer Balogh
Ordinate, USA
A common testing framework for computerized spoken language tests in multiple languages

Aukje Bergsma and Henk Kuijper
Citogroep, The Netherlands
Using the CEFR

Sibylle Bolton, Goethe-Institut, Germany; Peter Hardcastle, ALTE UK; and Francesca Pelliccia, Universita per Stranieri di Perugla, Italy
Test comparability and construct compatibility across languages

Jenny Bradshaw
National Foundation for Educational Research, UK
Judgment of standards: the use of the bookmarking method in standard-setting

Gilles Breton
CIEP, France
Diplôme initial de langue française (DILF)

Cécile Bruley-Meszaros
Université René Descartes – Paris 5, France
Apprentissage du polonaise en France: mise en place d'un système d'évaluation

Tineke Brunfaut
University of Antwerp – Centre for Language and Speech, Belgium
Testing subject specific academic reading for students of Germanic languages

Simon Buckland and Tony Y P Lee
Wall Street Institute International, Spain
Maintenance of uniform assessment and attainment standard for ESL courses within a multilingual context

Han-Liang Chang and Shi-Hwa Wei
Language Training and Testing Center, Taiwan
Assessing language abilities of Japanese and European language majors at colleges in Taiwan

Roland Chesters and Marta Nuñez,
Foreign and Commonwealth Office, UK
Language of diplomacy: testing the language skills of the Foreign Office

David Coniam
The Chinese University of Hong Kong, Hong Kong
Raw scores as examination results: How far can they be relied upon?

Peter Davidson
Zayed University, UAE
The use of authentic assessment in an EFL context

Alan Davies
University of Edinburgh, Scotland, UK
Academic language proficiency testing: the IELTS solution

Emyr Davies
Welsh Joint Education Committee/WJEC, Wales, UK
Issues in the development of an entry level qualification for adult Welsh learners

Aneta Dimitrova
US Peace Corps, Bulgaria
Diversity and unification in a global language testing program

Karen Margrete Dregelid and Berit Halvorsen
Norsk spraktest, University of Bergen, Norway
Setting the proficiency levels A1, A2, B1 in tests in Norwegian as a second language

Thomas Eckes
TestDaF Institute, Germany
Assessing academic writing

Elena Eremenko
Moscow State University, Russian Federation
Neue Deutschtests im Rahmen des Präsdentenprogrammes für Aus- und Weiterbildung von Führungskrawften der Russischen Föderation.

Inna Erofeeva, Moscow State University, Russian Federation and Tatiana Nesterova and Evgenji Yurkov, St Petersburg State University, Russian Federation -
Test of Russian as a Foreign Language (TORFL): national and cultural diversity of test-takers

Peter Falvey
Consultant, University of Cambridge ESOL Examinations, England, UK
Setting and improving standards in researching and writing about testing: assistance for new researchers

Ina Ferbežar and Jana Zemljaric Miklavcic
University of Ljublijana, Slovenia
The new style of learning: distance learning of Slovene; a linguistics perspective

Neus Figueras
Department of Education, Generalitat de Catalunya, Spain
The Dutch CEF construct project: purposes, problems, results and implications

Ardeshir Geranpayeh
University of Cambridge ESOL Examinations, England, UK
The German Placement Test: issues in relating placement tests to the Common European Framework of Reference

Maurizio Gotti, Università di Bergamo, Italy and Carol Taylor Torsello, University of Padua, Italy
The CERCLU project for certifying language competence in Italian university language centres

David Graddol
The English Company (UK) Ltd, England, UK
The future of English and its assessment

Kate Green
Department for Education and Skills, UK
The Languages Ladder – steps to success

Tony Green
University of Cambridge ESOL Examinations, England, UK
The ESOL Common Scale Project: working towards a common scale for speaking

Sara Gysen, University of Leuven, Centre for Language and Migration, CNaVT, Belgium and Piet van Avermaet, University of Ghent, Belgium
Identifying and investigating parameters affecting language performance within a task-based language assessment approach

Hamid Reza Haghverdi
Khorasagan University, Iran
Construct validity of current listening comprehension tests

Liz Hamp-Lyons
University of Melbourne, Australia
Assessing writing: standards meets diversity

Claudia Harsch and Konrad Schröder
Universität Augsburg, Germany
Zur Verknüpfung der DESI-Kompetenzniveaus mit dem Gemeinsamen Europäischen Referenzrahmen

Roger Hawkey
Cambridge ESOL, England, UK
An impact study of a high-stakes test (IELTS): lessons for test validation and linguistic diversity

Stefan Hohbusch
Institut für Slavistik, Germany
Grenzen der Kompatibilität bestehender Sprachtests mit dem GeR

Krista Jack
Consultant, Canada
Text specifications, do they work?

Jean-Pierre Jeantheau
National Agency for Fighting Illiteracy, Lyon, France
Assessment of low levels of literacy in a national survey: the ANLCI module

Neil Jones
University of Cambridge ESOL Examinations, England, UK
Methods for constructing a multilingual framework: The Languages Ladder Project

Bernd Kast
Goethe-Institut, Germany
Profile deutsch A1-C2. Ein Hilfsmittel, das Unmogöliches will?

Hanan Khalifa
University of Cambridge ESOL Examinations, England, UK
Testing teaching knowledge: developing a quality instrument to support professional development

Mara Kokina
Naturalization Board, Latvia
Identifying and investigating parameters affecting language performance within a task-based language assessment approach – presentation of case from Latvia

Charalambos Kollias, Hellenic American Union, Greece and José Noijons, CITO, Netherlands
Pilot of CEF benchmark performances of spoken interaction

Christian Krekeler
Fachhochschule Konstanz, Germany
Languages for special academic purposes testing revisited

Antony Kunnan
California State University, USA
Towards a model of test evaluation; macro and micro analytical approaches

Gisella Langé
Ministry of Education, Regional Office for Lombardy, Italy
Painting a picture of quality in Lombardy: certifications, international examinations, European Language Portfolio

Anne Lazaraton
University of Minnesota, USA
Non-native speakers as language assessors: recent research and implications for assessment practice

Barbara Lazenby Simpson
Trinity College, Ireland
Immigrant adult language learners and the achievement of recognised accreditation

María Sol López Martínez and Cristina Suárez Gómez
Centro Ramón Piñeiro para a Investigación en Humanidades, Xunta de Galicia, Spain
La lengua gallega: aprendizaje y evaluación / A lingua galega: aprendizaxe e avaliación

Nele Maddens
Centre of Language and Migration, Leuven, Belgium
Developing an interlocutor instruction video for assessment of functional oral interaction

Waldemar Martyniuk, Language Policy Division, Council of Europe, France and Jagiellonian University, Poland and Joanna McPake, Scottish Centre for Information and Language Teaching and Research, UK
Promoting linguistic diversity? Community languages in Europe – learning, teaching, assessment

Mariane Mavel and Patrick Riba
CIEP, France
L'harmonisation du DELF et du DALF sur les niveaux du Cadre européen commun de référence pour les langues

Pilar Medrano, Spanish Ministry of Education, Spain and Teresa Reilly, British Council, Madrid, Spain
Assessing our young learners in the Spanish Ministry of Education/British Council Bilingual Project

Eli Moe
University of Bergen, Norway
Co-operation, constraints and consciousness – chaos or control? Relating reading tests to the CEFR

Montserrat Montagut
Generalitat de Catalunya, Catalonia, Spain
The revision of higher-level Catalan certificate and the Common European Framework of Reference for Languages

Günter Nold and Henning Rossa
University of Dortmund, Germany
Proficiency scaling in DESI listening and reading tests: task characteristics, item difficulty and cut-off points

Brian North, Eurocentres and EAQUALS, Switzerland and Barbara Stevens, University of Cambridge ESOL Examinations, England, UK
The EAQUALS – ALTE electronic ELP: A pilot project

José Ramon Parrondo
Instituto Cervantes, Spain
La evaluación en el ámbito hispánico: hacia un enfoque globalizador

Pavlos Pavlou
University of Cyprus, Cyprus
Implementing alternative assessment for young learners: advantages and disadvantages for children and teachers

John Pidcock
University of Cambridge ESOL Examinations, Catalonia, Spain
Quality assurance in speaking tests: evaluation of the University of Cambridge ESOL Examinations team leader system in Spain

Pawel Poszytek
Foundation for the Development of Education System, Poland
Relating Polish school leaving exam (Matura) to the CEFR

Christoph Prantl
Universität Wien, Austria
Kommunikatives Testen: Eine Untersuchung zur Validität direktar Tests am Beispiel des ÖSK

James E Purpura
Colombia University, USA
Re-examining grammar assessment in multiple-choice response format exams

Isaac Quist
International Baccalaureate Organization, Wales, UK
Administering language assessment in an international context: challenges for the international Baccalaureate Organization (IBO)

Dorlies Radike Thiel
Senatsverwaltung BJS, Germany
Working in Europe: the language skills required

Susanne Romaine
University of Oxford, UK
Linguistic diversity, sustainable development and the future of the past

Henny Rönneper
Ministerium für Schule, Jugend und Kinder des Landes NRW, Germany
Internationale Sprachzertifikate im schulischen Fremdsprachenunterricht

Rübeling Heinrich
WBT Weiterbildungs-Testsysteme GmbH, Germany
Identifying and investigating parameters affecting language performance within a task-based language assessment approach – presentation of case from Germany and Latvia

Diana Rumpite
Riga Technical University, Latvia
Assessment of ESP skills using the Common European Framework of Reference (CEFR)

Raffaele Sanzo
Ministero della Publica Istruzione, Italy
Over 60,000 primary teachers to acquire B1 level of competency in English: the Italian challenge

Joseph Sheils
Council of Europe, France
Language Testing and Citizenship Forum Opening: Council of Europe language policies for democratic citizenship

Elana Shohamy
Tel Aviv University, Israel
Language tests as covert policy tools in multilingual societies

Helen Spillett and Juliet Wilson
University of Cambridge ESOL Examinations
Considering young learners: the Cambridge Young Learners English Tests

Marko Stabej and Ina Febežar
University of Ljubljana, Slovenia
Identifying and investigating parameters affecting language performance within a task-based language assessment approach – presentation of case from Slovenia

Helen Sunderland, LLU+ London South Bank University, UK and Christine Taylor, NIACE, UK
Learning citizenship alongside language; a national pilot programme in the UK

Rita Süssmuth
Member of the Global Commission on International Migration and former President of the Bundestag, Germany
European and national debates about language assessment and citizenship: fostering integration and preventing exclusion

Lynda Taylor
University of Cambridge ESOL Examinations
Linguistic diversity: language varieties and their implications for testing and assessment

Geoff Tranter
WBT Weiterbildungs-Testsysteme GmbH, Germany
Specific requirements for tests for schoolchildren

Ülle Turk
University of Tartu, Estonia
Comparing examinations across languages: Year 12 examinations in Estonia

Maria Tzevelekou
Institute of Language and Speech Processing, Greece
Proficiency in Greek of children of the Turkish speaking minority residing in Western Thrace

Cyril Weir
University of Surrey, Roehampton, UK
A socio-cognitive approach to test validation

Bernadette Williamson
University of the South Pacific (USP) Fiji Islands
Setting and attaining standards for an EAP proficiency test in the multilingual South Pacific Islands

Jessica Rowwhei Wu
The Language Training and Testing Centre, Taiwan
The use of English language tests in the Taiwanese context – current situations and issues